RESEARCH METHODS IN EDUCATION AND PSYCHOLOGY

0803958277

0803958277

RESEARCH METHODS IN EDUCATION AND PSYCHOLOGY

INTEGRATING DIVERSITY WITH QUANTITATIVE & QUALITATIVE APPROACHES

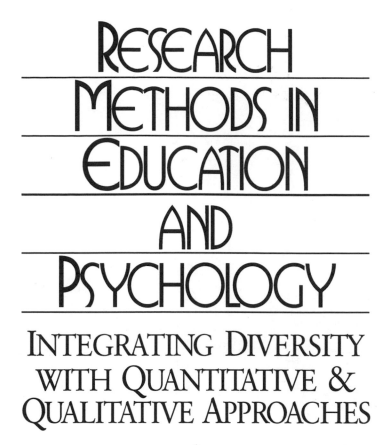

DONNA M. MERTENS

SAGE Publications
International Educational and Professional Publisher
Thousand Oaks   London   New Delhi

For information:

SAGE Publications, Inc.
2455 Teller Road
Thousand Oaks, California 91320
E-mail: order@sagepub.com

SAGE Publications Ltd.
6 Bonhill Street
London EC2A 4PU
United Kingdom

SAGE Publications India Pvt. Ltd.
M-32 Market
Greater Kailash I
New Delhi 110 048 India

Printed in the United States of America

Library of Congress Cataloging—in-Publication Data

Mertens, Donna M.
    Research methods in education and psychology: Integrating
diversity with qualitative & quantitative approaches / Donna M.
Mertens.
       p.   cm.
    Includes bibliographical references and index.
    ISBN 0-8039-5827-7 (cloth: acid-free paper). — ISBN
0-8039-5828-5 (pbk.: acid-free paper)
    1. Education—Research—Methodology.   2. Psychology—Research—
Methodology.   I. Title.
LB1028.M3966   1997
370'.7'2—dc21   97-4890

This book is printed on acid-free paper.

00 01 02 03 04 10 9 8 7 6 5

Acquiring Editor:	C. Deborah Laughton
Editorial Assistant:	Eileen Carr
Production Editor:	Astrid Virding
Production Assistant:	Karen Wiley
Copyeditor:	Linda Gray
Typesetter/Designer:	Christina M. Hill
Cover Designer:	Candice Harman
Print Buyer:	Anna Chin

Contents

8. History and Narrative Study of Lives   193

11. Data Collection   285

Preface

When I studied about research in my graduate classes many years ago, only one approach to research was taught—a quantitative approach that emphasized closed-ended surveys and experimental designs. My basic statistics courses were taught in the agriculture department, with no emphasis on the messiness that enters into research when you study people compared to animals or types of fertilizers. As I began conducting research studies myself in the messier world of people and educational and psychological policies and practices, I found that a piece of the puzzle was missing. I felt compelled to study the principles of qualitative approaches to research to get a more complete understanding of the phenomenon that I was researching. Later in my career, I began teaching at Gallaudet University and doing research for the deaf community. At this time, I began to search for approaches to research that could more accurately capture the experiences of people who were not exactly in the mainstream of society.

The idea for a different way of looking at research actually emanated from my work as a teacher of educational psychology. I came across Carol Gilligan's (1982) book *In a Different Voice* in which she made the point that Kohlberg's theory of moral development had been developed based on data collected only from boys and young men. To further our understanding of the process of moral development, Gilligan explored responses to moral dilemmas by a group of females. Thus, Gilligan's work planted the seed that research needed to include people of both genders and that perspectives might be different for males and females on important, fundamental developmental issues.

Reading Gilligan's work led me to seek out other researchers who approached their work from a feminist perspective (e.g., Reinharz, 1992). I was especially interested in exploring the question, What does it mean to conduct research from a feminist perspective? Having worked with deaf people for many years, I could immediately see many parallels between the feminists' statements concerning discrimination and oppression based on gender and the experiences of people with disabilities. Another important source of information for me were the writings of racial and ethnic minorities on more culturally sensitive approaches to research (e.g., Stanfield & Dennis, 1993).

As I struggled to put the pieces of the puzzle together, I found the organizing framework that I was seeking in the work of Patti Lather (1992) and Guba and Lincoln (1994) in their discussion of paradigms of research. They make clear that researchers' views of the world (i.e., their chosen paradigms) underlie their choices of research approaches. It is not simply a choice of method: Should I use quantitative or qualitative approaches to research, or should I mix the methods? Researchers make methodological choices based on their assumptions about reality and the nature of knowledge that are either implicitly present or explicitly acknowledged. The goal of this book is to guide researchers in identifying their own assumptions and examining for themselves the implications of choices about research methodology based on those assumptions.

It is my position that the newer paradigms add to our understanding of how to conduct more valid research. They should not be viewed as replacements for the older approaches to research. As a research community (whether we create or use research), we should be constantly building on the information we have from the past. If we know some things about how to conduct surveys from past experience, it is not wise to throw that out just because those learnings came from the original paradigm of research. If we can learn about how to conduct better surveys from feminists, racial and ethnic minorities, people with disabilities, and their advocates, then we should listen to what they are saying. *I believe that knowledge is cumulative and we learn by listening.*

Organization of This Book

This book is organized according to the logic of conducting a research study. Researchers must first examine their underlying assumptions about the nature of reality and knowledge to make sensible decisions about all of the other steps in the research process. Chapter 1 contains an explanation of the major research paradigms and their associated assumptions. Students who understand the research paradigms and their assumptions will not only be prepared to make methodological decisions about their own research, they will also be prepared to engage meaningfully in the debates in the research community about the most appropriate ways to approach the business of research. In addition, the topic of ethics is discussed in Chapter 1 as a fundamental principle that researchers must keep in the front of their minds as they begin to walk down the research road. Ethical issues are integrated into all of the chapters because they are of central concern throughout the research process.

In Chapter 2, the nuts and bolts of conducting a literature review and formulating a research problem are explained. This chapter has value for all students of research, whether they are preparing to conduct their own research or if they view themselves as consumers of research. Even students whose current self-perceptions are that they will use only the research that others produce may find that in future years they will be involved in a research team. This text will prepare them to participate in a meaningful way on such a team.

A variety of approaches to systematic inquiry are explained in Chapters 3 through 9, including experimental and quasi-experimental research, causal comparative and correlational research, survey research, single-case research, qualitative methods, history and narrative study of lives, and evaluation. Although the book is somewhat oriented to a step-by-step process of how to do research, each chapter also contains perspectives from the three major paradigms, along with a discussion of issues that are controversial, depending on one's worldview.

The final chapters help the student complete the research process. In Chapter 10, issues of the definition and selection of samples are explained, along with specific ethical concerns when working with human beings in a research context. Both quantitative and qualitative data collection strategies are discussed in Chapter 11, along with standards for judging the quality of the data collected from a variety of perspectives. In Chapter 12, quantitative and qualitative choices for data analysis are presented and issues related to data interpretation and reporting of research results are discussed. Students are also instructed in how to write a research plan, including a management plan and a budget for research that they might propose for thesis or dissertation requirements or for external funding.

Audiences for This Book

This book is designed for the advanced undergraduate student, master's students, and beginning doctoral students in education and psychology. It can be used by those who will plan and conduct research as well as by those who see their main goal as learning to locate, read, and critically evaluate research. Students will use the book differently, depending on their ultimate goal (to be an independent producer of research, a member of a research team, or a consumer of research). For students in the latter two categories, this book is quite comprehensive and could be used as a stand-alone text.

For advanced students who are preparing to conduct independent research, additional course work and resources are necessary. This book provides the foundation for making decisions about what additional study would be necessary. For example, students may need additional course work in statistics or psychometrics, because these topics are discussed at a conceptual level rather than as "how-to-do-it." References are cited throughout the text that would lead to more depth in specific methodologies, such as survey research or focus groups. Many researchers who teach qualitative approaches to research believe that students should have a mentor to teach them to conduct field work. These are ideas for expanding a student's expertise in different aspects of research once they have acquired the foundational information to guide them in the most appropriate directions.

Pedagogical Features

The following pedagogical features are found in this text:

- At the beginning of each chapter, students are given a list of the main ideas contained in that chapter. This can be used as an advance organizer for the students, as well as for an outline for students to keep themselves situated as they move through the complex process of learning about research.

- In many chapters, specific research studies are summarized, providing a realistic context for the discussion of the points throughout the chapter.

- In many chapters, step-by-step processes are explained for conducting that part of the research process.

- In every chapter, perspectives from the major paradigms are included as they relate to that chapter's topic, along with discussion of controversies that exist within the broader research community.

- Questions for critical analysis are included in each chapter that students can apply in the critical analysis of extant research studies as well as in the critical evaluation of their own planned research processes.

- Each chapter closes with questions for discussion and activities for application, providing students with an opportunity to further their understandings of the concepts presented in that chapter.

- An outline for the preparation of a research proposal is contained in the appendix and can be used by those students who will be preparing a research proposal either as part of the course requirements, for the purpose of completing a thesis or dissertation, or for requesting funds to support research.

Acknowledgments

Many people helped me through the years that this book has been in process. I want to thank the members of my professional organizations, especially Anna Madison, Joanne Farley, Bessa Whitmore, Carole Truman, Molly Ingle, and Susan Lopez, because they have inspired me through their own work in creating more inclusive and transformative models of research. Thanks also to Lester Horvath for his advice and references related to accessing the World Wide Web search engines.

I also want to thank the faculty members, graduate students, and office support staff at Gallaudet University who helped me in so many ways, especially Kay Meadow-Orlans, Vera Follain-Griselle, Janice Irizarry-Sierra, Glenda Mobley, Bonnie Neuhaus, Susanne Morgan, Jennifer Pullen, and Kat Steele. My thanks go also to the many graduate students who attended my classes and challenged, encouraged, and inspired me to produce a textbook that contained representation of the voices of struggling groups.

For their careful and thorough reviews, I wish to thank the following: Ruth Ault, Susan E. Dutch, William A. Firestone, Craig Frisby, Evelyn Jacob, Valerie Janesick, Andrea Karkowski, Linda Mabry, Aleta Meyer, Jim Scheurich, and Bob Wilson.

Thank you to my editor, C. Deborah Laughton at Sage, who believed in me and helped me as a professional and a friend. Thanks also to Linda Gray, Eileen Carr, and the other staff members at Sage who helped get this book into print by offering professional advice and support in a friendly manner. Robyn Ertwine deserves special recognition as my indexer and friend.

I want to save my warmest thanks for my husband, Jim Hopper, and my sons, Nathan (age 8) and Jeffrey (age 5), for accepting the sacrifices a family inevitably experiences when "Mom" is writing a book. I am inspired to try to make the world a better place because of the magic I find in the faces of my children.

In This Chapter

■ *Various definitions of research are provided, and a distinction is made between research and evaluation.*

■ *Definitions for important research terminology are provided.*

■ *Three major paradigms are explored in terms of their philosophical assumptions and methodological implications: postpositivist, interpretive/constructivist, and emancipatory.*

■ *Different perspectives on the politics of acceptance for the various paradigms are illustrated through contrasting statements concerning the concept of objectivity as it is currently being debated in the research community.*

■ *Ethical issues in research are discussed in terms of the definitions from different professional organizations, such as the American Psychological Association, the American Educational Research Association, and the American Evaluation Association, as well as from the various pardigmatic perspectives.*

1

An Introduction to Research

In the late 1800s, the prevailing myth held that men were more intelligent than women. Mary Calkins, a psychologist, conducted experiments at Wellesley College in 1887 that demonstrated that women are just as intelligent as men (Furumoto, 1980).

Which is better instructional practice for teaching reading to second- or third-grade Hispanic students with learning disabilities: a traditional basal approach with a high level of drill and practice or an interactive conversational approach that consists of dialogue between the student and teacher? Echevarria's (1995) comparison of these two approaches indicated that children in both conditions were equally able to answer comprehension questions about what they read; however, the level of concept development was higher in the interactive, conversational approach.

Nearly half of American Indian students who enter kindergarten do not graduate from high school. In an extensive study of American Indian women who do graduate, Bowker (1993) reports that the single most important factor as to whether a girl stayed in school and graduated was the link with a caring, competent adult who not only modeled appropriate behaviors but also encouraged the adolescent and served as an advocate when necessary.

Why Bother?

Life is complex; the world is not perfect. Many different kinds of people live on this planet, and educators and psychologists do not know the best ways to educate or counsel large groups of people who have a history of poor achievement in school and who suffer a poor quality of life in terms of low pay, poor working conditions, high rates of unemployment, and other social and psychological disadvantages. The brief descriptions of research findings presented at the beginning of this chapter illustrate the complexity of educational and psychological problems that confront researchers in our society, and they provide a glimpse into the role that research can play in identifying issues in need of additional research and providing insights into how to change the life experiences of those who suffer oppression.

This is not meant to imply that research in and of itself can solve all the world's problems, nor is it meant to suggest that all research must be oriented toward social action. There are methods for designing research that make it more likely to be useful to educators, psychologists, administrators, policymakers, parents, and students; these are discussed in this text. There are also research studies (termed *basic research*) that do not attempt to have immediate application in a social setting. Nevertheless, the trend in education and psychology is to move even basic research out of the laboratory into more real-life settings to increase the usefulness of the results (Kaestle, 1993).

What Is Research?

Research is one of many different ways of knowing or understanding. It is different from other ways of knowing, such as insight, divine inspiration, and acceptance of authoritative dictates, in that it is a process of *systematic inquiry* that is designed to collect, analyze, interpret, and use *data* to understand, describe, predict, or control an educational or psychological phenomenon or to empower individuals in such contexts. The exact nature of the definition of research is influenced by the researcher's theoretical framework and by the importance that the researcher places on distinguishing research from other activities or different types of research from each other.

For example, Langenbach, Vaughn, and Aagaard (1994) distinguish research from other activities, such as reading literature as a preparation for class, writing a paper, or developing a journalistic story, by stipulating that research influences theory. The role of theory is to establish relationships between or among constructs that describe or explain a phenomenon by going beyond the local event and trying to connect it with similar events. Examples of theories abound in education and psychology, such as theories of personality, learning, and moral development.

Langenbach et al. use the connection to theory as a way of distinguishing research from evaluation in that evaluation uses methods of systematic inquiry to know or understand a phenomenon; however, they assert it is not tied to theory. The relationship between research and evaluation is not simplistic. Much of evaluation can look remarkably like research and vice versa. Both make use of systematic inquiry methods to collect, analyze, interpret, and use data to understand, describe, predict, control, or empower. Evaluation is more typically associated with the need for information for decision making in a specific setting, and research is more typically associated with generating new knowledge that can be transferred to other settings. In practice, a large gray area connects evaluation and research; therefore, much of what is said in terms of methodology in this text has applicability for both types of inquiry. Those variables unique to evaluation are described in a later chapter.

Research Terminology

A number of important terms used in research have specific meanings within the research context that differ from their everyday or commonsense meanings. If you have studied research before, you might be familiar with these terms. However, it is almost impossible to talk about research without having at least a rudimentary understanding of these terms. Therefore, if you are new to the researcher's world, you should stop and review the terms and definitions presented in the box labeled "Research Terminology: Definitions and Examples."

Approach Taken in This Book

The main focus of this text is to examine, from a variety of theoretical perspectives, the process of systematic inquiry that constitutes research in education and psychology. The typical process for planning and conducting a research study is displayed in the box labeled "Steps in the Research Process." The research process is rarely as linear as this figure suggests; the process can be very iterative in nature. Although these steps are used to organize the information in this text, in reality, the researcher may take one step forward, three steps back, and then jump to Step 4, only to find it necessary to revisit Step 2.

Typically, research methods textbooks address quantitative research methods (research that measures variables in a quantifiable way) *or* qualitative research methods (research that captures holistic pictures using words). (These definitions are overly simplistic; they are expanded in later chapters).

A few texts address both. This text sets these methods within three major theoretical paradigms (ways of viewing the world) and their philosophical assumptions. Two of these paradigms (postpositivist and interpretive/constructivist) are commonly included in research methods texts. The emancipatory paradigm is more of a newcomer in the research community and includes the perspectives of feminists, ethnic-racial minorities, persons with disabilities, and their advocates. These three paradigms are explained in the next section on the history of research.

Why get tangled up in theory, philosophy, and politics? Why not just explain the methods? Why bring in the viewpoints of feminists, ethnic minorities, and persons with disabilities regarding research practice? *This is very important.* A researcher's theoretical orientation has implications for every decision made in the research process, including the

■ **RESEARCH TERMINOLOGY: DEFINITIONS AND EXAMPLES**

1. *Subject-participant:* The individual you are studying is the subject or participant. Often, the subject-participant in educational and psychological research is a student, client, teacher, administrator, or psychologist, but it could also be an animal or a textbook. For example, in Doren, Bullis, and Benz (1996) we read, "Participants were students with disabilities who were identified by their schools as in their last year of high school or who had dropped out of high school sometime during what would have been their last year" (p. 8).

2. *Independent variable, predictor variable:* The independent or predictor variables are the variables on which the groups in your research study differ, either because you have exposed them to different treatments (independent variable) or because of some inherent characteristics of the groups (predictor variable). When the researcher deliberately manipulates a treatment[a] (e.g., introduces social skills training for one group but not the other), treatment is called the *independent variable.* Common independent variables in education and psychology include variations in methods of teaching or therapy. If the researcher is interested in the effect of differences in an inherent characteristic, the variable is more frequently called a *predictor variable.* For example, in studies of gender differences, gender is the predictor variable.

3. *Dependent variable, criterion variable:* The dependent or criterion variable is the variable that the researcher is interested in measuring to determine how it is different for groups with different experiences (dependent) or characteristics (criterion). The *dependent variable* gets its name because it depends on what the researcher does with the independent variable. The researcher manipulates an independent variable (treatment) and exposes groups to differing amounts or types of it and then measures a dependent variable to see if it is different for the different groups. When working with a predictor variable (inherent characteristic or nonmanipulated variable), the measurement of "effect" is called a *criterion variable.* Common dependent or criterion variables in education and psychology include academic achievement, social skills, personality measures, and income after leaving school.

4. *Experimental and control groups:* In certain types of research, the researcher can divide the subjects-participants into two or more groups to test the effect of a specific treatment (independent variable). For example, a researcher might want to test the effect of providing social skills training to students with disabilities by comparing outcomes for students who receive such training with those who do not. The group that receives the training is called the *experimental group.* The comparison group that does not receive the training is called the *control group.* In true experimental research, participants are randomly assigned to conditions—that is, they have an equal and independent chance of being assigned to either the experimental or the control group.

5. *Population and sample:* The *population* is the group to whom you want to apply your results. The *sample* is the group that you have chosen from your population from which

choice of method. It is true that many researchers proceed without an understanding of their theoretical paradigm or philosophical assumptions. However, Skrtic (1991) reminds us that the danger is not that research is atheoretical but, rather, that it rests on an unexamined, unrecognized theory. Therefore, to plan and conduct your own research, read and critique to collect data. For example, 2,150 students met the criteria established in the Doren et al. (1996) study mentioned in the first definition in this box. That group of 2,150 students represented the population for the study. The researchers selected a 20% sample and collected data from 422 students. The 422 students constituted the sample for this study.

6. *Generalizability and transferability: Generalizability* refers to the researcher's ability to generalize the results from the sample to the population from which it was drawn. The ability to generalize results depends on how representative the sample is of the population. The degree of generalizability can be discussed in statistical terms depending on the type of sampling strategy that the researcher uses. In some types of research, the researcher emphasizes the total context in which the research took place to enable readers to make judgments as to the *transferability* of the study's results to their own situations.

7. *Statistically significant:* Statistical significance is important in studies in which comparisons between groups or estimations of sizes of relationships between variables are made. If groups are compared on a dependent variable (e.g., social adjustment), a test of statistical significance can be used to determine if the observed difference between the groups is too large to occur plausibly as a result of chance alone. On the basis of the laws of probability, a difference that is too large to attribute to chance is called statistically significant. Researchers in education and psychology will sometimes say that their results are statistically significant at the .05 or .01 level. These levels refer to the researchers' confidence that similar results would probably be obtained if the study were repeated using other samples drawn from the same population.

8. *Extraneous variable:* Researchers are typically very interested in the effect of their independent (or predictor) variables on the dependent (or criterion) variables. But social phenomenon are complex and are influenced by many variables other than those of central interest to the researchers. These other variables that can influence the effect of the independent or predictor variables are called *extraneous variables.* For example, a researcher might be very interested in testing the effectiveness of a new therapeutic or teaching approach. However, the subjects-participants might have varying degrees of enthusiasm for the different treatments. The counselors or teachers might be strongly wedded to the traditional approach, or they might be intrigued by the new ideas represented in your experimental treatment. Thus, it may be the extraneous variable of their enthusiasm that determines which approach produces the more desirable outcome rather than the approach itself. Other common extraneous variables can be associated with culture, gender, disability, ability, and ethnicity differences between groups. ■

NOTE: a. A researcher can study the effect of a treatment without manipulating it or comparing groups who do and do not receive it. This is commonly done in qualitative and descriptive research studies.

the research of others, and join in the theoretical and methodological debates in the research community, you need to understand the prevailing theoretical paradigms, with their underlying philosophical assumptions.

■ STEPS IN THE RESEARCH PROCESS

Step 1: Identify own worldview (Chapter 1)

↕

Step 2: Problem sensing (Chapters 1 & 2)

↕

Step 3: Literature review; research questions (Chapter 2)

↕

Step 4: Identify design (quantitative/qualitative/mixed) (Chapters 3, 4, 5, 6, 7, 8, & 9)

↕

Step 5: Identify and select sources of data (Chapter 10)

↕

Step 6: Identify and select data collection methods and instruments (Chapter 11)

↕

Step 7: Data analysis, reporting, and utilization (Chapter 12)

↕

Step 8: Identify future directions (Chapter 12) ■

Major Paradigms in Research: A Brief History of Research

A *paradigm* is a way of looking at the world. It is composed of certain philosophical assumptions that guide and direct thinking and action. Trying to categorize all educational and psychological research into a few paradigms is a complex and, perhaps, impossible task. Table 1.1 displays three of the major paradigms, along with a list of the variety of terms used to describe each. I provide you with the alternative labels listed in Table 1.1 because you will find different labels used in different texts. For example, some authors use the label *qualitative* rather than *interpretive/constructivist* for that paradigm (see Langenbach et al., 1994). I explain the rational for my choice of the major paradigm labels in the next section.

Guba and Lincoln (1994) identify three questions that help define a paradigm:

---

1. The ontological question asks, What is the nature of reality?

2. The epistemological question asks, What is the nature of knowledge and the relationship between the knower and the would-be known?

3. The methodological question asks, How can the knower go about obtaining the desired knowledge and understandings?

TABLE 1.1 Labels Commonly Associated With Different Paradigms[a]		
Positivism/Postpositivism	*Interpretive/Constructivist*	*Emancipatory*
Experimental	Naturalistic	Critical Theory
Quasi-experimental	Phenomenological	Neo-Marxist
Correlational	Hermeneutic	Feminist
Causal comparative	Symbolic interaction	Race specific
Quantitative	Ethnographic	Freirean
	Qualitative	Participatory
		Transformative

SOURCE: Adapted from Lather (1992).

a. Lather placed poststructuralism and postmodernism in yet a fourth paradigm, which she labeled *deconstructivist*.

Three of the major paradigms in the research community are described in the next section. The lines between them are not altogether clear in practice. However, to guide their thinking and practice, researchers should be able to identify the worldview that most closely approximates their own. Answers to the paradigm-defining questions are summarized for each paradigm in Table 1.2.

Positivism/Postpositivism

The dominant paradigm that has guided educational and psychological research has been *positivism* and its successor *postpositivism*. Positivism is based on the rationalistic, empiricist philosophy that originated with Aristotle, Francis Bacon, John Locke, August Comte, and Emanuel Kant. The underlying assumptions of positivism include the belief that the social world can be studied in the same way as the natural world, that there is a method for studying the social world that is value-free, and that explanations of a causal nature can be provided. Reichardt and Rallis (1994) write that this type of logical positivism was discredited shortly before World War II and was replaced by postpositivism. Research methodologists such as Campbell and Stanley (1963, 1966) and Cook and Campbell (1979) embraced postpositivism's assumptions. Cook and Campbell (1979) write,

> We share the postpositivist's belief that observations are theory-laden and that the construction of sophisticated scientific apparatus and procedures for data presentation usually involve the explicit or implicit acceptance of well-developed scientific theories, over and above the theories being tested. However, we reject the position that observations are laden with only a single theory or paradigm. (p. 24)

TABLE 1.2 Basic Beliefs Associated With the Major Paradigms			
Basic Beliefs	Positivism/ Postpositivism	Interpretive/Constructivist	Emancipatory
Ontology (nature of reality)	One reality; knowable within probability	Multiple, socially constructed realities	Multiple realities shaped by social, political, cultural, economic, ethnic, gender, and disability values
Epistemology (nature of knowledge; relation between knower and would-be known)	Objectivity is important; researcher manipulates and observes in dispassionate, objective manner	Interactive link between researcher and participants; values are made explicit; created findings	Interactive link between researcher and participants; knowledge is socially and historically situated
Methodology (approach to systematic inquiry)	Quantitative (primarily); interventionist; decontextualized	Qualitative (primarily); hermeneutical; dialectical; contextual factors are described	More emphasis on qualitative (dialogic), but quantitative design could be used; contextual and historical factors are described, especially as they relate to oppression

SOURCE: Adapted from Guba and Lincoln (1994).
NOTE: In contrast to Guba and Lincoln's choice of "critical theory and related ideological positions" to label the third paradigm, I chose to label this "emancipatory" because of critical theory's close association with Marxist theory.

Based on the rationale presented by Reichardt and Rallis (1994), this text refers to this theoretical perspective as it is currently applied in education and psychology as the postpositivist paradigm.

An example of research conducted within the postpositivist paradigm is summarized in Sample Study 1.1. The study has been summarized according to the main categories typically included in a report of research in this paradigm—that is, research problem, question, methods (participants, instruments, and procedures), results, and conclusions. The researchers acknowledge several limitations to their work, such as low representation of people from minority populations, use of a numeric scale to summarize complex variables such as social skills, and lack of inclusion of qualitative, contextual data concerning variables such as general unemployment in a specific locale or the nature of the adolescents' experiences with various types of victimization (e.g., physical abuse, robbery) and participants' responses to those experiences. Despite these limitations, their study does provide a preliminary insight into the relation between the disability status of serious emotional disturbance and personal-social achievement to victimization.

The answers to the paradigm-defining questions for postpositivism are as follows:

Ontology. The positivists hold that one reality exists and that it is the researcher's job to discover that reality (naive realism) (Guba & Lincoln, 1994). The postpositivists concur

---

SAMPLE STUDY 1.1 *Summary of a Postpositivist Research Study*

Research problem: Very little is known about the victimization experiences of adolescents with disabilities, yet previous research has suggested that people with mental retardation are vulnerable to economic, psychological, and physical abuse.

Research question: What are the predictors of victimization for a sample of adolescents with disabilities in transition from high school to adult life?

Method: Students with disabilities and their parents in two U.S. Western states were interviewed during the students' last year in school and once again when students were 1 year out of school.

Participants: Participants were students with disabilities who were identified by their schools as in their last year of high school or who had dropped out of high school sometime during what would have been their last year (sample size = 422).

Instruments and procedures: A fixed-response interview was conducted by telephone with students and their parents by trained interviewers. Predictor variables were selected based on previous research; these included gender, minority status, serious emotional disturbance (SED), specific learning disability (SLD), dropout status, family socioeconomic status, parent rating of academic skills, and a rating of personal-social skills. The outcome variable of victimization was defined as experiencing more than one of the following: being teased or bothered, having something stolen from them, or being hit hard or beat up.

Results: The following characteristics were associated with a greater likelihood of being victimized during the first year out of school: prior victimization while still in school in the previous year, being female, having low postschool personal-social achievement, and individuals with both SED and an arrest record within 1 year of leaving school.

Discussion: The greatest risk for victimization was for the group who had a serious emotional disturbance and low personal-social achievement. The authors recommend increasing social skill training directed to this specific group in terms of appropriate ways to behave in community settings where victimization could occur.

SOURCE: Based on Doren, Bullis, and Benz (1996).

---

that a reality does exist but that it can be known only imperfectly because of the researcher's human limitations (critical realism). Therefore, researchers can discover "reality" within a certain realm of probability. They cannot "prove" a theory, but they can make a stronger case by eliminating alternative explanations (Reichardt & Rallis, 1994).

The ontological assumption in the Doren, Bullis, and Benz (1996) research study exemplifies the postpositivist approach in that the researchers were able to create a list of the variables that might be associated with victimization based on previous research in the area. They converted both their predictor variables and the criterion variable (victimization) into quantitative variables so that they could conduct a statistical analysis to determine the strength of the relationship between the predictor variables and the criterion variable within a specified level of probability.

Epistemology. In early positivist thinking, the researcher and the subject of the study were assumed to be independent; that is, they did not influence each other (Guba & Lincoln, 1994). Postpositivists modified this belief by recognizing that the theories, hypotheses, and background knowledge held by the investigator can strongly influence what is observed (Reichardt & Rallis, 1994). This paradigm holds that objectivity is the standard to strive for in research; thus, the researcher should remain neutral to prevent values or biases from influencing the work by following prescribed procedures rigorously.

The epistemological assumption of the postpositivist paradigm is exemplified in the Doren et al. (1996) study in that the researchers used interviewers who had been trained to follow exactly the same procedures for asking questions of the respondents and for recording their responses. To standardize the responses, the goal was to ask exactly the same question, in the same way, to each of the people being interviewed. The researchers used a fixed-response format for the questions on the interview instrument. The researchers checked the interviewers' performance to ensure that they were coding responses in the same way.

Methodology. As mentioned previously, positivists borrowed their experimental methods from the natural sciences. Postpositivists recognized that many of the assumptions required for rigorous application of the scientific method were not appropriate for educational and psychological research with people; therefore, quasi-experimental methods (*quasi-experimental*—sort of like experimental, but not exactly) were developed (Campbell & Stanley, 1966; Cook & Campbell, 1979). In other words, many times it is not possible to randomly assign subjects to conditions (as one can with plots of land for a study of fertilizers, for example); therefore, researchers devised modifications to the experimental methods of the natural sciences in order to apply them to people. Although qualitative methods can be used within this paradigm, quantitative methods tend to be predominant in postpositivist research.

A postpositivist approach to methodology is evident in the Doren et al. (1996) study in that the researchers used a modification of the experimental methods associated with this paradigm. The researchers could not randomly assign students to conditions (e.g., gender or level of personal-social achievement); however, they did conduct group comparisons based on these inherent characteristics of the participants. The researchers summarized complex variables such as socials skills into numeric scales. As mentioned previously, the researchers acknowledged the limitations of their study in that they did not include qualitative, contextual information, such as the general employment conditions in a specific locale; nor did they describe the nature of the adolescents' experiences with various types of victimization or the participants' responses to those experiences.

Interpretive/Constructivist Paradigm

Despite the recognition by postpositivists that facts are theory laden, other researchers questioned the underlying assumptions and methodology of that paradigm. Many different labels have been used for the interpretive/constructivist paradigm, which can be seen from the sample list in Table 1.1. Tesch (1990) identifies 26 different types of qualitative research (the method most closely associated with the interpretive/constructivist paradigm). The interpretive/constructivist label was chosen for this paradigm because it reflects one of the basic tenets of this theoretical paradigm; that is, reality is socially constructed. The constructivist paradigm grew out of the philosophy of Edmund Husserl's phenomenology and Wilhelm Dilthey's and other German philosophers' study of interpretive understanding called *hermeneutics* (Eichelberger, 1989). Hermeneutics is the study of interpretive understanding or meaning. Historians use the concept of hermeneutics in their discussion of interpreting historical documents to try to understand what the author was attempting to communicate within the time period and culture in which they were written. Interpretive/constructivist researchers use the term more generally to interpret the meaning of something from a certain standpoint or situation.[1] An example of an interpretive/constructivist research study is presented in Sample Study 1.2.

The basic assumptions guiding the interpretive/constructivist paradigm are that knowledge is socially constructed by people active in the research process, and that researchers should attempt to understand the "complex world of lived experience from the point of view of those who live it" (Schwandt, 1994, p. 118). The interpretive/constructivist paradigm emphasizes that research is a product of the values of researchers and cannot be independent of them. The answers to the paradigm-defining questions for the interpretive/constructivist approach are as follows.

Ontology. Reality is socially constructed. Therefore, multiple mental constructions can be apprehended, some of which may be in conflict with each other, and perceptions of reality may change throughout the process of the study. For example, the concepts of disability, feminism, and minority are socially constructed phenomena that mean different things to different people.

Schwandt (1994) describes what he calls "everyday" constructivist thinking in this way:

> In a fairly unremarkable sense, we are all constructivists if we believe that the mind is active in the construction of knowledge. Most of us would agree that knowing is not passive—a simple imprinting of sense data on the mind—but active; mind does something with those impressions, at the very least forms abstractions or concepts. In this sense, constructivism means that human beings do not find or discover knowledge so much as construct or make it. (p. 125)

But constructivist researchers go one step further by rejecting the notion that there is an objective reality that can be known and taking the stance that the researcher's goal is to understand the multiple social constructions of meaning and knowledge.

In terms of ontology, the Merten (1996) study (summarized in Sample Study 1.2) exemplifies the interpretive/constructivist paradigm in a number of ways. First, the re-

SAMPLE STUDY 1.2 *Summary of an Interpretive/ Constructivist Research Study*

Research problem: Previous research on adolescent rejection has focused on the causes of rejection. Merten's (1996) study focused on the responses of adolescent boys to rejection.

Research questions: What changes did the boys make and how effective were those changes in altering their rejected status? How did the rejected students construe their rejection? What did they understand to be the reasons for their rejection and how did their evaluation of those reasons guide their decisions whether to change?

Method: In this longitudinal study, an ethnographic approach was used to examine the responses to peer rejection of junior high school boys during seventh and eighth grades.

Participants: Four boys who were frequently mentioned by their peers as being examples of rejected students were the focus of this study. The researchers did conduct interviews with 160 students (male = 77; female = 83) to identify the 4 "rejected" students, as well as to collect data from the broader school community.

Procedures: Three teachers were given 3 months of intensive training in ethnography before school started. The ethnographers taught one class per semester, and spent time observing students in the cafeteria, library, halls, and other school settings. Their observations were tape-recorded and later transcribed, as were the tape-recorded interviews with the students. The interviews were open-ended and lasted about 40 minutes for each student. The same individuals were interviewed many times (resulting in approximately 600 interviews), and the questions were modified each time to provide a running account of the students' experiences handling the transitions in domains such as relationships with friends, peers, teachers, and family.

Results: Each of the four boys' responses are detailed in the journal article. The boys experienced harassment in the forms of teasing, ridicule, or being tripped or spit at. The boys' responses ranged from trying to become "invisible" (withdrawing, daydreaming), to denying friendship with other rejected students, to intentionally choosing not to act "babyish" by breaking adult (school) rules (e.g., cheating, lying, swearing).

Discussion: The boys changed their behaviors in response to the rejection; however, the changes they made were largely ineffective. Only one boy was successful in changing his image during eighth grade by surpassing what his peers would do and doing something that no one with his reputation would be expected to do. He responded directly and forcefully by yelling at his antagonists, broke school rules, and generally negated the image of his "babyish" label.

SOURCE: Based on Merten (1996).

searcher allowed the concepts of importance in the study to emerge as they had been constructed by the participants. He studied "rejection," not as he conceptualized it but, rather, as it was constructed by the students in the study. Thus, the term *mels* was used to describe the boys who had been rejected because this was the term used by their peers. "The term 'mel' was short for Melvin and referred to a boy who was considered to be more child-like than adolescent, vis-à-vis the dominant peer standards of junior high school" (p. 7).

The author's ontological assumptions are also evidenced in his discussion of his decision to use the interpretive/constructivist approach. Merten (1996) acknowledges that

> taking this approach was not to claim this was the only way to make sense of these data. For example, running through the data were incidents that could be interpreted from a variety of developmental perspectives. Nevertheless, the present interpretation of mels' responses to rejection emphasized *their* construction of their rejection and how the *meanings* of the options they saw themselves having, in turn, influenced the responses they made. (p. 9)

Epistemology. The inquirer and the inquired-into are interlocked in an interactive process; each influences the other. The interpretive/constructivist therefore opts for a more personal, interactive mode of data collection. For example, one special education teacher conducted a qualitative research study in collaboration with a university researcher in which she discussed with her students with mild learning disabilities how they could more effectively respond to the demands in the mainstream classroom (Davis & Ferguson, 1992). She then used their ideas to structure the intervention that was the focus of her qualitative study.

The values that influence the investigator are made explicit. For example, the concept of least restrictive environment (LRE) in special education exemplifies the connection between facts and values. The federal government defined LRE as inclusion of students with disabilities in regular education classes as much as possible. However, deaf advocates contended that because of communication barriers, even with qualified interpreters, inclusion in regular education would be socially isolating and hence restrictive to deaf students.

The concept of objectivity is replaced by confirmability (Guba & Lincoln, 1989). The assumption is made that data, interpretations, and outcomes are rooted in contexts and persons apart from the researcher and are not figments of the imagination. Data can be tracked to its sources, and the logic used to assemble interpretations can be made explicit in the narrative.

The interpretive/constructivist epistemological assumptions were also evident in the Merten (1996) study of adolescent boys. At the start of the study, he was focused on the social relationships between early adolescents in a junior high school and how they negotiated the transition between elementary and high school. As a result of extensive observational and interview data, he chose to study the rejection experiences of a small group of adolescent boys. Thus, by a process of interaction between the researcher and the participants, the central focus of the study emerged.

Merten (1996) does not make a claim of objectivity in the sense of personal distance from the students in his study. Rather, he supported the validity of his claim by the multiple sources of data that he used and the multiple methods that he used to collect the data. He also provided multiple examples of direct quotes from the students to support the inferences that he drew from the data.

Methodology. Qualitative methods such as interviews, observations, and document reviews are predominant in this paradigm. These are applied in correspondence with the assumption about the social construction of reality in that research can be conducted only through interaction between and among investigator and respondents (Guba & Lincoln, 1994). This interactive approach is sometimes described as hermeneutical and dialectical in that efforts are made to obtain multiple perspectives that yield better interpretations of meanings (hermeneutics) that are compared and contrasted through a dialectical interchange involving the "juxtaposition of conflicting ideas, forcing reconsideration of previous positions" (Guba & Lincoln, 1989, p. 90).

Eichelberger (1989) describes the methodological work of the interpretive/ constructivist (hermeneutical) researcher as follows:

> They want to know what meaning people attribute to activities . . . and how that related to their behavior. These researchers are much *clearer* about the fact that they are *constructing* the "reality" on the basis of the interpretations of data with the help of the participants who provided the data in the study. They often carry out their research much as anthropologists do in their studies of culture. They do a great deal of observation, read documents produced by members of the groups being studied, do extensive formal and informal interviewing, and develop classifications and descriptions that represent the beliefs of the various groups. (p. 9)

The methodological implication of having multiple realities is that the research questions cannot be definitively established before the study begins; rather, they will evolve and change as the study progresses. In addition, the perceptions of a variety of types of persons must be sought. For example, in special education research, the meaning of total inclusion needs to be explored as it has been constructed by regular and special education administrators and teachers, parents who have children with and without disabilities, and students with differing types and severity of disabilities (see Keller, Karp, & Carlson, 1993; Mertens, 1992). Finally, the interpretive/constructivist researcher must provide information about the backgrounds of the participants and the contexts in which they are being studied.

Some of the methodological strategies that were used in the Merten (1996) study of adolescent boys that exemplify the interpretive/constructivist paradigm include the following: (a) Multiple data collection strategies were used, most of which resulted in qualitative data. The researcher conducted extensive interviews (over 600 hours) and observations over a 2-year period of time. (b) The interview questions evolved over time and were adjusted based on each previous interview to develop for each individual a running account of his or her experiences handling the transitions in various domains. (c) The author explained the context of the study in great detail in terms of the type of community, economic factors, ethnic diversity, and school characteristics. (d) The focus of the study was to explain the process of rejection and the boys' responses to the rejection from their own point of view.

Emancipatory Paradigm

The interpretive/constructivist paradigm has been criticized not only by positivists and postpositivists but also by another group of researchers who represent a third paradigm of research: the emancipatory paradigm. This group includes critical theorists, participatory action researchers, Marxists, feminists, ethnic minorities, and persons with disabilities (the active subjects of the research), among others. I rejected the label "critical theory" for this paradigm (in contrast to Guba & Lincoln, 1994) because of critical theory's close association with Marxist theory. The emancipatory researchers argue that the interpretive/constructivist paradigm did change the rules; however, it did not change the nature of the game. Interpretive/constructivist researchers still consist of a relatively small group of powerful experts doing work on a larger number of relatively powerless research subjects. The emancipatory paradigm directly addresses the politics in research by confronting social oppression at whatever levels it occurs (Oliver, 1992; Reason, 1994b). Thus, emancipatory researchers go beyond the issue of the powerful sharing power with the powerless and relinquish control of the research to the marginalized groups (Foster, 1993a).

Researchers who were concerned about a number of different issues and events developed the emancipatory paradigm. Some of these stimulating concerns and issues are discussed next.

Why the Emancipatory Paradigm Emerged

1. The emancipatory paradigm arose because of dissatisfaction with the dominant research paradigms and practices and because of a realization that much of sociological and psychological theory had been developed from the White, able-bodied male perspective and was based on the study of male subjects. Gilligan (1982) notes that theories that were formerly thought to be sexually neutral in their scientific objectivity have been found to reflect a consistent observational and evaluative bias. Examples of the dominant theories in psychology that were developed using the male as the norm include Freud's theory of personality, McClelland's theory of motivation, Kohlberg's theory of moral development, and Perry's theory of college student development. As these theories were reexamined from the feminist perspective, a new level of awareness developed as to women's life experiences.

2. Similar to the overall population in the United States, the total school-age population is becoming poorer and more racially and ethnically diverse (Morra, 1994). For example, in the 10 years spanning 1980 to 1990, the number of poor Hispanic children grew by over 43%, increasing by 481,000 to 1.6 million. This increase in the diversity of children in schools and in the overall population has contributed to an increased interest in multicultural education (Banks, 1993) and ways to conduct race-sensitive research.

3. Discussions at the American Psychological Association meeting about cross-cultural counseling revealed that some ethnic-minority psychologists believe that White researchers who study their communities do so without an understanding or caring for the people who

live there (Mio & Iwamasa, 1993). Minority researchers expressed the view that their work had not been respected and that counseling and psychotherapy have failed to recognize the important contributions of minority authors. A special issue of *The Counseling Psychologist* (Stone, 1993) explores ways that psychologists who conduct research can be more sensitive to ethnic-minority issues.

4. Differences in school achievement by gender, race, class, and disability have been documented in previous research studies. One possible explanation is based on genetic or biological factors. However, Campbell (1989) suggests that the differences could be accounted for by the choice of test and test items, parental and teacher expectations, differential course taking, and differential treatment in the same classes and different experiences outside school. For example, males in elementary and secondary schools are called on more frequently and receive more praise, acceptance, remediation, and criticism than do female students (Sadker & Sadker, 1986).

5. Padilla and Lindholm (1995) point out the absence of literature found in "standard guild journals" of the American Psychological Association and the American Educational Research Association on children of African American heritage or of any other ethnic group. They cite Graham's (1992) review of journal publication practices for *Developmental Psychology* and the *Journal of Educational Psychology* between 1970 and 1989. Graham reports that published articles employing African American participants in those two journals decreased over the 19-year time period, from 8.1% to 6.1% in the *Journal of Educational Psychology* and from 8% to 4.6% in *Developmental Psychology*. Padilla and Lindholm (1995) argue that there is a need for more culturally sensitive research with ethnic minorities based on a paradigm shift with different assumptions than are found in the postpositivist or interpretive/constructivist paradigms.

6. A need exists for informed practitioners to form partnerships with researchers to plan and conduct research and evaluation studies in a meaningful way. The most common complaint about research is that there is no link to practice (Kaestle, 1993). For research to be meaningful, it must be forged from the felt needs of the practitioners who are sophisticated enough to work as partners in the research process.

The philosophical base of the emancipatory paradigm is quite diverse, reflecting the multiple positions represented in that paradigm. For example, Tong (1989) identifies seven different varieties of feminist thought, each with its corresponding philosophical base. A number of ethnic minorities have written that mainstream feminists are not representative of their views (e.g., Collins, 1990; James & Busia, 1993; Stanfield & Dennis, 1993), thus adding to the complexity of identifying *the* philosophical base of the emancipatory paradigm.

Three strands of feminist research identified by Olesen (1994) provide insight into the major philosophies that drive the emancipatory paradigm:

1. Standpoint theorists stress that all knowing substantively involves the standpoint or social and historical context of the particular knowers (Alcoff & Potter, 1993). Important standpoint theorists include Harding (1993), Hartsock (1983, 1985), and Dorothy Smith (1987). According to Harding (1993), standpoint theory is important in societies such as ours that are stratified by race, ethnicity, class, gender, sexuality, or some other variables that shape the structure of society. She states,

Knowledge claims are always socially situated, and the failure of dominant groups critically and systematically to interrogate their advantaged social situation and the effect of such advantages on their beliefs leaves their social situation a scientifically and epistemologically disadvantaged one for generating knowledge. (p. 54)

She continues: "Standpoint epistemology sets the relationship between knowledge and politics at the center of its account in the sense that it tries to provide causal accounts to explain the effects that different kinds of politics have on the production of knowledge" (pp. 55-56). Much, although not all, of standpoint theorists' work proceeds from a Marxist orientation, examining the researchers' role in the power structure (Olesen, 1994).

2. Feminist empiricists follow the norms of the postpositivist and interpretive/constructivist paradigms with the caveat that women's lived experiences are central to the research process. Thus, they share the philosophical base of these paradigms, while at the same time borrowing ideas about social justice and oppression from emancipatory theorists. According to Harding (1993), feminist empiricists believe that "sexism and androcentrism could be eliminated from the results of research if scientists would just follow more rigorously and carefully the existing methods and norms of research—which, for practicing scientists, are fundamentally empiricist ones" (p. 51).

3. Postmodern feminist thought is rooted in the philosophies of poststructuralism and postmodern thinkers such as the French feminists Cixous, Irigaray, and Kristeva, and Foucalt, Lyotard, and Bandrillard (Olesen, 1994; Sands & Nuccio, 1992). Textual analysis and the role of text in sustaining the integration of power and oppression has been a central focus of postmodern feminist research. Richardson (1994) explores the idea of writing as a method of inquiry in itself in that researchers can learn things about themselves and their topics through the process of writing.

The emancipatory paradigm (as exemplified by the varieties of feminist thought) is broad and far from a unified body of work. Martusewicz and Reynolds (1994) describe the commonality of concern for feminist theories as "understanding and improving the lives and relations between women and men, economically, socially, culturally, and personally" (p. 13). Feminists generally agree that, historically, women have not enjoyed the same power and privileges as men, either in the public or private sphere. Women live their lives in an oppressive society; this concept of oppression links the voices of those who work in the emancipatory paradigm.

Similar themes emerge from the writings of African American scholars. Gordon (1995) writes,

The Black challenge to Western ideological hegemony is older than both critical and feminist discourse and was born of the need for intellectual, ideological, and spiritual liberation of people who lived under both the racist domination and sexist patriarchal subordination to which both the critical and feminist discourse react and refer. (p. 190)

She does criticize the critical and feminist scholars as follows:

> The blind side of critical and feminist discourses is their inability, unwillingness, or complete lack of awareness of the need to focus on the conceptual systems that construct, legitimize, and normalize the issues of race and racism. This is demonstrated through the flagrant invisibility in their works of the critical and cultural model generated by the subjugated oppressed group from its own experiences within a dominant and hostile society. (pp. 189-190)

She does not see sufficient attention being given to the African American critical and liberatory pedagogy in most feminist discourse.

Although no unified body of literature is representative of the emancipatory paradigm, four characteristics are common to the diverse perspectives represented within it and serve to distinguish it from the postpositivist and interpretive/constructivist paradigms (Mertens, Farley, Madison, & Singleton, 1994):

1. It places central importance on the lives and experiences of the diverse groups that, traditionally, have been marginalized (i.e., women, minorities, and persons with disabilities). Kelly, Burton, and Reagan (1994) suggest that researchers not limit study to the lives and experiences of women but study the way oppression is structured and reproduced. Researchers must focus on how oppressed groups' lives are constrained by the actions of oppressors, individually and collectively, and on the strategies that oppressed groups use to resist, challenge, and subvert. Therefore, studying oppressed people's lives also means that a study of the oppressors' means of dominance must be included.

2. It analyzes how and why inequities based on gender, race or ethnicity, and disability are reflected in asymmetric power relationships.

3. It examines how results of social inquiry on inequities are linked to political and social action.

4. It uses an emancipatory theory to develop the program theory and the research approach. A program theory is a set of beliefs about the way a program works or why a problem occurs. Different types of program theories and their influence on the research process are explored in Chapter 2 (see especially Table 2.7).

An example of a research study conducted within the emancipatory paradigm is summarized in Sample Study 1.3. This study was chosen because it focuses on the least powerful in the school system, the low-income and minority students, and analyzes the resulting inequities in terms of the asymmetric power relationships that exist between the student and the school staff. The authors make specific recommendations for linking the results of their study to social and political action. They used an emancipatory approach to develop the theory as to why low-income and minority students were more likely to be in low-ability classes for non-college-bound students by directly examining the school's role in maintaining a society that is stratified by race and social class.

SAMPLE STUDY 1.3 *Summary of an Emancipatory Research Study*

Research problem: Low-income and minority students are more likely to be in low-ability classes for non-college-bound students. Little is known about how schools actually match particular students to tracked courses in high schools.

Research questions: What are the effects on students' course taking of educators' judgments about what courses are best for students, students' and parents' choices, and the constraints and opportunities inherent in schools' own cultures and the larger social and policy context? What are the factors that contribute to the racial, ethnic, and social class patterns of curriculum participation?

Method: The researchers studied three comprehensive senior high schools in adjacent communities within a major West Coast urban center, using a quantitative and qualitative case study approach.

Participants: Interviews were conducted with the district curriculum director, the district vocational education coordinator, the school principal, assistant principals, or deans responsible for overseeing curriculum or counseling; all of the counselors; approximately 15 teachers; and a number of students from both vocational classes and academic classes in various tracks at two of the schools.

Instruments and procedures: They analyzed student handbooks, course descriptions, and master schedules and conducted on-site interviews and observations. They designed the interview protocols as they proceeded, to incorporate knowledge gained in preceding interviews. Background and transcript data were collected for all students who were seniors any time during the 1987-1988 school year.

Results: Most teachers believed that there was little hope for improvement once a student reached high school because the students either lacked essential basic skills or appropriate motivation. Given this widespread perception of stability in students' intellectual capacity, the schools saw their job as offering programs that accommodate rather than alter their students' abilities and motivation. The most successful students were placed in better classes and, once placed, were likely to continue along this advantaged track. Racial groups were identified with specific tracks in most teachers' minds, indicating that Latinos had low representation in higher-level courses because they were "culturally disinclined" to aspire to postsecondary education.

Discussion: Curriculum opportunities are not based on an open, merit-based system. Differences in course participation flowed, in large part, from perceptions that educators held about race and social class differences in academic abilities and motivation. In these schools, the common belief was that Asian students were high in ability and motivation and Latino students lacked the ability and family values needed for higher education.

SOURCE: Based on Oakes and Guiton (1995).

With that lengthy introduction to the emancipatory paradigm, and in full recognition of its diverse and emerging character, the answers to the three defining questions are as follows.

Ontology. Like the constructivist paradigm, multiple realities are recognized in the emancipatory paradigm. However, the emancipatory paradigm stresses the influence of social, political, cultural, economic, ethnic, gender, and disability values in the construction of reality. In addition, it emphasizes that that which seems "real" may be reified structures that are taken to be real because of historical situations. Thus, what is taken to be real needs to be critically examined via an ideological critique in terms of its role in perpetuating oppressive social structures and policies.

In Oakes and Guiton's (1995) study of high school tracking, the ontological assumptions of the emancipatory paradigm are evident in that the researchers attempted to uncover the influence of social, political, cultural, economic, ethnic, and gender values in the determination of school placements. The school personnel stated that their policies were to make placement decisions on the basis of merit alone (without consideration for other factors, such as income or ethnicity). Yet the teachers expressed the perception that there was little hope for improvement in high school because the students lacked essential basic skills or they held negative attitudes. Race, ethnicity, and social class were used as a basis for signifying a student's ability and motivation, thus influencing curriculum decisions. For example, Latinos at all three schools were almost always judged as the least well suited for academic work and were most often associated with low-track academic courses and vocational programs.

Epistemology. The relationship between the knower and the would-be known (i.e., the researcher and participants) is viewed as interactive. Harding (1993) recommends that the researcher use a methodology that involves " 'starting off thought' from the lives of marginalized people" (p. 56). This would reveal more of the unexamined assumptions influencing science and generate more critical questions.

The relationship should be empowering to those without power. Thus, research should examine ways the research benefits or does not benefit the participants (Kelly et al., 1994).

Feminist objectivity means "situated knowledge" (Haraway, 1988)—that is, recognizing the social and historical influences on that which we say we know. Harding (1993) argues that politically guided research projects have produced fewer partial and distorted results (as in sexist or racist) than those supposedly guided by the goal of value neutrality. Objectivity in this paradigm is achieved by reflectively examining the influence of the values and social position of the researcher on the problems identified as appropriate for research, hypotheses formulated, and key concepts defined.

In the Oakes and Guiton (1995) study of high school tracking, the epistemological assumptions of the emancipatory paradigm can be seen. They conducted on-site interviews and observations, as well as analyzing many written documents, such as course descriptions and master schedules. In addition, the authors focused on the lives of marginalized people (i.e., students of low ability and ethnic-minority status). They made recommendations that would lead to greater empowerment of those with the least power. And they were very sensitive to the social and historical influences on the placement decisions and the school personnel's construction of race and ability.

Methodology. Emancipatory researchers are pluralistic and evolving in their methodologies. The empiricists who work within the emancipatory tradition tend to use quantitative methods; however, they emphasize a need for more care and rigor in following existing methods commonly associated with the postpositivist paradigm to avoid sexist, racist, or otherwise biased results (Eichler, 1991; Harding, 1993). Other emancipatory researchers use a wide diversity of methods; many make use of qualitative methods such as interviews, observations, and document review within an emancipatory framework (Reinharz, 1992). In emancipatory research that comes from the participatory action research tradition, it is viewed as essential to involve the people who are the research "participants" in the planning, conduct, analysis, interpretation, and use of the research. A common theme in the methodology is inclusion of diverse voices from the margin.

Oakes and Guiton (1995) exemplified the emancipatory methodology by combining quantitative and qualitative methods of data collection. As mentioned in the epistemology section for this paradigm, the researchers analyzed printed documents such as course descriptions and master schedules. They also conducted on-site interviews and made observations at the schools. They interviewed a wide-ranging, cross-section of the staff and students from the schools to obtain the representation of "diverse voices." They collected quantitative data in the form of students' standardized achievement test scores and the number of courses taken within each track (vocational or college prep). Thus, they used a variety of data sources and several data collectors who conducted interviews and observations at each site. They had at least two researchers who coded and sorted the data into categories or themes.

The Politics of Acceptance: The Objectivity Debate

As stated in the history of research section of this chapter, the oldest paradigm for educational and psychological research is the postpositivist paradigm. The second paradigm to enter this research world was the interpretive/constructivist paradigm, and the most recent is the emancipatory paradigm. In years past, the professional literature contained many attacks by postpositivists on interpretive/constructivists (and vice versa). These still occur, but they are far less common. Critical pieces about the emancipatory paradigm are frequently seen in mainstream publications in which the "old guard" expresses concern about the loss of objectivity and the inclusion of politics in the research process as it is represented in the emancipatory paradigm. The nature of this debate is illustrated in the following statements that exemplify part of the discussion about the concept of objectivity as it is viewed from the three paradigmatic perspectives.

Postpositivist. Krathwhol (1993) uses the label of "analyzer" to represent the position that favors experimental research designs. He describes this view on objectivity as follows:

Analyzers prefer carefully designed studies. Experimenting is their main technique, but they may also do natural or field experiments. . . . They place considerable emphasis on science as a method of reducing or eliminating the biasing effects of personal values on observations and try to be value-free. (p. 635)

Interpretive/Constructivist. Guba and Lincoln (1989) provide the following thoughts about value-free objectivity:

Values permeate every paradigm that has been proposed or might be proposed, for paradigms are *human* constructions, and hence cannot be impervious to human values. Values enter an inquiry through such channels as the nature of the problem selected for study . . . the choice of paradigm for carrying out the inquiry, . . . the choice of instruments and analysis modes, the choice of interpretations to be made and conclusions to be drawn, and the like. (p. 65)

Emancipatory. Fine (1994a) explicates the political nature of research as it is viewed by the emancipatory (in her case feminist, activist) perspective:

Some researchers fix themselves self-consciously as participatory activists. Their work seeks to unearth, disrupt, and transform existing ideological and/or institutional arrangements. Here, the researcher's stance frames the texts produced and carves out the space in which intentional surprises surface. These writers position themselves as political and interrogating, fully explicit about their original research and where their research took them. (p. 17)

Critique of Emancipatory Position. In direct response to Fine's words, Patai (1994) writes the following:

Feminism, today, as it conflates politics and education and effaces any distinction between political agendas and the protocols of research, is in danger of suppressing—it already dismisses—any calm, reflective stance that sees some strengths in the effort (however difficult to achieve) to set biases aside and that still regards research as a valuable and satisfying endeavor. (p. 62)

Response to Criticism. Fine's response to Patai's criticism contained these thoughts:

I offer no apology for the belief that ideological questions are saturated in biography and politics and that they should be. I do want to be clear, however, about a point raised by Patai and by critics from the New Right. Researchers on the Left may begin with a set of intellectually and politically charged questions, but this does not mean that we force "ideological alignment." When we listen closely to each other and our informants, we are surprised, and our intellectual work is transformed. We keep each other honest to forces of difference, divergence, and contradiction. (pp. 30-31)

Harding (1993) makes the argument that the socially situated basis for knowledge claims and feminist standpoint epistemologies (emancipatory) require and generate stronger standards for objectivity than do those that turn away from providing systematic methods for locating knowledge in history:

The starting point of standpoint theory—and its claim that is most often misread—is that in societies stratified by race, ethnicity, class, gender, sexuality, or some other politics shaping the very structure of society, the *activities* of those at the top both organize and set limits on what persons who perform such activities can understand about themselves and the world around them. . . . So one's social situation enables and sets limits on what one can know; some social situations—critically unexamined dominant ones—are more limiting in this respect, and what makes these situations more limiting is their inability to generate the most critical question about recorded beliefs. (p. 55)

Thus, she concludes that the researcher who "starts off thought" from marginalized lives is actually imposing a stronger objectivity by soliciting viewpoints that have been ignored in past research.

Ethics in Research

Ethics in research should be an integral part of the research planning and implementation process, not viewed as an afterthought or a burden. Increased consciousness of the need for strict ethical guidelines for researchers occurs each time another atrocity is discovered under the guise of research. The Nazi's medical experiments, the CIA's experimentation with LSD, the Tuskegee experiments on Black men with syphilis, and the U.S. government's administration of radioactive substances to uninformed pregnant women stand as examples of the worst that humankind can do to each other. Ethical guidelines in research are needed to guard against such obvious atrocities as these; however, they are also needed to guard against less obvious, yet still harmful, effects of research. In Sieber's (1992) guide to planning ethically responsible research, she identified problems such as deception and invasion of privacy that must be given serious consideration in research planning.

Some of the major organizations that have codes of ethics include the American Psychological Association (1982), the American Educational Research Association (1985a), the American Evaluation Association (Shadish, Newman, Scheirer, & Wye, 1995), Council for Exceptional Children (1983), and the Conference of Executives of American Schools for the Deaf (1979). The American Educational Research Association also publishes *Guidelines for Eliminating Race and Sex Bias in Educational Research and Evaluation* (1985a).

Copies of these statements can be obtained by contacting the headquarters of the various organizations.

The National Commission for the Protection of Human Subjects in Biomedical and Behavioral Research (1978) identified three ethical principles and six norms that should guide scientific research in their landmark report titled *The Belmont Report*. The three ethical principles include the following:

1. *Beneficence:* Maximizing good outcomes for science, humanity, and the individual research participants and minimizing or avoiding unnecessary risk, harm, or wrong

2. *Respect:* Treating people with respect and courtesy, including those who are not autonomous (e.g., small children, people who have mental retardation or senility)

3. *Justice:* Ensuring that those who bear the risk in the research are the ones who benefit from it; ensuring that the procedures are reasonable, nonexploitative, carefully considered, and fairly administered

The six norms of scientific research include these:

1. Use of a *valid research design:* Faulty research is not useful to anyone and is not only a waste of time and money but cannot be conceived of as being ethical in that it does not contribute to the well-being of the participants.

2. The *researcher must be competent* to conduct the research.

3. *Consequences of the research must be identified:* Procedures must respect privacy, ensure confidentiality, maximize benefits, and minimize risks.

4. *The sample selection must be appropriate* for the purposes of the study, representative of the population to benefit from the study, and sufficient in number.

5. The participants must agree to participate in the study through *voluntary informed consent*—that is, without threat or undue inducement (voluntary), knowing what a reasonable person in the same situation would want to know before giving consent (informed), and explicitly agreeing to participate (consent).

6. The researcher must inform the participants *whether harm will be compensated.*

The topic of informed consent is discussed further in Chapter 10 on sampling.

One ethical problem that has been debated in the research community is the appropriateness of using deception. The justification put forward for the use of deception is usually that the results of the study would be compromised because people would alter their behavior if they knew what the researcher was really investigating. Most professional associations' ethical guidelines for psychologists and educators prohibit the use of deception unless it can be justified and the effects of the deception "undone" after the study is completed. The "undoing" of deception is supposed to be accomplished by the following means:

1. *Debriefing* the research participants after the research study, which means that the researcher explains the real purpose and use of the research.

2. *Dehoaxing* the research participants in which the researcher demonstrates the device that was used to deceive the participants. The researcher's responsibility is to attempt to allay a sense of generalized mistrust in educational and psychological research.

3. Guarding the *privacy and confidentiality* of the research participants.

4. Obtaining *fully informed consent.*

Guba and Lincoln (1989) view the allowance of deception in research settings as one of the main failings of the postpositivist paradigm. They point out that the professional associations' codes of ethics that focus on harm are inadequate to guard against the harm that results from discovering that you have been duped and objectified. Such harm includes "the loss of dignity, the loss of individual agency and autonomy, and the loss of self-esteem" (p. 121). They point out the contradiction in using deception to serve the search for "truth" through science. The requirement for fully informed consent and use of deception also creates a contradiction for the researcher. How can people give their fully informed consent to participate in a research study if they do not know what the real purpose of the research is?

Guba and Lincoln (1989) argue that such deception cannot be a part of the constructivist paradigm because the goal is to collect and debate the various multiple constructions of the different constituencies affected by an issue. Nevertheless, researchers functioning within the interpretive/constructivist paradigm are not immune to ethical challenges. The following excerpt provides one example of an ethical dilemma that arose during a study that was conducted within the parameters of the interpretive/constructivist paradigm. Gary Fine and Kent Sandstrom (1988) describe the following situation in their study of White preadolescent boys:

> One day I was driving some boys home, we passed some young Blacks riding bicycles in that almost entirely White suburb. One boy leaned out the car window and shouted at the "jungle bunnies" to "go back where you came from." The ethical problem was what to do or say in reaction to this (and similar) behaviors. In this instance (and others), I offered no direct criticism, although a few times when the situation was appropriate, I reminded the boys of the past prejudices against their own ethnic groups [Irish American]. (pp. 55-56)

Fine comments that he made the judgment not to react to these racist comments because he wanted the children to continue to trust him. This raises other ethical issues in terms of how far researchers should go to engender the trust of their informants. Fine and Sandstrom raise the questions: Should you smoke a joint? Join in a gang fight? Commit a crime?

By presence and tolerance of drug use, racist behavior, and so on, are you supporting that behavior? Fine and Sandstrom (1988) comment that "one must wonder whether the researcher who 'enables' drug dependency or who permits crimes to occur is really acting in accord with the presumption of 'doing no harm'" (p. 68).

Cultural Issues and Ethics

The emancipatory paradigm emerged because of dissatisfaction with research conducted within other paradigms that was perceived to be irrelevant to, or a misrepresentation of, the lives of people who experience oppression. Sieber (1992) writes, "Clearly, sound ethics and sound methodology go hand in hand" (p. 4). Greater concern about the rights and welfare of research participants generally leads to greater involvement of the participants themselves in the research process—one of the basic tenets of the emancipatory paradigm.

Scholars writing from the perspectives of feminists, ethnic minorities, poor people, and people with disabilities have commonly expressed dissatisfaction with both the postpositivist and interpretive/constructivist paradigms of inquiry (Lather, 1992; Mertens et al., 1994; Oliver, 1992; Steady, 1993). Mertens (1995) identified three characteristics of the emancipatory paradigm with ethical implications for methodological choices:

1. Traditionally silenced voices must be included to ensure that groups marginalized in society are equally "heard" during the research process and the formation of the findings and recommendations.

2. An analysis of power inequities in terms of the social relationships involved in the planning, implementation, and reporting of the research is needed to ensure an equitable distribution of resources (conceptual and material).

3. A mechanism should be identified to enable the research results to be linked to social action; those who are most oppressed and least powerful should be at the center of the plans for action in order to empower them to change their own lives.

Sieber (1992) notes a need for increased cultural sensitivity, collaboration, respect, and the tailoring of the research procedures to the population being studied. Because of the difficulty of becoming a community insider in a "foreign" culture, the researcher can choose to collaborate with community leaders and organizations, such as churches and schools. There must be an honest desire to communicate effectively, respect the community members, and share the decision making.

Pollard (1992) suggests that researchers adapt ethical guidelines that were based on developments for cross-cultural research when working with people from minority communities in the United States. Although the cross-cultural ethical standards were developed to guide researchers in other countries, they have applicability for research with Native Americans, Native Alaskans, Hispanic, African Americans, and other minority populations. Pollard provides an example of the application of cross-cultural ethical principles through his research with the American deaf community. Cross-cultural ethical principles require collaboration between the researcher and the host community. In the American deaf community, representatives of the host community could be identified through various national organizations, such as the National Association of the Deaf or Self-Help for Hard of Hearing People. Collaboration should not be limited to conversations with leaders; these initial contacts can be viewed as a way of enhancing access to other members of the deaf community.

Other cross-cultural ethical principles require that the researcher communicate the intended research agenda, design, activity, and reports with members of the host community. The research should be designed in such a way as to bring benefit to the host community and to foster the skills and self-sufficiency of host community scientists. The visiting researcher should strive to conduct the research on an equal-status basis with the host community scientist.

Marín and Marín (1991) and Zambrana (1995) provide examples of the importance of cultural sensitivity in research with Latino populations in terms of the ethical implications for conducting worthwhile and meaningful research. Marín and Marín (1991) suggest that people of Hispanic heritage may be reluctant to participate in research studies for a number of reasons, such as concerns about immigration status, previous experience with oppressive governments, or experience with unscrupulous commercial firms that take advantage of their lack of familiarity with credit or money-lending schemes. Nevertheless, researchers may find Hispanics willing to participate in research endeavors because of their cultural value of promoting positive and cooperative social relations. Researchers should be careful not to take advantage of this generous spirit. To ensure that participation is indeed voluntary, the researcher should strive to make contact with the participants through their community leaders in comfortable settings, so that the participants truly understand their right of refusal to participate.

Merging Paradigms

In practice, many researchers combine the use of quantitative and qualitative methods, so on the surface at least, it appears that a merger of paradigms is possible. Reichardt and Rallis (1994) argue that postpositivists and interpretive/constructivists share more compatibility than incompatibility and that depictions of paradigms such as that in Table 1.2 emphasize differences more than similarities. On the other hand, Guba and Lincoln (1994) maintain in their chapter in the *Handbook of Qualitative Research* and in their earlier writings that the paradigms are basically incompatible (they used the word *incommensurable*). However, in an article that was written only months after their chapter in the *Handbook,* they state that they have begun to have second thoughts (Lincoln & Guba, 1994).

They suggest the possibility of developing a new paradigm *in the future* that looks at everything as a matter of degree rather than dualistically (e.g., something is either real or it is not).

Because the field of research has not yet reached this point in its development, this text presents the existing paradigms and their assumptions as starting points for thought. Researchers should be aware of their basic beliefs, their view of the world (i.e., their functional paradigm), and the way these influence their approach to research.

In this book, quantitative and qualitative methods are explained, and the viewpoints of the various research paradigms are incorporated into the descriptions of methods. The intent is to provide as full a picture as possible of what is considered to be "good" research methodology from a variety of perspectives. This text cannot provide an in-depth discussion of the philosophical underpinnings of each perspective, each approach to research, data analysis, or construction of measurement instruments. References are provided in appropriate chapters for more in-depth information on these topics.

■ *Questions and Activities for Discussion and Application*

1. One definition of research is provided in this text. Think about your own understanding of what it means to do research. Modify the definition provided or create a new definition that reflects your understanding of the meaning of the term *research*.

2. Three paradigms that are currently guiding research in education and psychology are presented in this chapter. Write a short paper that reflects your own ideas regarding where you stand in terms of the options for paradigms of research. Do you find yourself intrigued by or more comfortable with one than another? Do you find yourself somewhat in the middle? Are you withholding judgment until you know more? What else do you want to know? Discuss your position in terms of the ontological, epistemological, and methodological assumptions of each paradigm.

3. What is your opinion concerning merging of paradigms? What do you envision as being required for a merger to occur (if you think it is possible)?

4. Identify research studies that exemplify different paradigms. Categorize these studies according to the paradigm they represent. What were the distinguishing characteristics that led you to conclude that each belongs to the paradigm you selected (e.g., what are the underlying characteristics that define an emancipatory research study)?

5. Is it appropriate to use the "umbrella term" *oppression* to include the experiences of women, ethnic minorities, and persons with disabilities? Why or why not?

6. One unresolved issue in the paradigm discussion relates to the tension between objectivity and relativism. Postpositivist scholars teach the student to value objectivity and the discovery of objective truth. But in the interpretive/constructivist and emancipatory paradigms, multiple viewpoints are sought, with special efforts made to represent the views of the oppressed. The ontological assumption is not that there is one reality waiting to be discovered but that there are multiple realities, depending on whose viewpoint you are soliciting. This ontological assumption has been labeled "radical relativism" by some who feel that interpretive/constructivist and the emancipatory research results only in "opinions" that cannot be substantiated. How do you resolve this dilemma for yourself?

a. Padilla and Lindholm (1995) frame the question as follows:

> The *nomothetic* approach seeks confirmation of general laws and uses procedures that parallel the physical sciences. In contrast, the *ideographic* approach seeks to uncover a particular event in nature or society. Since its initial formulation the nomothetic-ideographic debate has been recast in terms of universalistic and relativistic principles. The universalist view rests on the assumption that concepts and methodologies are basically valid across cultures. Conversely, the relativist view maintains that concepts and methodologies do not necessarily have universal validity, and that they may be appropriate only within a restricted cultural setting. (p. 98)

What is your viewpoint on this issue?

b. In Gitlin's *Power and Method* (1994), two quotes highlight the tension between researchers who think that objectivity is possible and desirable and those who recognize the inherent nature of politics in research:

> Feminism, today, as it conflates politics and education and effaces any distinction between political agenda and the protocols of research, is in danger of suppressing—it already dismisses—any calm, reflective stance that sees some strengths in the effort (however difficult to achieve) to set biases asides and that still regards research as a valuable and satisfying endeavor not in need of quite so much postmodernist angst. (Patai, 1994, p. 62)

In response to Patai's call for "intellectual independence," Michelle Fine (1994a) writes in that same volume that

> feminist scholars across disciplines, situate themselves proudly atop a basic assumption that all research projects are (and should be) political; that researchers who represent themselves as detached only camouflage their deepest, most privileged interests. (p. 15)

Discuss.

7. Are there fundamental differences between/among groups, or are these differences exaggerated? For example, between males and females? Persons of different ethnicities? Persons with disabilities and those without?

8. How can the research community address the issues of oppression and group differences in access to power without engendering greater divisiveness?

9. Who should and can do emancipatory research? Harding (1993) writes the following in answer to this question:

> But the subject of every other liberatory movement must also learn how gender, race, class, and sexuality are used to construct each other in order to accomplish their goals . . . it cannot be that women are the unique generators of feminist knowledge. Women cannot claim this ability to be uniquely theirs, and men must not be permitted to claim that because they are not women, they are not obligated to produce fully feminist analyses. Men, too, must contribute distinctive forms of specifically feminist knowledge from their particular social situation. (p. 67)

Do you agree or disagree with Harding? State your reasons.

10. How can a researcher from a dominant group (i.e., one with power) conduct meaningful research about those of differing race, class, gender, and disability? How can researchers conduct an inquiry on the same cultural group that they are a member of? How can those with less power "study up" the members of groups with more power?

11. It is not clear whether the emancipatory paradigm is to replace existing paradigms or to be an alternative paradigm in conducting research. Is it suggested as an alternative or preferred paradigm in conducting evaluations or research concerning marginalized groups? Or is it a paradigm to be integrated into the existing research methodologies, regardless of the research focus? Some researchers will argue that this paradigm is incompatible with "scientific research methods." What is your response to this argument?

12. Critically analyze the meaning in the following discussion of the impact of a quantitative versus qualitative approach to research (accepting the authors' assumption that a quantitative researcher would use a hypothesis and a qualitative researcher would use a question):

> Aside from specific impact on design of the study, the general advantage of the hypothesis over the question is that it permits more powerful and persuasive conclusions. At the end of a study, a research question never permits the investigator to say more than "Here is how the world looked when I observed it." In contrast hypotheses permit the investigator to say, "Based on my particular explanation of how the world works, this is what I expected to observe, and behold—that is exactly how it looked! For that reason my explanation of how the world works must be given credibility." When a hypothesis is confirmed, the investigator is empowered to make

arguments about knowledge that go far beyond what is available when a question has been asked and answered. (Locke, Spirduso, & Silverman, 1993, p. 15)

13. Critically analyze the message being communicated in the following passage: "For many graduate students, the process of becoming comfortable with the qualitative way of thinking about problems requires adopting a view of the world that is alien to the fundamental canons of empirical thought" (Locke et al., 1993, p. 108).

Note

1. Schwandt (1994) provides detailed background on the philosophical base of the interpretive/constructivist paradigm, and Guba and Lincoln (1989) devoted an entire book to explaining the underlying assumptions of constructivism.

In This Chapter

■ *Two major reasons for conducting a literature review are explained: as a basis for conducting your own research or as an end in itself.*

■ *A nine-step process for conducting a literature review is outlined:*

  1. *Problem identification and source of research topics*

  2. *Review of secondary sources to get an overview of the topic*

  3. *Development of a search strategy, including identification of preliminary sources and primary research journals, and accessing personal networks*

  4. *Conducting the search*

  5. *Obtaining sources*

  6. *Reading and preparing bibliographic information and notes on each article*

  7. *Evaluating the research reports*

  8. *Analyzing the research findings and synthesizing the results*

  9. *Using the literature review to gain a conceptual framework and to formulate research questions, hypotheses, or both*

■ *Issues and questions related to the critical analysis of literature reviews are presented.*

2

Literature Review and Research Problems

Why would you be interested in doing or reading a literature review? After all, when teachers were asked what they did when they were faced with a problem, they reported that their biggest source of information was the teacher down the hall (Kaestle, 1993). Suppose you were working with students who were Hispanic and were having difficulty learning to read. How would you address that challenge? Echevarria (1995) decided to do more than ask the teacher down the hall. She began by conducting a literature review of reading instruction practices, especially as they have been applied to culturally and linguistically diverse special education populations. She used her literature review as a basis for designing a study of effective reading instruction with a group of second- and third-grade Hispanic children with learning disabilities.

When asked, Why do a literature review? a somewhat cynical answer may have popped into some of your minds. Why do a literature review? It is required for my research class, or I have to do a dissertation. Then, again, some of you may have more socially redeeming motivations, such as wanting to change the world or improve your practice of a profession.

Literature reviews are important as a research tool, especially in emerging areas, with populations that typically yield small samples (e.g., special education research often does), or in areas that represent value-laden positions adopted by advocacy groups. Literature reviews are also valuable in light of the knowledge explosion and the consequent impossibility of reading everything. Therefore, it is good that someone does literature reviews.

Major Reasons for Doing Literature Reviews

There are two major reasons for conducting literature reviews: to conduct primary research oneself (or as a part of a team) or as an end in itself.

Literature Reviews for Planning Primary Research

Almost every report of a primary research study begins with a review of the literature. The purpose of the literature review section of a research article is to provide the reader with an overall framework for where this piece of work fits in the "big picture" of what is known about a topic from previous research. Thus, the literature review serves to explain the topic of the research and to build a rationale for the problem that is studied. For almost 200 years, researchers have known that more research is needed:

> In research the horizon recedes as we advance, and is no nearer at sixty than it was at twenty. As the power of endurance weakens with age, the urgency of the pursuit grows more intense. . . . And research is always incomplete. (Mark Pattison, 1813-1884, as cited in the *Oxford Dictionary of Quotations,* 1979, p. 370)

Researchers use the literature review to identify a rationale for the need for their own study. Some of the specific rationales for your research that might emerge from your literature review include the following:

1. You may find a lack of consistency in reported results across the studies you have chosen to review and undertake research to explore the basis of the inconsistency (Eagley & Wood, 1994). For example, Born (1993) chose to study site-based management and shared decision making because the outcomes of previous research were unclear: "Though some schools have experienced frustration, bureaucratic snags, chaos, and outright failure, some have been successful" (p. 66).

2. You may have uncovered a flaw in previous research based on its design, data collection instruments, sampling, or interpretation. For example, Lips (1993) notes the gender-sensitive nature of tests used to support differences between males and females in mathematics skills.

3. Research may have been conducted on a different population than the one in which you are interested, thus justifying your work with the different population. For example, Sullivan, Vernon, and Scanlan (1987) note that incidence data on sexual abuse were available for the general population but not for deaf children.

4. You may document an ongoing educational or psychological problem and propose studying the effect of an innovative intervention to try to correct that problem. For example,

B. T. Anderson (1993) notes the ongoing problem of underrepresentation of minority women in scientific careers, thus supporting the need to investigate the effectiveness of intervention programs to rectify the situation.

5. Uncertainty about the interpretation of previous studies' findings may justify further research. For example, Eagley and Carli (1981) reported that the sex of the researcher influenced the size of differences associated with specific psychological characteristics. They found that male authors, more often than female authors, tended to report that women were more influenced by others than were men and that women were less accurate than men at decoding nonverbal messages.

As mentioned previously, a literature review can be used at the beginning of the study to explain what is known about your topic and provide a rationale for the study you are planning. In addition, the literature review can be used to help in the design of the study by providing guidance as to appropriate sample size or identifying promising data collection practices or instruments that can be used in your study. Morse (1994) points out that qualitative researchers should be well prepared in their topic so that they can pick up on subtle clues in interviews and follow up on pertinent points. They should know the literature to be able to recognize statements made in an interview that relate to phenomenon described by other researchers. In addition, extant literature can be used to guide you in the interpretation of your results. For example, knowing the results of other studies can reveal whether your results are smaller, typical, or larger than those obtained by other researchers (Eagly & Wood, 1994).

When your purpose is to plan your own research study, the number of studies that you actually cite in your literature review may be fairly limited due to space limitations (for authors who publish in journals) or because the review is considered a learning activity (in your own course work). Typically, primary research articles published in journals contain 20 to 30 references of primary research. The number of citations may be quite limited for a course activity or more extensive if you are preparing a proposal for a thesis or dissertation. The exact number varies, depending on the purpose of the literature review and the extant literature. The primary criteria for inclusion should be centrality to your topic, within whatever constraints are imposed by instructors, advisers, or publishers.

Use of the literature review to plan and conduct a study requires that you critically evaluate the research that you read. This critical analysis can form the basis for your rationale or for your choice of data collection procedures. Criteria for evaluating primary research studies are provided at the end of this chapter.

Review of Literature as an End in Itself

The review of literature can be seen as an end in itself, either to inform practice or to provide a comprehensive understanding about what is known about a topic. The process for conducting this type of literature review varies, depending on your purpose. If your purpose is to *improve your professional practice,* you will want to base your literature review on the problem you encountered in your profession. Therefore, when you look to the literature for a solution, you may rely on other people's literature reviews, or you may seek out primary research reports until you find one that seems to fit your situation. For example,

B. T. Anderson (1993) reviewed literature for the purpose of proposing a model intervention program to increase the representation of minority women in scientific careers.

When a literature review is conducted to provide a *comprehensive understanding* of what is known about a topic, the process is much longer. For example, Scarr and Eisenberg (1993) reviewed almost 200 references in their review of child care research, Sadker and Sadker (1991) include over 400 references in their review of gender issues in education, and Schofield (1991) has a similar number of references in her review of literature on school desegregation and intergroup relations.

In Cooper and Hedges's (1994a) edited volume, *The Handbook of Research Synthesis,* they explain how to conduct an *integrative research review,* which they define as a "research syntheses attempt to integrate empirical research for the purpose of creating generalizations" (p. 5). They provide an extensive explanation of how to conduct a comprehensive review of literature and how to combine the results of studies that present their results in the form of statistical data for theory testing. The general approaches to an integrative research review are explained in Chapter 12 of this text; however, the student who wishes to conduct a comprehensive integrative research review would be well-advised to check Cooper and Hedges's *Handbook* (see especially Chapter 29 by Miller & Pollock, 1994).

Whether your purpose is to improve your practice or to provide a comprehensive understanding of a topic, it is important to critically evaluate the research that you read. Criteria for the evaluation of literature reviews are discussed at the end of this chapter.

The Search Process

No matter what the reason for the literature review or the paradigm within which the researcher is working, many aspects of the literature review process are the same. A general outline for conducting a literature review is provided in the box labeled "Steps in the Literature Review Process." Some of the differences in the process that emanate from paradigm choice include the following:

1. With the postpositivist paradigm, the researcher who plans to conduct quasi-experimental research needs to be able to develop a hypothesis (best guess as to the outcome of the planned research) based on previous research.

2. With an interpretive/constructivist orientation, the researcher should have a good understanding of previous research but remain open to possible emerging hypotheses that would require examination of additional literature during the study (Marshall & Rossman, 1989).

3. In the emancipatory paradigm, the researcher should consult with persons who have experienced oppression and seek out literature that represents their viewpoints (Harding, 1993).

In the following section, the commonalities in the search process are described, along with a recognition of appropriate caveats that differentiate work within alternative paradigms.

■ STEPS IN THE LITERATURE REVIEW PROCESS

Step 1: Identify a research topic

Step 2: Review secondary sources to get an overview of the topic: for example, *Review of Educational Research, Harvard Educational Review, Psychological Bulletin, Review of Research in Education, Annual Review of Psychology*

Step 3: Develop a search strategy:

   Identify appropriate preliminary sources and relevant journals to search (see Tables 2.1, 2.2, and 2.3)

   Identify primary research journals and use the ancestry approach

   Access personal networks

Step 4: Conduct searches and select titles

Step 5: Obtain sources

Step 6: Read and prepare bibliographic information and notes

Step 7: Evaluate the research reports

Step 8: Analyze the research findings and synthesize the results

Step 9: Use the synthesis to develop a conceptual framework, research questions, and/or hypotheses ■

Step 1: Identify Research Topic

Two pieces of advice should guide (novice) researchers as they begin their literature review process. They should be flexible in their conceptualization of the research problem being investigated, and they should begin with a broad idea and be prepared to narrow it down as they progress through the search (Krathwohl, 1993). Sometimes, students choose topics for research that turn out to be not very researchable (in that no one else has conceptualized the problem quite that way), and as they begin reading and seeing what is available, their ideas change as to what they want to investigate. Also, if the topic definition is too narrow, it may not be possible to identify any previous research that addressed that specific topic. Therefore, be flexible and start broadly.

Sources of Research Topics

A research topic can emerge from a wide variety of sources, including the researcher's interests, knowledge of social conditions, and observation of educational and psychological problems, challenges that arise in one's professional practice; readings in other courses; talking to other researchers; or funds available to conduct specific research topics (sponsored research). Any of these is appropriate as a source to help identify the primary research topic.

For researchers interested in conducting a comprehensive review of literature for its own sake, another criterion must be met: They must study topics that appear in the literature (Cooper, 1989).

For sponsored research, the researcher needs to clarify with the funding agency what the research problem is (Hedrick, Bickman, & Rog, 1993). Often, students can apply for funding to support their own research, usually with a faculty sponsor. When applying for funds, it is important to know what the agency is interested in sponsoring and to tailor one's research interests to match those of the agency. Other students might work as research assistants to faculty members who have received financial support from an outside agency.

Scholars working in the emancipatory paradigm have been instrumental in stimulating research on a variety of topics that had previously received little attention, such as spouse abuse, sexual abuse, sexual harassment, homophobia, unpaid labor, and motherhood and child care. For emancipatory research, Harding (1993) recommends beginning with marginalized lives. The researcher might want to involve persons affected by the research through informal or formal means such as focus groups in the definition of the research problem (Mertens, Farley, Madison, & Singleton, 1994). Hedrick et al. (1993) also recommend this strategy, although they did not offer their suggestion in the context of the emancipatory paradigm.

Step 2: Review Secondary Sources to Get an Overview

A good literature review written by someone else can provide you with an overview of what is known about your chosen topic. Specific places that you can look for literature reviews include the following:

1. Journals that typically publish literature reviews, such as *Review of Educational Research, Harvard Educational Review,* and the *Psychological Bulletin.*

2. Books that contain literature reviews:

   a. *Review of Research in Education:* This series is published annually by the American Educational Research Association. Each volume contains a series of chapters on diverse topics, such as race, culture, and education; curriculum and schooling; learning and performance; and test validity and educational indicators (Vol. 19, Grant, 1993b); curriculum, history and philosophy, and teacher education (Vol. 18, Grant, 1993a); and assessment, politics, and school decision making; gender and race; and moral education (Vol. 17, Grant, 1991).

   b. National Society for the Study of Education yearbooks: Two volumes are published on a specific topic annually. Recent topics include bilingual education (Arias & Casanova, 1993), gender and education (Biklen & Pollard, 1993), the arts and education (Reimer & Smith, 1992), the changing contexts of teaching (Lieberman, 1992), the care and education of America's youth (Kagan, 1991), evaluation and education (Mclaughlin & Phillips, 1991); and schooling and disabilities (Biklen, Ferguson, & Ford, 1989), and curriculum (Jackson & Haroutunian-Gordon, 1989).

   c. The *Annual Review of Psychology* contains literature reviews on topics of interest in psychology and education, such as counseling or learning theory.

   d. *Research in Race and Ethnic Relations* is published annually to address race relations and minority and ethnic group research.

e. Other handbooks have been published on specific topics:

Gaylord-Ross, R. (Ed.). (1990, 1992). *Issues and research in special education* (Vols. 1-2). New York: Teachers College Press.

Ponterotto, J. G., & Casas, J. M. (1991). *Handbook of racial/ethnic minority counseling research.* Springfield, IL: Charles C Thomas.

Wang, M. C., Reynolds, M. C., & Walberg, H. J. (Eds.). (1987-1989). *Handbook of special education: Research and practice* (Vols. 1-3). Oxford, UK: Pergamon.

Wang, M. C., Reynolds, M. C., & Walberg, H. J. (1990). *Special education research and practice.* Oxford, UK: Pergamon. [Condensed version of *Handbook of special education,* Volumes 1-3]

Step 3: Develop a Search Strategy

Three substeps are included in developing a search strategy: (a) identify preliminary sources, (b) identify primary research journals, and (c) access personal networks. These are explained below. Decide what is the best strategy for you to follow in your search process, and remember, stay flexible.

Identify Preliminary Sources

Preliminary sources include databases, abstracts, and indexes that contain a compilation of bibliographic information (and sometimes abstracts) for a wide range of topics and are accessible in print form, on compact disks (CD-ROM), or through an on-line service. Examples of the most frequently used preliminary sources are listed in Table 2.1. Additional abstract and index services that specifically target marginalized groups include *African Urban & Regional Science Index, Feminist Periodicals, Studies on Women Abstracts,* and *Women Studies Abstracts.*

World Wide Web (WWW) sites are a more recent development in the realm of literature searching. There are many search sites on the Web, and new ones appear with some regularity. In the December 1996 issue of *PC Magazine,* the editors' top three choices for search engines[1] were Excite, HotBot, and Yahoo! (Singh & Lidsky, 1996). The editors recognized the advanced searching power of AltaVista, but they point out that Yahoo! is integrated with the AltaVista search engine. So if your query fails at Yahoo!, it is automatically run again using the AltaVista engine. The search process on the WWW sites generally employs Boolean logic (explained later in this chapter) but can differ a bit from site to site. Because this is such a dynamic area, it is best to check *PC Magazine* or some other computer source both to find out what sites are recommended and to determine appropriate search strategies for those sites. One word of caution: The WWW sites do not have a peer review system to screen what is accepted (as most professional journals do); therefore, scholars raise questions about the quality of information available from those sources. In addition, the Web sites are not designed to contain information specifically about research in education and psychology as are the other databases described in this chapter.

TABLE 2.1 Most Frequently Used Preliminary Sources

Bibliographic Index	Lists bibliographies that have been published separately or as part of books or journals that have at least 50 or more citations. Available in print or as an on-line service.
Psychological Abstracts	Contains citations and abstracts from over 1,300 journals and psychology-related dissertations. The electronic version of *Psychological Abstracts* is called PsycINFO and is available on CD-ROM.
Dissertation Abstracts International	All dissertations and thesis (since 1962), regardless of topic, are included in this source. It is available on-line and on CD-ROM.
Educational Resources Information Center (ERIC)	ERIC consists of two parts. Both are combined in the ERIC database that is available on CD-ROM and on-line:[a] Current Index to Journals in Education (CIJE), which includes about 700 educational journals Resources in Education (RIE which includes research reports and other reports of educational significance, such as conference proceedings and curriculum materials)
Exceptional Child	Quarterly publication of abstracts prepared by the Council for Exceptional Children on issues related to disabilities and giftedness; it includes over 200 journals, dissertations, and other print and nonprint resources. It is currently available in print and through on-line searching. A CD-ROM version is expected to be available in 1998.
NTIS (National Technical Information Service)	A source of government reports from many government agencies and government-sponsored research projects. It is available on CD-ROM. FEDRIP (Federal Research in Progress) is another NTIS database that contains information about research projects still in progress.
Social Science Citation Index	A forward search of citation indexes of the Institute for Science Information. It lists works that cite a relevant article identified by other means.
Education Index	Includes over 400 periodicals, educational publications, journals, yearbooks, and monographs that tend to focus on higher education. It is available in print and on CD-ROM.
Child Development Abstracts	Includes abstracts from professional periodical and reviews books related to growth and development of children. Published by the Society for Research in Child Development; currently available only in print.

a. The citations contained in CIJE are primarily from peer-reviewed journals (i.e., the manuscripts are reviewed by experts in the field prior to acceptance for publication). The citations in RIE are much more of a "mixed bag." Because peer review is not used as a screening mechanism for documents accepted in RIE, you need to be cautious in your assessment of the quality of materials located in the RIE database.

The computerized databases are a tremendous resource for the researcher in the literature review phase of a project. A researcher can identify thousands of references by only a few key strokes on the computer. Because of the tremendous coverage provided by the databases, the researcher should plan to include a search of appropriate databases in the literature review process.

One important limitation should be noted about the available databases. You can get out of them only what was put into them. In other words, the databases are selective about the journals they include. For example, many of the best known feminist journals are not included in the databases. A survey of 17 feminist journals indicated that only 3 are included in ERIC (see Table 2.2). Some of the feminist journals listed in Table 2.2 might not be considered appropriate for inclusion in ERIC because their content is not directly related to education or psychology. However, readers who are not familiar with feminist journals might find the list helpful as a way of broadening their resource base. For example, *Hypatia* publishes mainly philosophical work and thus would be of interest to those who want to delve more deeply into that aspect of feminist theory. And *camera obscura* publishes work that could be of interest to scholars in educational media or social learning theory (in the study of the power of media to shape cultural expectations by gender).

Identify Primary Research Journals

Additional primary research articles can be identified by examining the reference lists found at the end of relevant journal articles or books. Cooper (1989) calls this the "ancestry approach" (p. 43). You can also go directly to journals that you know publish articles related to your topic. This is especially important in light of the selectivity of the databases discussed in the previous section. Researchers who are working from an emancipatory paradigm should be aware of the journals that deal with issues specific to marginalized groups, such as those in Table 2.2 for feminists, as well as journals such as *Latin American Perspectives, Hispanic Journal of Behavioral Sciences, Journal of Multicultural Counseling and Development, Journal of Negro Education,* and *Journal of Black Studies.* A special issue of *Disability, Handicap & Society* was devoted to the concept of the emancipatory paradigm in research with people with disabilities, and *The Counseling Psychologist* (Stone, 1993) devoted an entire issue to the topic of the White American researcher and multicultural counseling (Vol. 21, No. 2). A more extensive list of special education journals can be found in Table 2.3.

Personal Networking

Additional resources can be found by talking to people who are doing work in areas related to your interest. This can include people at your own institution or those you meet through professional associations such as the American Educational Research Association, the American Evaluation Association, or the American Psychological Association. Talking to people who have completed related work can reveal sources that you were unaware of, such as unpublished research reports, and provide you with leads from work that is "in progress" for that researcher.

Step 4: Conduct Search

In conducting the search, you should access your personal network and also check the table of contents and abstracts in appropriate journals. The remainder of this section focuses on the search strategy as it applies to accessing preliminary sources.

TABLE 2.2 Feminist Journals

camera obscura	A journal of feminism and film theory.
differences	Devoted to feminist cultural theory. "Affiliated with the Pembroke Center for Teaching and Research on Women at Brown University." This journal has been noted for being related to poststructuralist theory.
Feminist Studies	The first academic journal (started in 1972); "the oldest continuously publishing feminist journal." Based at the University of Maryland. "An interdisciplinary journal, publishing pieces on literature, art, history, psychology, and even poetry and fiction." The journal takes a particular interest in theoretical debates in feminism.
Feminist Teacher[a]	Dubbing itself a "reader-developed magazine," *Feminist Teacher* aims to provide a forum for the exchange of ideas about the theory and practice of nonsexist teaching at all levels, preschool through graduate school. Topics examined include science and math teaching, sexual harassment in academia, making students aware of ableism, teaching about women in introductory courses in American politics, and celebrating women's history. In addition to feature articles, the quarterly publishes a directory of Feminist Teacher Network members, news reports, resource lists and bibliographies, calls for papers, and conference notices.
Gender and Education	Three volumes per year, published in England on topics related to sex equity and discrimination in education.
Genders	Focusing on art, literature, film, and television. Based out of the University of Colorado. Interested in feminism and men and masculinity. Controversial topics.
Gender and Higher Education in the Progressive Era	The impact of women's presence on university campuses did not become evident until the Progressive Era 1890–1920.
Gender & History	A quarterly based at Radcliffe College that is devoted to historical questions about gender relations.
Gender & Society	The official publication of the Sociologists for Women in Society, this journal focuses on the social and structural study of gender as a basic principle of the social order and as a primary social category, with emphasis on theory and research from micro- and macrostructural perspectives. It is multidisciplinary in nature and includes research in the areas of anthropology, economics, history, political science, social psychology, and sociology.
Hypatia	One of the best known journals for its devotion to feminist philosophy approach. Articles include topics such as male friendship, ecology, and feminism and the body. "We publish people who are not strictly philosophers."
Initiatives	Published quarterly by the National Association for Women in Education. Each issue is thematic; recent themes included women in math and science, and sexual harassment.
Journal of Women's History	Covers new research on women's history. Promotes scholarship about women in all time periods that is broadly representative of national, racial, ethnic, religious, and sexual grouping.
NWSA (National Women's Studies Association) Journal	Interdisciplinary articles that "link feminist theory with teaching and activism" (since 1988).

TABLE 2.2 Feminist Journals	
Sex roles: A Journal of Research	Examines sex roles for males and females. Includes educational and psychological topics such as spouse abuse, self-perception, aggression, and teacher behavior.
Signs: Journal of Women in Culture and Society[a]	An academic journal that "helped pave the way" for other feminist journals such as *differences* and *Genders*. Published by the University of Chicago Press. Recognized for covering a vast array of areas "from esoteric literary theory to practical politics."
Women's Studies International Forum	Multidisciplinary journal for the rapid publication of research communications and review articles in women's studies. Supplement: *Feminist Forum*
Women's Studies Quarterly	Publishes essays that connect feminist theory and scholarship to teaching and curriculum development, research, or political action in women's studies.

a. These feminist journals are included in the ERIC database; the others on this list are not in ERIC.

Preparing to Search Preliminary Sources

Select the preliminary sources that you think contain the best information on your topic (see Table 2.1). Then identify key terms that will help you locate the literature included in the database of choice. One way that researchers select key terms is to find one primary research article that is "exactly" on target and identify the terms used to describe that article.

A search strategy based on using the ERIC CD-ROM system is used to illustrate this process. The search strategy is similar when using other databases and indexes, such as PsycLIT. Most databases give you four choices for searching: title, author, subject, or key words. The title and author choices are fairly self-explanatory and not usually used in the beginning of a literature review because you are not seeking a specific article. The subject

TABLE 2.3 Selected Journals Containing Special Education Resource Information	
American Annals of the Deaf	*Disability & Society*
American Journal on Mental Retardation	*Journal of Autism and Developmental Disorders*
Annals of Dyslexia	*Journal of Early Intervention*
Australia and New Zealand Journal of Developmental Disabilities	*Journal of Learning Disabilities*
Journal of Special Education
Behavioral Disorders	*Journal of Speech and Hearing Research*
British Journal of Special Education	*Journal of Speech of the Association for Persons With Severe Handicaps*
Canadian Journal of Special Education	
Career Development for Exceptional Individuals	*International Journal of Disability*
Education and Training in Mental Retardation	*Learning Disability Quarterly*
Exceptional Children	*Mental Retardation*
Exceptionality: A Research Journal	*Research in Development Disabilities*
Development and Education	*Volta Review* (deafness)

TABLE 2.4 Journal Citation From ERIC	
Accession No.:	EJ448540
Title:	The Effects of Psychotherapy on Behavior Problems of Sexually Abused Deaf Children
Author(s):	Sullivan, Patricia M.
Source:	Child Abuse and Neglect: The International Journal v16 n2 p. 297-307 1992
Clearinghouse No:	EC603367
Document Type:	Journal articles. Reports—research
Major Subjects:	Behavior problems; child abuse; deafness; outcomes of treatment; psychotherapy; sexual abuse
Minor Subjects:	Effect size; intervention; program effectiveness; residential schools; sex differences
Abstract:	This study assessed the effectiveness of a broad-based psychotherapeutic intervention with about half of a group of 72 children sexually abused at a residential school for the deaf. Findings indicated a powerful treatment effect, with boys and girls differing in the specific areas of improvement following therapy.
Language:	English
Availability:	UMI

and key word choices need a bit of explanation. *Subject* words are those that were used by the people who work for the database to categorize that item. These words are contained in a thesaurus, such as the *Thesaurus of ERIC Descriptors*. Each item in the database has a field associated with it that contains subject words that an indexer selected, and that is the field that is searched when you choose a subject word strategy. *Key* words, on the other hand, allow researchers to choose words that reflect their own vocabulary in the description of the topic. When the computer searches for these terms, it uses a "free text" strategy; that is, it searches anywhere in the document for the words that you enter (i.e., the title, descriptors, or abstract fields). Advantages and disadvantages accrue to whichever search strategy is chosen.

The easiest way to start is to use a key word strategy to determine if the words that you think are appropriate produce references that match your conceptualization of the problem. For example, for the topic of sexual abuse in residential schools for the deaf, I started with the key words *sex?* and *deaf?* (there is a good reason, explained later, for the inclusion of the *?* and the word *and* in this search specification). This resulted in 162 entries. One of the entries was Sullivan's (1992) article, "The Effects of Psychotherapy on Behavior Problems of Sexually Abused Deaf Children." An examination of that entry revealed that its descriptors included *sexual abuse, deafness,* and *child abuse* (see Table 2.4).

I used some of these descriptors, still in a free-text mode, to narrow my search. My next search asked for *sex? abuse* and *deaf?* This yielded seven studies that were more directly related to my topic. If you have difficulty finding references using your own key word vocabulary, check a thesaurus of terms to determine how the indexers might have conceptualized your topic. Use of subject descriptors can be helpful in narrowing down a search, as long as the descriptors are defined in a way that is compatible with your topic. They can also be helpful in broadening a search by suggesting other terms that could prove fruitful in searching.

Now, why include a *?* in the search terms, and what is the importance of the *and* in the list? You can refine your search in the following ways:

---

1. Truncate the terms you use. This has the effect of broadening the search to include any terms that begin with the letters that you enter, no matter how they end. In ERIC, the truncating symbol is a *?*. Therefore, entering *sex?* would include *sex, sexual, sexes,* and so on, and *deaf?* would include deaf, deafness, deafened, and so on.

2. Use Boolean or positional operators to combine terms. Boolean logic allows you to use the words *and, or, not,* and *xor* (one but not both words are in a record). Thus, asking for *sex? abuse and deaf?* yields references in which both terms appear in the same record. The *or* operator yields references that have either or both words in the same record. So, I could have asked for *sex? abuse or child abuse and deaf?*. This would have given me all the records that contain *sex? abuse* or *child abuse* and *deafness*. For example, I could have broadened my search by including *deaf? or hearing-imp?*. This would have resulted in all references that had either *deaf, hearing-impaired, hearing impaired,* or *hearing impairment* in their records.

   Positional operators include *same, with, adj,* and *near,* and they limit retrieval by specifying how near key words must be to each other. *Same* means that both words must be in the same field of the same record; *with* means both words are in the same section of the same field of the same record; *adj* requires that the words must be next to one another (adjacent) in the order specified; and *near* finds references in which words are next to one another in any order (e.g., *sex abuse* or *abuse sex*).

3. There are other ways to limit the search, such as by year of publication or limiting the field that is searched (e.g., title only). Certain *stop* words are not allowed to be used as key words (e.g., *about, all, its*), but all of these things can be learned by reading the on-line instructions. As you get into using a database, it is always a good idea to read the on-line instructions to see what can be accomplished and how.

4. Obviously, the search process can be broadened by inclusion of additional databases or indexes. For example, when I searched PsycINFO using the same descriptors (i.e., *sexual abuse* and *deaf*), I identified three additional references that did not overlap with those found in ERIC.

Interpreting What You See

With an ERIC search, you can locate two types of documents: journal articles and other references (not journals). Journal articles are noted by an EJ (education journal) number at the top of the record; other references are noted as ED (education document). An example of each with an explanation of the codes is presented in Tables 2.4 and 2.5.

TABLE 2.5 ED Document Citation From ERIC	
Accession No.:	ED293245
Title:	Dormitory Program Review: A Model for External Analysis
Author(s):	Kellogg, Robert C.
Publication Date:	1987
Note:	A presentation to the Joint Meeting of the Convention of American Instructors of the Deaf and the Conference of Educational Administrators Serving the Deaf, Inc. (Santa Fe, NM, June 28-July 2, 1987)
Clearinghouse No.:	EC202094
Audience:	Administrators; practitioners
Document Type:	Reports—descriptive. speeches, conference papers
Major Subjects:	Child abuse; counselor client ratio; counselor training; deafness; residential institutions; sexual abuse
Minor Subjects:	Attendants; discipline policy; dormitories; elementary/secondary education; group experience; in-school suspension; policy formation; program evaluation; recordkeeping; resident advisers; school policy; sex education; staff development
Identifiers:	Nebraska School for the Deaf; independent living; program review
Abstract:	Systematic review of dormitory programs at residential schools for the deaf can alleviate existing problems and prevent new ones. Allegations of sexual misconduct and child abuse, in particular, have raised serious concerns about the adequacy of staff training and experience and the maintenance of appropriate student-staff ratios to provide necessary supervision. The model presented in this paper, developed at the Nebraska School for the Deaf, recommends that each dormitory program should have a policy and procedures manual that is part of the overall school policy system. Much attention is focused on the importance of accurate recordkeeping regarding disciplinary actions taken and the procedures used to discipline students, including an in-school suspension process, incident reports, privilege or behavior cards, positive parenting activities, and reward systems. Dormitory individualized education plans (IEPs) are prepared to meet all requirements outlined by P.L. 94-142 and have provided a bridge between school and dormitory programs. Other areas covered include sex education, independent living programs, staff career ladders and pay, and administrative structure to enhance a two-way flow of communication between administrators and staff. Copies of the Nebraska dormitory IEPs and bibliography and resource list are appended. (VW)
Language:	English
Country of Origin:	U.S., Nebraska
Availability:	EDRS Price—MF01/PC03 Plus Postage

Selecting Titles

Most databases provide an abstract of the articles listed. By scanning these abstracts, you can make a decision as to the worth of obtaining the complete article.

Step 5: Obtain Titles

Most libraries have lists (print or computerized) that list their holdings. If the journal you seek is held by your library, you are in luck. Go to the shelves and read the article. However, if your library does not have the item, you may avail yourself of an interlibrary loan service. If you provide complete bibliographic information, the librarian can determine which other library has the article and make a request to have it sent to you. There is often a small charge for this service. In some libraries, this capability is available by an on-line request as you are doing your search. The computer may ask you if you want to order the document, and then it will tell you how much it costs to obtain. You have the option of agreeing to pay the cost, and if you agree, the library that holds the reference is electronically contacted and asked to transmit the article to your library. Amazing! (The researcher's equivalent to Home Shopping Network.)

If you have chosen to review an ED document from an ERIC search, that document is available for your review on microfiche in the library. The microfiche are organized in ascending order according to their ED numbers, so they are easy to find.

Step 6: Read and Prepare Bibliographic Information and Notes

Once you have the article in hand, scan the document to determine if it is really what you want. If you decide that it is relevant to your topic, you will want to record bibliographic information and notes on each article. This can be done electronically or manually, using old-fashioned note cards. Woodworth (1994) provides a good explanation of how to set up a computerized database for meta-analytic literature reviews. Either way, the information that you should look for is about the same.

Bibliographic Information

The most important thing to remember in recording bibliographic information is to be complete and accurate. Some of the problems associated with recording bibliographic information have been reduced because of the capability of printing such information directly from the computer screen. However, if you have hundreds of printouts, you may want to record the information on index cards. (I do not always have a computer with me when I want to record bibliographic information, so index cards are handy.)

Although several options are available for the format of recording bibliographic information, the most common style for education and psychology is based on the American Psychological Association's (1994) *Publication Manual.* This is the basic format for a journal citation:

Author's Last Name, Initials. (date of publication). Title of journal article. *Title of Journal, volume number,*(issue number), page numbers.

For example,

Sullivan, P. M. (1992). The effects of psychotherapy on behavior problems of sexually abused deaf children. *Child Abuse and Neglect: The International Journal, 16*(2), 297-307.

There are differences, however, in citation style associated with different types of documents (e.g., books, chapters in books, government reports, etc.), so the student is advised to obtain a copy of the APA *Publication Manual* to guide the compilation of bibliographic information.

Notes on Each Study

Exactly what notes are written for each study vary greatly and depend on the nature of the study, the purpose of the review, and the intended use of the data. If the researcher intends to conduct a comprehensive literature review of studies that report their results in statistical form, the use of coding forms and computerized databases is recommended (Stock, 1994; Woodworth, 1994).

For empirical research studies, the following outline can be helpful:

---

1. Problem addressed

2. Paradigm of researcher(s)

3. Design, including

  a. Sampling strategy

  b. Characteristics of participants

  c. Data collection instruments and methods

4. Data analysis strategy

5. Results

6. Conclusions

7. Your own evaluation (including strengths and weaknesses and ideas for your own research, such as promising methodological or conceptual suggestions). (The evaluation of research reports is Step 7. However, once you have evaluated the research report, you should return to your note cards or files and enter your own assessment of the strengths and weaknesses of the research.)

Step 7: Evaluate the Research Reports

You will be learning how to evaluate research as you progress through this text. A comprehensive listing of questions for critical analysis for evaluating primary research is provided in the appendix. The questions are organized according to the sections of the research report (e.g., introduction, method, etc.), with additional specific questions relevant to each approach to research (e.g., experimental, quasi-experimental, etc.).

Step 8: Analyze the Research Findings and
Synthesize the Results

Two main options exist for the synthesis of research studies: narrative and statistical methods. The choice of the type of synthesis depends on the type of extant research literature on a topic and on the purpose of the researcher. In this chapter, I focus on the narrative approach to synthesizing literature. The statistical approach is explored in Chapter 12.

Narrative Synthesis

A narrative synthesis is appropriate for studies that use a qualitative design as well as for quantitative studies. In a narrative synthesis, the writer must organize the studies in a conceptually logical order and provide sufficient detail about the studies to support relevant critical analysis of them. The amount of detail provided (as well as the number of studies cited) will be influenced by the purpose of the literature review. For example,

1. Typically, the literature review section of a journal article includes a limited number of references that are selected on the basis of relevancy to the problem at hand, presenting a balanced picture, and establishing a rationale for the reported research.

2. A literature review for a research proposal is usually more extensive. If the research proposal is for a thesis or dissertation, it is expected to be quite comprehensive in most universities.

Ogawa and Malen (1991) propose the use of the exploratory case method as a way of conducting narrative reviews and suggested the use of the criteria "rigor" as the appropriate standard for assessing the quality of such reviews. They use the term *rigor* to mean "adherence to principles and procedures, methods, and techniques that minimize bias and error in the collection, analysis, interpretation, and reporting of data" (p. 267). The exploratory case method is implemented in a narrative review by treating each document as a data point that must be "scrutinized, summarized, and utilized in a relatively unencumbered but systematically executed search for emergent themes and patterns. The summations of diverse documents are then analyzed and aggregated in order to develop conclusions about the literature and inferences about the phenomenon of interest" (p. 271).

Patton (1991) recognizes that Ogawa and Malen's emphasis on the standard of rigor might be appropriate for research done within the scholarly community (the academy, so to speak). However, he suggests that the standard of "utility" might be more appropriate in other types of inquiry. For example, in program evaluation, information should be presented in a manner that is useful to the client, decision makers, stakeholders, and participants. Therefore, a literature review is judged to be "good" if it is viewed as useful by these constituencies.

Yin (1991) suggests that the exploratory case study method might not be the appropriate model for synthesizing narrative literature because this method typically requires use of both document-based data and field-based data. He proposes either consideration of grounded theory (Strauss & Corbin, 1990) or borrowing data synthesis strategies from historians (e.g., Neustadt & May, 1986). Methods based on grounded theory can apply to evidence collected in a library, data collected in the field, or both. Its aim is to build theory and identify emergent categories about a substantive topic (thus emphasizing the use of qualitative data). Thus, grounded theory could be used to synthesize evidence based solely on document review. For more on this topic, the reader is referred to Chapter 7 on qualitative approaches to research.

Step 9: Use the Literature Review

The narrative-statistical synthesis serves as a basis for the literature section of a research proposal or report. The appendix contains an outline for a research proposal for a thesis or dissertation. It is important for the proposal writer to realize that each institution and sponsoring agency has its own requirements for proposal writing, so it is best to check with those sources before proceeding with writing. Proposal writers must also realize that in this synthesis of research they are "selling" their ideas to a research committee, institutional review board, or funding agency. So above all, make it clear why the research is important (based on what is known from the extant literature).

Conceptual Framework and Program Theory

In some ways, the conceptual framework is like the chicken and egg controversy. A researcher's original conceptual framework influences the planning and conducting of the literature review. However, if a researcher keeps an open mind throughout the literature review process, a more sophisticated and (often greatly) modified conceptual framework should emerge. Mertens et al. (1994) discuss the influence of the theoretical framework on the choice of research questions and its implications for action. On the basis of work by Villegas (1991) on theoretical frameworks used to explain differential achievement by ethnic minority students, Mertens et al., derived four different research questions that illustrate this point (see Table 2.6). The IQ deficit theory and the cultural deficit theory reflect the postpositivist paradigm in the type of research questions and research approaches. The cultural difference theory reflects the constructivist paradigm, and the power inequity theory reflects the emancipatory paradigm.

These various explanations for poor academic achievement by ethnic minority children exemplify alternative theories that might be held by the researcher or by the research sponsor or participants. Researchers must be aware of their own personal theoretical base as well as that of the sponsors and the participants. For example, Davis (1992) notes that research on African American families often depicts them as deviant, pathological social organizations unable to fulfill the major responsibilities of socializing their members for productive roles in society (the deficit model). The conclusion based on this model, then, is that this undersocialization leads to negative outcomes such as low academic achievement, juvenile delinquency, drug abuse, and teenage pregnancy. Davis notes that this conclusion is reached by ignoring the data that "informs us of the unique and often precarious position of African Americans" (p. 59). Over one third of the African American population in the United States lives at or near the poverty level. It is the economic condition and its implications (e.g., inadequate housing and food, poor sanitation, overcrowding) that bring about negative consequences such as poor health, family violence, and delinquency. Thus, the use of a

TABLE 2.6 Influence of Different Theoretical Frameworks on Research Questions

Theory	Sample Research Question	Recommendations for Action
IQ deficit theory	Are minorities genetically inferior to White students?	Remedial education, but the problem is really "in" the child.
Cultural deficit theory (sociocultural deficits in home life)	Is there a higher rate of single-parent families among minorities? How do Black and White parents compare in discipline techniques?	Remedial education, but the problem is really "in" the family.
Cultural difference theory	What is the nature of language use at home and at school in terms of asking and answering questions or in seeking help?	Build on students' prior experiences; increase their language use structures.
Power inequities (school failure is rooted in a struggle for power: schools play a role in the preservation of the socioeconomic order)	How can we teach minority students so they do not continue to be oppressed?	Explicitly teach minority children the means to access power, including linguistic forms and ways of talking, writing, and interacting. Teach them to value ethnic characteristics and that the culture of the dominant group is not necessarily superior.

SOURCE: Based on Villegas (1991).

theoretical framework that starts with the marginalized lives allows researchers to understand the experiences of oppressed groups.

Morse (1994) also notes that the theoretical framework in qualitative inquiry is used to focus the inquiry and give it boundaries rather than to serve as *the* guide for data collection analysis. Deductive analysis based on a static theoretical framework violates the assumption of qualitative inquiry. The theoretical framework should be viewed as a conceptual template with which to compare and contrast results, not seen as establishing a priori categories for data collection and analysis.

Research Questions and Hypotheses

The literature review serves as a foundation for forming research questions. Hedrick et al. (1993) suggest that the research questions operationalize the objectives of the proposed research. They focus the research hypotheses and clarify what information needs to be collected from what sources under what conditions.

Framing the research questions can be a difficult task for beginning researchers. Hedrick et al. (1993) present a taxonomy for categorizing research questions that includes four categories of questions: descriptive, normative, correlational, and impact. Each is briefly discussed in the following section.

1. *Descriptive* research questions are designed to produce information about what is or has been happening in relation to the target of the research. For example, the researcher might want to describe certain characteristics of the participants in an intervention. Alternatively, the researcher might be interested in describing the prevalence of a particular disability within an identified domain (e.g., What is the prevalence of mental retardation in Black middle school children?).

2. *Normative* research questions go beyond description and require that the information generated in response to the descriptive research question be compared with some standard or expected observation. For example, in special education there are minimum requirements regarding most aspects of the service delivery system. A normative research question might ask, Were individual education plans (IEPs) in place before the placement was made, in accordance with the minimal service delivery requirements?

3. *Correlative* research questions are used to identify relationships to enable the explanation of phenomena. As Hedrick et al. (1993) point out, data derived in response to such questions indicate the strength and direction of a relationship between two or more variables, not causality. For example, the special education researcher might ask, What is the relationship between the size of family and the presence of emotional disturbance in siblings? If a strong, positive relationship is found, this would not lead to the conclusion that large families cause emotional disturbance in siblings. Such a relational finding would suggest the need for further study to uncover the causal relationships.

4. *Impact* research questions represent the last category offered in the Hedrick et al. (1993) taxonomy. Here, the researcher's aim is to identify effects, to establish causal links between an independent variable (the intervention) and a dependent variable (the anticipated change). According to Hedrick et al.'s framework, the researcher might investigate two types of effects: simple and relative. Research on the impact of an intervention (praise) on a behavior (learning a definition) is one example of a simple impact study (Stinson, Gast, Wolery, & Collins, 1991). Their research question asked, "Do students with moderate retardation who are praised immediately after correct sight reading learn more word definitions than students who receive delayed praise?" If the researchers chose (and this is good practice) to explore the impact of the intervention on other related outcomes (e.g., self-esteem), additional questions could address relative effects.

Impact questions can then be reformulated and stated as hypotheses. A hypothesis is an if . . ., then . . . statement. For example, a hypothesis might state this: "If students are exposed to a particular intervention, they will behave in a certain, predictable manner." A sample hypothesis for the Stinson et al. study cited above might read this way: "If students with moderate retardation receive a praise statement after correct sight-word readings, they will learn more definitions than students who receive delayed praise." This is known as a directional hypothesis because it is stated in the direction of the expected outcome. A researcher could choose to state a *null* hypothesis—that is, a statement that did not specify the expected direction of the outcome. The previous hypothesis could be restated as a null hypothesis as such: "There will be no difference in the number of definitions learned for students with moderate retardation who receive a praise statement after correct sight-word readings compared to those who receive delayed praise."

In summary, the literature review serves many purposes. It establishes a historical perspective on the intended research, provides a vision of the need for additional research, and enables the researcher to develop a conceptual framework for the research. This framework allows the researcher to generate research questions and hypotheses to guide the design and conduct of the research. In qualitative research, typically, the researcher will refine, modify, add, and even discard questions throughout the progress of the study (Morse, 1994). Therefore, qualitative researchers are advised to begin with broader questions that can be modified in response to discoveries made during the study. No matter which research paradigm or approach is used, the literature review is an essential ingredient in the research process.

Critical Analysis of Literature Reviews

The criteria for critically analyzing literature reviews depends (again) on the nature of the review being analyzed. A literature review that serves as an introduction to a primary research study reported in a journal would be subject to a different type of scrutiny than would an integrative literature review. The researcher should be aware of potential biases in literature reviews.

Publication Bias

There is a greater tendency for research with statistically significant results (i.e., those showing group differences larger than chance) to be published. Research studies that show no differences either are not submitted by the authors or are rejected more frequently by journal editors (Begg, 1994; Campbell, 1989). Campbell suggested that this publication bias leads to an exaggerated concept of differences between males and females. Begg recommended tracking down (or determining if authors of literature reviews tracked down) unpublished studies on the topic to correct for this bias. However, he also cautioned that the quality of the unpublished data may be suspect because it has not been through a review process. For this reason, he recommended a conservative interpretation of literature review results (especially meta-analyses).

Variable Quality in the Primary Research Studies

Matt and Cook (1994) focus on threats to inference from research syntheses based on the quality (or lack thereof) of the primary research studies included in the review. They point out weaknesses commonly found in quantitative research studies that could be used in a statistical synthesis of previous research findings. In assessing the conclusions reached in any literature review, the reader should be cognizant of the quality of the studies included. Researchers interested in substantively critiquing a review based on a statistical synthesis of findings are referred to Matt and Cook's chapter in the *Handbook of Research Synthesis* (Matt & Cook, 1994).

Inclusion-Exclusion Decisions

Researchers can bias the results of a literature review by excluding data that is methodologically questionable, based on their own personal, subjective judgment (Ogawa & Malen, 1991). Or they may present conclusions that are more firm and clear-cut than is justified because of the exclusion of studies with "murky" results. Without a clear specification of the method used to search for research and of the criteria used for inclusion or exclusion, it is difficult to judge the quality of a review.

► *Questions for Critically Analyzing Literature Reviews*

The following questions can be used to determine if a literature review is satisfactory. In preparing your answers to these questions, look for evidence in the article to support your answers:

1. The purpose of the literature review is to place the current research into the "big picture" of what is known and not known about a specific topic. What is the big picture into which this study fits? What is the central topic? How is the researcher conceptualizing the problem?

2. What is the nature of the literature cited?

   a. Is the review current, using research that is recent enough to have applicability to the proposed research?

   b. Is the review based predominately on primary research rather than on secondary or opinion pieces?

   c. Does the review provide a critical analysis of existing literature, recognizing the strengths and weaknesses of previous research?

   d. Is the literature review well-balanced, presenting evidence on both (or all) sides of the issue?

3. Is the review free from the biases of the reviewer? Is there any evidence in terms of emotional language, institutional affiliation, funding source, and so on to suggest that the reviewer might be biased?

4. Does the review establish a need for the study? What is the author's rationale for why this study is needed? What do we know? What do we need to know? Why is this study important?

5. What is the theoretical framework and what are the research questions? Does the review provide enough information to support the researcher's theoretical framework and research questions posed?

6. Does the review provide sufficient information to guide the research procedures, including the identification of subject participants, selection of data collection and analysis processes, and use of appropriate reporting strategies?

7. Was the information in the literature review judged to be useful to you as a consumer of research or as a researcher? Can you make a judgment as to the usefulness of the information for other audiences, such as the client, sponsor, stakeholder, or participants?

8. Are sources cited inclusive of "marginalized" voices? Are citations made that reference viewpoints of those with the least power?

To really have a basis for critically analyzing research, it is helpful to have a broad experience with different types of research as well as with a number of studies that represent the same research approach. Of course, such breadth and depth takes time to achieve. Nevertheless, a long journey begins with a single step. Throughout this text, you will be encouraged to identify full research articles that relate to your area of interest and to critically analyze those studies. The ability to critically analyze research is also a skill that becomes more holistic with experience.

When you are at the beginning stages of learning critical analysis, it is helpful to look at each section of the research study. So in this chapter, we focus on the introductory section that includes the literature review and research problem, hypothesis, questions, or objectives. Later, you will be able to look at other aspects of the article, such as how the author handled certain aspects of data collection, or analysis, or credibility building, or ethics. You can then do comparisons across studies on these dimensions, analyzing how and why texts differ, how they relate to theoretical readings, whether the authors are justified in their methods or presentations, and how they can help you in your own decisions about research. With each research article that you review, you will increase your ability to determine the quality of the author's work and the validity of the findings.[2]

■ Questions and Activities for Discussion and Application

1. What is the difference between a primary source and a secondary source? When and why would you choose to use one or the other? Have you been able to locate a secondary source on your topic of interest?

2. What search strategies have you found to be particularly effective in locating research on your topic of interest? Have you used networking? Professional associations? Why would these be important resources? What computerized databases have you used? Do you feel comfortable in using the computer to search for articles of interest for your research topic? (Can you identify the essential steps in conducting a literature review?) Have you sought out journals or other sources of information (e.g., direct dialogue with individuals who are experiencing oppression) that represent the "emancipatory perspective" in research?

3. Cooper and Hedges (1994a) recommend that researchers limit their literature review efforts to "mainstream" journals on the grounds that these represent the

"cream of the crop" of research efforts. Emancipatory researchers might contend that this would result in a bias because the viewpoints of oppressed people might not be represented in those journals. Where do you stand on this issue?

4. When writing a literature review for the purposes of planning a research study, what are some of the uses that the literature review can serve for you?

5. Why is a literature review especially important in areas that (a) are emerging, (b) typically have small samples (e.g., special education research) or (c) represent value-laden positions adopted by advocacy groups (e.g., meta-analysis of gender differences)?

6. What are the advantages and disadvantages of selecting either a narrative or statistical option for synthesizing research results? Discuss in terms of (a) quality of research studies used to reach conclusions, (b) the size of differences between groups, and (c) the limitations of meta-analysis (is this concept clear to you?).

7. When conducting qualitative research, some texts advise against conducting a comprehensive literature review because it may bias the researcher to see "what others say they saw" instead of looking with fresh eyes. What do you think?

8. How much and what kind of information should you include about each study in your literature review? About your literature review search method?

9. What are your rules for inclusion and exclusion of studies in your literature review?

10. Using the criteria at the end of Chapter 2, critique different kinds of literature reviews (e.g., narrative literature review, meta-analytic literature review, or a literature review that is used to introduce a primary research study).

11. Locate several empirical research studies. Identify the following features of the study: (a) the paradigm that the researchers used, (b) the research problem, (c) the theoretical framework that underlies the study, and (d) the research questions or hypothesis.

12. In the design of an experimental study, Locke, Spirduso, and Silverman (1993) recommend choosing a directional hypothesis over a null hypothesis for the following reason: "Many arguments favor the use of directionality because it permits more persuasive logic and more statistical power" (p. 61). What is your reaction to this statement?

13. Students of research are sometimes given conflicting advice about the topic and site for their own research. The following quotations exemplify such conflicts. Where do you stand on these two issues (e.g., choice of a research topic and setting) and why?

> The key to selecting a qualitative research topic is to identify something that will hold one's interest over time. New investigators can best identify such a topic by reflecting on what is a *real* personal interest to them. (Morse, 1994, p. 220)

Using . . . personal experiences as the impetus for a research study is not *wrong,* but it is best if the researcher is aware of his or her possible motives for conducting the study, as such experiences may give the study a particular bias. Of even more concern is the possibility that the researcher, when meeting and interviewing participants who have had the same experience, may have many unresolved feelings emerge and may be emotionally unable to continue with the study. (Morse, 1994, p. 221)

One common instance of the problem of investigator biography occurs when graduate students . . . design a study that requires them to return to the context of public education and play the role of unbiased spectator. . . . This particular problem is difficult to overcome and is precisely why it sometimes is best to select problems in a context with which the investigator has had little previous experience. (Locke et al., 1993, p. 114)

When injustice persists with no evidence of unhappiness, rebellion, or official grievance, we need to study the reasons why. . . . Faculty, staff, and students in the feminist and African-American communities have argued . . . that the *absence* of grievance substantiates the very depth of and terror imposed by harassment. Feminist research must get behind "evidence" that suggests all is well. (Fine, 1992, p. 23)

14. Students receive different kinds of advice as to how much literature to review and at what stage of the research process this should occur. What is your reaction to the following pieces of advice:

     When you have enough sense of the conversation to argue persuasively that the target for your proposed study is sound, and that the methods of inquiry are correct, you know enough for the purpose of the proposal. (Locke et al., 1993, p. 68)

Morse (1994) recommends reading in the general area of the inquiry once a topic has been selected:

     At this stage, the researcher should become familiar with the literature, with what has been done generally in the area, and with the "state of the art." He or she should develop a comfortable knowledge base without spending an extraordinary amount of time on minute details or chasing obscure references. (p. 221)

Notes

1. *Search engine* is the term used in the technology literature for search sites.
2. I am indebted to the comments of an anonymous reviewer for this framing of critical analysis.

In This Chapter

■ *The importance of experimental design in the postpositivist paradigm is discussed.*

■ *Concerns are expressed about experimental research by scholars in the emancipatory paradigm.*

■ *Independent and dependent variables, experimental and control groups, random assignment, and internal and external validity are defined.*

■ *Threats to internal and external validity are explained, along with ways to minimize these threats.*

■ *Research designs are diagrammed and explained for single-group, experimental, and quasi-experimental studies.*

■ *Other design issues are discussed, such as the type of treatment variable, ordering effects, and matching subjects.*

3

Experimental and Quasi-Experimental Research

Quantitative research is rooted in the positivist/postpositivist paradigm, which holds that the purpose of research is to develop confidence that a particular knowledge claim about an educational or psychological phenomena is true or false by collecting evidence in the form of objective observations of relevant phenomena (Borg & Gall, 1989). Research design can be defined as a process of creating an empirical test to support or refute a knowledge claim. Two tests of knowledge claims exist in the positivist/postpositivist paradigm: (a) Is the knowledge claim true in this situation (internal validity)? (b) Is the knowledge claim true in other situations (external validity or generalizability)?

Knowledge claims concerning internal validity require some complex thinking. Suppose you have a child in a first-grade classroom who generally refuses to sit in his seat and pushes so hard on the paper when he tries to write that the paper tears. When he does sit in his seat, he bangs his head on the desk. It does not matter whether you are the parent, teacher, counselor, or school administrator, you want to be able to identify the variables that cause the behavior and figure out a treatment that results in more appropriate in-school behavior. You might formulate a wide variety of hypotheses as to why these behaviors are occurring. You might speak with other staff members and find out that they have observed similar behaviors with other children. You might consult the literature and find that such behaviors could result from a lack of self-confidence in a school setting or from frustration associated with a learning disability or a develop-mental delay. The recommended courses of action could be to try to build the child's self-confidence, change teaching strategies to address the learning disability, or lessen the demands on the child until maturation occurs.

If you are operating in the postpositivist paradigm, you might design a research study in which you decide to administer a selected treatment (e.g., a program designed to build self-confidence) to one group of children and another similar group of children would not get the treatment. Suppose that the group of children who received the treatment improved their behavior more than the other group. How can you claim that it was your "treatment" that caused the observed change in behavior? For the researcher to make a knowledge claim that this treatment caused this effect, certain tests of internal validity must be met. These tests of internal validity are the subject of a major portion of this chapter.

Most quantitative research is of two types: studies aimed at discovering causal (or correlational) relationships and descriptive studies that use quantitative data to describe a phenomenon. Six types of quantitative research approaches are explained in this text: single-group experimental, and quasi-experimental designs (Chapter 3); causal comparative and correlational strategies (Chapter 4); survey research (Chapter 5); and single-case designs (Chapter 6).

Importance of Experimental Design

The importance of experimental research within the postpositivist paradigm is evident in the following quotations:

> The best method—indeed the only fully compelling method—of establishing causation is to conduct a carefully designed *experiment* in which the effects of possible lurking variables are controlled. To experiment means to actively change *x* and observe the response *y*. (Moore & McCabe, 1993, p. 202)

> The experimental method is the only method of research that can truly test hypotheses concerning cause-and-effect relationships. It represents the most valid approach to the solution of educational problems, both practical and

theoretical, and to the advancement of education as a science. (Gay, 1992, p. 298)

These authors maintain that experimental research is the only type of research that can truly establish cause-and-effect relationships, although they do recognize that there are many educational problems for which the experimental method is inappropriate. Feminists have interpreted such statements as evidence of a hierarchy of prestige in research methods (Reinharz, 1992). Some issues are not amenable to experimental research; thus, certain types of reform become extremely difficult to achieve if experimental research is accorded this exclusive position in the "truth hierarchy."

Researchers in the postpositivist paradigm recognized the complexity of establishing a definitive cause-and-effect relationship with social phenomenon. The underlying logic calls for controlling as many variables as possible and then systematically manipulating one (or a few) treatment variables to test the effect. The control of many variables (such as differences in background characteristics of the participants) can result in an oversimplification that distorts how the phenomenon occurs in the real world. Yet it is the controlling of many variables that allows the researcher to claim that one variable had a specific effect. Thus, the researcher in this paradigm works within a tension between control and manipulation (changing one or a few variables at a time), and representation of a phenomenon in the real world. The fundamental assumption of this paradigm is that a researcher needs to eliminate possible alternative explanations to make a knowledge claim that one variable caused a change in another. Even with the careful control of variables and the systematic manipulation of the treatment variable, researchers within this paradigm are careful to acknowledge that their results are "true" at a certain level of probability and only within the conditions that existed during the experiment. The knowledge claim is strengthened when the results can be demonstrated repeatedly under similar conditions.

Emancipatory Perspectives Regarding Experimental Research

Emancipatory researchers are divided as to the appropriateness of using single-group, experimental, and quasi-experimental designs for educational, psychological, and sociological research. Reinharz (1992) cites a number of criticisms of this type of research by feminists.

1. Carlson (1972) characterizes experimental research in the social sciences as rigid control and manipulation of variables that is characteristic of a male, agentic style of research rather than of a feminine, communal mode. Concerns arise because of experimenter control of the decision making regarding appropriate treatments without consultation with the participants who will be affected by the treatment.

2. Sexist bias can influence every stage of the research process, including the formation of the research question, the review of literature, choice of a design, selection of a sample, and data collection, analysis, interpretation, and reporting (Eichler, 1991). Some researchers believe that sexist bias can be eliminated by following the rules of postpositivist research more stringently. Others believe that a fundamentally different approach is needed.

3. A number of major educational and psychological theories were based on male subjects only or were constructed with a male bias (see discussion in Chapter 1 on this topic).

Equally true, research done with all-White populations is generalized to minority populations.

4. The laboratory setting of some research studies is viewed as "unnatural" and not capable of reflecting the complexity of human experience. Phenomenologists and cultural theorists argue that the detached "objectivity" of experimental research cannot adequately explain the complexity of social life (Fine & Gordon, 1989).

5. Experimental studies decontextualize human behavior to simplify the interpretation of causality. Haaken (1988) uses the field dependence-independence research as an example of "breaking down social reality into small units and focusing on a limited set of discrete interactions while ignoring social context" (p. 312). Field dependence-independence, developed by Herman Witkin in 1954 as a part of an investigation of visual perception, refers to a person's ability to separate a stimulus from its embedding context. In the experiment, a person in a dark room is asked to place a luminous rod, suspended in a tilted frame, into a vertical position. The subjects who relied on the placement of the frame for their positioning of the rod were labeled as field dependent; those who relied on their own bodily and postural cues were labeled as field independent. Field dependence was said to be linked to such personality traits as passivity, dependence, and conformity. (A further discussion of this research in relation to sex differences is included in Chapter 4.)

6. One of the most serious criticisms raised by many feminists and other ethicists concerns the use of control groups. An ethical problem emerges with the use of control groups in that the experimental group receives the treatment, but the control group does not. Feminists raise the question, Is it ethical to deny "treatment" to one group on a random basis?

7. Experimental researchers are expected to use a standardized procedure for writing reports that "discourages the use of the first-person singular, eliminates reference to actual people, and attributes actions to concepts" (Reinharz, 1992, p. 95). Although the fourth edition of the American Psychological Association's (1994) *Publication Manual* no longer includes this recommendation, much published research has followed this style of writing.

Reinharz (1992) notes that those feminists who do not oppose the use of experimental methods have used them to expose myths about the inferiority of women as well as to raise consciousness on a number of other issues. These feminists recognize that experiments have utility as a powerful tool for achieving feminist goals through policy formation. For example, Fidell (1970) reported that attaching a woman's name or a man's name to a fictional set of application materials for a psychology professorship yielded higher ratings for the male. Thus, experimental methods were used to support the hypotheses of discrimination based on sex.

Although Reinharz (1992) acknowledges the usefulness of experimental methods for feminists, she also warns those interested in social change not to rely solely on the results of such research:

> We should also recognize that society is unlikely to be willing to change *even if* experimental research does provide information suggesting that change is needed. . . . Putting one's eggs in the basket of so-called definitive research is a very risky strategy to use to achieve social change. (p. 108)

Scott-Jones (1993) discusses problems faced by members of ethnic minority communities related to the use of experimental designs that deny treatment to one group (the control group) to test the effect of an intervention. She cited as an example the Tuskegee experiments that were conducted by the U.S. Public Health Service from 1932 to 1972. African American men with syphilis were not given treatment so that researchers could study the disease's progress. The participants were poor and illiterate and did not know they had syphilis (Jones, 1992). When the U.S. Senate learned of this project, it was motivated to pass the National Research Act, which established institutional review boards charged with the responsibility of overseeing ethical issues in research (see Chapter 10 for further discussion).

Nevertheless, Scott-Jones (1993) maintains that many low-income minority children participate in no-treatment control groups by the de facto requirements of experimental research designs. Thus, children who need the treatment most do not receive it. She discussed the following possible resolutions for the ethical dilemmas associated with experimental designs:

1. Give the potentially beneficial treatment to the control group at some time point after the experimental group received it. (This is not acceptable in situations in which children need specific interventions at specific times in their development. Delay in receiving the intervention may result in prolonging the undesirable conditions and, possibly, irreversible delays in development.)

2. Have two (or more) potentially beneficial treatments so all participants receive some intervention.

3. Compare the treatment group outcome to some carefully chosen standard.

4. Conduct intra-individual comparisons rather than cross-group comparisons.

5. Use individual base-lines as comparison standards.

6. Include minority researchers as part of the research team.

These criticisms of and reflections on the experimental approach to research are meant to elucidate the thinking that has emerged from scholars in the emancipatory paradigm. The strength of the research world at this historical moment is the debate and dialogue that is occurring across paradigms.

Single-Group, Experimental, and Quasi-Experimental Designs

Any parent, teacher, counselor, or administrator who encounters a student who cannot read or cannot read as well as one thinks he or she should, experiences a complex challenge to figure out how to improve reading performance. Is the poor performance due to a skill deficit, inappropriate instruction, lack of home support, resistance to pressure to perform, insufficient reinforcement for efforts made, a lack of maturity or "readiness to read," or what? Educators and psychologists have wrestled with this question and, through the use of systematic explanatory designs, attempted to find ways to improve reading performance.

Malone and Mastropieri (1992) tackled the problem of improving reading comprehension with a group of children who had learning disabilities. In addition to the many possible explanations for poor reading performance listed in the preceding paragraph, previous research suggests that reading comprehension may be lower for children with learning disabilities because of visual-perception problems, auditory-processing deficits, or verbal-coding deficits. Out of all this complexity, Malone and Mastropieri decided to focus on testing the effect of teaching children to summarize what they had just read (summarization condition) and to monitor their use of that strategy (summarization with monitoring condition) on the children's reading comprehension.

In this example, the *independent variable* (i.e., the variable that is manipulated) is the approach to teaching. It has three levels: summarization, summarization with monitoring, and traditional. The *dependent variable* (i.e., the variable that will be affected by, that "depends on," the independent variable) is reading comprehension. The groups that get the new teaching strategy (summarization and summarization with monitoring) are the *experimental groups* (sometimes called treatment groups), and the group that gets the traditional instruction is the *control group*. If the participants are *randomly* assigned to the experimental and control groups, you have a true experimental design. *Random assignment* means that every person has an equal chance of being in either the experimental or control group. This can be done by pulling names out of a hat, throwing dice, using a table of random numbers, or flipping a coin.

Experimental research is fundamentally defined by the direct manipulation of an independent variable. Thus, the Malone and Mastropieri (1992) study exemplifies experimental research in that the researchers themselves decided how to operationalize the experimental treatment. They operationally defined the summarization training condition by teaching students a strategy for recognizing important information in a text by asking themselves two questions: (a) "Who or what is the paragraph about?" and (b) "What is happening to them?" (p. 273). Students were then taught to write a summary sentence that tells what the paragraph is about in a few words. Malone and Mastropieri hypothesized that students who had received the training in summarization strategies would recall more information than students taught by traditional methods.

In the next section, I discuss the terms *internal validity* and *external validity*, ways to minimize threats to internal and external validity by using various research designs with examples from education and psychology, and challenges associated with the application of these designs in educational and psychological research.

Internal Validity

Internal validity means that the changes observed in the dependent variable are due to the effect of the independent variable, not to some other unintended variables (known as *extraneous variables, alternative explanations,* or *rival hypothesis*). If extraneous variables are controlled, the results can be said to be due to the treatment, and therefore, the study is internally valid. Campbell and Stanley (1963) identified eight extraneous variables that can threaten internal validity.

1. *History.* History refers to events that happen during the course of the study that can influence the results. For example, suppose you are investigating the effectiveness of various reading strategies. During your study, the principal announces that she will give a certificate for a free ice-cream cone for every book that the school children read. This *event* could have an impact on the children's ability to comprehend what they read; however, it is *not* the treatment that you have in mind. History can be controlled by having a control group that is exposed to the same events during the study as an experimental group, with the exception of the treatment. If this magnanimous principal had made such an offer to the students during the Malone and Mastropieri (1992) study, *all* of the students would have "read for ice cream," and thus, its effect would be assumed to balance out and leave only the effect of the experimental treatment.

2. *Maturation.* Maturation refers to biological or psychological changes in the participants during the course of the study. This might refer to changes such as becoming stronger, more coordinated, or tired as the study progresses. For example, the children in your reading study might become tired after reading the first passage. This fatigue might cause them to perform more poorly on the second passage. However, the children in the control group should also experience a similar maturational change, and thus, its effect should balance out. Maturation is controlled by having a control group that experiences the same kinds of maturational changes but that does not receive the treatment.

3. *Testing.* Testing is a threat to validity that arises in studies that use both pre- and posttests and refers to becoming "test-wise" by having taken a pretest that is similar to the posttest. That is, the participants know what to expect, learn something from the pretest, or become sensitized to what kind of information to "tune into" during the study because of their experience with the pretest. Testing is a potential threat to validity only in research studies that include both pre- and posttests. Malone and Mastropieri (1992) relied only on posttests of reading comprehension, so this would not be a threat to the validity of that outcome measure. However, they did include a pre- and postquestionnaire to identify which strategies the children typically used to help them decide what information was important to remember. Simply reading the questions about how they make such decisions might have prompted the children to be more aware of using strategies to help remember things they read. Once again, all the children in the study took both pre- and posttests, so the effect of pretesting should balance out.

4. *Instrumentation.* Instrumentation is another threat to validity in studies that use both pre- and posttests, and it arises when there is a change in the instrument between the pre- and posttests. It is possible that one test might be easier than the other test, and then changes observed on the dependent variable are due to the nature of the instrument, not to the independent variable. Instrumentation is a potential threat to validity only when the instrument used for data collection changes from one observation time period to the next. Examples of such situations include using a different test for pre- and posttesting or collecting qualitative data by observation can be associated with changes in the researcher

as instrument. Malone and Mastropieri (1992) addressed this threat by using the same questionnaire for pre- and posttesting the strategy use behavior.

5. *Statistical regression.* Statistical regression is a threat to validity that occurs when the researcher uses extreme groups as the participants (i.e., students at the high or low end of the normal curve). For example, if you select students who score at the 25th percentile on an achievement measure and test them again on a similar measure at the conclusion of the study, their scores could increase simply because of statistical regression rather than because of your treatment. This is due to the role that chance plays in test scores. We cannot measure achievement with 100% precision. Therefore, there is always an element of error in any measurement. If the researcher selected students from the bottom of the normal curve, then by chance, it is most likely that their scores will go up (because they are already at the bottom, it is unlikely that they will go down). This threat to validity is a problem only in studies that use a pretest to select participants who are at the lowest or highest ends of the normal curve and then test them again using that instrument for the dependent measure.

6. *Differential selection.* If participants with different characteristics are in the experimental and control groups, the results of the study may be due to group differences, not necessarily to the treatment or the independent variable. For example, in your hypothetical study of reading instruction, the experimental group might include children who are older than the students in the control group. If the experimental group scores higher than the control group on your outcome measure (dependent variable), how would you know if it was due to your treatment or to their age difference (which is confounded with variables such as maturity, length of time exposed to reading, or opportunity to learn). Malone and Mastropieri (1992) controlled for differential selection effects by first dividing the students by sex and grade and then randomly assigning the students to one of three conditions. They did this to ensure that the students were equally distributed by sex and grade within the conditions. Differential selection is theoretically controlled by the random assignment of participants to conditions because differences should balance out between and among groups.

7. *Experimental mortality.* Experimental mortality refers to participants who drop out during the course of the study. It becomes a threat to validity if participants differentially drop out of the experimental and control groups. For example, suppose you have a new strategy for teaching reading to learning disabled students during a special summer program. The experimental group gets the new strategy and the control group gets the traditional approach. During the study, many of the higher-ability students drop out of the experimental group. At the end, the scores for the lower-ability students who complete the experimental treatment are higher than scores for all of the students in the control group. Can you say that your program was successful? Maybe, maybe not. It could be that the program is successful for the lower-ability students but is dreadfully boring for the higher-ability students. This threat is controlled by having a pretest that allows the researcher to determine if people who drop out of the study are systematically different from those who complete it. Malone and Mastropieri (1992) do not mention if any students dropped out of their study; therefore, it is not possible to judge if this is a threat to its validity.

8. *Selection-maturation interaction.* Selection-maturation interaction combines the threats to validity described previously under differential selection and maturation; however, maturation is the differential characteristic that causes the groups to differ. For example,

suppose that the students with learning disabilities in the experimental group are older than those in the control group. The difference in their reading achievement might be due to this maturational characteristic rather than to the educational treatment.

Cook and Campbell (1979) extended this list of extraneous variables by adding the following additional items.

9. *Experimental treatment diffusion.* People will talk, and if the ideas they hear sound interesting, they might just try to use them themselves. If the treatment group is in close proximity to the control group, it is possible that the control group participants may learn about the independent variable and begin using some of the ideas themselves. This would cloud the effect of the treatment. The researcher should conduct observations of selected classes to determine if the control group has become contaminated and should also conduct interviews with the participants to determine their perceptions of what they were doing. Wilson and Sindelar (1991) addressed this problem by assigning participants to treatment groups by school so that within-school contamination would be avoided. Malone and Mastropieri (1992) conducted their study over a 3-day period, thus minimizing the possibility for treatment diffusion.

10. *Compensatory rivalry by the control group.* This threat is also known as the John Henry effect that is based on the folk tale of the railroad worker who was pitted against a machine. John Henry wanted to prove that man was superior to the machine, so he tried extra hard. He did beat the machine and then he died. (Let this be a warning to the control group.) Some individuals who think that their traditional way of doing things is being threatened by a new approach may try extra hard to prove that their way of doing things is best. Malone and Mastropieri (1992) arranged for all treatments to be delivered individually in a quiet room near the students' regular classroom, so the students were probably unaware that they were in a "control" group.

11. *Compensatory equalization of treatments.* Members of a control group may become disgruntled if they think that the experimental group is receiving extra resources. To keep everybody happy, a principal may decide to give extra resources to the control group. This could cloud the effect of the treatment.

12. *Resentful demoralization of the control group.* This is the opposite of the John Henry effect. The control group may feel demoralized because they are not part of the "chosen" group, and thus, their performance might be lower than normal because of their psychological response to being in the control group. Members of a control group could become quite angry if they find out that they are not going to receive an experimental treatment. If that happened, the control group in that setting could not be considered to be "unbiased."

External Validity or Generalizability

External validity is the extent to which findings in one study can be applied to another situation (Borg & Gall, 1989). If the findings from one study are observed in another situation, the results are said to be generalizable or externally valid. The concept of population validity (i.e., to whom you can generalize the results based on sampling strategies) is described in Chapter 10. Bracht and Glass (1968) describe another type of external validity, termed *ecological validity,* that concerns the extent to which the results of an experiment can be generalized from the set of environmental conditions created by the researcher to other environmental conditions. They identified 10 factors that influence ecological validity:

1. *Explicit description of the experimental treatment.* The independent variable must be sufficiently described so that the reader could reproduce it. This is a common criticism in educational and psychological research, particularly as it applies to instructional or therapeutic interventions. Asking questions such as, "Is mainstreaming effective?" or "Does behavior modification work?" is really absurd because there are so many ways that such interventions can be implemented.

2. *Multiple-treatment interference.* If participants receive more than one treatment, it is not possible to say which of the treatments, or which combinations of the treatments is necessary to bring about the desired result. For example, Stevens and Slavin (1995) conducted a study to determine the effect of a cooperative elementary school model that used an overarching philosophy to change school and classroom organization and instructional processes. Their independent variable was the school's overarching philosophy. The experimental (treatment) variable was the cooperative school model that included using cooperative instructional strategies, full-scale mainstreaming of students with learning disabilities, teachers using peer coaching, teachers planning cooperatively, and parent involvement in the school. Because all of the treatments were applied simultaneously, it would not be possible to isolate the effects of the different components.

3. *Hawthorne effect.* The Hawthorne effect derives from a study at the Western Electric Company (Roethlisberger & Dickson, 1939) of changes in light intensity and other working conditions on the workers' productivity. The researchers found that it did not matter if they increased or decreased the light intensity, the workers' productivity increased. Seemingly, the idea of receiving special attention, of being singled out to participate in the study, was enough motivation to increase productivity.

4. *Novelty and disruption effects.* A new treatment may produce positive results simply because it is novel, or the opposite may be true. A new treatment may not be effective initially because it causes a disruption in normal activities, but once it is assimilated into the system, it could become quite effective.

5. *Experimenter effect.* The effectiveness of a treatment may depend on the specific individual who administers it (e.g., the researcher, psychologist, or teacher). The effect would not generalize to other situations because that individual would not be there.

6. *Pretest sensitization.* Participants who take a pretest may be more sensitized to the treatment than individuals who experience the treatment without taking a pretest. This is especially true for pretests that ask the participants to reflect on and express their attitudes toward a phenomenon.

7. *Posttest sensitization.* This is similar to pretest sensitization in that simply taking a posttest can influence a participant's response to the treatment. Taking a test can help the participant bring the information into focus in a way that participants who do not take the test will not experience.

8. *Interaction of history and treatment effects.* An experiment is conducted in a particular time replete with contextual factors that cannot be exactly duplicated in another

setting. If specific historical influences are present in a situation (e.g., unusually low morale because of budget cuts), the treatment may not generalize to another situation.

9. *Measurement of the dependent variable.* The effectiveness of the program may depend on the type of measurement used in the study. For example, one study of the effects of mainstreaming might use multiple-choice tests and conclude that mainstreaming doesn't work; another study that uses teachers' perceptions of behavior change might conclude that it is effective.

10. *Interaction of time of measurement and treatment effects.* The timing of the administration of the posttest may influence the results. For example, different results may be obtained if the posttest is given immediately after the treatment as opposed to a week or a month afterward.

As briefly mentioned at the beginning of this chapter, a tension always exists between internal and external validity. To achieve perfect internal validity (e.g., the control of all extraneous variables), the laboratory is the perfect setting—a nice, clean, sterile environment in which no variables operate except those that you, as the researcher, introduce. To achieve perfect external validity, the research should be conducted in the "outside" world, in the clinic, classroom, or other messy, complex, often noisy environment in which the practitioner will attempt to apply the research results. Of course, all the "noise" in the outside world plays havoc with the idea of testing the effects of single variables while eliminating the influence of other variables.

For example, some research in memory processes is conducted in laboratories (usually with college students enrolled in beginning psychology courses). A researcher conducting basic research to determine the optimal number of items a person can recall might be pleased to report (and publish) that participants can remember 7 items better than 10 when they are presented in black letters on white background and flashed individually on a wall for a specified period of time. A teacher might view those results as minimally applicable to helping her students remember that different schedules of reinforcement yield different expectations for maintaining and extinguishing behaviors—her students' memory tasks are more complex than the researcher's laboratory ones. As researchers move to increase the external validity of their work, they sacrifice internal validity. Nevertheless, there is room for both types of research, as well as a need to build bridges between them. Some of the cooperative inquiry approaches to research have been developed with this in mind—for example, making the intended users of the research part of the research team. (See Chapter 7 in this text and also Reason's, 1994b, chapter in the *Handbook of Qualitative Research* for further discussion of cooperative inquiry.)

Researchers who work in a laboratory setting need to acknowledge the limitations of their work, especially as it applies to external validity. In addition, they need to strive to make explicit the context within which the research was conducted so that practitioners can better judge its applicability to their own setting.

Other Threats to Validity

Two other threats to validity deserve mention here because of their prevalence in educational and psychological research. The first is *treatment fidelity* in which the implementer of the independent variable (e.g., a teacher, counselor, or administrator) fails to follow the exact procedures specified by the investigator for administering the treatments (Borg & Gall, 1989). Researchers should try to maximize treatment fidelity by providing proper training and supervision and to assess it by observations or teachers' logs. Wilson and Sindelar (1991) trained their teachers in five 1-hour sessions over 2 weeks prior to the study. The teachers had to score over 80% on three demonstrations by acting out the part of the instructor. Also, scripts were provided for the lessons, and prescribed examples were provided.

The second problem concerns the *strength of the experimental treatment.* An experiment to determine the effectiveness of an innovative teaching or counseling strategy can last for a few hours or for days, weeks, months, or years. It may not be reasonable to expect that students' learning, attitudes, self-concepts, or personalities can be affected by an experiment of short duration. If the study results do not show evidence that the treatment was successful, this may not mean that the approach is ineffective but simply that it was not tried long enough. Interventions designed to change behaviors, attitudes, and knowledge often require more time than would be possible in a short experiment of one or two sessions.

Research Designs

Research design can be thought of as answering the question, Who gets what when? It involves decisions about how many groups to have and how many times to administer the dependent variable with an eye to controlling threats to validity.

Three types of research designs are explained: single-group, experimental, and quasi-experimental. For each of these designs, a coding system is used with the following symbols:

R = Random assignment of subjects to conditions
X = Experimental treatment
O = Observation of the dependent variable (e.g., pretest, posttest, or interim measures)

Generally, internal threats to validity are controlled by means of the research design. For example, history and maturation can be controlled by having a control group, and differential selection can be controlled by random assignment to conditions.

Single-Group Designs

Three single-group designs are briefly described here. For a more in-depth discussion of research design options, see Campbell and Stanley (1963) or Cook and Campbell (1979).

One-Shot Case Study. In the one-shot case study, the researcher administers a treatment and then a posttest to determine the effect of the treatment. The one-shot case study is depicted as follows:

X   O

For example, a researcher could study the effects of providing peer tutors for students with learning disabilities ability on math performance. Here, the experimental treatment (X) is the use of peer tutors, and the dependent variable is math performance (O). This design is subject to the threats of history, maturation, and mortality (if subjects drop out) because there is no control group and no pretest. If the students score well on the math test, you would not know if it was the result of having a peer tutor because you did not pretest their math knowledge. Even if you think the students are performing better in math, you could not be sure it was your experimental treatment that caused their enhanced performance. Other events (such as having the opportunity to play math-based computer games) might have been the "cause," thus constituting a threat to validity based on history. Maturation is an uncontrolled threat to validity in this design because the students could have matured in their ability to understand numerical concepts. This design is very weak and does not allow for a reasonable inference as to the effect of the experimental treatment.

One-Group Pretest-Posttest Design. The researcher administers a pretest, then the treatment, and finally a posttest in the one-group pretest-posttest design. This design is represented as follows:

O   X   O

For example, the researcher could administer a pretest of math problems (O), then provide peer tutoring to students with learning disabilities (X), and measure math ability again after the intervention (O). This design is stronger than the one-shot case study because you can document a change in math scores from before the treatment to after its application. However, this design is open to the threats of history and maturation, in that the children could have experienced an event (e.g., math-based computer games) or a maturational change (e.g., maturing in their ability to understand numerical concepts) that could result in a change in their math scores. Without a control group who might have had the same experiences except for exposure to the experimental treatment, you are limited in your ability to claim the effectiveness of your treatment (i.e., peer tutoring). This design can also be open to the threats of testing (if the students do better on the posttest simply because it is the second time they are taking the test) or instrumentation (if the pre- and posttests were different). Mortality is not a threat because you have pretest data on the students at the beginning of the experiment, and thus, you could determine if those who dropped out were different from those who completed the study.

Although this design does have many weaknesses, it may be necessary to use it in a situation in which it is not possible to have a control group because the school would not allow differential provision of services. Borg and Gall (1989) state that this design is justified under circumstances in which you are attempting to change attitudes, behavior, or knowledge that are unlikely to change without the introduction of an experimental treatment (e.g., few students learn research design "incidentally," without direct instruction).

Time Series Design. This design involves measurement of the dependent variable at periodic intervals. The experimental treatment is administered between two of the time intervals. This design is depicted as follows:

O O O O X O O O O

For example, the researcher could give weekly math tests (O O O O), then institute a peer tutoring program for students with learning disabilities (X), and follow up with weekly math tests after the intervention (O O O O). This design is based on the logic that if the behavior is stable before the introduction of the experimental treatment, and it changes after the treatment is introduced, the change can be attributed to the treatment. The biggest threat to this design is history because the experiment continues over a period of time, and there is no control group who might experience the "historical event" but not the treatment. In this example, you might find that performance in math prior to the peer tutoring is consistently low. If you found improved performance after peer tutoring, you would need to be sensitive to other historical events that might have led to the improvement, such as math-based computer games, distribution of free calculators, or exposure to a new, fun-filled math television program.

The time series design does provide for control of several threats to validity. For example, it is unlikely that maturation would be a threat if the scores were found to be consistently low before treatment and consistently high after treatment. If maturation was having an effect, it is likely that it would be reflected in a more erratic pattern in the pretest scores. The same logic can be applied to ruling out testing as a threat to internal validity in this study. If repeated testing, in and of itself, was having an effect, it would be evident in an erratic (or gradually increasing) pattern during the pretesting period. Differential selection is not a problem in studies in which the same persons are involved in all of the measurements and treatments.

Experimental Designs

Three experimental designs that use control groups and random assignment of participants are briefly described here.

Pretest-Posttest Control Group Design. In this design, participants are randomly assigned to either the experimental group or the control group. It is depicted as follows:

R O X O

R O   O

The experimental group receives the treatment and the control group receives either no treatment or an alternative treatment (to avoid threats to validity such as the John Henry effect or compensatory equalization). This design controls for the effects of history, maturation, testing, instrumentation, and experimental mortality by the use of control groups and for differential selection by the use of random assignment to conditions.

If Malone and Mastropieri (1992) had used only two groups (trained vs. traditional), the strategy use portion of their study would exemplify the pretest-posttest control group design. Remember, the researchers in this study were interested not only in the students' improvement in recall of what they read but also in determining if the students increased their use of the strategies in which they were trained. They used a pretest-posttest control group design to study the impact of their experimental treatment on strategy use. The group who received the strategy-use training are the experimental group and are depicted in the top line of the design, where

R — Indicates they were randomly chosen to participate in the training
O — Indicates they were pretested on their use of strategies prior to training
X — Indicates they received the summarization training
O — Indicates they were posttested on their use of the strategies.

The control group is depicted in the second line of the design. They were also randomly assigned to their condition (*R*), were pretested on their use of strategies (*O*), and then participated in traditional reading comprehension instruction. The blank space in the second line between the two Os is used to indicate that this group did not receive the experimental treatment. They were also posttested at the end of the study to determine their use of the summarization strategies.

Thus, the design would look like this:

$$R \quad O \quad X \quad O$$

$$R \quad O \quad \quad O$$

Malone and Mastropieri (1992) were able to conclude that students who participated in the training had increased their use of summarization strategies at greater than a chance level. They attributed the increase to their experimental treatment because students who were in the control group and had not been exposed to the treatment did not increase their use of the strategies. They ruled out the possibility of threats to validity such as history, maturation, and testing because the control group would have shared all of these same experiences. Thus, even if the students had been exposed to "Reading Is Wonderful Week" during the experiment, all of the students would have experienced that. Theoretically, the only difference in their experience during the experiment was exposure to the experimental treatment. Instrumentation was ruled out as a threat to validity because the dependent measure was recorded as student responses to a printed form that did not change from pre- to posttesting. The researchers also ruled out experimental mortality because they had a pretest and they could determine if there were systematic differences in the characteristics of students who completed the study and those who dropped out. Finally, they were not concerned about differential selection because the students were randomly assigned to the experimental and control groups. Thus, they assumed that any differences in background characteristics in the two groups would be balanced out by the random assignment. If the researchers had chosen the participants on the basis of extreme pretest scores, the use of random assignment to experimental and control groups would also control the effect of regression. It would be assumed that the control group would regress as much as the experimental group, and thus, the effect of this threat to validity would be balanced out by the design.

Posttest-Only Control Group Design. This design is similar to the pretest-posttest control group design except that no pretest is given. It is depicted as follows:

$$R \quad X \quad O$$

$$R \qquad O$$

It controls for the threats to validity in the same way as the previously discussed design, except that mortality can be a problem, if people drop out of the study.

Again, assuming that Malone and Mastropieri (1992) had limited themselves to two conditions for their independent variable, the reading comprehension portion of their study would exemplify the posttest-only control group design. The R indicates the random assignment of students to experimental or control conditions. The X indicates the treatment that the experimental group received—that is, the training in summarization strategies. The O indicates the measure of the students' recall of the stories that they read during the study. The blank space between R and O on the second line of the design indicates that the control group did not receive the experimental treatment.

Malone and Mastropieri (1992) concluded that the students who participated in the training were able to recall more than those who had not been trained. They attributed their higher level of performance to the training because they had controlled for history, maturation, and testing by having a control group that shared all of the same experiences, except exposure to the experimental treatment. Campbell and Stanley (1966) state that a pretest is not necessary because "the most adequate all-purpose assurance of lack of initial biases between groups is randomization" (p. 25). Thus, differential selection is not a problem in studies that use this design. It would be assumed that randomization would also result in the equalization of mortality effects, although the astute researcher would want to monitor the pattern of dropouts from the study. Finally, without the use of a pretest, the threats of testing and instrumentation disappear.

Single-Factor Multiple-Treatment Designs. This design is an extension of the control group, randomized designs presented previously, but the sample is randomly assigned to one of several conditions (usually three or four groups are used). Because three conditions were actually used in Malone and Mastropieri's (1992) study, the pre- and postintervention strategy use portion of their study exemplifies the single-factor multiple-treatment design. As mentioned previously, the students were randomly assigned to one of three conditions:

X_1 = Summarization training
X_2 = Summarization training with self-monitoring
Control group = Traditional reading comprehension instruction

Thus, their design could be depicted as follows:

$$R \quad O \quad X_1 \quad O$$

$$R \quad O \quad X_2 \quad O$$

$$R \quad O \qquad \quad O$$

The Os represent the pre- and postquestionnaire on strategy use that was administered before training and after all other posttesting. They controlled for the internal threats to validity by randomly assigning students to conditions and by having comparison groups (two experimental groups and one control group).

Solomon 4—Group Design. This design was developed for the researcher who is worried about the effect of pretesting on the validity of the results. The design looks like this:

$$R \quad O \quad X \quad O$$

$$R \quad O \qquad O$$

$$R \qquad X \quad O$$

$$R \qquad \qquad O$$

As you can see, the researcher combines the pretest-posttest control group design with the posttest-only control group design. Because half the participants receive the pretest and half do not, the researcher can test the effect of taking the pretest and thus eliminate that threat to validity without sacrificing the valuable information that can be obtained from a pretest. The disadvantage of this design is that it necessitates having four groups and thus increases the number of participants that one would need to test.

Factorial Design. Researchers who choose the experimental approach grapple with the issue of the complexity of reality and how to represent that complexity while still reducing their choice of variables in their studies to a manageable number. One way to include more than one variable is to include multiple *independent* variables. Such designs are known as *factorial designs,* and each independent variable is called a *factor.*

For example, returning to the Malone and Mastropieri (1992) study of reading comprehension, I have already introduced you to their first independent variable: instructional strategy (A), which had three levels. They also had a second independent variable: question type (B) which had two levels. Thus, as a factorial design, their study could be depicted as a 3 × 2 design (two independent variables, one with three levels and one with two levels). The factors and their levels are as follows:

$A =$ Instructional strategy
    $A_1 =$ Summarization training
    $A_2 =$ Summarization training with self-monitoring
    $A_3 =$ Traditional reading comprehension instruction
$B =$ Question type
    $B_1 =$ Summary-related items
    $B_2 =$ Nonsummary-related items

The question type variable levels were designed to test the effect of the instructional strategies for different types of recall. Half of the items on the recall measures were related to the summary information for each paragraph that the students read (B_1); the other half related to nonsummary information (B_2).

Thus, in conducting the analysis for a factorial design, the researcher tests the effects of the main variables, as well as their possible interaction:

$$A$$

$$B$$

$$A \times B$$

$A \times B$ refers to the interaction between A and B. In the Malone and Mastropieri (1992) study, the main effect for instructional strategy (A) was statistically significant, thus suggesting that the treatment was effective. The main effect for question type (B) was not statistically significant. However, the interaction effect ($A \times B$) was statistically significant, suggesting that the treatment was differentially effective, depending on the condition. Although this discussion foreshadows the information presented in Chapter 12, I will not keep you in suspense as to this interpretation.

Malone and Mastropieri state that

> Treatment Condition × Question Type interaction revealed that the summarization group performed at a higher level on nonsummary items, the monitoring group performed at a comparable level on both summary and nonsummary items, while the traditional group performed at a higher level on the summary-related items. (p. 275)

Often, a graphic presentation of interaction effects is useful to interpretation.

Factorial designs are quite common in experimental research because they allow researchers to test for effects of different kinds of variables that might be expected to influence outcomes, such as grade level, age, gender, ethnicity or race, or disability type.

As you can see, there are multiple variations on the number of variables and how they can be put together into a design for research. The main limitation in the number of variables arises from the number of participants needed for each condition (a topic addressed in Chapter 10) and the resulting complexity in interpretation of the results (see Chapter 12). If your head was swimming a bit at trying to "see" the $A \times B$ interaction, the level of complexity is greatly enhanced by adding a third variable (C), such that effects would be tested for the following:

$$A$$

$$B$$

$$C$$

$$A \times B$$

$$A \times C$$

$$B \times C$$

$$A \times B \times C$$

Let your mind wander around the thought of adding yet a fourth variable and reach your own conclusions as to why researchers tend to limit their factorial designs to two or three factors.

Quasi-Experimental Designs

Quasi-experimental designs are those that are "almost" true experimental designs, except that the participants are not randomly assigned to groups. In quasi-experimental research, the researcher studies the effect of the treatment on intact groups rather than being able to randomly assign participants to the experimental or control groups.

Stevens and Slavin (1995) conducted a research study on the effect of cooperative learning in elementary schools. Their actual design was quite complex; however, I use selective variables from their study to exemplify the quasi-experimental designs. Their main independent variable was the overarching philosophy of the school. There were two levels:

X = Cooperative elementary schools
Control = Traditional elementary schools

Because the school's cooperation was necessary for the implementation of the experimental treatment, the researchers were unable to randomly assign schools to conditions. Therefore, their design is *quasi*-experimental because they were working with intact groups. Although Stevens and Slavin had numerous dependent measures of the students' achievement, attitudes, and social relations, for purposes of this illustration, I focus on the social relations measure that asked students to list the names of their friends in the class.

Two quasi-experimental designs are briefly described here.

Static-Group Comparison Design. This design involves administering the treatment to the experimental group and comparing its performance on a posttest with that of a control group. It is depicted as follows:

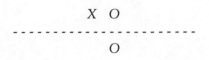

The dotted line is used to indicate that the participants were not randomly assigned to conditions.

The two main threats to this design are (a) differential selection because the groups might differ initially on an important characteristic and (b) experimental mortality if participants drop out of the study. It is very important with this design to collect as much background information as possible about the two groups to determine how they differ.

If Stevens and Slavin (1995) had asked the students to list the names of their friends *only* at the end of the treatment period (2 years), *then* their design could be depicted as follows:

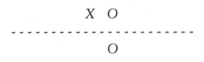

where *X* is the cooperative education treatment and the blank space on the next line under *X* indicates the control group that continued with the traditional school philosophy. The Os here represent the posttest of social relations, which in this example, is assumed to have been given only at the end of the study.

As mentioned before, the two main threats to internal validity for this design are differential selection and experimental mortality. Stevens and Slavin attempted to control for background differences by selecting comparison schools from a pool of schools that matched the treatment schools on the mean California Achievement Test for Total Reading, Total Language, and Total Mathematics. They also tried to control for ethnic and socio-economic background of the students by selecting comparison schools from the same or similar neighborhoods. They presented statistics indicating that the student populations were fairly similar in terms of ethnicity, socioeconomic status, and percentage of learning disabled students.

The researchers also investigated the educational practices at treatment and comparison schools and concluded that both allocated the same amount of time to reading, language arts, and mathematics instruction daily. They also used similar basal reading programs; however, the treatment schools did not use the adjunct materials, such as workbooks, provided by the basal publishers. By providing this kind of detail about the schools, Stevens and Slavin (1995) tried to satisfy that differential selection was not a serious threat to the internal validity of their study.

Information relevant to experimental mortality was reported by Stevens and Slavin (1995) in that the study started with 1,012 students and ended 2 years later with 873 students. This attrition in their subject pool could warn of a threat to validity, especially if the researchers had not used a pretest. In actuality, Stevens and Slavin did use a pretest, and that leads us to the next quasi-experimental design.

Nonequivalent Control Group Design. This design is similar to the static-group comparison design except for the addition of a pretest. It is depicted as follows:

$$O \quad X \quad O$$
$$\text{-----------------------}$$
$$O \qquad O$$

This design controls for differential selection and mortality somewhat by the use of the pretest. The researcher would be able to determine if the two groups differed initially on the dependent variable.

Because Stevens and Slavin (1995) actually did ask the students in their study to list their friends *before* the study started, the design could be depicted as follows:

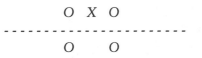

with the Os representing the social relations pre- and postmeasures. Thus, they were able to establish that there was no statistically significant difference in the number of friends listed by students in the treatment and control groups prior to the intervention.

Other Design Issues

Type of Treatment Variables

In this chapter, I have focused almost exclusively on *manipulable* variables—the type of variable that is under the control of the researcher, such as counseling or instructional strategies. Such variables are at the heart of experimental design research. Other types of variables are more difficult to manipulate because of logistical, ethical, or genetic factors. For example, people cannot be randomly assigned to be males or females, or to be Caucasian, African American, or Latino. The effects of such variables might be very important to investigate, but because they cannot be manipulated, different approaches to research have developed, such as casual comparative and correlational research, which are described in the next chapter. Nevertheless, these nonmanipulable variables can be combined with manipulable variables in experimental studies that use factorial designs.

Ordering Effects

In some research studies, a researcher might be concerned that exposure to one treatment before another would have different effects than if the treatments had been administered in reverse order. Researchers who are concerned about the ordering effects of treatments can choose to use a counterbalanced design in which some of the participants receive one treatment first and some receive the other treatment first. After measuring the dependent variable once, the administration of treatments can be reversed for the two groups.

For example, suppose a team of researchers had developed a strategy for teaching science using either "virtual reality" technology for animal dissection or the traditional approach. They might divide their sample in half and teach one half a unit using the virtual reality first, followed by a unit taught in the traditional mode. The other half of the participants would participate in the traditional mode first and then the virtual reality condition.

Matching

In research in which randomization is not possible (in this chapter, quasi-experimental designs), a researcher might choose to try to match participants on variables of importance— for example, gender, age, type of disability, level of hearing loss, or ethnicity. By matching pairs between the treatment and control groups, the researcher can control for some extraneous variables (e.g., older children tend to be more mature). Problems always arise in matching in trying to find a "perfect" match. Participants for whom no match can be found must be eliminated from the study. Matching on more than one variable can be quite problematic.

Echevarria (1995) used a modified counterbalanced design in which all the participants in her study participated in all conditions to avoid the problems associated with matching students. Her independent variable was instructional practice for teaching reading to second- or third-grade Hispanic students with learning disabilities. She had two levels of the independent variable: instructional conversation (IC) and traditional basal approach. She described her design as follows:

> The study consisted of five IC lessons and five basal lessons, counterbalanced to provide random presentation. Counterbalancing yielded the following sequence: Lesson 1, basal; lesson 2, IC; lesson 3, basal; lesson 4, IC; lesson 5, IC; lesson 6, basal; lesson 7, IC; lesson 8, basal; lesson 9, basal; lesson 10, IC.
>
> The procedures used in the study solved a problem common in working with system-identified special education subjects: Given the individual nature of the students' learning characteristics, it would have been problematic to match the five subjects with controls on such variables as ability level, language proficiency, and disability characteristics. Variables such as time of day, seating arrangement and reading text were held constant. (p. 539)

Thus, Echevarria was able to avoid the problems of matching and the differential selection threat to internal validity by exposing all participants to all conditions.

Challenges to Using Experimental Designs in Educational and Psychological Research

Many challenges face the researcher who would like to use an experimental design to investigate educational and psychological phenomenon. Several of these factors include school policies restricting differential treatment, difficulty in identifying appropriate comparison groups, small sample sizes, sampling bias, and ethical considerations. Because of these problems, some researchers have turned to single-subject designs (described in Chapter 6) and qualitative designs (see Chapter 7).

▶ *Questions for Critically Analyzing Single-Group, Experimental, and Quasi-Experimental Designs*

▶ *Internal Validity*

1. *History.* Could events (other than the independent variable) have influenced the results?

2. *Maturation.* Could biological or psychological changes in study participants (other than those associated with the independent variable) have influenced the results?

3. *Testing.* Could the participants have become "test-wise" because of the pretest?

4. *Instrumentation.* Was there a difference between the pre- and posttests?

5. *Statistical regression.* Were extreme groups used?

6. *Differential selection.* Did the experimental and control groups differ in ways other than exposure to the independent variable?

7. *Experimental mortality.* Did participants drop out during the study?

8. *Selection-maturation.* Was differential selection a problem based on the biological or psychological characteristics of the sample?

9. *Experimental treatment diffusion.* Were the treatment and control groups close enough to share ideas?

10. *Compensatory rivalry by the control group.* Did the control group try extra hard?

11. *Compensatory equalization of treatments.* Were extra resources given to the control group?

12. *Resentful demoralization of the control group.* Was the control group demoralized because of being "left out"?

▶ *External Validity (Ecological Validity)*

(See Chapter 10 on population validity)

1. Was the experimental treatment described in sufficient detail?

2. Were multiple treatments used? Did they interfere with each other?

3. Was the Hawthorne effect operating?

4. Was the treatment influenced by being novel or disruptive?

5. What was the influence of the individual experimenter?

6. Were the participants sensitized by taking a pretest?

7. Were the participants sensitized by taking a posttest?

8. Was there an interaction of history and treatment effects?

9. What was the influence of the type of measurement used for the dependent variable?

10. What was the influence of the time period that elapsed between the treatment and the administration of the dependent variable?

▶ *Other Threats to Validity*

1. Were steps taken to ensure the treatment was implemented as planned?

2. What was the influence of the strength of the treatment?

3. Was it ethical to deny treatment to the control group?

■ *Questions and Activities for Discussion and Application*

1. Through a computerized literature search or by going directly to the main journals that publish empirical, quantitative research studies, identify five research studies, each of which uses a slightly different design. Be sure to include both experimental and quasi-experimental studies. For each study, do the following:

   a. Identify the research problem.

   b. Identify the independent and dependent variables.

    c. Categorize the study as experimental or quasi-experimental.

    d. Explain the basis for your categorization.

    e. Draw the design that depicts the administration of treatment and dependent measures.

    f. Critique the studies using the questions for critical analysis at the end of this chapter.

2. Brainstorm a number of different problems that would be appropriate for experimental or quasi-experimental research.

3. Select one research problem and do the following:

    a. Identify the independent and dependent variables.

    b. Sketch a design that could be used to study your research problem.

    c. Explain how your design would satisfy the questions for critical analysis for experimental and quasi-experimental research.

4. Under what circumstances would you *not* recommend using experimental or quasi-experimental approaches to research? What kind of alternative approach would you suggest?

In This Chapter

■ *The types of variables appropriate for causal comparative and correlational research are explored.*

■ *Challenging issues in this type of research are discussed that relate to focusing on group differences, group identification, the fallacy of homogeneity, and the post hoc fallacy.*

■ *Steps for conducting causal comparative research are outlined.*

■ *Correlational research is described in terms of challenges and steps for conducting both relationship and prediction studies, with special attention given to statistical decisions for analysis of data.*

■ *Questions for critically analyzing causal comparative and correlational research are presented.*

Causal Comparative and
Correlational Research

The school psychologist announced to the faculty that the school would participate in a research study to compare the effect of a new strategy for improving students' self-concepts. To control for the differential selection effects, all the names of the students in the school would be put in a hat and then randomly assigned to the high- and low-self-concept groups. Of course, this example is absurd. You can't assign people to different self-concept levels at random. Many characteristics of individuals are not manipulable—for example, disabilities, gender, ethnicity, age, cognitive abilities, and personality traits, such as aggression or anxiety. Causal comparative and correlational research strategies represent two approaches that are appropriate for studying such nonmanipulable variables.

Types of Variables

A variety of types of variables are appropriate for causal comparative and correlational research:

1. Inherent characteristics (organismic)—for example, gender, ethnicity, age, disability, socioeconomic class, ability, personality traits.

2. Characteristics that should not be manipulated for ethical reasons—for example, illegal drug use, cigarette smoking, alcohol consumption.

3. Characteristics that could be manipulated but that are not—for example, school placement, social promotion to the next grade, participation in psychotherapy.

When studying such characteristics, a researcher can use a causal comparative or a correlational approach. These types of research are quite common in education and psychology because of the frequency of comparisons of persons with different characteristics (such as gender, race, and disabilities). Although both approaches explore cause-and-effect relationships between variables, neither involves the experimental manipulation of treatment variables, and therefore, the results cannot be used as proof of a cause-and-effect relationship.

For example, Mexican American and European American college students were compared on the basis of their willingness to use, and their perceptions of the effectiveness of, four different alcoholism treatment programs (Atkinson, Abreu, Ortiz-Bush, & Brewer, 1994). The researchers found that Mexican Americans and European Americans reported being equally willing to use alcoholism treatment programs; however, the Mexican Americans perceived all four treatment programs to be more effective than did European American students. The authors did not conclude that Mexican American ethnicity causes a higher degree of perceived effectiveness. Rather, they speculated that cultural differences between the two groups might result in different ratings. To explore this hypothesis, they administered an acculturation scale on which low scores represented identification with Latinos and Hispanics and high scores represented European American identification for language use, media, and ethnic social relations. Their hypothesis was supported because the Mexican Americans with high acculturation scores rated the treatment effectiveness in a manner similar to the ratings of the European Americans. Atkinson et al. note that these results raise questions as to why current findings suggest that Mexican Americans tend to underuse, or prematurely terminate from, alcoholism treatment programs. They suggest alternative explanations, such as the use of college students (rather than recovering alcoholics) in their sample; counselor characteristics, such as ethnicity, cross-cultural competence, and credibility; and economic and physical inaccessibility of services. Thus, the authors did not assume causality but explored alternative hypothesis for explaining the study's results.

Although both causal comparative and correlational research are used to study phenomenon involving the inherent characteristics of participants, there is an important difference between the two approaches: Causal comparative research focuses on making group comparisons (e.g., comparing academic achievement in groups with high vs. low self-concepts). Although correlational research can also be used to make group comparisons, its main focus is on providing an estimate of the magnitude of the relationship between two variables (e.g., examining the relationship between the level of self-concept and academic achievement). The difference in focus of the two types of studies leads to a difference in the kinds of conclusions that can be drawn. In the causal comparative study, the researcher might conclude that a group of students with high self-concepts differed significantly on academic achievement compared with a group with low self-concepts. In a correlational study, a researcher might conclude that there is a strong, positive relationship between self-concept and academic achievement.

Inherent Characteristics: Challenging Issues

By their very nature of comparing individuals who differ based on inherent characteristics, such as ethnicity, gender, socioeconomic class, or disabling conditions, these approaches to research have serious implications for researchers in terms of how the research questions are framed and the basis that is used for group definition.

Focusing on Group Differences

As Campbell (1988, 1989), Fine and Gordon (1989), and others (Shakeshaft, Campbell, & Karp, 1992) have pointed out, the focus of much gender-related research has been on gender differences. Campbell (1988) notes, "Even the sound of 'sex similarities' sounds new and strange" (p. 5). These researchers point out that focusing on sex differences obscures the many areas in which males and females overlap.

Researchers have noted that gender differences in academic abilities, even in the areas of verbal and mathematics skills, have narrowed between males and females (Hyde, 1990). Lips (1993) used this basis of "no differences" in math abilities and aptitude to explore why women are underrepresented in mathematics and the physical and engineering sciences. Now, you might ask, how did the myth that males are superior in mathematics attain such stature as a scientific fact? Campbell (1988) proposes a number of factors related to research design and reporting that might help explain the focus and seeming credibility of differences between the sexes.

Campbell (1988) attributes the focus on gender differences to an artifact associated with the origins of research designs in the social sciences rooted in an agricultural model designed to investigate differences in effect of treatments on variables such as crop size and quality. Although this is an appropriate approach for research in agriculture, it fails to accommodate the needs of a researcher who is exploring the complexity of human beings in that it does not allow an examination of similarities *and* differences. Thus, the model is incomplete and inadequate for gaining knowledge about males and females or about people from minority groups and Whites. The second artifact of the research process that leads to an overemphasis on differences arises from the practice of journals in education and psychology to publish studies in which *statistically significant differences* are found (a term defined in Chapter 1 and discussed more fully in Chapter 12). Campbell (1988) points out that finding differences

> has been what counts in terms of publication, dissemination and ultimately research survival. Studies not finding significant differences are FOUR times less apt to be finished. Even when they are finished, they are less likely to be published than studies in which significant differences are found. (p. 3)

Fine and Gordon (1992) present a different basis for criticism of gender difference research. They write that "this almost exclusive construction of gender-as-difference functions inside psychology as a political and scientific diversion away from questions of power, social context, meaning, and braided subjectivities" (p. 8). They suggest that what is needed is a new language, because the issues are less about sex as biology or even gender as social construction and more about the politics of sex-gender relations that can transform oppressive social arrangements. Although sex and gender may feel biological or psychological, the more important focus is on the political implications.

Group Identification

A second area of challenge for the researcher in the causal comparative and correlational approaches to research is the definition of who belongs in which group. This is more a problem with race, class, and disability-related research at present than with gender-related research. Definitions of race and ethnicity somewhat parallel those of sex and gender; that is, one is considered to have a biological basis and the other a socially constructed basis. However, Stanfield (1993a) identifies the difficulties in answering questions such as, What is a White person? or What is a Black person? as stemming from the "extensiveness of ethnic mixing that has occurred in the United States in reciprocal acculturation and cultural assimilation processes, if not in miscegenation experiences" (p. 21).

Problems arise in terms of which basis for categorization to use. Stanfield (1993a) recognizes that most classifications of racial identity are based on skin color and other phenotypic characteristic: For example, a person who has dark skin, woolly hair, and a broad nose is readily identified as an African American. The problems for a researcher arise when the skin color of the African American person becomes lighter so that he or she might "pass" for European American or with people of mixed-race descent who do not readily identify with any of the standard racial categories.

Qualitative researchers tend to construct the meaning of a person's racial identity based on the respondents' self-perceptions of race and ethnicity and their influence on one's life experiences. Quantitative researchers, on the other hand, have tended to rely on statistical categories derived from government documents and survey coding. Stanfield (1993a), however, warns both groups of researchers that they have no way of knowing "whether an informant's expressed racial identification is a response to the objectified categorization derived from learning experiences in a race-saturated society or merely a subjective admission" (p. 18).

Bias can result when the method of determining racial or ethnic identity does not adequately represent the complexities of the situation. For example, if research is done on Latino populations and the respondents are selected based on a Spanish surname, children of Latino fathers who use the names of their fathers would be included but not the children of Latino mothers (Shakeshaft et al., 1992). The practice of lumping together biological and social definitions of race under a common racial label results in a biased sample. This is the situation that results when children of a Black and a White parent are identified as African American.

The use of a socially constructed, self-identification of race or ethnicity by authors such as Jensen (1969) and Herrnstein and Murray (1994) is problematic in terms of the types of genetically based interpretations that they offer. As Campbell (1989) notes, "When social definitions of race are used, *no* conclusions about genetic or biological differences can be made" (p. 11).

Stanfield (1993a) raises some important questions for researchers who choose to work in the causal comparative or correlational mode with respect to race and ethnicity:

- How do we conceptualize identity issues in race and ethnicity research that go beyond reified, simplistic stereotyping?

- How do we use official data sources with care in exploring racial identity questions, realizing the problematics of aggregate data and ill-defined circumstances of self-reporting versus actual self-identity?

- If we have to categorize people to understand who they are and how they define themselves, how do we do so in this area of research more in terms of self-definitions than in terms of what popular cultural folk wisdom dictates?

- How do we incorporate understanding in research designs regarding the interactional aspects of identity formation in dominant and subordinate populations that would make such considerations much more sociological? (p. 24).

The U.S. Office of Management and Budget (OMB) has recognized the complexity of multiracial groups and other individuals who do not neatly fit into existing categories for race on federal forms (Skrzycki, 1994). The OMB is currently struggling with how to collect and code information for people who might have one White and one African American parent or who might be from South America but are not Hispanic. The options they are considering include the following:

1. Add a new "multiracial" category
2. Add an "other" category
3. Provide an open-ended question to probe for information on race and ethnicity
4. Add categories for Native Americans, Native Hawaiians, and Middle Easterners

Other federal agencies are also struggling with this issue. For example, the U.S. Bureau of the Census and the Centers for Disease Control are considering changing the racial categories they use by allowing people to identify themselves as mixed race or by adding new categories for minorities, such as Cambodians or Arab Americans (Wheeler, 1995).

The whole debate over racial or ethnic identity is further complicated by the conflict between the reality of social oppression based on such phenotypic characteristics as skin color and the realization that no single gene can be used to define a race. The American Anthropological Association passed a resolution saying that "differentiating species into biologically defined 'races' has proven meaningless and unscientific" (cited in Wheeler, 1995, p. A9). Anthropologists have replaced the concept of race with a focus on how people identify themselves, by geographic origins or by other means.

Despite all the problems associated with categorizing people according to race or ethnicity, disabling conditions, and (sometimes) gender, researchers need to be aware of the benefits that have accrued from cross-group comparisons. Causal comparative and correlational research have been used to document oppression based on skin color and other phenotypic characteristics. Discontinuing such research based on the rationale that our understanding of race, gender, and disability is limited needs to be weighed against the benefit associated with revealing inequities in resources and outcomes in education, psychology, and the broader society.

Fallacy of Homogeneity

Campbell (1989) and Stanfield (1993a) both discuss the fallacy of homogeneity—that is, assuming similarities within racial and ethnic groups on other characteristics, such as socioeconomic class. Much of the research done in cross-race comparisons ignores the generally higher socioeconomic class associated with people of European American descent. Teasing out the effects of race and poverty is a complex and difficult task (if not impossible).

Problems similar to those associated with race can be found in Mertens and McLaughlin's (1995) discussion of the identification of persons with disabilities (p. 60).

Post Hoc Fallacy

Problems with the identification of group differences in causal comparative and correlational research occur with such regularity that researchers have developed a specific name for the inappropriate attribution of causation in such studies—that is, the post hoc fallacy (Campbell, 1989). The types of studies discussed in this chapter (e.g., comparisons of males and females, European Americans and African Americans) are particularly susceptible to the post hoc fallacy, and therefore, competing explanations for the results should be carefully examined. Lips's (1993) study is one example of causal comparative research that examined numerous competing explanations for differences in male and female participation in mathematics and engineering careers. Her study is used in the following section to explain strategies for conducting causal comparative research (see Sample Study 4.1 for a summary of Lips's study).

Causal Comparative Research

The steps for conducting causal comparative research are similar to those outlined in Chapter 1 for any research undertaking:

1. Identify a research problem.
2. Select a defined group and a comparison group.
3. Collect data on relevant independent and dependent variables and on relevant background characteristics.
4. Analyze and interpret the data.

SUMMARY STUDY 4.1 *Summary of a Causal Comparative Study*

Research problem: Compared with men, women are underrepresented in mathematics and science careers.

Research question: For people who have strong positive feelings about math and science, what are the gender differences in self-rated likelihood of pursuing a career in physical sciences or engineering?

Method: Male and female college students were asked to respond to yes-or-no questions on a computer screen related to their feelings about their own inclinations toward math and science and their interest in a career in the physical sciences or engineering.

Participants: Ninety-seven college students (55 females, 42 males) participated in the study.

Instruments and procedures: The researcher used computer-programmed and timed assessments. The first part involved yes-or-no responses to short self-descriptive phrases, including 13 related to mathematics and science affirmations, such as "good with numbers." The career portion of the assessment items related to a large number of careers, including some specific to mathematical, physical, and engineering sciences were presented. Again, a yes-or-no format was used to determine the likelihood that the respondent would pursue this career.

Results: For physical and engineering science careers, the pattern for women and men diverged sharply at high-interest levels. For men, a strong general endorsement of science and mathematics was significantly and positively predictive of an increasingly strong likelihood of interest in a career in the physical sciences and engineering. For women, there was little or no relationship between self-described interest in and liking for science and mathematics and self-reported likelihood of pursuing a career in the physical and engineering sciences.

Discussion: Lips suggests that future research is needed to explore factors that may be necessary to heighten women's chances of choosing scientific and engineering careers, such as psychological support at some critical juncture, a minimum number of female faculty, or a visible number of female student peers in departments such as science, mathematics, and engineering.

SOURCE: Based on Lips (1993).

First, a research problem is identified. Lips (1993) notes that women are underrepresented in mathematics and science careers. She speculates on possible causes for this discrepancy:

1. Differences in ability and performance might explain the discrepancy. But Lips rejected this because of the small to modest differences supported by previous research. Even small differences by gender are suspect because of the gender-sensitive nature of the measuring instruments, such as the SAT-M. Also, comparisons of group means resulted in biased estimates of true differences because the males' scores were "pulled up" by a relatively small group of high-scoring outlier men.

2. Social forces such as low peer and faculty support might lower the extent to which girls and women value achievement in math and science.

3. Females might feel personally alienated from the subject matter, methods of science, or both, thus leading to the development of a self-view that does not include interest in math or science. If this is the reason for underrepresentation in these fields, Lips reasons that redress could be made by establishing policies and procedures focused on awakening (or reawakening) women's self-perception of their abilities and interests in math and science.

Lips decided to pursue this problem in terms of the gender differences in the relationship between self-affirmed inclination toward mathematics and science and likelihood of choosing careers in the physical sciences and engineering.

The *second step* is to select a defined group and a comparison group. The researcher has a number of options for creating the groups that yield more or less control over the differential selection threat to internal validity. Because causal comparative research compares the performance of two (or more) intact groups, the threat of differential selection must be addressed. If the two groups differ significantly on characteristics other than the explanatory variable (e.g., gender), those other (extraneous) characteristics might explain the difference between the groups.

Some strategies that researchers can use to control the threat of differential selection include the following:

1. Matching on particular characteristics of relevance (discussed further in Chapter 10)

2. Using a statistical technique such as analysis of covariance to control for preexisting differences (discussed further in Chapter 12)

3. Eliminating subjects with specific characteristics (e.g., those with multiple disabilities)

4. Analysis of subgroups

The creation of homogeneity by elimination of people with specific characteristics comes at a cost in restricting the generalizability of the findings to that "homogeneous" population.

For her study, Lips (1993) chose 97 college-level students (55 females, 45 males). In causal comparative research, the researcher will often form subgroups based on other variables of interest (e.g., ethnicity) to better understand the phenomenon. Lips decided to explore inclinations for careers in the physical sciences and engineering for students with different self-affirmed inclinations toward math and science. She created five subgroups based on their self-affirmed math-science inclination: low, low-average, average, high-average, and high. Thus, she was able to determine if the self-reported likelihood of a career in physical science and engineering varied across levels of inclination toward these fields.

The *third step* involves collecting data on the independent and dependent variables as well as on relevant background characteristics. Lips (1993) asked her participants to respond to short, self-descriptive phrases, including 13 related to math and science affirmation, such as "good with numbers," and a yes-or-no format to reflect the likelihood of pursuing careers in various fields (including physical and engineering sciences).

The *fourth step* includes analyzing and interpreting the data. She reported that men and women with low levels of inclination shared low interests in careers in physical science and engineering. However, men with high inclinations reported high career likelihood, but women with high inclinations did not indicate high career likelihood. Thus, she concluded that for these women, liking mathematics and sciences did not positively predispose them to a career in the physical sciences and engineering.

As is necessary in causal comparative research, Lips (1993) explored alternative explanations for her results:

- A need to be aware of the effect of a scarcity of other women on women in math and science classes
- Perceived social norms and pressures associated with being a member of a highly visible minority
- Experiencing stereotyping and fewer opportunities for affiliation and social support
- Gender bias and inequities in the classroom

Thus, Lips's study demonstrates that a comparison of male and female characteristics would oversimplify interpretations if subgroup analysis and alternative explanations are not pursued.

Correlational Research

Correlational studies can be either *prediction* studies or *relationship* studies. In prediction studies, the researcher is interested in using one or more variables (the predictor variables) to predict performance on one or more other variables (the criterion variables). For example, kindergarten test scores can be used to predict first-grade test scores, if there is a strong relationship between the two sets of scores. In prediction studies, it is important to be aware of any other variables related to performance on the criterion variable. Relationship studies usually explore the relationships between measures of different variables obtained from the same individuals at approximately the same time to gain a better understanding of factors that contribute to a more complex characteristic.

It is important to realize that the correlation coefficient can range between plus and minus 1.00. The closer the correlation coefficient is to plus or minus 1.00, the stronger the relationship. A positive correlation means that the two variables increase or decrease together. For example, a positive correlation might exist between age and reading skills for deaf children, meaning that older children tend to exhibit higher reading skills. A negative correlation means that the two variables differ inversely; that is, as one goes up, the other goes down. For example, reading skills may be higher for children with less severe hearing losses—for example, as hearing loss goes up, reading skills go down. If the correlation coefficient is near zero, no relationship exists. For example, lipreading ability might be unrelated to reading skills in deaf children.

A word of caution should be entered here regarding the inadvisability of assuming cause and effect from correlational data. It is possible to calculate a correlation coefficient between any two sets of numbers:

- The number of PhDs in a state and the number of mules (it is strongly negative)
- The number of ice-cream cones sold and the number of deaths by drowning (it is strongly positive)
- The number of churches and bars in the same vicinity (it is strongly positive) (Beins, 1993)

There are obvious explanations other than causality for these correlations. Such high correlations that are due to some third variable (such as rural areas, hot weather, urban crowding) are called *spurious*. Nevertheless, it should be remembered that a high correlation does not in and of itself negate the possibility of a causal relationship (to wit: smoking and lung cancer).

An extension of this word of caution about assumptions of causality centers around the finding by researchers that the sum is somehow larger than the parts. In other words, even though a strong relationship may be found between a set of variables and an outcome measure, it is not always possible to then achieve the desired outcomes by manipulating the set of prediction variables. Wittrock (1986) uses the failure of the "input-output" model for effective teaching to make this point. He notes that researchers were able to find strong correlations between various teacher behaviors, such as use of positive reinforcement and student achievement. However, when teachers were trained to increase their use of such behaviors, corresponding increases in student achievement did not occur. He attributes the failure of the correlational approach to inappropriate theoretical assumptions that did not recognize cognitive variables inside the teacher and student and to contextual variables outside the teacher-student dyad.

Steps in Conducting Correlational Research: Relationship Studies

1. Identify an appropriate problem.
2. Identify variables to be included in the study.

3. Identify the appropriate research participants.
4. Collect quantifiable data.
5. Analyze the data and interpret the results.

The *first step* in correlational research, as in all other approaches, is to identify an appropriate problem. Remember, correlational research can be either for prediction purposes or to explain relationships between variables. Steps for conducting a relationship study are explained here, and the following section contains information specific to prediction studies.

One example of a relationship study is Solberg, Valdez, and Villarreal's (1994) investigation of variables related to Hispanic students' adjustment to college (see Sample Study 4.2 for a summary of this study). Their problem arose from the observation that Hispanic students had not fared well in postsecondary education; therefore, the researchers were interested in identifying variables related to college adjustment for this population.

The *second step* is to identify the variables to be included in the study. The variables in correlational research are sometimes called *explanatory* or *predictor* variables instead of independent variables because they are not experimentally manipulated. The dependent variable is then termed the *outcome* or *criterion* variable.

One advantage of correlational research is that several variables can be included in one study (more easily than in experimental or causal comparative designs). (Of course, the number of variables is moderated by sample size. The recommended number of participants per variable is 15, at a minimum.) However, the choice of variables should be done using a theoretical framework rather than a shotgun approach[1] (Borg & Gall, 1989). A researcher should give considerable thought to the variables chosen for inclusion for explanatory purposes. It is possible to "pour" many variables into the computer and then focus on those that come out statistically significant. Because statistics work on the theory of probability, with enough variables, it is probable that some will appear to be significant. It is more important that researchers include those variables that they have reason to believe are related to the outcome variable, based on previous research and theory.

In the Solberg et al. (1994) study, the authors wanted to test a "diathesis-stress" model that posits that mental health functions as an interaction between the amount of stress a person experiences and individual characteristics such as acculturation and social supports that could serve to minimize a person's negative experience of stress. Thus, theoretically, social support should moderate the relationship between stress and adjustment such that a person who perceives that social support is available will have a better adjustment level than someone without such support. Thus, the researchers used this theoretical model to select their independent (predictor or explanatory) variables: stress, social support, and cultural pride. Their dependent (criterion) variable was college adjustment.

The *third step* is to identify appropriate participants. Borg and Gall (1989) suggest that the groups be homogeneous or that subgroup analyses be done because variance in the criterion variable may be explained by different sets of variables for different subgroups. For example, in explaining high school dropout behavior for females, early pregnancy is an important variable; for males, economic need is a stronger predictor.

SUMMARY STUDY 4.2 *Summary of a Correlational Study of Relationship*

Research problem: Previous research suggests that Hispanic students had not fared well in postsecondary education; therefore, researchers were interested in identifying variables related to college adjustment for this population.

Research question: What is the relationship between Hispanic students' adjustment to college and individual characteristics, such as stress levels, acculturation, and social supports?

Method: The researchers used a correlational approach, collecting quantitative data on explanatory variables (stress, social support, and cultural pride), and examined their relationship to the participants' level of college adjustment.

Participants: The participants included 126 men and 268 women who attended a public university and who identified their family's country of origin as Mexico, a Latin American country, or an island in the Caribbean.

Instruments and procedures: Quantitative, paper-and-pencil scales were used to measure all variables. For example, stress level was measured using a 30-item scale that asked questions such as, "How often have you experienced difficulty trying to fulfill responsibilities at home and at school?" (p. 233). Students indicated their responses on a 5-point scale from 0 (*never*) to 4 (*very often*).

Results: Both stress and social support were significantly related to college adjustment; cultural pride was not found to be a significant variable. Academic and social stress and social support combined to account for 59% of the variance in college adjustment.

Conclusions: The diathesis-stress model was not supported in that social support was not found to buffer individuals from the negative effects of stress. "This research indicated that intervention and prevention programming aimed at addressing social factors such as living in the local community, handling relationships, and availability of social support are areas that are likely to have a positive impact on retention efforts targeted for Hispanic populations" (p. 237).

SOURCE: Based on Solberg, Valdez, and Villarreal (1994).

Solberg et al. (1994) chose to use 126 men and 268 women who attended a public university and who identified their family's country of origin as Mexico, a Latin American country, or an island in the Caribbean. They did not conduct subgroup analysis to determine if men's or women's college adjustment were explained by different patterns of variables.

The *fourth step* is to collect quantifiable data. For example, students' stress levels in the Solberg et al. (1994) study were measured using a 30-item scale that asked such questions

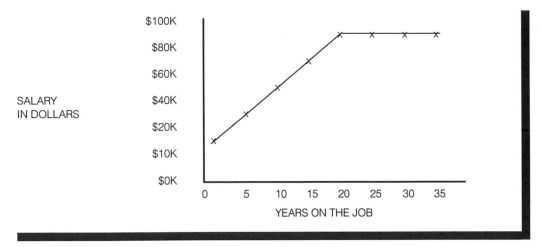

Figure 4.1.

as "How often have you experienced difficulty trying to fulfill responsibilities at home and at school?" (p. 233). The students indicated their responses on a 5-point scale from 0 (*never*) to 4 (*very often*).

The *fifth step* is to analyze the data and interpret the results. The researcher has a number of options for correlational analysis, including simple correlation, regression analysis, multiple regression analysis, discriminant function analysis, canonical correlation, path analysis, and factor analysis. These analytic techniques are described in Chapter 12. In this chapter, I explain some of the issues related to the use of statistical techniques for correlational research studies.

Graphs and Curvilinear Relationships. No matter what statistic is chosen, the researcher should always start with a graphic display of the relationships between the variables. One reason for this is that it gives you a commonsense base for interpreting the correlation coefficients that are subsequently calculated. Another *very* important reason is that simple correlation analysis is based on the assumption of a linear relationship between the variables. For example, as one's number of years in a job increases, one's salary increases. However, if a curvilinear relationship is depicted in the graph, simple correlation is an inappropriate statistical choice. For example, if a sample's ability to increase its earnings was restricted (because it had reached a "ceiling" within the organization or whatever), the relationship would be represented as shown in Figure 4.1.

The correlation coefficient would be low, suggesting a lack of relationship, when in actuality, a curvilinear relationship exists.

Choice of a Correlation Coefficient. The choice of a correlation coefficient depends on the scale of measurement. For variables with a continuous scale, the Pearson product-moment coefficient is typically used. For rank level data, Spearman's rho can be used. For nominal (dichotomous) data, a biserial correlation coefficient can be used. These are explained in more depth in Chapter 12.

Size and Interpretation. The interpretation of the size of the correlation depends on the purpose of the study. For relationship studies, a test of statistical significance can be applied to a correlation coefficient (see Chapter 12 for further discussion of this concept). For prediction studies, generally, a correlation above .60 is considered to be adequate for group predictions, and above .80 for individual predictions (e.g., school placement decisions).

Common or Explained Variance or r^2. Interpretation of correlation coefficients is often based on the amount of *common* or *explained variance* found by squaring the correlation coefficient. The explained or common variance refers to the variation in one variable that is attributable to its tendency to vary with the other (Gay, 1992). For example, Solberg et al. (1994) obtained a correlation coefficient of −.74 between stress and college adjustment scores for the Hispanic college students. Therefore, they reported that stress accounted for 40% of the variance in college adjustment. If stress was perfectly correlated with college adjustment, the two variables would have 100% common variance (and a correlation coefficient of −1.00). Because many variables other than stress influence college adjustment, the two variables have 40% shared or common variance.

Multiple Regression and Ordering Variables.[2] The order of entry for variables in multiple regression equations is important. When the predictor variables are correlated (a situation called *collinearity*), the amount of variance that each independent variable accounts for can change drastically with different orders of entry of the variables. Although there is no "correct" method for determining the order of variables (Kerlinger, 1973), the researcher must decide on a rationale for entry. If the researcher is interested in controlling for the effects of background characteristics before testing the effects of a treatment, it makes sense to enter the background characteristics first (e.g., see Andrews & Mason, 1986). Then the treatment variable will explain what is left of the variance.

Other possible rationales for entering variables include the following:

1. Enter the variables in order of their highest correlation with the criterion variable.
2. Enter them in chronological order.
3. Enter them in an order established by previous research.
4. Use a theoretical base for ordering.

To test their diathesis-stress model, Solberg et al. (1994) first entered the cultural pride variable into a hierarchial regression, followed by social support, stress, and the Social Support × Stress interaction term. They stated that if the entry of cultural pride and social support was statistically significant, the hypothesis of a direct relationship would be supported. However, for the diathesis-stress model to be considered, stress must also be directly related to adjustment, and the interaction of social support and stress would have to be significant.

In hierarchical regression, R^2 is generated as the amount of explained variance accounted for by the entry of variables in the equation. In the Solberg et al. (1994) study, statistical significance was determined by the level of R^2 change and whether the predictor or interaction term was significant (i.e., beta value) at the time it was entered into the equation. The R^2 changed from .00 to .21 with the entry of social support and from .21 to .58 with entry of the stress variable. These changes in R^2 indicated that stress and social support were significantly related to college adjustment. However, no significant changes in R^2 were found with the cultural pride variable or the interaction term of social support and stress. Thus, their diathesis-stress model was not supported in that social support was not found to buffer individuals from the negative effects of stress.

Discriminant Function Analysis. This statistical technique is used to predict group membership on the basis of a variety of predictor variables. For example, a number of different test scores could be used to see if they can discriminate between individuals who have mental retardation, learning disabilities, or no educational disability. Or it could also be used to see if measures of self-esteem, social skills, and participation in recreational activities can discriminate between people who are lonely or not lonely.

Canonical Correlation. Canonical correlation is also used to determine group membership; however, it can be used with multiple independent (explanatory or predictor) *and* multiple dependent (criterion) variables. For example, explanatory variables such as sex, socioeconomic status, and educational level can be combined with criterion variables such as income, employment, and prestige to determine if any discernible patterns emerge that could be used to separate people into groups.

Path Analysis. Path analysis is used when a researcher wants to test a causal theoretical model. For example, based on previous research, a casual model of academic achievement could be developed that included various student background characteristics (e.g., sex, ethnic status, presence or degree of disability), and instructional process variables (e.g., teacher expectation, degree of sensitivity to cultural differences). The researcher must specify the model in advance and then test to estimate the strength and direction of the relationships.

Factor Analysis. Factor analysis is an empirical way to reduce the number of variables by grouping variables that correlate highly with each other. For example, Solberg et al. (1994) identified 30 items related to stress. They factor-analyzed their participant's responses to these 30 items and determined that stress could be understood in terms of these factors: social stress, academic stress, and financial stress. Thus, they were able to reduce the number of variables from 30 to 3 (based on factor scores). For factor analysis, at least five participants per variable is recommended.

Cross-Validation. Perhaps all research seemingly could merit from replication to substantiate that the results are not a fluke. However, because of the lack of control and manipulation in correlational research, it is advisable to *cross-validate* the results of correlational analysis with a separate, independent sample. For example, would the stress variable divide into the same three factors if data were collected from another, similar sample?

Correlational Studies: Prediction

An example of a correlational study for predictive purposes is summarized in Sample Study 1.1. Doren, Bullis, and Benz (1996) were interested in making predictions as to which young adults with disabilities were more likely to be victimized within 1 year of leaving high school. In predictive correlational studies, the procedures are very similar to relationship studies. However, a few differences should be noted.

The *first step* is to identify the research problem. Doren et al. (1996) note that previous research suggests that people with mental retardation are vulnerable to economic, psychological, and physical abuse. They wanted to know more about the variables that might be used to predict who might become a victim.

The *second step* is to identify the variables to include in the study. Doren et al. (1996) selected variables based on previous research, including gender, minority status, serious emotional disturbance, specific learning disability, dropout status, family socioeconomic status, parent rating of academic skills, and a rating of personal and social skills.

In prediction studies, the researcher who focuses on one predictor variable (e.g., score on the Graduate Record Exam [GRE]) needs to be aware of the multiple criteria used to select people for admission to graduate school. A simple correlation between GRE scores and graduate school grade point average (GPA) would probably be low for a number of reasons:

1. Many criteria are used to select people for graduate school, including their undergraduate GPA, letters of reference, and personal position statement.

2. The range of scores for those accepted is restricted on a predictor variable such as the GPA.

3. The range of scores in the graduate school GPA (the criterion variable) is very restricted. (In many graduate schools, only A's and B's are acceptable for continuation in the program. If a student gets a C, he or she can be put on probation or dismissed.)

Thus, a high correlation between GRE and graduate school GPA could be obtained if a random sample of people took the GRE, all were accepted into graduate school, and all were allowed to remain in the program, no matter what grades they got. Not a likely scenario.

Researchers who conduct predictive correlational studies must be concerned not only with the number of predictor variables but also with the reliability and range of the criterion variable.

The *third step* is to identify appropriate participants for the study. Doren et al. (1996) included 422 adolescents from two Western states. The samples represented their respective populations in each state by primary disability category and gender. Population data on minority status was not available in the state's databases.

The *fourth step* is to collect quantitative data. One big difference that should be noted about prediction studies is that a time period must be allowed to elapse between the predictive variables and the criterion variables. In a prediction study, there is a need for an appropriate time delay between the measurement of your explanatory (predictor) variable(s) and your criterion variable. For example, suppose you wanted to use children's scores on a reading readiness measure to predict their ability to read at the end of first grade. You would need to administer the reading readiness measure at the beginning of the school year and then wait until the end of the school year to measure their reading abilities.

The researchers in the predictive study of victimization, quantified all the data concerning predictor and criterion variables. For example, victimization was coded as occurring if the students or their parents reported that the adolescent had experienced more than one of the following: being teased or bothered, having something stolen from him or her, or being hit hard or beaten up. The quantification of this variable allowed them to conduct the statistical analysis necessary for the prediction model. However, the researchers did acknowledge that this quantification was not able to capture the true nature of the adolescents' experiences of victimization. In terms of time delay, the researchers were able to interview students and parents once during the students' last year in school and once again when students were out of school for 1 year (Doren et al., 1996).

The *fifth step* is to analyze the data and interpret the results. The statistical choices for prediction studies are similar to those for relationship studies. One difference in predictive studies concerns the amount of variance that can be explained in the criterion variable. If predictor variables are to be useful, they should (in combination) explain about 64% of the variance in the criterion variable. This would translate into about .8 correlation between one predictor and one criterion variable. In the Doren et al. (1996) study, the researchers did not report the amount of variance accounted for by their model. However, they did report that a person who was both characterized as having a serious emotional disturbance and low on personal and social achievement was 20.48 times more likely to experience victimization.

► *Questions for Critically Analyzing Causal Comparative and Correlational Research*

1. Is a causal relationship assumed between the independent (predictor) variables and the dependent (response) variable? What unexpected or uncontrollable factors might have influenced the results? What competing explanations are explored?

2. How comparable are the groups in causal comparative studies?

3. Did the authors address group similarities and differences?

4. How did the authors operationally define who belonged in each group—for example, based on ethnicity or race or on disability? How did they address the issue of self-reporting versus actual self-identity? How were issues related to multiracial people addressed?

5. How did the authors address the fallacy of homogeneity?

6. How did the authors avoid the post hoc fallacy?

7. After the initial groups were defined, were subgroup analyses conducted, based on age, sex, socioeconomic status, or similar variables?

8. Could a third variable cause both the independent (predictor) and dependent (criterion) variables?

9. For correlational studies, what was the rationale for choosing and entering explanatory or predictor variables? What was the percentage of variance explained by the explanatory or predictor variables?

10. If a predictive relationship was studied, was the predictor variable the only criteria used to select participants in the study? Would combining the predictor variable with other screening criteria improve its predictive validity? (A predictive validity coefficient of about .8 is needed for an accurate prediction.)

11. What is the reliability of the criterion variable (compared with the test used to make the prediction)? Is there a restricted range for the criterion variable?

12. Were the results cross-validated with a separate, independent sample?

■ Questions and Activities for Discussion and Application

1. Through a computerized literature search or by going directly to the main journals that publish empirical, quantitative research studies, identify four research studies, two that use a causal comparative approach and two that use a correlational approach. For each study do the following:

   a. Identify the research problem.

   b. Identify the independent or predictor and dependent or criterion variables.

   c. Categorize the study as causal comparative or correlational.

   d. Explain the basis for your categorization.

   e. Critique the studies using the questions for critical analysis at the end of this chapter.

   f. For each study, note how the authors addressed the challenges of focusing on group differences, group identification, the fallacy of homogeneity, and the post hoc fallacy.

2. Brainstorm a number of different problems that would be appropriate for causal comparative or correlational research.

3. Select one research problem and explain how you would approach it using a causal comparative approach:

a. Identify the independent and dependent variables.

b. Explain how your approach to the study would satisfy the questions for critical analysis for causal comparative research.

4. Select one research problem and explain how you would approach it using a correlational approach:

a. Identify the independent or predictor and dependent or criterion variables.

b. Explain how your approach to the study would satisfy the questions for critical analysis for correlational research.

5. Under what circumstances would you *not* recommend using causal comparative or correlational approaches to research? What kind of alternative approach would you suggest?

Notes

1. A shotgun scatters the "shot" in a broad area; it does not hit a precise area. Thus, likelihood of hitting something is increased with a shot gun, but it may not be the precise thing that you intended to hit.

2. A sophisticated understanding of statistical practices is necessary to actually conduct multiple regression and make decisions about ordering variables. Nevertheless, you should be aware of the potential problems associated with inappropriate ordering of variables in research that uses this type of analysis.

In This Chapter

■ *Steps for conducting a survey research study are outlined, including the design phase, the sampling plan, designing the questionnaire, and conducting the survey.*

■ *Construction of different types of questions is considered, such as demographic, threatening and nonthreatening behavioral, knowledge, and attitude questions.*

■ *Response rate considerations are described.*

■ *Notes specific to phone and personal interviews address specific issues related to those approaches.*

■ *Issues related to the emancipatory perspective are discussed.*

■ *Questions for critical analysis of survey research are presented.*

Survey Research

Surveys can be thought of as methods used for descriptive research or as data collection methods used within other research designs. For example, a survey used to collect data for comparisons of income between deaf and hearing high school graduates represents the data collection technique used within a causal comparative research design. I have chosen to devote an entire chapter to this approach to research because surveys are used pervasively in educational and psychological research and because many design issues are an integral part of the planning and conduct of surveys.

Surveys are a familiar part of most peoples' lives in the sense that their results are often cited in the popular media, such as newspapers, magazines, and television programs. You should be aware of the strengths and limitations of survey research compared with other research strategies. Surveys are good because they allow collection of data from a larger number of people than is generally possible when using a quasi-experimental or experimental design. However, unlike most qualitative research approaches that involve direct observation of behavior, surveys rely on individuals' *self-reports* of their knowledge, attitudes, or behaviors. Thus, the validity of the information is contingent on the honesty of the respondent. You might assume that people who do not give an honest answer have something to hide. However, as can be seen in the following quotation from popular comedian George Burns, people might not know the answer, or they might not know that they do not know the honest answer.

> If you were to go around asking people what would make them happier, you'd get answers like a new car, a bigger house, a raise in pay, winning a lottery, a face-lift, more kids, less kids, a new restaurant to go to—probably not one in a hundred would say a chance to help people. And yet that may bring the most happiness of all. (Burns, 1984, p. 141)

Surveys can be conducted for a wide variety of purposes. If you are planning to conduct a survey, the first step is to define the purpose of the survey.

Design Phase

During the design phase, the researcher should begin to articulate the purpose(s) of the survey, state specific objectives, consider the types of information needed, and evaluate design options. Two of the study summaries included in Chapter 1 of this text provide you with an overall picture of research that used surveys to collect data. The postpositivist research study of victimization experiences of adolescents with disabilities chose to use telephone interviews (see Sample Study 1.1). The emancipatory research study of high school tracking used personal interviews (see Sample Study 1.3).

Purpose

Surveys can be used for a wide variety of purposes:

- The American Association of University Women's (AAUW) Educational Foundation commissioned Louis Harris and Associates to survey public school students in Grades 8 through 11 concerning their experiences of sexual harassment in school (AAUW, 1993).

- The U.S. General Accounting Office (GAO) surveyed businesses and government agencies to determine the extent to which the accessibility standards outlined in the Americans With Disabilities Act (ADA) were being met (U.S. GAO, 1993).

- Many surveys have been conducted to examine the relationship of participation in a variety of educational placements for a variety of populations:

  Shapiro and Lentz (1991) conducted a survey of graduates from a secondary-level vocational-technical program who had learning disabilities to determine their postsecondary educational and employment experiences.

  MacLeod-Gallinger (1992) compared the labor force, occupation, and earning outcomes between men and women in a survey of deaf high school graduates.

The National Longitudinal Transition Study of Special Education Students was conducted by SRI International for the Office of Special Education Programs, U.S. Department of Education, to examine the secondary and postsecondary education, employment, and personal independence experiences of youths with disabilities (DeStefano & Wagner, 1991).

- Surveys have been used extensively in the study of the effects of integrating students with disabilities into general education classes (e.g., Janney, Snell, Beers, & Raynes, 1995).

- Feminist researchers have used surveys to investigate issues such as child care, housework, parenting, sexual harassment, and violence against women (Reinharz, 1992; M. Smith, 1994).

- Perceptions of the "chilly" climate on campus were investigated for university faculty and staff and were analyzed in terms of associations between climate perceptions and demographic characteristics such as race and gender (Dewey, Cashin, Stockdale, & Shearer, 1994).

- A survey of African American fifth graders was used to explore the relationship between the influence of Africentric values, self-esteem, and Black identity on drug attitudes (Belgrave et al., 1994).

- Interviews were conducted with the residents of a Mexican border town to investigate their social and economic survival strategies (McKee, 1992).

A number of national surveys are conducted in the United States on a regular basis, such as the labor market statistics generated by the Bureau of Labor Statistics and the Bureau of the Census; basic data about health conditions, use of health service, and behaviors that affect the risk of illness from the National Health Interview Survey carried out by the Bureau of the Census for the Public Health Service; and rates of crimes and people's concerns and fears about crime from the National Crime Survey (Fowler, 1993). The Center for Assessment and Demographic Studies at Gallaudet University conducts the Annual Survey of Hearing Impaired Children and Youth, which includes demographic, audiological, and educationally related information about the students and program information about the schools they attend.

A good first step in starting a survey is to write the purpose of the survey in 25 words or less. This purpose can then be expanded in terms of specific objectives that the survey will strive to address. In the U.S. GAO (1993) study of the ADA, the researchers translated their general statement of purpose into the following four questions:

- To what extent were businesses and state and local government facilities accessible to persons with disabilities just as the ADA took effect?

- What were the most common barriers remaining?

- To what extent were owners and managers aware of their responsibilities under the ADA?

■ What barrier-removal efforts had owners and managers made between the passage and effective date of the ADA? (p. 2)

A second example of specifying objectives is found in the AAUW's (1993) survey of sexual harassment in America's schools. They asked,

■ How widespread is sexual harassment in school?

■ Who is doing it . . . and to whom?

■ Where is it happening?

■ What forms does it take?

■ How are kids affected by it—what happens to their attitudes toward school and their ability to learn, grow, and achieve? (p. 3)

Specification of such objectives can then be used as a basis for further methodological decisions.

Design Considerations

In survey research, the researcher has a choice between simple descriptive, cross-sectional, and longitudinal approaches. The *simple descriptive* approach is a one-shot survey for the purpose of describing the characteristics of a sample at one point in time. The *cross-sectional* design involves examining the effects of several groups at one point in time (e.g., first-, third-, and fifth-grade students). *Longitudinal* designs survey one group or cohort of subjects at different points in time (e.g., 1 year, 2 years, and 3 years after leaving school). Cross-sectional designs have the advantage of collecting information in a shorter time frame. The disadvantage is that the experience of the students who are now in the fifth grade may have been different in the first grade, compared with students who are now in first grade. The advantage of longitudinal research is that it follows the same (or highly similar) subjects over a period of time. The disadvantage is that it takes a long time to do it, and conditions may not be the same for students who are graduating 3 years later. Short of a time warp, there is no easy solution to these problems other than acknowledging the limitations of individual studies.

The descriptive design is exemplified in the previously cited studies of ADA implementation, the integration of students with disabilities, perceptions of a chilly climate, fifth-graders' attitudes toward drug use, and survival strategies for residents of a Mexican border town. Longitudinal designs were used in the surveys of postsecondary experiences. For example, Shapiro and Lentz (1991) conducted follow-up surveys at 6, 12, and 24 months after graduation.

Cross-sectional surveys are sometimes used to compare responses across different grade levels. For example, the AAUW (1993) survey of students in Grades 8 through 11 represents a cross-sectional approach.

Particularly with special education students, the researcher must be aware that progression from one grade to another may not be the most appropriate way to measure passage of time. The students' individual education plans (IEPs) often define goals for individual growth rather than for progression from grade to grade; thus, longitudinal research with these populations would more appropriately focus on age rather than grade.

Data Collection Choices

In survey research, the researcher has a choice of mail, telephone, personal interviews, e-mail, or a combination of these as a method of collecting data. The method selected depends on the purpose of the survey, the nature of the data to be collected, cost factors, and the size and characteristics of the sample. Advantages and disadvantages are associated with each approach. For example, mail surveys are good for collecting detailed information in a closed-ended format, the cost is relatively low, and they can allow a respondent to consult records before responding (e.g., checking on the level of expenditure within specific categories). The disadvantages of mail surveys is that they are generally associated with lower response rates than phone and personal interviews, and the surveyor does not have an opportunity to probe for more in-depth answers or to determine if the respondent understood the questions appropriately. Phone interviews are also good for collecting open-ended responses, and they are generally associated with a higher response rate than are mail surveys. However, they are more costly than mail surveys. In phone interviews, the surveyor does have the opportunity to probe for additional information; however, one cannot observe the interviewees' body language and their contextual surroundings as a part of the interview. The most costly type of interviewing is the personal interview. With this type of interview, the advantages are that the interviewer can use a less structured approach, conduct the interview in a more conversational style, and probe more easily for understanding and additional information. Personal interviews are generally associated with the highest response rates.

Braverman (1996) reports that the sensitivity of the topic appeared to be related to accuracy of responses for different data collection strategies. He referenced two studies that compared responses to questions about substance abuse that were asked in telephone interviews, face-to-face interviews, and self-administered (nonmail) questionnaires (Aquilino, 1994; Fendrich & Vaughn, 1994). In both studies, the strongest evidence of underreporting occurred in the telephone survey mode. Aquilino suggests that the underreporting may be due to respondent confidentiality concerns and lack of opportunity to build trust in the telephone mode. Face-to-face interviews provide a greater opportunity to build trust; self-administration offers greater response anonymity.

Feminist Perspectives

Reinharz (1992) notes that many feminists view survey research as a rigorous and scientifically sound method that has credibility with many people in the social science community and with the public at large. However, other feminists express deep distrust of survey research and other statistically based forms of research. Feminists' criticisms of quantitative, closed-ended survey research are based on the problem of oversimplifying complex issues by reducing them to a limited number of questions and response options. Some researchers try to address these concerns by asking many questions that attempt to get at some of the details of the events and by including participants' verbatim comments in the text.

Reinharz (1992) suggests that the conflict between adherence to strict scientific (postpositivist) procedures and a desire to work within an emancipatory framework can be resolved by using what she calls a "dual vision" (p. 93). She describes the dual vision as a way of embracing contradictions that synthesizes the political and scientific. The concept is described in Reinharz's citation of Roberta Spalter-Roth and Heidi Hartmann's (1989) work. They design their work so that it meets the standards of the mainstream social science community of validity, reliability, objectivity, and replicability. However, they are influenced by their principles of feminist methodology in that they challenge the rigid dichotomies between researcher and researched and between activist and truth seeker. In practice, this means that they use largely quantitative methods and cost-benefit analysis when appropriate. They also view research as political and use their expert stance to legitimate feminist ideas, thus rejecting the part of the objectivity canon that distances the production of knowledge from its uses and applying a constituency test to see if research will be of use to grassroots and advocacy groups.

Other feminist researchers have turned to interviewing as their data collection method of choice for the following reasons (Reinharz, 1992):

- Interviewing allows for free interaction between the researcher and the interviewee and includes opportunities for clarification and discussion.

- The researcher can explore people's views of reality and make full use of differences among people.

- Interviewing provides access to people's ideas, thoughts, and memories in their own words.

- The researcher is able to verify emerging themes and interpretations and can incorporate new questions as needed.

Disability Perspectives

Combinations of methods can result in better response rates. For example, Bowe (1991) adapted the mail survey method for use with blind people. He sent the questionnaire to the respondents and then telephoned them to ask them to arrange for a sighted reader's assistance or to use a magnifying glass to read the print. He achieved a 49% response rate using this method. Freeman, Goetz, Richards, and Groenveld (1991) also conducted a survey with blind people, but they used a lengthy, individual interview that was 15 pages long in a semistructured format. They reported an 85% response rate. Their respondents reported that they welcomed the opportunity to share information and feelings, often for the first time.

Sampling Plan

Identification of the Respondents

Identify the respondents who have the information you want. When you conduct a survey, you should inquire as to who has access to the kind of information you need. You might choose to collect the information from the person who experienced an event, from another person (such as a parent or responsible adult), or by examining records (such as a student's file). Your choice of the source of information will depend on the following factors.

1. Who has access to the information. You may need to inquire to find out who would have access to the kind of information that you need.

2. The characteristics of the people who have experienced the event in terms of age or disabling conditions. If the child is very young or has moderate to severe disabilities that would prevent meaningful participation, it may be necessary to ask the parent or responsible adult for the information. Fine and Sandstrom (1988) provide some insights for interviewing children within a participant observation context. Researchers should be aware that federal legislation requires parents' permission before asking children controversial questions.

3. The type of information needed can help determine the best source of that information. For example, a parent would most likely be aware of whether or not the child is employed, the type of job he or she has, and how much the child is being paid. Thus, they could serve as a proxy to be interviewed if the child was unavailable. However, parents might be a less reliable source for attitudinal information, such as the child's satisfaction with the job. School records are valuable as sources of information regarding courses taken and graduation status.

School records are often used as a source of information in survey research. DeStefano and Wagner (1991) compared parent and student survey responses with various types of information that are commonly available through school records. They found that parents were sometimes unaware that their child took vocational training, even when it was reflected on the school record. On the other hand, the school records reflected a sizable number of students who could not be accounted for in terms of school completion; they were reported as "withdrawn," "moved," or "status unknown." Students in these categories accounted for more than 13% of secondary school leavers with disabilities in the 1986-1987 school year (U.S. Department of Education, 1989). In the National Longitudinal Transition Study (NLTS), parents indicated that 62% of the unclassifiable students had dropped out; thus, reliance on school records would have underestimated the dropout problem. Parents were also confused by what constitutes graduation from high school. The NLTS study revealed that 60% of parents whose children had "aged out" reported that their children had graduated.

Another related issue involves who is asked which questions on the basis of assumptions that the researcher might make. Smith (1993) reports that White people are commonly asked their opinions about Black people and racism but that Black people are not asked race relations questions. He hypothesized that researchers located the race problem in the minds of White people and assumed that Black peoples' opinions on racial matters were obvious. Another reason that researchers gave for not asking Black people questions about racial interviews was concern over the effect on the validity of the data of having a White researcher asking such questions of Black respondents. Thus, because of the narrow focus of questions that Black people were asked and the predominantly White field staff members, the issues of concern to Black people were "historically as invisible in surveys as were Blacks themselves" (p. 220). The issue of who can collect data from whom is raised again in a later section of this chapter.

In longitudinal studies, the researcher must also decide which type of group will be followed over the years. Here are three possible choices:

1. Trend analysis involves studying the same general population but not the same individuals.

2. Cohort analysis involves studying the same specific population but not necessarily the exact same individuals.

3. Panel analysis involves following the exact same individuals over the time period of the study.

Population Definition

Once the general nature of the respondents has been identified, it is time for the researcher to become more specific about the information sources. Thus, the conceptual definition of the population must be translated into operational terms.

Sampling Decisions

If *probability sampling* procedure is used, researchers need to specify to whom the results will be generalized. If a *purposeful sampling* procedure will be used, the researcher needs to provide sufficient details about the people in the study to communicate to the reader their important characteristics. Serious bias can occur in the interpretation of results from a survey that does not make explicit its sampling strategy and the characteristics of the respondents. For example, parents' satisfaction with a drug and alcohol prevention program might appear to be artificially high if a researcher surveys only parents of children who completed the program. To get a more balanced view, parents of children who dropped out of the program should also be surveyed. It is very important to make explicit the sampling strategy and the characteristics of the sample.

Sampling procedures are described in Chapter 10. These include probability sampling (simple random sampling, systematic sampling, clustered sampling, and stratified random sampling) and purposeful sampling (e.g., a "snowball" strategy that involves asking each person who is interviewed to suggest names of additional people who should be interviewed, usually with some guidance as to the nature of the characteristics being sought).

When using a probability sampling approach, the researcher needs to specify a *sampling frame*—that is, a list of the people who have a chance to be selected. A sample can be representative only of the population included in the sampling frame; therefore, it is important to provide evidence concerning how well the sampling frame corresponds to the population (Fowler, 1993).

Braverman (1996) lists the following sources of error in sampling for surveys:

1. Coverage errors arise in two circumstances: (a) people who should be in the sampling frame are *not* there, or (b) people who are truly ineligible (i.e., they are not

members of the target population) are in the sampling frame. A coverage error could occur if you are surveying parents of deaf children and a parent's name is omitted from the sampling frame because the school has not updated its records. Or you might be interested in surveying only hearing parents with deaf children. If the school does not identify parents' hearing status, you may have deaf parents with deaf children inappropriately included in your sampling frame.

2. Nonresponse error occurs when someone refuses to be interviewed or to complete the questionnaire or cannot be reached (e.g., incorrect address or phone number). Response rate considerations are discussed later in this chapter.

3. Sampling error occurs because each sample drawn from a population is somewhat different from any other sample that could be drawn. The probability-based sampling strategies discussed in Chapter 10 are designed to statistically control for sampling error.

Sampling Minority Populations

A few ideas about sampling strategies with minority populations can guide the researcher in decisions about survey research with this population. Smith (1993) notes that in a soundly constructed national, cross-sectional survey, Blacks should turn up proportionately. However, a statistically valid national sample of 1,500 cases produces only about 150 Black respondents. Smith identifies two important results associated with the small size of this subsample:

1. Results based on the subset of Blacks will be less reliable. The margin of error for Whites would be approximately 3%, whereas that for Blacks would be 20%.

2. The small subset of Blacks could not be broken down further into other subgroups for analysis. This serves to further reinforce the myth that the Black community is homogeneous.

Thus, to reduce the margin of error and permit subgroup analyses, the survey researcher should plan to oversample minority populations.

Smith (1993) also discusses strategies for modifying sampling strategies to obtain sufficient representation of Black minorities. If sampling is being conducted on the basis of households in a community, the researcher must acknowledge that Black Americans are not evenly distributed over the landscape and therefore are usually expensive to locate and interview.

Modern national probability samples are constructed on the basis of size criterion—the estimate of the *total* population in any given geographic area. A given place (i.e., county, SMSA, primary sampling unit, segment, or block) has a probability of being included in a sample that is roughly proportionate to its size. Many places end up in a sample on such a basis, but they may have few Blacks; therefore, a majority of the households might be disqualified from any survey interested solely in Blacks. Moreover, when looking particularly for Blacks, one tactic is to over-represent systematically places having higher *concentrations* of them. (p. 225)

Smith (1993) recommends that this strategy be modified to take into account both the properties of Blacks in the areas' boundaries and its total population. He argues that this procedure would be more efficient than oversampling because many of the areas chosen would have large numbers, if not a majority of Blacks. In those areas where there are few Blacks, interviewers could stop searching for them once the expected number of interviews with Blacks was reached. He described an experiment that was conducted as a part of the 1982 General Social Survey in which the selection probabilities were proportional to the size of the Black population at every stage with high-quality results.

James and Busia (1993) (in *Theorizing Black Feminisms*) recognize that traditional random sampling strategies would not result in representative samples of Black Americans. They recommend going through churches in Black communities to reach this population. This strategy was also used to reach minority populations in a study of homelessness in Seattle (Jane Reisman, August 1994, personal communication) and smoke detector use in homes (Margaret Neilly, January 1995, personal communication).

Random Digit Dialing

Random digit dialing (RDD) is a technique that researchers use in selecting samples for telephone surveys (Fowler, 1993). It involves identifying areas to be sampled (at random) and their corresponding area codes and exchanges (the first three digits of the phone number). Then the last four digits of the number to be dialed could be generated at random according to the number of units needed in the sample. It is possible to identify which exchanges are used primarily for residential telephones and to focus the sampling on that subgroup.

The National Black Election Study (NBES) (cited in Smith, 1993) modified the RDD technique to conduct a telephone interview with a national sample of Black Americans. The NBES pilot study results indicated that given an equal probability design in which every phone in the United States had the same chance of being selected, the eligibility of working numbers for Black households would be too low and thus too costly. To solve this problem, the NBES assigned all telephone exchanges to one of three following Black household density strata:

1. High Black density: exchanges in all large SMSAs with a Black population of 15% or more

2. Medium Black density: exchanges in small SMSAs and in all of Alabama, Florida, Georgia, Louisiana, Mississippi, North Carolina, South Carolina, and Virginia

3. Low Black density: all remaining exchanges

The selection rate was adjusted to the density of the Black population in each area. For example, in the high-density stratum, the selection rate was three times that for the low-density stratum. The rate for the medium-density stratum was twice that of the low-density stratum.

Designing the Questionnaire

Before undertaking the task of designing a questionnaire, researchers should do what they should always do before making data collection decisions: Review the literature! Check to see what else has been done from which you might be able to borrow (with appropriate citations and permissions, of course). Many of the national survey organizations publish their questionnaires, and these are available in databases such as ERIC or Psychological Abstracts or from the organizations themselves.

If you decide that you need to develop your own questionnaire, a few general directions are in order, followed by specific suggestions related to different types of questions.

---

1. Outline the various topics you want to include in your survey.

2. Explain to yourself why you are asking each question.

3. Decide on the degree of structure that is most appropriate (e.g., open vs. closed formats or some combination of these). Closed formats include questions in which the respondent chooses from a list of possible options (e.g., multiple-choice questions, true-false questions, or a checklist). Open formats are questions that allow respondents to answer in their own words. Here are examples of each format:

Closed Format

What are your child's preferred activities during a free play period (check all that apply)?

_____ Fantasy play with action figures

_____ Coloring or painting

_____ Fantasy play with dolls

_____ Physically active outdoor play (e.g., swinging, climbing)

_____ Playing board games

Open-Ended Format

What are your child's preferred activities during a free play period?

4. If you plan to use a closed format, such as a multiple-choice question, be sure that you ask the questions, in an open format, of a pilot group first. You can then use their answers to develop the response options. This will help ensure that you have included all reasonable response alternatives. Did you include the right options? Are they all-inclusive, or do you allow for the respondent to enter additional options, if necessary?

5. Generally, avoid psychologically threatening questions. Of course, you cannot avoid psychologically threatening questions if your topic of interest is a sensitive area; however, you should be aware that this type of question should be handled differently. I advise you to read the section later in this chapter on "Threatening Behavioral Questions" before attempting this type of survey question. Many people react defensively when asked about topics such as citizenship (Did you vote?), morality (Did you attend church on Sunday?), social responsibility (Did you help the homeless?), illnesses (Have you been treated for a mental illness?), illegal activities (Have you used illegal drugs?), sexuality (Have you ever had a homosexual

experience?), and finances (How much money do you make?). In many cases, psychologically threatening questions have "socially desirable" answers, and to appear socially appropriate, people may misrepresent their actual attitudes, behaviors, or knowledge. Parents of children with disabilities can find questions about their child's disability threatening, especially if the diagnosis is recent or they have not fully accepted their child's condition.

6. *Clarity* is paramount. Make sure that all the items mean the same thing to all the respondents. This may or may not be possible to do (especially recognizing the social construction of reality). If you are using terms that are commonly open to multiple meanings, you can improve clarity by providing a definition of the terms as you intend them to be understood in your survey. For example, *mainstreaming* is a term commonly used in surveys about the placement of students with disabilities, and it is open to many different interpretations. The researcher should provide a definition of this term for the respondent to be sure that everyone is interpreting it in a similar manner.

7. Short items are generally preferable to long items.

8. Negative wording should be avoided (e.g., which of these are not contributors to violence against women?).

9. Avoid items that ask about more than one idea. Ask about only one idea in each question. For example,

> Do you believe that services provided to teenage mothers should include supplements for child care, psychological services, and training?

   a. Yes

   b. No

10. Avoid jargon and big words. You should know the approximate reading level of your intended respondents and design your questionnaire accordingly. Also, you should assume that the respondent needs any acronyms spelled out (at least the first time they appear in the questionnaire). This is a problem that can be reduced by pilot testing the questionnaire.

11. Avoid biased or leading questions. I used to have a congressional representative who had very well-known views on military spending. For some reason, he used to send questionnaires out to his constituency to ask their views about this topic. (The reason I am not clear as to why he asked is that I am sure that he would not change his views no matter what I said.) But the questions were asked in a way that suggested the answer that he was looking for. For example,

> Do you think that we should increase military spending in view of the threat to national security that is posed by America's enemies who could attack us at any time?

   a. Yes

   b. No

12. Emphasize *critical* words by using italics or underlining or bold letters. This is much easier to do now with fancy font options in word processing programs.

Formatting the Questionnaire

Here are a few hints about the physical appearance of your questionnaire:

1. Make it attractive: For example, use colored ink, colored paper, different type styles.

2. Organize and lay out the questions so that they are easy to answer.

3. Be sure to number the items and the pages.

4. Put the name and address of the person to whom the questionnaire is to be sent at the beginning and end of the questionnaire, even if a self-addressed envelope is included. You would be surprised at how many times the questionnaire and the envelope become separated, and a well-intentioned respondent is unable to return your survey because she does not know where to send it. (Does this sound like personal experience?)

5. Include brief, clear instructions. Specify what to do with the completed questionnaire.

6. Use examples before any item that might be confusing (especially important if this involves *ranking* responses). Show respondents exactly what you want them to do.

7. Organize the questions in a logical sequence (i.e., group related items together).

8. Begin with a few interesting and nonthreatening items.

9. Do *not* put the most important items at the end of a long questionnaire.

10. Avoid using the words *questionnaire* or *checklist* on your forms. (I have found the title "Response Form" to be useful, because it suggests what I want the respondent to do.)

Pilot Test the Questionnaire

Pilot testing your questionnaire means that you try it out with a small sample similar to your intended group of respondents. You can follow these steps in the pilot test:

1. Select a pilot sample that is similar to your population.

2. In formatting the questionnaire, you may want to modify it a bit if necessary to allow room for comments to be written on the pilot version.

3. Instruct your pilot respondents that you are interested in their reactions to the process and questions and encourage them to note any ambiguities or response options that are not included.

4. Follow the procedures for administration that you plan to use in your study (i.e., if it is a mail survey, ask the pilot group to read the survey and answer it first without asking you any questions). Kelly, Burton, and Regan (1994) adapted the traditional process of piloting that asks individuals to "pretend" that they are participants in the study. Instead, they ask the pilot participants to tell them what they think the questions mean and to suggest ways of rewriting them if they are unclear or too complex. They also include a section at the end of every questionnaire where participants can record any additional questions they think should have been asked.

5. When the data are collected,

    a. Read the comments.

    b. Check the responses item by item. Look for blanks, unexpected answers, clusters of responses that suggest misinterpretation of questions, and so on.

    c. Do a brief analysis. Do you have the information that you need?

    d. Add, change, or delete any questions as needed.

Krosnick, Narayan, and Smith (1996) suggest that researchers be on the lookout for the following types of response patterns that could bias their results:

1. Question order effects that occur when responses to a question could be pushed one way or another by asking a prior question on a related topic.

2. Response order effects that occur when the order of response options affects people's choices among them.

3. Acquiescence—the tendency to agree with items in the survey.

4. No-opinion filter effects that offer people a "don't know" option because it is easier to claim ignorance on a topic than to formulate an opinion.

5. Status quo alternative effect when respondents are offered a "keep it the same as it is now" option.

Language Differences Between the Researcher and the Respondent

When the language of the researcher is different from the respondents, the usual method of constructing the instrument is to rely heavily on collaboration with native-speaking colleagues. A process of back translation is often used in which the native speaker is asked to translate the instrument (either alone or in a committee), and the instrument is then retranslated into the language of the source document to ensure that the original intent was preserved.

McKay et al. (1996) suggest that the process of back translation can result in an instrument that is stilted, awkwardly worded, or even incomprehensible. They recommend extending the back translation with a strategy called *decentering* that entails modifications to the source document wording to accommodate concepts that are not directly translatable. Thus, the language in *both* the source document *and* the translated documents are subject to change until comparable questions are achieved in both languages. McKay and her colleagues reported that their experiences with national surveys with Hispanic populations in the United States had underscored the importance of language adaptations based on country of origin, geographic region in the United States, and educational level of the respondents.

McKay et al. (1996) conducted a statewide study of alcohol and drug prevalence in which they translated the survey into six languages other than English. They described their lessons learned in this process as follows:

First, avoid literal translations. While these are grammatically correct and follow the wording of the original text, they may be too formal for the average speaker, convoluting the language to borderline comprehensibility. Next, when creating the source language instrument, avoid the use of slang and technical terms, which may not translate well into other languages. Also, keep modifiers and examples to a minimum. Modifiers and examples used to increase comprehension in the source instrument added to the difficulty of translating the instrument. Some examples simply did not translate while others were foreign to the different cultures. The examples also tended to get very long in translation, exacerbating an already existing problem of length. Next, try to use questions, phrases, and examples that are culturally sensitive and that fit the life experiences of the persons to be interviewed. To be sensitive to the linguistic style of the target community, ask the translators to indicate which questions might be offensive or missing important polite phrases necessary for good form in an interview. Finally, as with any survey instrument, thorough pretesting of all aspects is the best way to discover potential pitfalls in a translated questionnaire. (pp. 102-103)

McKee (1992) cautioned that surveyors may fail in their research despite precautions related to the translation of the instruments, essentially for reasons that go beyond the actual language used. McKee conducted an interview-based survey in a small town on the Mexican border. Her results illuminate the need to integrate a sociolinguistic, contextual perspective in this type of research. She used the following question to explore the peoples' notion of "fate": "Does it seem to you that things happen because they are destined (*son cosas del destinos*) or because people struggle to bring them about" (p. 357)? Based on a linguistic and semantic analysis of their responses, McKee was able to refute the stereotypical perception of fatalism and passivity that has been attributed to Mexican Americans in other research studies. Although 22% of respondents did state that they believed things happen because they are fated to do so, the majority of the respondents used the term *destino* to distinguish between circumstances they were powerless to control and those they believed they had a chance to affect. In addition, she noted nearly everything about the way the people live indicates that they consistently struggle, plan, and adapt to changing circumstances to gain a measure of control over the forces that affect their lives.

She cautioned researchers in cross-cultural studies to be careful in their interpretations of data and to base them on a thorough understanding of the culture that produced them. Because survey research decontextualizes words through its very nature, the researcher must be careful to interpret the words in light of particular cultural circumstances.

Special Types of Questions

Many different organizational frameworks could be used to describe different types of questions. In this chapter, I discuss the following types: demographic, nonthreatening behavioral, threatening behavioral, knowledge, and attitudinal question types.

■ **DEMOGRAPHIC QUESTIONS**

1. Which of the following categories best describes where you live?

   a. City of 100,000+

   b. Suburb of a city

   c. Town of 50,000 to 100,000

   d. Town of 10,000 to 50,000

   e. Town of 5,000 to 10,000

   f. Town of 1,000 to 5,000

   g. Town of less then 1,000

   h. Rural area

2. What is your sex?

   a. Male

   b. Female

3. What is the month, day, year of your birth?

   Month_____Day_____Year_____

4. How old were you on your last birthday? _____

5. What is the highest level of formal education you have obtained?

   a. Elementary school or less

   b. Some high school

   c. High school graduate

   d. Some college

   e. Associate, two-year college degree

   f. Four-year college degree

   g. Postgraduate degree started

   h. Postgraduate degree finished

6. Current marital status

   a. Now married (including common-law marriages)

   b. Widowed

   c. Divorced

   d. Separated

   e. Never married (including annulments) ■

Demographic

This is the part of the questionnaire commonly labeled "Background Information" and that asks about the personal characteristics of the respondents. Although the design of demographic questions might seem relatively simple in light of the many standardized questionnaires that have asked such questions, they are not entirely unproblematic. Some questions seem to serve researchers fairly well, such as are shown in the box labeled "Demographic Questions." However, other background characteristics are a bit more controversial or difficult to identify precisely. As mentioned in Chapter 4 on causal comparative and correlational research, race, class, and disability represent complex iden-tifications.

The suggestions (found in Chapter 4) for handling race identification include the following:

---

1. Add a "multiracial" category (and leave a blank line with the instructions "Please explain").
2. Add an "other" category (and leave a blank line with the instructions to "Please specify").
3. Provide an open-ended question to probe for information on race and ethnicity.
4. Add some categories not traditionally included, such as Native American, Native Hawaiian, and Middle Easterner.

Macias (1993) explored distinctions related to language and ethnic classification of language minority students in relation to Chicano and Latino students. He noted that federal surveys do not systematically collect comparable English language proficiency data across states and school districts for describing the English proficiency of language minorities or Latinos. He suggested that researchers explore ways to more consistently identify language use and proficiency and ethnicity. He identified several important constructs for researchers to consider including non-English language background, non- or limited-English proficient, English difficulty, and linguistically isolated households.

The collection of demographic data about disabilities can be aided by knowledge of the categories as they are defined in the federal legislation, Individuals With Disabilities Education Act (IDEA):

- Specific learning disabilities
- Speech or language impairments
- Mental retardation
- Serious emotional disturbance
- Multiple disabilities

■ Hearing impairments

■ Orthopedic impairments

■ Other health impairments

■ Visual impairments

■ Deaf-blindness

■ Autism

■ Traumatic brain injury

In addition to reviewing the legislation itself, a useful source of information is a data dictionary published by the U.S. Department of Education (1993) that includes definitions of key terms in special education legislation.

The reader should be aware that the terms used in the IDEA legislation are not without controversy (Mertens & McLaughlin, 1995). For example, heterogeneity exists within all categories, such that "other health impairments" includes people with heart conditions that interfere with their educational performance as well as those with the more recently recognized disability labeled Attention Deficit Hyperactivity Disorder (ADHD). In addition, the measures used to identify a person's disability (such as learning disability) are not perfect. For example, using the existing classification system, 85% of normal-functioning children could be classified as learning disabled (Ysseldyke, Algozzine, & Epps, 1983).

Nonthreatening Behavioral Questions

Nonthreatening behavioral questions ask people about behaviors that are typically performed and easily talked about. The closed- and open-ended format questions about children's play behavior presented earlier in this chapter exemplify this type of question. Here are a few thoughts to keep in mind:

1. Aided recall may help. This means that you might ask a general question and provide the respondent with a list of potential behaviors or put examples of the kinds of behaviors that you mean in the question.

2. Especially with behavioral questions, it might be helpful to put a time period in the question. This is called "bounded recall" and could be worded "In the last year . . ." or "In the last week . . ." It is best to avoid asking about "usual" behavior, because this is ambiguous. M. Smith (1994) reports that the boundary chosen can have a significant effect on the reported prevalence of behaviors. He found that if women were asked about having been raped in the last 12 months, the incidence appeared to be 16 per 10,000. However, when the boundary on the question is "any time in their lifetime," then the incidence rises to 8 of 100. He commented, "It makes little sense to exclude a woman as a victim of violence simply because she did not report having been assaulted during the 12 months immediately prior to the survey" (p. 113). Of course, I have strayed into the threatening behavioral category in

this discussion; however, my comments do illuminate the effect of using different boundaries in behavioral recall questions of any type.

3. If you want detailed information about low-salience behavior, a diary approach might be useful. For example, the major survey firms that investigate people's television watching habits have found that a daily diary is useful for people to record what they are watching.

4. Specify whose behavior you are interested in. Is it the individual, the entire household, the staff of the school, the oldest sibling, or someone else?

Influence of Theoretical Framework on Survey Questions. Oliver (1992) provides an excellent contrast in questions that represent a "blame-the-victim" theory versus an "emancipatory" theory for surveying people with disabilities. He used sample questions from the Office of Population Census and Surveys (OPCS) in Great Britain as examples that locate the problem of disability within the individual:

- What complaint causes your difficulty in holding, gripping, or turning things?
- Are your difficulties in understanding people mainly due to a hearing problem?
- Have you attended a special school because of a long-term health problem or disability?

He contrasted these questions with those that reflect the location of the problem elsewhere:

- What defects in the design of everyday equipment like jars, bottles, and tins cause you difficulty in holding, gripping or turning them?
- Are your difficulties in understanding people mainly due to their inabilities to communicate with you?
- Have you attended a special school because of your education authority's policy of sending people with your health problem or disability to such places?

Thus, researchers indicate their theoretical perspective in the framing of the survey questions themselves.

Threatening Behavioral Questions

The notion of threatening behavioral questions was introduced earlier in this chapter. Any questions that potentially elicit a defensive reaction in the respondent fit this category. For example, most people feel a bit uncomfortable talking about how much alcohol they drink (especially if they feel they drink a bit too much). The following are a few hints about asking such questions:

1. Open-ended questions are usually better than closed-ended questions on frequency of socially undesirable behaviors. Respondents tend to avoid extremes and so might choose a midlevel response to a close-ended question in terms of frequency just to appear "not too deviant." M. Smith (1994) reports that open-ended questions were superior in building interviewer-respondent rapport in surveys about violence against women. He speculated that the open format

> may reduce the threat of a question about violence, because it allows the respondent to qualify her response, to express exact shades of meaning, rather than forcing her to choose from a number of possibly threatening alternatives. For another, open questions may reduce the power imbalance inherent in the interview situation . . . because open questions encourage interaction and collaboration between interviewer and respondent. (p. 115)

2. In contrast to the general rule that was presented earlier about length of questions, *longer* threatening questions are generally better than shorter ones. It seems to give people some time to recover from their initial shock that the researcher would ask about such a topic, and they can begin to formulate their response in whatever carefully selected words they choose. Here is an example of *long* "threatening" question.

> We know that some kids drink alcohol and some kids don't. Some might drink alcohol a little bit, and some a lot. Some might have a few drinks now and then, whereas others drink to get drunk. Some kids drink alone and others drink with their friends. Some kids drink wine or beer, and others drink the harder stuff like whiskey and gin. How about you? Have you drunk any alcohol in your life?

3. Use words that are familiar to respondents. This can be accomplished by asking respondents what words they use for certain people, things, or activities. For example, the researcher might say, "There are a lot of different ways to talk about buying illegal drugs. Some people say they "scored," others use other terms. What words do you use when you talk about someone buying illegal drugs?" The researcher can then use the words that are most communicative with that respondent.

4. Other ways of allowing respondents to indicate their answers can increase their honesty. For example, people may insert their answers into sealed envelopes or they may use a card-sorting procedure. For example, the National Opinion Research Center (cited in Sudman & Bradburn, 1982) used a card-sorting activity to determine people's perceptions about the seriousness of different types of crimes. They gave each respondent a ruler divided into six categories; one end of the ruler was labeled "least serious," and the other end "most serious." The respondents were then given a stack of cards with different types of crimes (e.g., stealing, passing bad checks, etc.) and asked to sort the cards by laying them on the appropriate space on their "ruler."

5. The wording of the question can suggest to the respondent that it is all right for him or her to reveal some aspect of their behavior that might not be socially desirable. Possible phrasing might include the following:

> "Many people have taken a drink . . ."
>
> "Such behaviors occur with different frequencies . . ."
>
> "Some doctors recommend drinking a glass of wine . . ."
>
> "Did you ever happen to . . ."

"Many people complain that the tax forms are just too complicated . . ."

These phrases suggest that even if respondents have engaged in socially undesirable behavior, they are not alone and are free to focus on the frequency of their own behaviors.

6. Survey researchers who are asking about sensitive topics may find that using multiple measures will enhance the reliability and validity of their results. Again, referencing M. Smith's (1994) work on surveys of violence against women, he notes that respondents sometimes do not mention being victimized when the interviewer first broaches the subject. Rather, this information surfaces toward the end of the interview, usually in answer to another, related question. He suggested that this may happen because the respondents either remember a previously forgotten incident or have second thoughts about their initial decision not to disclose. Thus, providing them with a second or third opportunity to disclose may reveal the true extent of victimization.

Knowledge Questions

These are the questions typified by those found on tests in school. These questions ask how much a person knows about a particular subject. Henry (1996) recommends using knowledge questions in surveys to understand the people's knowledge and sentiments about public policies and programs. He contends that researchers could obtain information through the use of this strategy that would be useful in interpreting the meaning of respondents' expressed opinions. If the public's knowledge of social conditions and policy is limited, that affects the interpretation of their expressed opinions.

For example, the Georgia State University of Applied Research Center conducted a survey of a nationwide sample of U.S. residents to ascertain their knowledge of public issues such as the economy, health insurance, social welfare, education, and the federal budget (Henry, 1996). At the time the survey was conducted, only 21% of the public knew that the average stay on welfare was 2 to 5 years. And less than half of the respondents knew that more children than seniors live in poverty. The public had inaccurate information about the social conditions related to this issue and the size of the problem. As the country's elected officials struggle with welfare reform, the public is expressing their opinions on this very important policy issue without much factual data.

A few suggestions for writing and using knowledge questions in surveys follow:

1. Use a knowledge question as a screen before you ask an attitude question. For example, you might ask someone if he or she approves or disapproves of the U.S. policy concerning provision of educational benefits to individuals with disabilities. The interpretation of responses should be different for those who actually know what that policy is compared with those who have an opinion about many things about which they know very little.

2. Use an appropriate level of difficulty. Just another reminder; know your population and its general reading level and presumed knowledge levels about various topics.

3. When possible, reduce the level of threat of knowledge questions by asking, "Do you happen to know . . .?" No one likes to look stupid.

4. One technique that political scientists have used is the name recognition list—just to see if people are reporting opinions about someone they really know or someone they are pretending to know. For example, a list of candidates for office could also include the researcher's spouse and brother-in-law. If people claim to know these people as well as the presidential candidates, their responses should be considered suspect.

5. Usually, mail surveys are not appropriate for knowledge questions, because the person could go look up the answer.

Attitude Questions

1. Make sure that the attitude object is clearly specified. For example, asking people's opinions about mainstreaming is not very sensible if the people don't know the meaning of the term. The researcher could probe with such comments as "Explain to me what you think the question is asking . . ." Or the respondent can be given a definition of the concept, as mentioned earlier.

2. Consider asking about the three components of attitudes—for example, affective (like vs. dislike: How does the person *feel* about this), cognitive (knowledge: What does the person *know* about this), and action (What is the person willing *to do* about this).

3. Assess attitude strength (e.g., How much do you like or dislike . . .?).

4. Avoid questions that include more than one concept (e.g., Would you vote for me and peace or my opponent and war?).

5. Generally, use bipolar questions rather than unipolar ones (e.g., Are you in favor of or opposed to . . .? Are you satisfied or dissatisfied with . . .?).

6. Start with the answer to the bipolar question, then move on to measure degree of positive or negative attitude. For example,

   Question 1: Are you in favor of, opposed to, or don't you care?

   If in favor:

   Are you strongly in favor or moderately in favor . . .?

   If opposed:

   Are you strongly opposed or moderately opposed . . .?

7. Do not use more than five points on the rating scale, unless you can give the person a visual aid with the options presented on it.

8. Ranking should be limited to no more than five alternatives and should be done only when the individual can see or remember all the alternatives.

9. More complex ratings can be achieved by card-sorting procedures.

Letter of Transmittal

A letter of transmittal can be used as a cover letter for mail surveys or as an introductory "warning" letter for a phone or personal interview survey. In addition to specifying the purpose of the survey, the most important function that a letter of transmittal can serve is to give the respondent a good reason to return your questionnaire.

In a review of 19 studies that focused on the effect of the cover letter, the majority reported no impact of the cover letter on response rate (Katz, Green, & Kluever, 1995). These researchers conducted an empirical study of 265 graduates or current students in a doctoral program in education to explore possible reasons that cover letters have not been found to be influential variables. They reported that 18% of the respondents said that they did not read the cover letter. Of the remaining 82% who *did* read it, 27% reported that it was convincing, 28% said somewhat convincing, and 45% reported the cover letter was unconvincing.

Katz et al. recognize the limitation of their one study with a specific sample; however, their results were consistent with the other 19 reviewed studies as to the cover letter effect. Nevertheless, you have to have one, because it is expected by the respondents.

Here are some hints related to establishing motivation for responding to a question-naire:

1. Appeal to authority: Send the letter out under the most well known and respected person's signature (with his or her permission, of course); make the letter "look" official.

2. Appeal to self-interest: "You are one of the few people with the intelligence (information, background, etc.) to be able to help us with this problem."

3. Appeal to professional interests: "This is a very important question in our profession (our society, our state, etc.)."

4. Appeal to altruism: "The results of this survey will be used to solve one of our nation's most pressing problems."

5. Appeal to curiosity: Offer to send a copy of the results.

6. Appeal to greed: Offer to send a monetary incentive.

7. Appeal to a sense of connection with you: Enclose a tea bag and ask them to have a cup of tea with you while they jot down their thoughts; enclose a pencil to make it easier to sit down and start writing.

Other things to keep in mind when writing a transmittal letter should be to specify the time frame in which the study is taking place. If it is a mail survey, specify the date by which the form should be returned and to whom (and to which address) it should sent. (Mail surveys should always enclose a stamped, self-addressed envelope.) If it is an introductory letter for a phone or personal interview, be sure to indicate the date(s) on which the person can expect to hear from you, and then be sure that you call at that time.

Whatever your intended purpose for the letter, be sure that you use professional production techniques for it. A letter signed in a different color ink is more impressive than one that appears to have a copied signature.

Conducting the Survey

The following steps summarize the process of conducting the survey itself:

1. Be sure to send out an advance letter. (This can be the cover letter for a mail survey.) People who receive many phone calls (especially from solicitors) may choose not to talk with you or return your calls without an official letter that arrives in advance of your call.

2. Enclose the questionnaire with the transmittal letter for mail surveys.

3. Supervise the data collection. Watch the calendar. If the time specified for returns was 2 weeks, be sure that you have gone through your mail a few days after the 2-week time period. If you coded your questionnaires, you can check to see who has responded during the "first wave."

4. Send a follow-up to nonrespondents. You could follow this process:

   Send another letter and questionnaire a few days after the time limit to nonrespondents.

   Send a second follow-up (a postcard reminder).

   Call a select sample of nonrespondents (if it is possible to identify who did not return the survey and obtain a telephone number for them).

5. Control processing errors. Be sure to monitor questionnaires as they are returned and the data is entered. You should develop a checklist or matrix of some kind to keep track of which questionnaires come from which "wave" (i.e., the original mailing is the first wave; the first follow-up is the second wave, etc.) Be sure that you keep the returned questionnaires in some kind of organized fashion so that they are not misplaced when it is time to enter the data for analysis.

6. Enter the data into the database of your choice.

7. Clean up the data before you begin analysis.

The number of questions you ask in the telephone follow-up depends on the length of your initial questionnaire. Because the people you are contacting by telephone chose not to return your initial questionnaire, it is unlikely that they would be willing to answer all the questions in a telephone interview. However, they might be willing to answer two or three questions, and you could then compare their responses to those of your original respondents. If you choose the items judiciously, you could determine whether nonrespondents have any pattern of difference with the respondents that could affect generalizability of the results. This approach can be used even when return rates are fairly high. It cannot be used when your sample was chosen through an organization (such as a school or clinic) in such a way that you do not have access to names and phone numbers of nonrespondents. In that case, you could do an analysis on whatever information the school or clinic might be willing to release in aggregate form about the nonrespondents (if they can be identified) or about the population as a whole. For example, one school system allowed a survey to be conducted of parents of children with disabilities. However, they would not approve the release of the parents' names and phone numbers. Therefore, the researcher requested that the schools provide a frequency distribution of types of disability. Although this was not ideal, at least respondents could be compared against the population on this key variable.

Response Rate Considerations

Many different factors have been investigated as to what influences people to return mail survey forms or to agree to participate in your phone or personal interviews. Based on a meta-analysis of 115 studies of response rates for mail surveys, the following factors were associated with an increased return rate:

- Preliminary notification and follow-ups
- Appeals
- Inclusion of a return envelope
- Differences in postage (e.g., use of a first class stamp)
- Monetary incentives (Yammarino, Skinner, & Childers, 1991)

Be persistent. If you have a choice between spending extra money to use colored paper or having an additional follow-up mailing, choose the follow-up mailing. People will respond at a higher rate the more you "bug" them. (Although I am sure there must be some point at which frequent mailings would become counterproductive, I doubt that most researchers have the funds that would allow them to exceed that limit.)

Other suggestions for increasing response rates include these:

▶ Personal and phone interviews generally yield higher response rates than do mail surveys.

▶ Questionnaire length sometimes has an effect on response rates. Short questionnaires will be returned at a higher rate than long ones unless the respondent endorses the importance of the topic.

▶ Monetary and nonmonetary incentives can increase response rates.

▶ Sponsorship (through a respected organization or signature by a high-ranking administrator) can yield higher response rates.

► Good timing is *very* important, especially with populations that center around a school calendar. Avoid sending the questionnaires at the very beginning or end of a school year or around a holiday period.

► Be sure to make it easy to return the questionnaire by providing a stamped, self-addressed envelope (and maybe a pencil). Even your choice of stamps versus metered mail can influence response rates, especially if you are able to locate a stamp that has salience for your population. For example, the U.S. Postal Service printed stamps that depicted a deaf mother signing "I love you" to her child.

► Consider using an attention-getting delivery mode, such as express mail, special delivery, or airmail and, possibly, printing your questionnaire on brightly colored paper.

► Handwritten envelopes seem to attract more attention now than computer-generated address labels.

► Your follow-ups could be delivered via humorous postcards or telephone calls.

Phoenix (1994) provides some insights into other reasons for nonparticipation that might arise when working with people who live in poverty or who perceive that their ethnic group has not been served well by participation in research in the past. When she was interviewing Black women, several of her respondents refused to participate because of the way they had seen Black people "pathologized" in the past. Others voiced similar concerns and wanted to know how the information would be used. She found that she could obtain their cooperation to participate in the study if she carefully explained the intended uses of the information. She also found that a large number of the participants who had agreed to participate were repeatedly not at home at the time of their appointments. The reason for the high rate of broken appointments was not related to a lack of enthusiasm for the project. Rather, the women lived in cramped or poorly furnished government-assigned accommodations, and they chose not to spend much time there. As a result, they visited friends or family and returned home only when they felt they needed to. Therefore, repeated visits were necessary to complete the interviews.

Nonresponse is a serious issue for survey researchers, as illustrated by another observation from George Burns (1984).

> I've always suspected that people who have hobbies were happier than people who didn't. A few days ago to find out if I was right, I took my own private poll. I stood on the corner of Wilshire and Rodeo Drive, stopped ten people passing by and asked them if they had a hobby. Seven told me to mind my own business, and the other three didn't speak English. I guess Dr. Gallup must use a different corner. (p. 91)

A response rate of around 70% has generally been recommended as acceptable (Berdie, 1990; Gay, 1992). However, this recommendation is based on the assumption that respondents and nonrespondents are fairly similar. Jones (1995) used a computer simulation (called the Monte Carlo method) to test the effect of response rate and the assumed differences between respondents and nonrespondents (e.g., 0.0, 0.25, and 0.50 effect size for group differences). He found the following:

- If the assumption holds that the respondents and nonrespondents are similar (effect size is 0.0), even a 50% return rate would be acceptable.

- As the effect size increases, the reduced response levels resulted in increasingly biased estimates.

- When the effect size was moderate (e.g., 0.50), a response rate of at least 90% was needed.

This finding underscores the importance of following up nonrespondents—both to increase response rates and to estimate differences between respondents and nonrespondents.

Notes Specific to Phone Interviews

The following ideas should help you plan and conduct phone interviews:

---

1. It is usually a good idea to send an advance letter (unless you are using an RDD strategy, in which case you would not necessarily know the names and addresses of respondents).

2. Provide a brief explanation of your purpose, who you are, and what your expectations are.

3. Make sure that you are talking to the right person! You may find that your initial contact would prefer to refer you to someone else who would be more appropriate for your purposes.

4. Once you are sure that you are talking to the right person, make sure that this is a good time to talk. If not, schedule an appointment for a follow-up call. And be sure to return the call at the appointed time.

5. Try to keep the phone time to a short duration. (What is short? Who knows? But based on pilot testing, you should be able to give the respondent a rough estimate of the amount of time that the survey will take.)

6. On the telephone, it is sometimes best to use somewhat structured questions.

7. Establish rapport and move quickly. Be organized. Don't be shuffling papers trying to find out what to ask next.

8. Make your first questions fairly simple and nonthreatening.

9. Allow "don't know" as an option because of lack of knowledge.

10. Use an appropriate tone of voice (friendly and conversational). Sound enthusiastic, fresh, and upbeat. If you get tired, take a break. (No one wants to continue in a survey if you are asking questions with your head down on the desk from fatigue.)

11. Speak at an appropriate speed (sometimes, matching the respondents' speed will increase their comfort level).

12. Keep a log of calls made and their outcomes (e.g., busy, no answer, completed, follow-up appointment made) and date and time your notes.

13. *Before* conducting the survey, be sure to rehearse.

14. Set hour-by-hour goals (e.g., I want to make 5, 10, or 20 phone calls each hour). With a large telephone survey, it is easy to start feeling that you are not getting anywhere, so set your goals and you will see that you are making progress if you keep with it.

15. You can tape-record a phone call, but you must inform the respondent that you are doing so.

Notes Specific to Personal Interviews

Personal interviews are often associated with qualitative research. Although this is the topic of Chapter 7, I have included the lengthy "how-to" information in this chapter because of its connection with survey research.

The following ideas can guide you through the planning and conducting of personal interviews.

Preparing for the Interview

1. Learn the local language. This is a reiteration of the advice given in the section on threatening questions in this chapter; that is, the researcher should use terms familiar to the respondent: "What name do you use for . . ." (your school, your parents, your group of friends, your educational program, etc.)?

2. Hold an introductory meeting to share the purpose, discuss confidentiality issues, and get assurance that the person does want to participate. Then, schedule the interview at the respondent's convenience.

3. Make an interview schedule as best you can at the beginning of the study. This may include names, positions, or characteristics of the individuals you think you should interview. If it is important to talk with some people before others, this should be reflected in the schedule. How many people is it reasonable to interview in a day? That will depend on the nature of your survey, but bear in mind that this is hard work and you do need time to process what was said to you.

4. Make an interview guide. This can be very general (these are the types of issues that I think I should ask about) to very specific (I want to be sure I ask all these questions of everyone). Often, personal interviews raise issues that you had not previously considered and want to follow up with additional participants. So stay flexible as far as the interview guide goes.

5. Don't structure the interview guide around yes-or-no questions. This would defeat the purpose of having the person there to converse with. Plan to ask open-ended questions:

> How do you feel about the program?
>
> What is your opinion about the program?
>
> What do you think about the program?
>
> What is your role here?
>
> What are you trying to do in this program?

6. Plan to conclude with open-ended questions: "For example, is there anything that I didn't ask about that you think I should know? What didn't I ask about that I should have? Is there anything else that you wanted to tell me that hasn't come up so far?"

7. Definitely pretest your interview procedures.

8. If you are training interviewers, do the following:

> First, have the interviewers study the interview guide and learn about the interviewing conditions and logistics.
>
> Second, have the interviewers practice interviews and receive feedback until performance reaches a desired level. (Videotaping can help with this.)

Starting and Conducting the Interview

1. Start by establishing rapport: Briefly review the purpose of the interview, your credentials, and the information needed. Provide assurances of confidentiality.

2. Focus your attention on what the person is saying. Use your "extra mind" time to evaluate what they are saying. This would allow you to formulate more than one possible hypothesis about what is happening. Test your various hypotheses. Ask for clarification: For example, "You mentioned several things. Let me be sure I have this straight . . ."

3. Sequence the questions from general to specific. People need time to think about a question. Summarize what you have heard, then ask for specifics.

4. When asking for criticisms of a program, be sure to use a constructive framework to structure the questions: For example, "Are there any special factors about this problem that I should understand?"

5. Put answers in perspective: Ask for specific examples. Ask what opinions others might hold: For example, "Do administrators and teachers see this issue the same way?" Ask for definitions for words that a respondent might use, such as *impact, urgent, critical,* and *blunders.* Be wary of generalizations (e.g., the problem is staff incompetence), convoluted answers, or answers that fit preconceived notions too well. If respondents say that they want to talk "off the record," then put your pencil down and listen to what they have to say. Be sure to get their permission to continue taking notes when they are ready to go back "on the record."

6. A variety of different kinds of questions can be asked in interviews. (This is a slightly different conceptualization than that presented previously in the discussion of demographic, behavioral, knowledge, and attitude questions.) An interviewer might ask about these things:

Experiences or behaviors: For example, "What do you do?" It is possible to elicit description of experiences by asking questions such as the following:

If I were in this program, what kinds of things would I be doing?

Imagine that I am a new participant in this program, what kind of advice would you give me to help me get adjusted?

Imagine that I'm a new kid here. I just arrived today. What would you tell me so that I would know what to do and expect?

Opinion or value questions:

What do you believe is the problem here?

What do you think about that?

What would you like to see happen?

What is your opinion about that?

Feeling questions:

How do you feel about that?

How would you describe your feelings? Happy, anxious, afraid, intimidated, confident . . .?

Knowledge questions:

What services are available?

Who is eligible?

What are the characteristics of the clients?

Sensory questions:

What do you see? hear? touch? taste? smell?

What is said to you?

Background questions:

What is your training in?

What positions did you hold prior to this one?

How long have you been in this program?

7. Ask only one question at a time.

8. Avoid asking "why" questions. Some people view these as threatening. To avoid a possible defensive reaction, try wording the questions in one of these ways:

What was it that attracted you to the program?

What other people played a role in your participation?

9. Try using role play or simulation questions: For example, "Suppose I was a student in your classroom, what kinds of activities would I be involved in to learn to read?"

10. Avoid disagreements, sarcasm, playing "Can you top this?" correcting facts and dates. Admit an error if you make one.

11. Record the interview if possible and always take notes if possible in case of a technological failure with the recording equipment.

Concluding the Interview

1. Ease into the conclusion by summarizing what you have just heard.

2. Explain what you plan to do with the data.

3. Thank the person for participating.

4. Probe gently (did I miss anything?)

5. Follow up with a phone call or letter thanking the person again and clarifying any confusions.

Compiling and Analyzing the Results

Allow at least twice as much time as you spent interviewing to go over the notes as soon as possible.

Emancipatory Perspectives on Interviewing

Feminists have explored a wide range of methodological issues related to interviewing as a data collection method in research. Reinharz (1992) cites the following issues:

- Duration of interviews
- Desirability of repeat interviews with the same respondent
- Number, sequencing, and type (closed, open, or both) of questions
- Ability of the interviewee to question the interviewer
- Standardization of the process or questions
- The location of the interview
- The method of recording the data
- Conducting the interview yourself or using trained interviewers
- Doing face-to-face or phone interviews

- Determining who will be present during the interview
- Doing interviews individually or in a group
- Whether or not the interviewer and interviewee know each other in advance
- Having the interviewee read the interview transcript and interpretation and modify the data and interpretations in the study

Feminists have reported that multiple, in-depth interviews build bonds and provide an opportunity to share transcripts and interpretations (Reinharz, 1992). The goal of multiple interviews is to increase the accuracy of the results.

Who Can Interview Whom?

Is it necessary for women to interview women? For deaf people to interview deaf people? For African Americans to interview African Americans? These are not simple questions, nor do they have simple answers. Reinharz's (1992) review of feminist methodologies suggests that woman-to-woman talk is different from that found in mixed-sex settings. Part of the decision as to the matching of gender for the interviewer-interviewee may be based on the subject of the survey. For example, M. Smith (1994) reports that the research team chose to use only female interviewers in a study of violence against women on the assumption that women would be more adept at establishing rapport and evoking candid responses to threatening questions about physical and sexual victimization.

Foster (1993b) frames the issue from her perspective as a hearing person doing research in the area of deafness with the following questions:

> One might reasonably question whether it is appropriate for a hearing person to design and conduct research with deaf people. Without an insider's understanding of deaf culture, can I even select the right questions for the study? If I do, can I design a study and interview informants without alienating them? Can I establish enough of a rapport that they will describe their experiences, perspectives and feelings to me? If I can and they do, will I be able to analyze the data without imposing my world view on the process? Will the results reported truly reflect the experience of those I interviewed, or will they be a reprocessed version, interpreted and framed within the perspective of the hearing, and—not insignificantly—dominant culture. (p. 1)

Her answers to her own questions (Foster, 1993a) indicated that it would not be necessary to be deaf to conduct research in deafness because what is important is a willingness to enter into meaningful dialogue with disabled people and to place control of the research agenda in their hands. She suggested several strategies that she used to improve the quality of her work: (a) choosing qualitative methods, (b) seeking advice from an advisory group with deaf representatives, (c) having her work reviewed by deaf colleagues, (d) conducting research in collaboration with deaf researchers, (e) using an interpreter who is fluent in the many varieties of sign language (e.g., American Sign Language, Total Communication, Signed English), and (f) acknowledging that we are all multipositional. Thus, although she might not share the characteristic of deafness with her respondents, commonalities can be found on other grounds, such as both being women, mothers, and so on.

Ann Phoenix (1994) reports that the intersection of race and social class of respondents with those of the researcher enter the interview situation in complex ways. Therefore, the recommendation to match the gender and race of the interviewers and respondents is overly simplistic. She conducted interviews in a research project titled Mothers Under Twenty in which the appointments for personal interviews were made during an advance phone call. She reported that some of the respondents were shocked to see a Black woman researcher show up to do the interview. She acknowledged that the complexity of the impact of race and gender on the interview itself and on respondents' reactions makes it difficult to say whether matching interviewees with interviewers on particular characteristics will produce better or richer data than not matching. She further commented:

> If different types of accounts about race and racism are produced with black and white interviewers, this is in itself important data and may be good reason for using interviewers of both colours whenever possible since it illustrates the ways in which knowledges are "situated." It is, therefore, not methodologically "better" *always* to have black interviewers interviewing black interviewees. Politically, this strategy may also lead to the marginalization of research on black people and of black researchers since it is then easy for white researchers to consider that black interviewers can only contribute to research on black informants. (p. 66)

Phoenix also raised issues that interviewers might encounter that would make conducting an interview more challenging. For example, some of her respondents made racist comments that indicated a distaste for Black people (especially Black men) but made an exception for her as the researcher. Also, in some studies, interviewers are asking questions written by someone else. Some of her respondents commented that the questions sounded like they had been written by a White person who did not really understand Black people's experiences.

Should the Interviewer and Interviewee Be Friends or Strangers?

Reinharz (1992) raises the issue of the comparative benefits of being friends or strangers in an interview situation. If the interviewer and interviewee were friends prior to the interview, the interviewee may feel greater rapport and be more willing to disclose information. However, there could be a feeling of greater safety with a stranger in that the respondent can say what he or she thinks and not see the interviewer again. In early feminist writings about interviewing, Oakley (1981) recommends that the interviewer invest her own personal identity in the research relationship by answering respondents' questions, sharing knowledge and experience, and giving support when asked. She found that reciprocity of this kind invites intimacy and could lead to long-term friendships with interviewees.

This characterization of researcher-as-friend is contentious. Babbie (1990) recommends that the interviewer assume a "neutral role" (p. 188), and Fowler (1993) recommends a role as a "standardized interviewer" (p. 107). Both writers assume that value is placed in trying to "neutralize" the effect of the interviewer so that differences in answers can be attributed to differences in the respondents' themselves. They suggest interviewers standardize the following:

- The way they present themselves and the study
- The way questions are asked
- The way answers are probed and recorded
- The way interpersonal aspects of the interview are handled

If interviewers follow these procedures and ask each question in the same way for each respondent, biasing effects of the interviewer will be avoided.

This description of the ideal interviewer contrasts sharply with the role of the interviewer that has developed in feminist literature.

Cotterill (1992) distinguishes between friendships and friendliness. In a study that involved interviewing both friends and strangers, she adopted a "friendly stranger" role with the respondents who were unfamiliar with her prior to the study. She found that they felt safe revealing things to her that they would not share with close friends or family because she was a stranger.

After listening to the women's stories, Cotterill was often moved to want to do something to help her respondents with their problems. However, she felt there was nothing that she could do that would not communicate a patronizing stance. Kelly et al. (1994) take a different position regarding the responsibility of the researcher to act in regard to perceived interests of the respondents. They have developed methods within the context of studying domestic violence in which they attempt to create knowledge in their respondents and encourage them to question oppressive attitudes and behaviors. Their interviews were designed to uncover responses that indicated a lack or awareness and then used probe questions to raise this directly. They stated, "The probes were directed towards exploring an individual's ignorance or prejudices, by encouraging them to reflect on how women's circumstances and needs may not be the same" (pp. 38-39). For example, where women were blaming themselves for abuse, the interviewers tried to help them explore their reasoning in more depth and to link this to the intention and behavior of the perpetrator, thereby opening up different ways of understanding. They concluded as follows:

> If we accept that conducting and participating in research is an interactive process, what participants get or take from it should concern us. Whilst we are not claiming that researchers have the "power" to change individuals' attitudes, behavior, or perceptions, we do have the power to construct research which involves questioning dominant/oppressive discourses; this can occur within the process of "doing" research, and need not be limited to the analysis and writing up stages. (pp. 39-40)

How self-disclosive should the interviewer be? How much information should an interviewer share about himself or herself during the interview? Reinharz (1992) recognizes a tension between engaging in a true dialogue with the respondent and possibly biasing responses by triggering "expected" responses. She recommended that interviewers be sensitive to possibly biasing the interviewee by the information that they choose to disclose about themselves.

Data Analysis With Survey Research

Data analysis techniques in general are discussed in Chapter 12. However, a few issues related to data analysis are specific to survey research:

1. If you have conducted a follow-up of nonrespondents (which you should do!), you can do a comparison between respondents and nonrespondents.

2. You can also do comparisons between those who responded on the first wave, second wave, and so on.

3. You do need to make decisions about how to handle missing data. If someone answered some, but not all, of the questions, can his or her responses be used anyway? Be sure to instruct data entry people and the computer as to how to represent and treat missing data.

4. Sometimes it is helpful, with quantitative data particularly, to take a clean copy of the questionnaire and fill in raw numbers for frequency counts, percentages, and measures of central tendency where appropriate.

5. Look for interesting findings that suggest extremes, trends, or patterns in the data.

6. Do cross-tabulations for subgroup analyses where possible.

7. Display the data using tables and graphs.

▶ *Questions for Critically Analyzing Survey Research*

1. Examine the wording of the questions. Could the way the question is worded lead to bias because the questions are leading?

2. Because surveys are based on self-reports, be aware that bias can result from omissions or distortions. This can occur because of lack of sufficient information or because the questions are threatening. Could self-report result in bias in this study?

3. Were any other response-pattern biases evident, such as question-order effects, response-order effects, acquiescence, no-opinion filter effects, or status quo alternative effects?

4. What was the response rate? Was a follow-up done with nonrespondents? If so, how did the respondents compare with the nonrespondents?

5. Who answered the questions? Was it the person who experienced the phenomenon in question? Was it a proxy? How adequate were the proxies?

6. If interviews were used, were interviewers trained? What method was used to record the answers? Was it possible or desirable to "blind" the interviewers to an "experimental" condition?

7. How did the surveyors handle differences between themselves and respondents in terms of gender, race or ethnicity, socioeconomic status, or disability? What consideration was given to interviewer effects?

8. If the survey instrument was translated into another language, what type of translation process was used? What kind of assurance do you have that the two forms were conceptually equivalent and culturally appropriate? How was accommodation made for language differences based on country of origin, geographic region, and education level of the respondents?

9. What sampling strategy was used? Was it appropriate to reach adequate numbers of underrepresented groups (such as ethnic minorities or low-incidence disability groups)?

10. Was the survey descriptive, cross-sectional, or longitudinal? How did this design feature influence the interpretation of the results?

■ Questions and Activities for Discussion and Application

1. Select a topic for a survey research study. Use that topic to exemplify how you could design a descriptive, longitudinal, and cross-sectional survey research study.

2. Do the following:

   a. Select a topic for a survey research study.

   b. Write a statement of purpose for the study.

   c. Write specific objectives that relate to your purpose.

   d. Decide if you would conduct your survey by mail, phone, or personal interviews.

   e. Justify your choice of data collection method.

3. Using a topic for a survey research study of your choice, draft a set of questions appropriate for use in a mail survey that exemplify the following types of ques-

tions: demographic, knowledge, behavioral (threatening *and* nonthreatening), and attitudinal.

4. Prepare a cover letter that you could use as part of your mail survey.

5. Using your cover letter, administer your questions for the mail survey to a small sample (in your class).

6. Take the questions generated in Question 3 and transform them into a set of questions that an interviewer could ask in a phone interview. Write some brief introductory comments.

7. In groups of four, role-play a phone interview, using the questions generated in Question 6. One person should play the respondent and one the interviewer. The other two should act as evaluators and provide feedback concerning the following:

   a. Making a statement of purpose, credentials, expectations, and anonymity

   b. Asking "is this a good time to talk?"

   c. Asking highly structured questions

   d. Establishing rapport

   e. Using an appropriate tone of voice

   f. Being assured that this is the right person to interview

   g. Being enthusiastic, fresh, and upbeat

8. Take the questions generated in Question 3 and transform them into a set of questions (or into an interview guide) that an interviewer could ask in a face-to-face interview. Write some brief introductory comments.

9. In groups of four, role-play a face-to-face interview, using the questions generated in Question 8. One person should play the respondent and one the interviewer. The other two should act as evaluators and provide feedback concerning the following:

   a. Making a statement of purpose, credentials, expectations, and anonymity

   b. Using open-ended questions

   c. Using probes on unclear responses

   d. Asking only one question at a time

   e. Avoiding "why" questions

   f. Avoiding disagreements

10. What is your opinion about the following:

    a. Standardizing the interview process

    b. Duration of interviews

    c. Desirability of repeat interviews with the same respondent

    d. Number, sequencing, and type (closed-ended, open-ended, both) questions

    e. Interviewees questioning the interviewer

    f. Standardizing the process or questions

    g. Where the interview takes place

    h. How it is recorded

    i. Doing it yourself or having an assistant

    j. Face-to-face or phone

    k. Who is present during the interview

    l. Doing it individually or in a group

    m. Should the interviewer and interviewee know each other in advance?

    n. Can the interviewee read the interview transcript (and interpretation) and modify the data and interpretations in the study?

11. Who can interview whom?

    a. Can women interview men? Can men interview women?

    b. Can White people interview ethnic minorities? Can ethnic minorities interview White people?

    c. Can people with disabilities interview people without disabilities? Can people without disabilities interview people with disabilities?

    d. Can women interview other women? Can men interview other men?

12. How do you address the following?

    a. Dominant groups using negative labels for nondominant group experiences

    b. Connection and empathy

    c. Interviewee-guided interviews

    d. Putting the interviewee at ease

    e. Doing reliability checks

13. Can you empathize with some respondents and not with others?

14. Should the interviewer be a friend or a stranger? Should the interviewer take action to help empower the interviewee (e.g., by raising consciousness of oppression)?

15. How much should you as the interviewer disclose about yourself during an interview?

16. Find several examples of survey-based studies. Critique them using the criteria found at the end of this chapter.

In This Chapter

■ *Possible uses for single-case research are explored.*

■ *Characteristics of single-case research are identified that enhance experimental validity, reliability, generalizability, and social validity.*

■ *Four design options are explained: phase change, alternating-treatment, multiple-baseline, and factorial designs.*

■ *Data analysis options are discussed.*

■ *Questions for critical analysis of single-case research are presented.*

6

Single-Case Research

Steve engaged in self-injurious behaviors (SIBs), including banging his head against hard surfaces and hitting his head with his hand or fist. Goh and Iwata (1994) noticed that Steve was able to avoid participation in his training program by engaging in these SIBs in that staff members terminated his training when they occurred.he experimenters wanted to design a research study that would test the effectiveness of a treatment to reduce Steve's SIB. A summary of Goh and Iwata's study is presented in Sample Study 6.1.

Single-case research is a type of research that closely follows the logic laid out in Chapter 3 for experimental and quasi-experimental research, with the exception that you are using an *N* of 1 (i.e., you have only one person—or a small number of persons—in your study). This type of research used to be called single-subject research, but the terminology has been changed to single-case research because of what Levin (1992) calls a humanitarian spirit that discourages using the term *subjects* for human beings who participate in research studies.

Single-case research is particularly appealing to researchers and practitioners in education and psychology because it is based on an interest in the effectiveness of an intervention for a single, particular individual. Thus, teachers in classrooms or psychologists in clinics can use this approach to conduct research in their own setting with particular

...ents or clients who have presented them with a challenging problem. The single-case design can be used to test the effectiveness of a specific instructional strategy or a therapeutic technique on behaviors such as learning word definitions, academic achievement, social behaviors, SIBs, aggression, property destruction, and disruptive behaviors. Many examples of single-case research studies from a variety of disciplines are published in journals such as *Behavior Therapy, Behaviour Research and Therapy, Journal of Applied Behavior Analysis, Journal of Behavior Therapy and Experimental Psychiatry, Journal of the Association for Persons With Severe Handicaps, Journal of Special Education, Journal of Learning Disabilities,* and *Exceptional Children.*

As in experimental research with multiple subjects, single-case researchers are concerned with ways to increase the validity, reliability, and generalizability of their findings. These and other related issues are discussed in the next section.

Quality Issues With Single-Case Research

Validity and Reliability

Kratochwill (1992) reviewed a number of research characteristics that improve the validity of inferences from single-case research. I summarize his main points here and provide examples of how these have been applied within a specific research study.

1. Typically, single-case research is based on observational data such as counting the number of correct spelling words or disruptive behaviors that occur in a specific period of time. The validity of the inferences that can be drawn are enhanced by the use of *objective data;* that is, data that can be counted with a high degree of accuracy and reliability should be used to measure the dependent variable(s) (Kratochwill, 1992). For example, Fox and Westling (1991) conducted a study designed to increase the quality of social interactions between parents and their children with profound disabilities. The quality of social interactions could be viewed as a vague, subjective dependent variable. However, Fox and Westling provide an objective definition of the behaviors they considered to be evidence of positive social interactions. For example, the observers were instructed to

> score if the child's behavior is directed to the parent. Includes touching parent, vocalizing to parent (indicated by gazing in parent's direction while vocalizing, moving body toward parent, reaching for the parent, etc.) It does not include parent's manipulation of body to change positions unless in a social game. (p. 170)

2. The validity of inferences from single-case research can also be enhanced by providing *repeated measurements* across all phases of the experiment—that is, not just one measurement of behavior before and after the intervention is applied (Kratochwill, 1992). Some researchers suggest that baseline observations be continued until a relatively stable level of responding can be established. Busk and Marscuilo (1992) recommend that at least

10 to 15 observations be made for each experimental phase of the study. In the Fox and Westling (1991) study, one parent-child dyad was taped in play interaction for 6 days before the intervention was begun. In a second parent-child dyad, the researchers noticed an increase in the social responses of the child during baseline. They speculated that the parents had increased their interaction with their child during playtime because the researchers had expressed an interest in their interactions at that time during their initial explanation of the study.

3. As in experimental research, greater credibility is given to studies based on *direct interventions* that are designed as part of the study rather than on ex post facto variables that are not part of the planned study (Kratochwill, 1992). Fox and Westling (1991) designed a training program to teach the parents how to use facilitative behavior, including imitating the child's verbal and nonverbal behaviors, elaborating on those behaviors, offering the child a choice of objects or stimuli, and engaging in social interaction games.

4. Kratochwill (1992) notes that the validity of inferences are enhanced when the target behaviors represent *problems of a long duration* and are unlikely to change without intervention. If the problems are of short duration, the behavior might change without any treatment. Fox and Westling (1991) note that "professionals who work with children who are the most severely disabled may instruct for many, many hours without seeing any change in child behavior" (p. 174).

5. Kratochwill (1992) states that *large and immediate impacts* should be evidenced when considering trend and level of change in the data. Levin (1992) takes issue with Kratochwill on this point and states that that criterion may not be applicable to all single-case research studies. Some studies may be designed to elicit a large and immediate impact; however, others may involve an intervention designed to produce small, delayed but genuine improvement (e.g., increasing homework time will improve performance; however, the impact may not be large and immediate). Therefore, he suggests that consideration be given to the practical and clinical significance attached to the size and immediacy of the effects.

6. The treatment should be *applied to several people* who differ on a variety of characteristics (Kratochwill, 1992). Fox and Westling (1991) applied their treatment to three dyads. They described the children and parents in enough detail to ascertain that, although all the children were classified as profoundly mentally handicapped by the school district, they also varied by age, gender, and the specific manifestation of their disabilities. Two mothers and one father participated in the training.

7. The procedures for the *treatment* should be *standardized,* formalized in written form, and monitored to ensure that they are implemented according to the plan (Kratochwill, 1992). Fox and Westling (1991) provide a written description of the sequence of the training program. They describe 2 days of training activities and note that the training sessions continue until the parent engages in facilitative behavior at least 3 consecutive days at frequencies above all baseline frequency data points. Thus, rather than "standardizing" the treatment such that each dyad receives exactly the same amount of it, the researchers based the amount of training on the demonstrated competency of the parents in the facilitative behaviors. This is a point of contention among single-case researchers, some of whom believe in this type of *response-guided experimentation;* that is, the experimental conditions are adjusted on the basis of the responses the person(s) makes during the experiment. Response-guided experimentation prohibits the use of randomization, a tech-

nique required for the use of statistical analysis of data. Therefore, researchers, who place greater importance on the ability of the researcher to statistically analyze the data, also place greater importance on randomization than on response-guided experimentation (Edgington, 1992).

8. *Multiple-outcome measures* that demonstrate a similar strong effect can be used to strengthen evidence of the effectiveness of the experimental treatment (Kratochwill, 1992). The researcher can also measure "nontargeted" behaviors to demonstrate a discriminative effect of the treatment.

9. Generalization of effect can be demonstrated by measurement of targeted and nontargeted responses, in conjunction with a *multiple baseline* across behaviors, persons, or settings. (These design options are explained in the next section of this chapter.) Levin (1992) cautions that the researcher should look for *discriminant validity* rather than generalizability across participants, behaviors, and settings. The experimental treatment should be judged to be successful only when applied to those behaviors or situations to which they are conceptually tied. He uses as an example different types of training to address different types of deviant behaviors. For example, discipline training in a biology class should be expected to affect disruptive behavior in that class, not necessarily a student's fear of snakes. He suggests that researchers also examine *transfer-appropriate processing* in that Treatment A might be more effective in modifying Behavior X, and Treatment B more effective for Behavior Y. For example, assertive discipline strategies might be more effective in reducing disruptive behaviors, and imagery desensitization therapy might be more effective for reducing fear of snakes.

10. Single-case research studies often involve more than one component in the experimental treatment. For example, four facilitative strategies were included in the parent training program in Fox and Westling's (1991) study (i.e., imitation, elaboration, choice, and social games). This is also common in educational settings in which an experimental treatment might combine a number of instructional strategies, such as directed instruction, reinforcement, and feedback. The researcher can attempt to *"dismantle" the joint effects* by using reversal on each treatment component, using a series of simultaneous treatment designs or by using a series of multiple-baseline designs (Barrios & Hartmann, 1988, cited in Kratochwill, 1992). None of these solutions is a perfect solution, both for theoretical and logistical reasons. It might be logistically impossible to formulate enough conditions to test the individual component effects; whatever results were achieved would depend on the exact ordering of the components as they were delivered in the various conditions, and the sum of the parts simply might not add up to the whole. Educators and psychologists design experimental treatments that they believe have integrity and for which all of the components are necessary to achieve the desired goal. If one component is removed, the experimental treatment might fail because of the lost integrity.

11. *Social validation* is a criterion used to judge the quality of the research from the perspective of its social importance, the social significance of the goals, and the appropriateness of the procedures (Storey & Horner, 1991). Although it is not specifically associated with the emancipatory paradigm, social validation is an important concept that fits well within that paradigm's basic philosophy if the people asked to do the ratings are those with the least power but who will be affected by the treatment. Typically, social validation

procedures have included people other than the researcher, educator, or therapist in the process. Questionnaires or interviews can be used to ask whether the goal is valuable, whether the outcome is valued, whether the process is acceptable, and what the optimal levels of performance might be. Storey and Horner (1991) reviewed the special education literature regarding social validation and raised a number of methodological questions that the researcher should consider:

- Who should do the rating for the social validity part of the research? (Options include staff, parents, experts, employers, students, clients, and people with disabilities.) How many people should be involved in the rating?

- Should the same people be involved in rating all aspects of the social validity of the study (i.e., social importance, social significance of the goals, and appropriateness of the procedures)?

- Should the raters be trained? If so, how and by whom?

- Were reliability and validity established for social validation instruments?

12. Reliability of observations needs to be established. This can be done by having two observers view the same behavioral segment (often on videotape) and comparing their behavioral counts. Fox and Westling (1991) trained two observers using videotapes of dyads in a play situation. During the study, they videotaped each observational session. The primary observer coded all the sessions. A secondary observer coded a sample of the sessions. Reliability was measured on 33% of baseline and 25% of training sessions. The mean occurrence reliabilities for the child-dependent measures averaged approximately 95%. They calculated the occurrence reliability by taking the total number of agreements for which both observers said the behavior occurred within an interval, dividing that by agreements plus disagreements, and then multiplying by 100.

Design Options

Four basic types of design options can be used in single-case research: phase change designs (sometimes called ABAB, reversal, or withdrawal designs), alternating-treatment design, multiple-baseline designs, and factorial designs. These different types of designs are described with examples in this section. The researcher who plans to conduct this type of research can find additional details and ideas in the following texts: Barlow and Hersen (1984), Borg and Gall (1989), Bullis and Anderson (1986), Kratochwill and Levin (1992), Odom (1988), and Tawney and Gast (1984).

Phase Change Designs

Phase change designs are based on the logic that if you can establish consistency in behavior *before* an intervention (the period *prior* to the intervention is labeled Phase A), then any change in behavior after the intervention is probably due to the treatment (the treatment period is labeled Phase B). The first observation period before the intervention is applied is also called the baseline period. A withdrawal component can be added to the design to determine if the behavior changes in the direction of the original baseline in the absence of the treatment. (This would again be labeled Phase A.) Assuming that the researcher wishes to see the desired behavior that was elicited by the treatment continue, he or she would then reinstate the treatment. (This would be labeled Phase B.) Thus, if the researcher included these four phases in the study, the design would be called a withdrawal, reversal, or ABAB design.

Goh and Iwata (1994) used a reversal design in a study of SIB in an adult with developmental disabilities (Steve—who was mentioned at the beginning of this chapter). As mentioned in the summary of this study, which appears in Sample Study 6.1, the experimenters had noticed that the SIB was being maintained by negative reinforcement (i.e., escape from his training program). Therefore, they decided to use extinction as the experimental treatment. They operationalized the treatment by physically guiding Steve to perform the desired task to completion when SIB occurred during a trial. The researchers first established a baseline (Phase A) of the frequency of SIBs. They then applied the intervention treatment (extinction) and counted the frequency of SIBs (Phase B). Following the introduction of the experimental treatment, they noted a "substantial burst" of responding at a variable and elevated rate before stable, low rates were observed. They then removed the experimental treatment (Phase A) and counted the number of SIBs In the final phase, they reintroduced the experimental treatment (Phase B). Again, they observed the substantial burst of responding, followed by stable, low rates of response.

More complex versions of the ABAB design can be used, especially if A and B represent two different treatments rather than absence or presence of treatment—for example, AA + BA. Or a researcher might choose to use a simpler versions of the ABAB design, such as AB.

Edgington (1992) notes that if the researcher intends to conduct statistical analysis on the resulting data, randomization should be included as a design element. Random selection from a population is not appropriate in single-case research because the experimenter is interested in a particular person, not just anyone. Thus, Edgington explored ways that the researcher could incorporate the elements of randomization into single-case designs. In reference to phase change designs, he suggested that if A and B represent two different treatments, the researcher should randomly assign the time periods during which each treatment would be introduced. If the simpler AB design was used, the researcher could randomly choose the point of intervention after sufficient baseline data had been collected. This notion allows for statistical analysis of the data but is in conflict with the response-guided principles of single-case research.

Although the AB design is weaker in terms of inference of causality than the ABAB design, such a choice would be justified if it is not possible to withdraw a treatment because of ethical reasons or because a skill has been learned or an attitude changed that cannot be unlearned by removing a treatment. Under these conditions, researchers may use either alternating-treatment designs or multiple-baseline designs.

SAMPLE STUDY 6.1 *Summary of a Single-Case Research Study*

Research problem: Developmentally disabled adults have been observed engaging in self-injurious behaviors (SIBs), including banging their heads against hard surfaces and hitting their heads with their hands or fists. One such adult, Steve, engaged in these behaviors to avoid participation in his training program.

Research question: How can the experimenters reduce Steve's SIBs?

Method: Goh and Iwata (1994) used a reversal design, using extinction as the experimental treatment. They operationalized the treatment by physically guiding Steve to perform the desired task to completion when SIB occurred during a trial.

Participant: One developmentally disabled adult named Steve was the participant in this study.

Instruments and procedures: The researchers first established a baseline (Phase A) of the frequency of SIBs. They then applied the intervention treatment (extinction), and counted the frequency of SIBs (Phase B). Following the introduction of the experimental treatment, they noted a "substantial burst" of responding at a variable and elevated rate before stable, low rates were observed. They then removed the experimental treatment (Phase A), and counted the number of SIBs. In the final phase, they reintroduced the experimental treatment (phase B). Again, they observed the substantial burst of responding, followed by stable, low rates of response.

Results: SIBs increased when the treatment was initially introduced (during the first 22 sessions), but decreased to almost zero during the next 12 sessions. A similar pattern of response was observed during the reversal period of the experiment.

Discussion: The experimenters demonstrated the effectiveness of their treatment by virtually eliminating the SIBs in one adult who had a long history of such behaviors.

SOURCE: Based on Goh and Iwata (1994).

Alternating-Treatment Designs

An alternating-treatment design involves two (or more treatments) that can be delivered in an alternating pattern, such as in the morning and afternoon, every other day, or every other week. Edgington (1992) described this design option as follows: "One method of blocking for an alternating treatments' single-subject design is to group the treatment times into successive pairs, within each of which we randomly determine which member of the pair will be subjected to a particular treatment" (p. 143).

For example, Grace, Sung, and Fisher (1994) used two different treatments to try to reduce the socially inappropriate behavior of an 11-year-old boy with severe mental retardation. The treatments were to punish only the most severe behaviors (A) or to punish both severe and less severe behaviors (B). The researchers could have used an alternating-treatment design to test the effectiveness of their two treatments by dividing the day into morning and afternoon and then randomly assigning which of the two treatments would be applied in the morning and afternoon of each day of the study. Their design could be depicted as follows:

	Day 1	Day 2	Day 3	Day 4	Day 5	Day 6
a.m.	A	A	B	A	B	B
p.m.	B	B	A	B	A	A

You can see that the difference between alternating treatments and the ABAB design is that in the alternating treatments, both A and B are given randomly throughout the experimental period. In contrast, in the ABAB design, only one treatment is applied during each phase of the experiment.

Multiple-Baseline Designs

Multiple-baseline designs involve repetition of the treatment across behaviors, settings, or people. Comparisons can then be made both between and within a data series (Kratochwill, 1992).

Multiple-Baseline-Across-Behaviors Design. In this design, the researcher chooses two different behaviors (e.g., requesting cereal and requesting milk) to target for change. A baseline is then established for both behaviors, and an intervention is implemented for the first behavior. If a change is observed in that behavior, the intervention is applied to the second behavior. For example, an experimenter could implement a training program to modify a child's mode of requesting cereal at snacktime. When that behavior changes in the desired direction, she could then apply the same treatment to the requesting-of-milk behavior. If the child showed an increase in the second behavior following treatment, added credibility is given to the effectiveness of the treatment.

Multiple-Baseline-Across-People Design. In this design, the researchers use one behavior and try to establish a change using the same independent variable (treatment) with more than one person. Tirapella and Cipani (1992) used a language training program designed to increase requesting behavior at snacktime. They used a multiple-baseline-across-people design because they were teaching a skill that they expected the children to retain. To test the effectiveness of their treatment, they established baseline for two children (Allen and Sary) by observing and counting the number of times the children requested snack items during the morning snack period before the treatment (i.e., training in requesting) was introduced. After 8 baseline sessions, the training strategy was implemented with Allen during snacktime. Sary received training after 16 baseline sessions.

Multiple-Baseline-Across-Settings Design. In this design, the researcher chooses one behavior, one independent variable, and one person and attempts to change that person's behavior in two or more situations. For example, if you have a student who is not interacting effectively in social situations, you could start by trying to modify his or her behavior in physical education class. You could focus on an operational, countable definition of effective social interaction and design an intervention for reinforcement of that behavior. Then you would identify two settings in which you desire to see an improvement in social interaction (e.g., homeroom and physical education class). You would then establish baseline for effective social interactions in both settings. The treatment (reinforcement) would be introduced into the first setting (e.g., homeroom), and you would count the number of effective social interactions observed for a specified period of time. After observing an improvement to the desired level in the homeroom setting, you would then apply your treatment in the physical education setting. If the student's behavior improved in both settings, this would provide evidence of the effectiveness of your independent variable.

Randomization in Multiple-Baseline Designs. To statistically analyze the results of multiple-baseline designs, Edgington (1992) reminds researchers of the need to incorporate randomization into the design. For multiple-baseline designs, he suggests that researchers randomly choose as follows:

Multiple Baseline Design	Randomization Strategy
Across People	Randomly determine which person will take the earliest intervention
Across Behaviors	Randomly determine which behavior will be subjected to the treatment first
Across Settings	Randomly determine in which setting the treatment will be applied first

Factorial Designs

Factorial designs are not commonly used in single-case research; however, it is possible to test the effect of two (or more) independent variables within a single-case study. For example, a researcher could investigate the differential effects of reinforcement treatments by identifying the independent variables as follows:

A—Type of reinforcement
    A1—Consumable
    A2—Nonconsumable

B—Timing of reinforcement
    B1—Immediate
    B2—Delayed

A factorial design in a single-case study would look like this:

	Consumable	Nonconsumable
Immediate		
Delayed		

Multiple observations would then be made within each of the four cells created by the design.

Data Analysis in Single-Case Research

Traditionally, data analysis of single-case research results has consisted of a visual display of the data (in graph form) and the researcher's skilled personal judgment to decide what the experiment shows. Much research has been conducted on the variables that influence visual analysis of graphed data. Parsonson and Baer (1992) acknowledge that much subjectivity is involved in the interpretation of visually displayed data; however, they argue that much of the research on the problems with visual analysis is flawed. The research typically involves asking raters to evaluate graphs without giving them any of the contextual information that a researcher normally uses in making interpretations, such as the study's aims, the special characteristics of the people in the study or those implementing the treatment, or the dependent and independent variables. Parsonson and Baer note that research based on abstract, content-free forms may not be appropriate to test the validity of inferences made by researchers based on visual analysis of data with full contextual information.

Edgington (1992) and Busk and Marscuilo (1992) both recommend the use of statistical tests for single-case research data as a supplement to visual inspection of the data. They recommend the use of randomization tests to measures of central tendency for changes in levels of behavior and to measures of slopes for changes in trends of behavior. As mentioned in the design section, the use of randomization statistical tests requires incorporation of randomization in the design of the study. This may be possible in some circumstances; however, it may be in conflict with the response-guided principle discussed earlier in this chapter. Readers who are interested in using statistical analysis in a single-case study are referred to Edgington (1992) and Busk and Marascuilo (1992) for discussion of the appropriate procedures.

Ottenbacher and Cusick (1991) investigated a method for improving agreement about the interpretation of visual data. They provided two groups of people with 21 single-case graphs. One group examined the graphs containing single-case data arrayed in the traditional format. The second group viewed the same graphs; however, theirs were supplemented with trend lines. The interrater agreement was higher for the trend line group than for the group relying only on visual analysis. The researchers suggest that visual interpretation of data may be improved by simple supplements to visually inspected charts.

Levin (1992) suggests that researchers might be able to answer the visual versus statistical analysis question by determining their answers to two other questions:

1. Is it necessary or important that an inferential statistical test be performed on the data?

2. If so, which statistical test is most appropriate in terms of both meeting the test's assumptions and providing the most sensitive assessment of intervention effects?

If, as an educator or psychologist, you are primarily concerned with achieving a predetermined level of behavior, you make the determination of what constitutes clinical or practical success. In that case, statistical analysis is unnecessary. However, if you are interested in assessing the likelihood of a particular intervention-based outcome, statistical analysis would be appropriate.

A researcher's decision as to the use of statistical or visual analysis has implications for the type of conclusions that can be made. Levin (1992) states,

> All else being equal, visual analysis of exploratory studies should be associated with more tentative, speculative statements; and replications or confirmed predictions with supporting probability-based statistical analyses (and, hopefully, substantial effect sizes) should be communicated with a greater sense of conviction. (pp. 221-222)

▶ *Questions for Critically Analyzing Single-Case Research*

1. What was (were) the dependent variable(s)? How was (were) it (they) operationally defined? Was (were) the dependent variable(s) operationally defined in terms of measures of objective data that could be counted with a high degree of accuracy and reliability?

2. How many observations were made in each phase of the experiment? Were they sufficient to establish a stable pattern of responding?

3. What was the independent variable? Was it a direct intervention specifically designed as part of the study?

4. Were the target behaviors representative of problems of long duration that were unlikely to change without direct intervention?

5. Were immediate and large effects of the interventions visible in the data following intervention? If not, was the behavior one that might justify small, delayed results?

6. Was a multiple-baseline design used, in that the treatment was applied to several people, behaviors, and settings? How diverse was the population to which the treatments were applied? Could the effect be attributable to the uniqueness of the individual in the study?

7. Were treatment procedures standardized, formalized in written form, and monitored to ensure that they were implemented according to plan? Could an argument

be made that the experimental procedures needed to be modified to meet the needs of the individuals in the study (response-guided experimentation)?

8. What dependent measures were used? Were multiple dependent measures or a single dependent measure used?

9. Were targeted and nontargeted responses measured in the study? Could discriminant validity be established in that the treatment was successful in appropriate situations but not in others? Was transfer-appropriate processing evidenced?

10. If the treatment consisted of more than one component, did the researcher attempt to dismantle the joint effects? How would dismantling the joint effects affect the integrity of the intervention?

11. Was social validation established for the quality of the research from the perspective of its social importance, the social significance of the goals, and the appropriateness of the procedures? Who was involved in rating the social validity? Were the people with the least power involved in the rating? Were all the same people involved in rating all aspects of the social validity? Were the raters trained? Were reliability and validity established for social validation instruments?

12. Were the people doing the behavioral observations trained? What was the level of reliability for the various behaviors? Was the level of reliability tested within all the phases of the experiment?

13. Was a baseline for behaviors established prior to intervention? Was the baseline period sufficient to indicate a stable level of responding?

14. If a reversal design was used, was the intervention discontinued for a sufficient period of time? Was the intervention then reinstated with the same desired results?

15. Were ethical issues considered in the choice of the design? Would ethical concerns preclude the use of a reversal design?

16. Was randomization used as a part of the design? Would response-guided experimentation preclude the use of randomization in the design?

17. Was the data visually or statistically analyzed or both? What was done in visual analysis to reduce the effect of subjectivity and bias? Were the appropriate statistics used?

■ Questions and Activities for Discussion and Application

1. Brainstorm a number of different problems that would be appropriate for single-case research.

2. Select one research problem and

   a. Identify the independent and dependent variables.

b. Sketch a design for a single-case research study using:

– A phase change design
– An alternating-treatment design
– A multiple-baseline-across-people design
– A multiple-baseline-across-behaviors design
– A multiple-baseline-across-settings design

c. Discuss the appropriateness, advantages, and disadvantages of each design for your chosen problem.

3. Through a computerized literature search or by going directly to the main journals cited in this chapter, identify five research studies—one for each of the main design types. For each study, use the "Questions for Critical Analysis" presented at the end of this chapter to analyze its strengths and weaknesses.

4. Choose a somewhat ambiguous concept, such as self-concept or social skills, and describe how you could operationalize it in an "objective, countable" way.

5. Identify three studies that investigated their social validity. Compare the methods and results of the three studies.

6. Under what circumstances would you *not* recommend the use of a reversal design? Give an example of such an instance.

7. For the following example

a. Identify the research design.

b. Critique the study using the appropriate criteria.

Rortverdt and Miltenberger (1994) investigated the effectiveness of high-probability requests and timeout as treatments for noncompliance that appeared to be maintained by contingent attention in two developmentally normal children. The introduction of high-probability requests increased compliance for one child but not the other. Timeout was effective with both children.

In This Chapter

- ■ *Reasons for choosing qualitative methods are explored.*
- ■ *Strategies for qualitative inquiry and their methodological implications are discussed, including ethnographic research, case studies, phenomenology, grounded theory, participative inquiry, clinical research, and focus groups.*
- ■ *General methodological guidelines are presented for qualitative research.*
- ■ *Criteria for critically analyzing qualitative research are provided.*

7

Qualitative Methods

Two studies summarized in Chapter 1 of this text exemplify qualitative approaches to research. In one study, the researcher noted that adolescent boys who had been labeled "nerds" or "dweebs" experienced rejection and loneliness (see Merten, 1996, summarized in Sample Study 1.2). Merten undertook a qualitative study using ethnographic techniques to study the students' response to rejection.

In the second study, the researchers noted that "economically advantaged Whites and Asians had consistently better access to courses that would lead them to college and higher status jobs compared with Latinos whose achievement was similar" (Oakes & Guiton, 1995, p. 28). Faced with this issue, Oakes and Guiton conducted case studies in three senior high schools in an attempt to understand how educators frame tracking decisions. This study is summarized in Sample Study 1.3

Qualitative methods are used in research that is designed to provide an in-depth description of a specific program, practice, or setting. Here is a "generic" definition of a qualitative study:

Qualitative research is multimethod in focus, involving an interpretive, naturalistic approach to its subject matter. This means that qualitative researchers study things in their natural settings, attempting to make sense of, or interpret, phenomena in terms of the meanings people bring to them. Qualitative research involves the studied use and collection of a variety of empirical materials—case study, personal experience, introspective, life story, interview, observational, historical, interactional, and visual texts—that describe routine and problematic moments and meanings in individuals' lives. (Denzin & Lincoln, 1994, p. 2)

The key words associated with qualitative methods include *complexity, contextual, exploration, discovery,* and *inductive logic.* By using an inductive approach, the researcher can attempt to make sense of a situation without imposing preexisting expectations on the phenomena under study. Thus, the researcher begins with specific observations and allows the categories of analysis to emerge from the data as the study progresses.

For example, Mac an Ghaill (1993) used qualitative methods to study the school experiences of Black youths in England. The study extended over 5 years and focused on youths of Asian and Afro-Caribbean parentage in an inner-city secondary school and a sixth-form college. At the start of the study, the researcher discovered that he was working from the perspective of Black students as a "problem." During the study, he changed his framing of the problem based on focusing on the students' perspective of the meaning and purpose of the school. He found that the teachers explained differences in the Asian and Afro-Caribbean examination results in terms of intrinsic cultural differences. Thus, he came to view the problem as the racism and sexism that were the primary blocks to learning.

His methodology consisted of taking extensive field notes based on daily observations and interviewing each of the students individually and in groups. He also followed up his observations by collecting materials from school reports and questionnaires on the students' attitudes toward school. About 9 months into the study, he began interviewing the students' parents in their homes. He said that, initially, he also looked at the parents' attitudes toward their children's schooling as problematic because it represented a conflict between their home and the dominant, White culture. On the basis of the students' perception of their relationships with their families, he came to reformulate his research questions to their parents, asking about their immigration to England, their housing and work situations, and their experience of and response to racism and sexism. Through this work, he came to view the students' resistance to racism at school as linked to their parents' resistance. Mac an Ghaill chronicles his changing understanding of the "problem" through his use of qualitative methods so that he shifted from viewing the problem in the schooling of Black youths from deficits in their culture to racism in the educational system that mirrors the racism in the wider society.

Basis for Selection of Qualitative Methods

Three of the possible reasons for choosing qualitative methods are explored in this chapter: (a) the researcher's view of the world, (b) the nature of the research questions, and (c) practical reasons associated with the nature of qualitative methods.

The Researcher's View of the World

Interpretive/Constructivist View

Guba and Lincoln (1989) state that you cannot tell a person's paradigm (view of the world) simply by the research methods that he or she chooses; however, a person's view of the world should influence his or her choice of methods. Thus, they distinguish between using qualitative methods within a postpositivist (they use the term *conventional*) paradigm and using them within the interpretive/constructivist paradigm. If researchers accept the ontological assumption associated with interpretive/constructivism that multiple realities exist that are time and context dependent, they will choose to carry out the study using qualitative methods so that they can gain an understanding of the constructions held by people in that context. Guba and Lincoln identify qualitative methods as the preferred methods for researchers working in the interpretive/constructivist paradigm; however, they also recognize that quantitative methods can be used within this paradigm when it is appropriate to do so.[1]

Emancipatory Views

People With Disabilities. Peck and Furman (1992) explored the importance of qualitative research in special education in terms of recent developments in the philosophy of science, the need for more holistic analysis of problems in policy and practice, and increased attention to descriptions of the world as experienced by individuals in the analysis of issues in special education. Many of the issues they raise apply to reasons for choosing qualitative methods for emancipatory research for the study of educational and psychological phenomenon in other settings as well.

First, Peck and Furman note that researchers have used qualitative methods to identify the fundamental roles of ideology, organizational dynamics, and the social-political process in shaping policy and practice in special education. They suggest that the most fundamental problem constraining the inclusion of children with disabilities in regular classes are less technical than political in nature. Therefore, focusing on the instructional process affecting children's behavior is less appropriate than addressing political issues. They contend that adherence to the postpositivist tradition of research is likely to lead researchers away from asking some critical questions about why children with disabilities are not succeeding in school. This ability to provide insight into the social-political process has been emphasized by feminists as well (Reinharz, 1992).

Second, Peck and Furman (1992) note the value of constructing some sense of the insider's view. They note that qualitative research has enabled the development of professional interventions in special education that are responsive to the cognitive and motivational interpretations of the world held by children, parents, and professionals. For example, definitions of aberrant or inappropriate behaviors can be reframed in terms of their functional meaning for a child.

Third, qualitative methods have led to insights into the cultural values, institutional practices, and interpersonal interactions that influence special education practice. For example, placement and categorizing children in special education are subject to these influences and can be understood only through a research process that can look at different levels of social ecology.

Ethnic Minorities. Stanfield's (1994) reflections on how to best study the experience of African Americans and other people of color include a proposal to reject the postpositivist paradigm and the accompanying quantitative methods. He criticizes researchers who study ethnic issues while still embracing the norms of logical positivist reasoning:

> This results in Afrocentrists' contradicting themselves by claiming to be producing knowledge sensitive to the experiences of African-descent peoples as a unique cultural population even as they insist on using Eurocentric logics of inquiry that reduce the knowable to the measurable or to evolutionary or linear variables. (p. 182)

He says that this contradictory way of thinking is especially evident in the work of Afrocentric psychologists who advocate for the refining of standardized testing instruments and apply evolutionary concepts of human development to Afrocentric experiences in child development studies.

Feminist Perspectives. Reinharz (1992) describes the diversity of viewpoints held by feminists regarding the use of qualitative methods in research. Some feminists reject postpositivism and quantitative methods as representations of patriarchal thinking that result in a separation between the scientist and the persons under study (Fine, 1992). This group believes that qualitative methods are the only truly "feminist" choice because they include the use of open-ended interviewing and ethnographic data collection to focus on interpretation, allow the immersion of the researcher in the social setting, and facilitate intersubjective understanding between the researcher and the participants. Reinharz (1992) acknowledges that fieldwork is important for correcting the patriarchal bias in social science research. However, she cautions that conducting research using qualitative methods is not inherently feminist. Furthermore, she states that qualitative methods such as fieldwork are not the only research methods that feminists can use.

The Nature of the Research Question

The nature of the research question itself can lead a researcher to choose qualitative methods. Patton (1990) identifies the following types of research questions for which qualitative methods would be appropriate:

1. The focus of the research is on the process, implementation, or development of a program or its participants.
2. The program emphasizes individualized outcomes.

3. Detailed, in-depth information is needed about certain clients or programs.

4. The focus is on diversity among, idiosyncracies of, and unique qualities exhibited by individuals.

5. The intent is to understand the program theory—that is, the staff members' (and participants') beliefs as to the nature of the problem they are addressing and how their actions will lead to desired outcomes.

Many of the criteria that establish the appropriateness of choosing qualitative methods parallel the conditions in special education. In special education, low-incidence conditions, such as deaf-blindness, cause sample sizes to be restricted or small. Students with disabilities are unique with diversity across categories of disabilities as well as within them.

In special education, each student's program, by definition, is deliberately designed to be unique to satisfy that student's needs. This is reflected in the requirements of the Individuals With Disabilities Education Act (IDEA), including an individualized education plan (IEP) for school-age students; an individual family service plan (IFSP) for children, birth through 3 years old; and an individual transition plan (ITP) required for all individuals by their 16th birthday. By definition, if not by legal mandate, the programs for special education students are diverse and idiosyncratic.

Practical Reasons

Patton (1990) describes another basis for choosing qualitative methods that is rooted in pragmatics associated with these methods rather than in the nature of the research questions themselves. He notes that the choice of qualitative methods might be appropriate under three conditions. First, because many educational and psychological programs are based on humanistic values, the intended users of the research may prefer the type of personal contact and data that emerge from a qualitative study. Intended users should be involved in the decisions about choice of methods so that they will find the results credible and useful.

Second, qualitative methods may also be chosen when no acceptable, valid, reliable, appropriate quantitative measure is available for the desired outcomes of a program. For example, qualitative methods were chosen in a study of the impact of training on Egyptian administrators' and teachers' attitudes toward people with disabilities (Mertens, Berkeley, & Lopez, 1995). No standardized measures were available to measure attitude change that were appropriate within the Egyptian culture. Therefore, data collected from observations and interviews were used to document the kinds of language used to describe people with disabilities throughout the project. The participants' comments regarding the use of sign language and the role of the deaf community in the education of deaf children provide one example of the documentation of changes in attitudes using qualitative methods.[2]

At the beginning of the project, the participants said things such as "We don't use sign language in our schools for the deaf because we know that it will interfere with the deaf child's learning to speak and use their residual hearing." They also asked the trainers to stop using sign language during the training (some of the trainers were deaf) because they found it "distracting."

By the middle of the project, some of the participants asked to be taught sign language. They were told that they would need to learn sign language from Egyptian deaf people so that they would learn the signs appropriate for their deaf school children. The trainers said that they could provide training in how to teach sign language to the deaf Egyptians.

By the end of the project, five deaf Egyptians had been trained in how to teach sign language and had begun teaching Egyptian sign language to the teachers and administrators. In the final evaluation, the participants commented that they had not had enough training in sign language yet and that more deaf people needed to be trained to teach sign language in their communities. Thus, we were able to document changes in attitudes that were manifest in changes of behavior without the use of quantitative measures.

A third reason for choosing qualitative methods might be to add depth to a quantitative study. For example, in survey research, respondents commonly indicate their answers by circling a number on a Likert-type, 5-point scale. Follow-up interviews can be used to determine the meaning attached to their numerical ratings (Lopez & Mertens, 1993).

Strategies for Qualitative Research

Many different types of qualitative research are practiced in educational and psychological research. In fact, Tesch (1990) identified 26 different types in her analysis. Rather than discuss all 26 types, I have chosen to focus on 7 strategies:

1. Ethnographic research
2. Case study
3. Phenomenological research
4. Grounded theory
5. Participative inquiry
6. Clinical research
7. Focus groups

The first six of these are described in the Handbook of Qualitative Research (Denzin Lincoln, 1994), and thus, their inclusion is based on the rationale that they represent the "state of the art" in educational and psychological qualitative research. The seventh strategy, focus groups, is in some ways a "horse of a different color" in that it might be viewed more as a data collection technique than as a qualitative research strategy. However, it is emerging as an important strategy, especially in evaluation research, and therefore, I decided to include it. (Two other qualitative strategies, historical and biographical, are addressed in a later chapter.)

Ethnographic Research

Tesch (1990) identifies ethnography as the most common type of qualitative method used in educational and psychological research. Ethnography can be defined as a research method designed to describe and analyze practices and beliefs of cultures and communities. For example, Keller, Karp, and Carlson (1993) and Mertens (1992) studied community and school contexts for the integration of students with disabilities in total-inclusion programs in their neighborhood schools. Sleeter (1994) conducted a 2-year ethnographic study of 30 teachers who participated in a staff development program in multicultural education to study their construction of the meaning of race.

Ethnographic research is guided by theory, either an explicit anthropological, psychological, or educational theory or by an implicit personal theory about the way things work (Fetterman, 1989). In ethnography, the researcher must be willing to abandon or modify a theory that does not "fit" the data. The focus of ethnography is to understand the culture from an *emic* (insider) and *etic* (outsider) perspective. Culture can be defined as the behavior, ideas, beliefs, and knowledge of a particular group of people. Thus, ethnographic research typically includes a study of the group's history, geography, kinship patterns, structures (i.e., the group configuration in terms of kinship or politics) functions (i.e., the social relations between group members), rituals, symbols, politics, economic factors, educational and socialization systems, and the degree of contact between the target and mainstream cultures.

Atkinson and Hammersley (1994) note a tension within the ethnographic community based on a questioning of the objectivity of social research. Historically, ethnographers have focused on understanding particular phenomena in their sociohistorical contexts (*ideographic* orientation) for the purpose of discovering (universal) sociocultural laws (a *nomothetic* orientation). However, the criticism of ethnographic representations of phenomenon as one possible construction of reality is that the method makes it impossible to produce "scientific knowledge" that is universally valid. Atkinson and Hammersley warn against a debilitating nihilism. They call for a "careful reassessment of the methodological and philosophical arguments surrounding the concept of science and of the relationship of science to this" (p. 252).

Atkinson and Hammersley portray traditional ethnographic work as the researcher's making the decisions about what to study, how to study it, and whose voice to represent in the written ethnography. They present the traditional goal of ethnographic research as the production of knowledge. They do note that this goal contrasts with that which emerges from other important influences (they name Marxist critical theory and feminism) that explore ways that research can contribute to the political struggles of oppressed groups, including working-class people, women, ethnic minorities, and people with disabilities.

Feminist ethnography includes the study of women's private domains, workplaces, and organizations, in addition to mixed-gender settings (Reinharz, 1992). Reinharz defined feminist ethnography as

> research carried out by feminists who focus on gender issues in female-homogeneous traditional or nontraditional settings, and in heterogeneous traditional and nontraditional settings. In feminist ethnography, the researchers are women, the field sites are sometimes women's settings, and the key informants are typically women. (p. 55)

Reinharz characterized the goals of feminist ethnography as the following:

1. To document the lives and activities of women, focusing on women as full members of their social, economic, and political worlds

2. To understand the experience of women from their own point of view, rather than trivializing their activities or interpreting them from the standpoint of men in the society

3. To interpret women's behavior as shaped by social context, such as their marital relations or the community values

Case Study

Some authors view the case study as one type of ethnographic (interpretive) research that involves intensive and detailed study of one individual or of a group as an entity, through observation, self-reports, and any other means (Langenbach, Vaughn, & Aagaard, 1994; Tesch, 1990). However, Yin (1994) points out that case studies are not identical to ethnographic research. Because of this distinction and the important role that case studies have played in educational and psychological research, methodological issues related to case studies are explored in more depth in this chapter.

Examples of case studies in special education can be found in Koppenhaver and Yoder's (1992) literature review of case studies related to individuals with physical disabilities and in Ferguson's (1992) case study of six students with severe autism. Yin (1993) also provides detailed examples of case study methods in educational partnerships, management information systems, high-risk youth programs, and substance abuse prevention. Reinharz (1992) reviews the use of case studies within the feminist perspective, and Oakes and Guiton's (1995) research serves as an example of a case study centered on ethnicity and social class in high school tracking decisions.

Stake (1994) recognizes the somewhat problematic situation that emerges in trying to define a case study as a unique form of research. To solve the problem, he uses the criterion that case study research is not defined by a specific methodology but by the object of study. He writes, "The more the object of study is a specific, unique, bounded system" (p. 237), the greater the rationale for calling it a case study. (Yin, 1994, disagrees with Stake's definition of a case study, arguing that it is too broad.) The U.S. General Accounting Office (1990) provided another useful definition of case study methods: "A case study is a method for learning about a complex instance, based on a comprehensive understanding of that instance obtained by extensive descriptions and analysis of that instance taken as a whole and in its context" (p. 14). The commonality in the definitions seems to focus on a particular instance (object or case) and reaching an understanding within a complex context. Differences of opinion exist as to whether case study is a method or a research design. In that a variety of methods are used to collect data within case study research, I opt to discuss case studies as one option in qualitative research strategy choices.

To study a case, Stake (1994) recommends data collection of the following types of information:

■ The nature of the case

■ Its historical background

- Other contexts, such as economic, political, legal, and aesthetic
- Other cases through which this case is recognized
- Those informants through whom the case can be known

The process of making comparisons with other cases is often left to the reader of the case study who comes to the report with preexisting knowledge of similar and different cases. Stake warns readers not to lose that which is unique about this case in an effort to find similarities with other cases. Some people view case study methods as leading to scientific generalizations, but Stake emphasizes the intrinsic interest in each case as being important.

Yin (1994) recommends starting a case study by developing a research design (as has been the prevailing logic in this book all along). He identifies the following steps in the development of the case study design:

---

1. *Develop the research questions* (first discussed in Chapter 2). Yin suggests that "how" and "why" questions are especially appropriate for case study research. Oakes and Guiton's (1995) guiding research question asked, How do educators frame tracking decisions for high school students? They had two subquestions:

   a. What are the effects on students' course taking of educators' judgments about what courses are best for students, students' and parents' choices, and the constraints and opportunities inherent in schools' own cultures and the larger social and political context?

   b. What factors contribute to the racial, ethnic, and social class patterns of curriculum participation?

2. *Identify the propositions (if any) for the study.* Propositions are statements akin to hypotheses that state why you think you might observe a specific behavior or relationship. All case studies may not lend themselves to the statement of propositions, especially if they are exploratory. However, Yin (1994) says the researcher should be able to state the purpose (in lieu of propositions) of the study and the criteria by which an explanation will be judged successful. Propositions help narrow the focus of the study—for example, educators' tracking decisions in high schools. Oakes and Guiton (1995) developed seven propositions that emerged from their findings from the fieldwork and transcript analysis. Examples of their propositions include

   "Proposition 1: Schools view students' abilities, motivation, and aspirations as fixed" (p. 10).

   "Proposition 4: Because race, ethnicity, and social class signal ability and motivation, they also influence career decisions" (p. 15).

3. *Specify the unit of analysis.* Specification of the "case" involves the identification of the unit of analysis—for example, an exemplary student or a challenging psychotherapeutic client. Some cases can be more complex and harder to define than an individual—for example, a program, an organization, a classroom, a clinic, or a neighborhood. Researchers need to base the design on either a single case or multiple cases and establish the boundaries as clearly as possible in terms of who is included, the geographic area, and time for beginning

and ending the case. Once the case has been identified, the unit of analysis can then be described within the context of the case. One unit of analysis may be selected or several. A holistic unit of analysis might be an individual's relationship with his or her parents. Other units of analysis might be added, such as individual projects within a program or process units, such as meetings, roles, or locations. Yin (1994) labels single-unit case studies as *holistic* designs and multiple-unit studies as *embedded* designs. Oakes and Guiton (1995), for example, chose three 4-year senior high schools located in adjacent communities within a major West Coast urban center as their unit of analysis.

4. *Establish the logic linking the data to the propositions.* Yin (1994) suggests that researchers attempt to describe how the data will be used to illuminate the propositions. He recommends use of a type of time-series pattern-matching strategy developed by Campbell (1975) in which patterns of data are related to the theoretical propositions. Oakes and Guiton (1995) analyzed student handbooks, course descriptions, and master schedules and conducted on-site observations and interviews. To ensure the validity of their findings, they used standard triangulation procedures throughout the study.[3] In Oakes and Guiton's written report, they organized the findings according to the seven propositions to provide an "eclectic explanation that blends existing theories for a multidimensional understanding of the dynamic interplay of structure and culture in tracking decisions" (p. 10).

5. *The criteria for interpretation of the findings should be explained.* No statistical tests are typically appropriate for use as a criterion for case study decisions. Yin suggests that researchers use judgment to identify "different patterns (that) are sufficiently contrasting" (p. 26) to compare rival propositions. Oakes and Guiton (1995) used their data to reject a simplistic, unidimensional view of curriculum offerings and student assignments. They found it necessary to integrate the various unidimensional theories (e.g., human capital theory) to understand the interplay of structural, cultural, and political factors. For example, they reported that "these three schools did not mechanistically sort students into college-prep or vocational courses in ways that blatantly discriminated against low-income and non-Asian minority students and that reproduce the economic and social order" (p. 29). Students were given choices about elective courses. However, if they chose easier academic courses or opted for a vocational track, "the school seemed to accept these choices and only rarely pressed low-income and minority students to stretch beyond their own or others' low expectations" (p. 29). The researchers suggest that future research on tracking include a broader perspective of three factors:

   a. Differentiated, hierarchical curriculum structures

   b. School cultures alternatively committed to common schooling and accommodating differences

   c. Political actions by individuals within those structures and cultures aimed at influencing the distribution of advantage. (p. 30)

In case study research, theory development is one essential part of the design phase. Yin (1994) defines theory as an understanding (or theory) of what is being studied. As noted in Chapter 2, the literature review is an excellent source for the identification of appropriate theories to guide the case study design.

Oakes and Guiton (1995) drew on competing theories in the literatures on how schools track students:

- Technical-structural (e.g., a match between tracking and the differentiated structure of the workforce)
- Cultural (e.g., norms regarding race, social class, and educational prospects)
- Political or individualistic (e.g., choice, parent pressure) theories to explain students' track assignments

Phenomenological Research

Phenomenological research emphasizes the individual's subjective experience (Tesch 1990). It seeks the individual's perceptions and meaning of a phenomenon or experien Typically, phenomenological research asks, What is the participant's experience like? intent is to understand and describe an event from the point of view of the participar feature that distinguishes phenomenological research from other qualitative rese' proaches is that the subjective experience is at the center of the inquiry.

Examples of the phenomenological approach in special education could the experience of being in a total-inclusion classroom is like or what the experi a student with a disability (or one without a disability) in an integrated class' contrast, an ethnographic approach to special education research could incl' of the impact of a program designed to facilitate integration of student studying the culture of the total-inclusion classroom, or studying i' children with or without disabilities.

Readers interested in the philosophical basis of phenomen' perspective are referred to Holstein and Gubrium (1994). Like Tes' Holstein and Gubrium emphasize the key characteristic of pher the way in which members of a group or community themselve around them. The researcher does not make assumptions exists apart from the individual. Rather, the focus is on unde and understand their own life spaces.

Holstein and Gubrium (1994) identify phenomer interpretive research strategies such as ethnometho which have at their core the qualitative study of re realm, the scientist's job is to discover the meanin individual. In ethnomethodology, the analyst fo nize, describe, explain, and account for their e example of ethnomethodological research t' topics, management of turn taking, and pra' a conversation.

Feminists have used ethnomethod' of language use in describing womer "intact" only if they reflect the (som to each other and living in the same

the family tends to convey a negative value to the many families represented by patterns other than that described. Many households are headed by single women who struggle against great odds (including those psychological stresses imposed by the socially constructed language) to raise their children in a positive manner.

Goode (1994) used ethnomethodology to study the social constructions of children who were born deaf and blind. He characterized the social constructions of the clinicians and direct-care staff of the children as bad patients or difficult custodial objects. Neither characterization took the children's own ideas or goals into consideration. As a consequence of their powerlessness to define their own situation, their lives resembled those of animals in training. Thus, Goode undertook the task of describing the experiential world of one of the children. His guiding research question was, "How is it possible for deaf-blind children without language and normally seeing-and-hearing adults with language to understand each other?" (p. 114). He explained his rationale for the choice of ethnomethodology to address this question in the following remarks:

> It has become my firm belief after participating in case-study research for more than twenty years that what is lacking in our current knowledge of human behavior is the most basic descriptive understandings. Our current emphasis on extremely refined techniques scientifically to dissect human existence is either premature or entirely misdirected. If we accept that we know as little about the construction of many everyday phenomena as we do about communication, then the choice for contemporary human science seems clear. It can continue to refine itself into pragmatic superfluity, or it can begin at the beginning and conduct the range of descriptive studies that are required. The current measurement-and-modeling orientation in research is an elegant preoccupation that human science can ill afford. . . . But even this single case displays the potential of ethnomethodology to reinvest the fullness and realness of everyday life back into the social and clinical sciences. It is this fullness that informs and grounds the program of ethnomethodological research and provides it with potential relevance to human services practitioners who require practical answers to everyday human problems, and to scientists who seek knowledge of everyday reality and its social construction. (p. 95)

information on ethnomethodology and conversational analysis, the reader is Holstein and Gubrium (1994).

Theory

ed theory was developed by Glaser and Strauss and can be described as thodology for developing theory that is grounded in data systematically nalyzed" (Strauss & Corbin, 1994, p. 273). The defining characteristic of is that the theoretical propositions are not stated at the outset of the study. ations (theory) emerge out of the data themselves and not prior to data

collection. Thus, the emergent theory is grounded in the current data collection and analysis efforts.

Because the initial or emerging theory is always tested against data that is systematically collected, this approach to research has been called the *constant comparative method*. It was created explicitly for the purpose of developing theory based on empirical data. On the basis of the viewpoints expressed by participants in the research, researchers accept the responsibility to interpret the data and use it as a basis for theory generation. The constant comparative method calls on the researcher to seek verification for hypotheses that emerge throughout the study (in contrast to other qualitative approaches that might see this as the role of follow-up quantitative research). Although Strauss and Corbin (1994) view grounded theory as a general method, applicable in quantitative and qualitative studies, their greatest impact has been in qualitative research. They explicate the processes and techniques associated with grounded theory in their book titled *Basics of Qualitative Research* (Strauss & Corbin, 1990).

The key methodological features include the following:

1. The researcher needs to constantly interact with the data; ask questions designed to generate theory and relate concepts. Make comparisons, think about what you see, make hypotheses, and sketch out miniframeworks to test ideas.

2. Use theoretical sampling—that is, select incidents for data collection that are guided by the emerging theory; as you ask questions of your data, you will begin collecting data that will help you fill in gaps in your theoretical formulation.

3. Use theoretical, systematic coding procedures, conceptualize how the substantive codes relate to each other as hypotheses to be integrated into a theory. Strauss and Corbin identify three types of coding decisions (open coding, axial coding, and selective coding), explained in Chapter 12 on data analysis.

4. Ask questions of your data that allow you to depict the complexity, variation, and nature of the relationships between variables in your study. Strauss and Corbin provide guidelines for increasing theoretical sensitivity, such as sitting with your data and asking questions such as, Who? When? Where? What? How? How much? and Why? Also, be sensitive to red flag words such as *never, always,* and *everyone.* Provide sufficient details so the reader can see the progression in your conceptual development and induction of relationships.

Participative Inquiry

Reason (1994b) discusses the emergence of a worldview that emphasizes participation as a core strategy in inquiry. Reason identifies two approaches to participatory research that differ in their fundamental assumptions of the role of the researchers and the influence of power on the researcher-participant relationships:

1. Cooperative inquiry that involves participation of all people in the research process but does not explicitly address power relations and the potential transformative effects of the research.

2. Participatory action research (PAR) that also involves all the people in the research process but does so with explicit recognition of power issues and a goal of transforming society.

Cooperative Inquiry. Cooperative inquiry is based on the importance of self-determination, and thus, all people are involved in the research as co-researchers. They contribute to the decision making through "generating ideas, designing and managing the project, and drawing conclusions from the experience, and *also* co-subjects, participating in the activity being researched" (Reason, 1994b, p. 326). The methodological implications of cooperative inquiry include the following:

1. Co-researchers identify a research problem and procedures that they want to work on together.

2. They implement their research procedures in everyday life and work.

3. They review and interpret the data and draw conclusions for change in practice or need for additional research.

Participatory Action Research. PAR emphasizes the establishment of liberating dialogue with impoverished or oppressed groups and the political production of knowledge. Fals-Borda and Ralman (1991) note that PAR is rooted in the culture of the common people, and they describe the role of the researcher as a change agent who embraces the concerns of oppressed people. The methodological implications arise from the need for dialogue between the more formally educated researcher and the cultural knowledge of the people. As in cooperative inquiry, the focus is on the people's participation in setting the agenda, participating in the data collection and analysis, and controlling use of the results. However, PAR emphasizes the use of methods that allow the voices of those most oppressed to be heard.

Thus, such research might take the form of community meetings and events that allow the oppressed people to tell their own stories, to reflect on their communities, and to generate ideas for change. The components of participation and dialogue can center on innovations that have been introduced into the community (e.g., a literacy training program or a mental health clinic). PAR can also make use of other more orthodox research methods, both quantitative and qualitative, as long as the sense making comes from the community.

The box labeled "Questions Related to Participatory Action Research" provides a list of questions researchers can ask themselves to determine to what extent they are doing PAR. The questions were prepared by Tanis Doe (1996) of the World Institute on Disability in Oakland, California. For additional readings on PAR, the reader is referred to DeKoning and Martin (1996), Gitlin (1994), Humphries and Truman (1994), and Reason (1994a, 1994b).

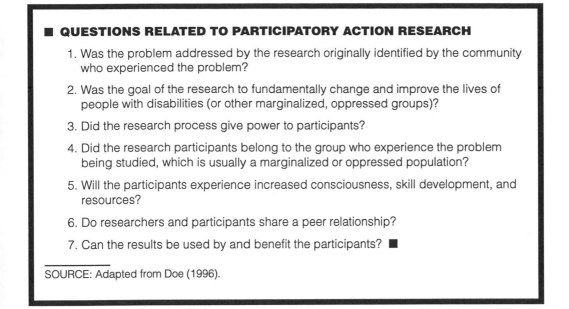

■ **QUESTIONS RELATED TO PARTICIPATORY ACTION RESEARCH**

1. Was the problem addressed by the research originally identified by the community who experienced the problem?

2. Was the goal of the research to fundamentally change and improve the lives of people with disabilities (or other marginalized, oppressed groups)?

3. Did the research process give power to participants?

4. Did the research participants belong to the group who experience the problem being studied, which is usually a marginalized or oppressed population?

5. Will the participants experience increased consciousness, skill development, and resources?

6. Do researchers and participants share a peer relationship?

7. Can the results be used by and benefit the participants? ■

SOURCE: Adapted from Doe (1996).

Clinical Research

Clinical research actually comes from the application of qualitative methods to biomedical problems (Miller & Crabtree, 1994). I include it primarily because of the close parallels between investigating the physician-patient relationship and the therapist-client relationship. Clinical research design was developed to adapt to the peculiarities of trying to understand a problem within a clinical context. Miller and Crabtree suggest that clinical qualitative research should investigate the physical, behavioral, cultural, historical, social, emotional, and spiritual ramifications of the following questions:

> What is going on with my *body?*
> What is happening with my *life?*
> Who has what *power?* (p. 342)

Through the use of in-depth interviews and participant observation, the researcher can come to understand the multiple forces that influence the effectiveness of different types of therapy.

Clinical research methods were developed to provide an additional avenue for understanding the efficacy (or nonefficacy) of prescribed treatments based on inclusion of the variables in the patient's everyday life. Much medical research is conducted using randomized designs that try to control or eliminate extraneous effects of everyday life. However, the physician who treats patients needs to prescribe treatments that take these variables into account. Clinical research uses qualitative methods to account for the effect of variables such as having young children to care for, restrictive insurance policies, or workers' compensation laws.

Focus Groups

Focus groups can be viewed as a data collection method or as a strategy for research. I introduce here only a brief description of focus groups as a strategy for research and elaborate on them as a data collection method in Chapter 11. Focus groups, in essence, are group interviews that rely, not on a question-and-answer format of interview but on the interaction within the group (Morgan, 1988). This reliance on interaction between participants is designed to elicit more of the participants' points of view (than would be evidenced in more researcher-dominated interviewing).

Using focus groups as a research strategy would be appropriate when the researcher is interested in how individuals form a schema or perspective of a problem. The focus group interaction allows the exhibition of a struggle for understanding how others interpret key terms and their agreement or disagreements with the issues raised. They can provide evidence of ways that differences are resolved and consensus is built.

Systematic variation across groups is the key to research design with focus groups. Examples include composing groups that vary on different dimensions:

1. Variation in the ordering of questions that the groups discuss

2. Variation in terms of characteristics such as age, ethnicity, gender, or disability

3. Using homogeneous groups versus heterogeneous groups (Warning: Hostility can result from bringing together two groups whose lifestyles do not normally lead them to discuss a topic together.)

4. Comparing responses of individuals who are brought back for more than one group (i.e., the same group meets several times together)

The group is considered the unit of analysis; therefore, the researcher must decide how many groups to have. This is the determinant of the degree of variability that will be possible. In market research, generally, no new ideas are forthcoming after three or four groups. Morgan (1988) concurs that only a few groups are necessary when the research is highly structured and exploratory; however, he recommends using six to eight groups if the goal is a detailed content analysis with relatively unstructured groups. (He does state that one group is never enough; two groups are viewed as a minimum number.)

General Methodological Guidelines

Because there is no one correct method for conducting qualitative research, Stainback and Stainback (1988) recommend that researchers describe their methodology in detail. There are multiple ways to structure and conduct a qualitative research study. Therefore, I discuss the process of designing and conducting such a study in terms of typical actions that occur in qualitative research and decisions that need to occur. This should not be interpreted as a lockstep approach to qualitative research. In a qualitative research proposal, the researcher needs to present a plan that includes a description of methods yet makes clear that changes will occur as the study progresses.

The reader who intends to conduct a qualitative research study is referred to other texts that explore this topic in more depth (Bogdan & Biklen, 1992; Fetterman, 1989; Guba & Lincoln, 1989; Lincoln & Guba, 1985; Marshall & Rossman, 1989; Patton, 1990; Yin, 1993, 1994).

Typically, qualitative researchers use three main methods for collecting data: participant observation, interviews, and document and records review. These methods are discussed in Chapter 11 on data collection. I list them here to provide context for my remarks about methodological guidelines.

The Researcher Is the Instrument

In qualitative research, the researcher is the instrument for data collection. Unlike a printed questionnaire or test that might be used in a quantitative study, the researcher is the instrument for collecting data. The qualitative researcher decides which questions to ask and in what order, what to observe, what to write down. Therefore, considerable interest has been focused on who the researcher is and what values, assumptions, beliefs, or biases he or she brings to the study. In general, qualitative research texts recognize the importance of researchers' reflecting on their own values, assumptions, beliefs, and biases and monitoring those as they progress through the study (perhaps through journaling or peer debriefing) to determine their impact on the study's data and interpretations.

In emancipatory research in particular, the issue has been raised as to the ability of men to study women, members of a dominant ethnic group to study minority ethnic groups, or people without disabilities to study persons with disabilities. This issue was touched on in Chapter 5 (on survey research) under the topic of interviewing people who are similar to or different from yourself. In this context, the issue is more broadly addressed. What can a person who is not a member of the group do to try to enhance the validity of the information collected from that group, especially if the researcher represents a dominant group?

M. L. Anderson (1993) raises these questions as a White woman who wanted to conduct a study of race relations in a community that was racially divided with a history of paternalism. She chose a senior center as her research site, and within that site, she chose to speak to African American women about their experiences. She reflected on the things that she did that led to gaining the trust of the women in the community. She spent many hours doing volunteer work at the senior center. She also did not pose herself as an "expert" on their lives. Rather, she presented herself as someone who was interested in learning about their lives. Foster (1993b) (a hearing researcher) also reported assuming this stance in conducting ethnographic work with deaf people.

M. L. Anderson (1993) reports sharing information about herself and her own feelings with the women. She describes her experiences as follows:

> In my project, despite my trepidations about crossing class, race, and age lines, I was surprised by the openness and hospitality with which I was greeted. I am convinced that the sincerity of these women's stories emanated not only from their dignity and honor, but also from my willingness to express how I felt, to share my own race and gender experiences, and to deconstruct the role of expert as I proceeded through this research. (p. 50)

She was an active volunteer in the senior center that these women regularly attended. Her participation in the everyday activities of the women's culture, both in the center and in their homes, resulted in conversations that were filled with emotional details of their lives.

Speaking for the Other

Going beyond the question of "Can a member of a dominant group legitimately study the experiences of an oppressed group?" lies the ethical issue of who can speak for another? The problems inherent in the role of the researcher speaking for the other was captured by bell hooks (1990) in the following passage that depicts a hypothetical conversation between a researcher and a participant:

> No need to hear your voice when I can talk about you better than you can speak about yourself. No need to hear your voice. Only tell about your pain. I want to know your story. And then I will tell it back to you in a new way. Tell it back to you in such a way that it has become mine, my own. Re-writing you, I write myself anew. I am still author, authority. I am still the colonizer, the speak subject, and you now at the center of my talk. (quoted in Fine, 1994b, p. 70)

Fine (1994b) warns that researchers can unwittingly or deliberately contribute to the continuation of oppression by presuming to speak for the groups in our research. Through collaborative construction of text, researchers can enable resistance to continued oppression. This topic is explored further in Chapter 12 in the section on reporting research results.

Focus on an Area of Inquiry

As discussed in Chapter 2, the qualitative researcher starts with a literature review that leads to the formulation of research questions. The important caveat, repeated here, is that the area of inquiry, as defined by the initial literature review and the research questions, should be viewed as tentative. The researcher must be open to a change of focus if that is dictated by the data emerging from the field experience.

Explore Research Sites

You can use information gathered from preliminary visits to potential research sites to convince a funding agency or a research committee that you are capable of conducting a qualitative study and to determine the site's accessibility and suitability (Marshall & Rossman, 1989; Stainback & Stainback, 1988). During your visits, you can conduct pilot work (with permission of the "gatekeepers" at the site) that will allow you to suggest possible activities, locations, and people (possibly defined in terms of positions within the organization) that you want to include in your study. Because of the ontological assumption of multiple realities, be sure to include in your list of people those with diverse viewpoints about the phenomenon of interest. Sampling procedures are discussed in Chapter 10. The researcher should be aware that data provided by participants may vary based on the place, activity engaged in, or social variables at the time of the data collection (Patton, 1990). The researcher should provide a description of the setting, research site, and the conditions operating at the time the data were gathered and report exactly how the participants were selected along with their characteristics.

Your initial pilot work may also give you an idea about the length of time needed to complete your study, in addition to the number of site visits that you will need to make. In some ethnographic texts, the length of a study is recommended to be between 6 months and 1 year (Fetterman, 1989); however, the time frame will be dictated by a number of factors. In some cases, the length of the program may be limited to a few months, and thus, the length of the study may correspond to the length of the program. In other cases, a funding agency will impose a limit of the amount of funds available and thus constrain the amount of time that the study can continue. The one guiding principle in the decision should be that the researcher avoids premature closure—that is, reaching inaccurate conclusions based on insufficient observations.

Gaining Permission

Before data are collected, the researcher must follow appropriate procedures to gain permission from the gatekeepers (typically defined as those with power in the organization or agency) of the organization or community. In organizational settings such as schools, clinics, or community agencies, formal procedures are established that define how permission is to be obtained. Issues surrounding such procedures are discussed further in the sampling chapter; however, the researcher should contact the organization or agency to determine their specific procedures.

The notion of entry into a setting by means of access granted by gatekeepers is problematic for researchers who work from an emancipatory perspective. Recall Sandra Harding's (1993) direction to start your research from marginalized lives and the key questions raised in the section of this chapter on PAR. The focus is on addressing problems that were originally identified by the community that experiences the problem (Doe, 1996). Thus, researchers operating within the emancipatory paradigm must consider strategies for entry into the community that has the least power.

Negotiating Entry

Morse (1994) provides practical advice for negotiating entry into sites for research. She suggests that the researcher visit a number of sites and "tentatively sound out administrators to determine if the proposed project would be welcomed and if researchers would be tolerated on site" (p. 222). She warned that administrators might be wary of research that was aimed at evaluating their personnel or institution or that might reflect badly on their organization. Administrators usually look for some assurances about the amount of control they will have over the research process and the use of the findings. The researcher needs to consider the nature of assurances that can be made without compromising the integrity of the research. The researcher also needs to learn about and adhere to the organization's review process in terms of protection of human beings and identification of costs to the organization. Talking with other researchers who have conducted research in this or similar settings can be quite helpful.

Entering the Field

The researcher needs to make plans to enter the field in the least disruptive manner possible, taking care to establish good rapport with the participants. As mentioned previously, this can be facilitated by accommodating yourself to the routines of the informants, establishing what you have in common, helping people out, displaying an interest in them, and acting like a person who belongs (and *being yourself*).

Warren (1988) identifies a number of variables that influence the researcher's entry into the field:

> The fieldworker's initial reception by the host society is a reflection of cultural contextualization of the fieldworker's characteristics, which include marital status, age, physical appearance, presence and number of children, and ethnic, racial, class, or national differences as well as gender. (p. 13)

Although Warren speaks primarily within the context of conducting research in other countries, all contexts have their own cultural norms and expectations based on various biological and socially defined characteristics of the people in them. The researcher should be sensitive to what these norms are and how they might affect the research work.

Role of the Researcher

In M. L. Anderson's (1993) examination of the role of the researcher within the context of being a White woman studying the experiences of African American women, she suggests that White researchers doing research on race and ethnicity "should examine self-consciously the influence of institutional racism and the way it shapes the formulation and development of their research, rather than assume a color-blind stance" (p. 43). Thus, she rejects the "unbiased, objective" scientific research stance in favor of one that recognizes the influences of the researcher's own status (e.g., race, gender, etc.) on the shaping of knowledge. This requires that researchers build more inclusive ways to discover the multiple views of their participants and adopt more personally interactive roles with them.

Whereas Anderson addresses issues related to a member of the dominant culture studying other adults who have less power, Fine and Sandstrom (1988) address the role of the researcher in the context of studying children. They discuss three possible roles that could be adopted in such studies, although they recommended that the age of the child is a critical factor in deciding which role to adopt:

1. *Supervisor:* Researchers can portray themselves as authority figures (typical adult role); however, this would not be conducive to conducting ethnographic research because it would most likely result in witnessing a limited range of behavior.

2. *Leader:* Researchers can still assume the "authority" role but have an added dimension of positive effect typically associated with leaders of children's activities (e.g., Scout leaders). This is an improvement over the supervisor role; however, it still focuses on the adult's frame of reference and thus restricts the range of observable behavior.

3. *Friend:* In this role, the researcher assumes no specific authority over the children; instead, the researcher attempts to establish a positive relationship with the children. Fine and Sandstrom believe that this role results in less sanctioning of the behavior being studied. It also requires that the participant observer treat his or her informants with respect.

Fine and Sandstrom (1988) discuss the following issues in regard to developing the friend role: First, researchers must provide the children with their reasons for being there. The researchers can be explicit and explain the complete and detailed purposes and hypotheses for the research. This could bias the research in that the kids may act in a way that could deliberately try to confirm or deny the researcher's hypotheses. The researchers could try for a "shallow cover"—that is, admitting that they are doing research on children's behaviors but not provide details. The problem with this role is that the children will develop their own ideas as to what the researcher is studying, and they may feel betrayed when they find out what the "real" reasons were. A third option would be to maintain "deep cover"—that is, not to tell the children that they are being observed; however, the researcher runs the risk of arousing suspicion and creating bad feelings after being "discovered."

A second issue related to the role of the researcher as friend is associated with the settings in which an adult would be viewed comfortably as a friend. For example, kids may feel comfortable with an adult present during many of their behaviors but not at a party where sexual behaviors could be observed.

A third issue in the researcher's role as friend is that of giving gifts or rewards. As a friend, the researcher might give companionship, praise, help with schoolwork, food, monetary loans, rides to activities, or movie tickets. Fine and Sandstrom warn researchers to be wary about using such gifts to manipulate their respondents or to allow the children to manipulate them by excessive demands for rewards (or loans and the like).

The age of the child is important in deciding which role to adopt. With very young children (preschoolers), the researcher could choose to act childlike or to just hang around and wait for gradual acceptance. The childlike behavior may thrill the children but "turn off" supervisors. With older children (preadolescent), the researcher could choose to assume the role of older sibling (big brother, big sister), student, journalist, or protector. With adolescents, the researchers can treat the children as people that they sincerely wish to get to know.

Warren (1988) discusses the role of the researcher as it has emerged in sociological and anthropological research. She notes that many times the role of the researcher is assigned by the respondents in terms of what they see as his or her proper place in the social order. Young unmarried women are often assigned the role of adoptive daughter or child (i.e., one who has to learn from the older community members). Reinharz (1992) notes that the role of daughter might be useful to gain entry but be in conflict with the competent researcher role. She suggests that the researcher ask herself, Can I function effectively within this role?

Other roles include sister or brother, spy, androgynous person, honorary male, or invisible woman. In her work in a drug rehabilitation clinic, Warren (1988) overheard one respondent say, "Aah, what harm can she do, she's only a broad" (p. 18).

Gender Issues

Sexual harassment is another issue that surfaces in fieldwork. This may take the form of sexual hustling, as well as assignment to traditional female roles and tasks in the field, such as "go-fer," or being the butt of sexual or gender jokes (Warren, 1988). The researcher's response to sexist treatment creates a tension in terms of "harmonious research relations in the field (based on the pursuit of knowledge and of career advancement) and the typically feminist politics of fieldworkers in academia (based on the struggle to overcome sexism)" (p. 38).

Reinharz (1992) suggests that the woman ethnographer who experiences sexual harassment might choose to avoid her harasser and thus accept the resulting alteration of her study. Or she might choose to overlook the harassment to avoid losing that informant. Reinharz also notes that women in field settings must be cognizant of the physical risks to which they are vulnerable, especially if working alone. At the same time, women researchers must be sensitive to the threat they may pose to men and the need to modify their behavior to gain access in a primarily male setting. Warren (1988) suggests that this is an area in which additional research is needed in terms of how best to respond to sexist situations.

Data Collection Methods

Many types of data collection methods can be used in qualitative studies. Specific methods are discussed in Chapter 11. I want to acknowledge that data analysis is generally considered to be an ongoing task during a qualitative study. However, for purposes of teaching you about how to do research, I discuss the techniques of qualitative data analysis in Chapter 12.

Critically Analyzing Qualitative Research

Criteria for judging the quality of qualitative research that parallel the criteria for judging positivist, quantitative research have been outlined by a number of writers (Guba & Lincoln, 1989; Stainback & Stainback, 1988). Guba and Lincoln equate credibility with internal validity, transferability with external validity, dependability with reliability, and confirmability with objectivity. They added the additional category of authenticity for qualitative research. In Lincoln's 1995 address to the American Educational Research Association, she listed a number of criteria for quality that have emerged from the emancipatory paradigm. In this section, each criterion is explained along with ways to enhance quality in research that uses qualitative methods. (See the box labeled "Criteria of Judging Quality in Qualitative Research" for a listing of these criteria.)

Credibility

Guba and Lincoln (1989) identify credibility as the criterion in qualitative research that parallels internal validity in postpositivist research. Internal validity means the attribution within the experimental situation that the independent variable caused the observed

■ **LISTING OF CRITERIA FOR JUDGING QUALITY IN QUALITATIVE RESEARCH**

Credibility (parallels internal validity)
    Prolonged, substantial engagement
    Persistent observation
    Peer debriefing
    Negative case analysis
    Progressive subjectivity
    Member checks
    Triangulation

Transferability (parallels external validity)
    Thick description
    Multiple cases

Dependability (parallels reliability)
    Dependability audit

Confirmability (parallels objectivity)
    Confirmability audit/chain of evidence

Authenticity
    Fairness
    Ontological authenticity
    Catalytic authenticity

Emancipatory
    Positionality or standpoint
    Community
    Attention to voice
    Critical reflexivity
    Reciprocity
    Sharing perquisites of privilege ■

change in the dependent variable. In qualitative research, the credibility test asks if there is a correspondence between the way the respondents actually perceive social constructs and the way the researcher portrays their viewpoints. A number of research strategies can be used to enhance credibility. A researcher should seek to use as many of these strategies as possible, because the goal is to provide evidence from a multiplicity of sources of the credibility of the research. Some researchers and users of research are uncomfortable with the lack of hard-and-fast rules for establishing credibility in qualitative research; therefore, it is incumbent on qualitative researchers to demonstrate through the use of multiple strategies that their research is credible.

Prolonged and Substantial Engagement. There is no hard-and-fast rule that says how long a researcher must stay at a site. When the researcher has confidence that themes and examples are repeating instead of extending, it may be time to leave the field. In a study of inclusion of a student with disabilities, Keller (1993) observed a girl with Down's syndrome from January through June of 1 year.

Persistent Observation. The researcher should observe long enough to identify salient issues. The researcher should avoid premature closure—that is, coming to a conclusion about a situation without sufficient observations. Keller (1993) had over 80 contacts with the school or the staff over a 6-month period.

Peer Debriefing. The researcher should engage in an extended discussion with a disinterested peer, of findings, conclusions, analysis, and hypotheses. The peer should pose searching questions to help the researcher confront his or her own values and to guide next steps in the study. Keller (1993) shared the narratives from his field notes with two other researchers involved in the school.

Negative Case Analysis. Working hypotheses can be revised based on the discovery of cases that do not fit. However, it should not be expected that all cases will fit the appropriate categories. Guba and Lincoln (1989) state that when a "reasonable" number of cases fit, negative case analysis provides confidence in the hypothesis that is being proposed. For example, suppose a researcher sees a pattern emerging that suggests that a top-down approach to a total-inclusion program creates resistance in the school staff (Mertens, 1992). The researcher could seek additional data for negative case analysis from a school that used a bottom-up approach to total inclusion. If resistance was identified in that setting as well, the researcher would need to revise the emerging hypothesis that administration style *alone* creates resistance. It may be one of many factors that contribute to resistance to change.

Progressive Subjectivity. The researcher should monitor his or her own developing constructions and document the process of change from the beginning of the study until it ends. The researcher can share this statement of beliefs with the peer debriefer so that the peer can challenge the researcher who has not kept an open mind but found only what was expected from the beginning. For example, a study of the social experiences of deaf high school students suggested that social isolation can be a very painful result of being the only deaf student (or one of a few) in a school (Mertens, 1989b). The emotional strength of this finding might have left the researcher biased against the integration of students with disabilities into regular classes. Consequently, in Mertens's subsequent work in total-inclusion research (1992), she needed to discuss this personal experience at the beginning and throughout the duration of the study so that she could keep an open mind and not be biased by previous experience.

Member Checks. This is the most important criteria in establishing credibility. The researcher must verify with the respondent groups the constructions that are developing as a result of data collected and analyzed. Member checks can be formal and informal. For example, at the end of an interview, the researcher can summarize what has been said and ask if the notes accurately reflect the person's position. Drafts of the research report can be shared with the members for comment. Mertens et al. (1995) established a daily feedback loop with trainers in special education who were deaf or blind or had no disabilities. She discussed the data that she had collected from the previous day to clarify their perspectives and to enhance her ability to represent their viewpoints accurately.

Triangulation. Triangulation involves checking information that has been collected from different sources or methods for consistency of evidence across sources of data. For example, multiple methods such as interviews, observation, and document review can be used, and information can be sought from multiple sources using the same method (e.g., interviews with different groups, such as program administrators, service providers, service recipients, and people who are eligible to receive services but are not currently doing so). Guba and Lincoln (1989) no longer support this notion of triangulation because it implies that it is possible (or desirable) to find consistency across sources, which contradicts the notion of multiple realities discussed earlier in this chapter. They say that triangulation can still be used to check on "factual data" (e.g., how many children are in a program), but they recommend the use of member checks for other types of data. Keller (1993) collected information by means of observations in classrooms, planning sessions, staff meetings, parent-teacher conferences, and IEP meetings. He taught three lessons in the classroom of the student in his study; he interviewed the student, her mother, and her teacher from her old school; and he held informal conversations with her regular and special education teachers and the principal. He combined the data from all of these sources to support his findings.

In specific reference to case study research, Yin[4] (1994) notes that internal validity is a concern only for causal or explanatory case studies in which the researcher is trying to determine if Event *X* caused Event *Y*. Descriptive or exploratory case studies do not attempt to make such causal assertions, and therefore, internal validity that is conceptualized as avoiding incorrect conclusions about causal relations is not relevant.

In addition, in case studies, no experimental variables are explicitly manipulated; therefore, causal relationships are established by inference based on interviews or documentary evidence. The researcher should be sure to explore rival explanations and to determine the convergence (or nonconvergence) of data from multiple sources in terms of supporting causal inferences.

Transferability: Thick Description and Multiple Cases

Guba and Lincoln (1989) identify transferability as the qualitative parallel to external validity in postpositivist research. External validity means the degree to which you can generalize the results to other situations. In qualitative research, the burden of transferability is on the reader to determine the degree of similarity between the study site and the receiving context. The researcher's responsibility is to provide sufficient detail to enable the reader to make such a judgment. Extensive and careful description of the time, place, context, and culture is known as "thick description."

Mertens (1990) studied the reasons that referrals were increasing to a special school that served several school districts in a rural area. She provided an in-depth description of the community in which the special school was located as well as of the sending and receiving schools by means of demographic and observational data. She observed in all the schools and provided a description of the physical setup of the classrooms and the processes of instruction that were used. Thus, readers could determine how similar their own conditions were to those reported by Mertens. A thick description of the context was important because the rural nature of the community had an impact on understanding the reasons for the increased referrals (e.g., in terms of ability to attract and retain qualified special education staff and inability to hire personnel to serve the needs of students with low-incidence disabilities in sparsely populated areas).

In case study research, Yin (1994) suggests that use of multiple cases can strengthen the external validity of the results. He also notes that the relationship between the case study and extant theories can lead to decisions about generalization from case study research.

Dependability

Guba and Lincoln (1989) identified dependability as the qualitative parallel to reliability. Reliability means stability over time in the postpositivist paradigm. In the constructivist paradigm, change is expected, but it should be tracked and publicly inspectable. A dependability audit can be conducted to attest to the quality and appropriateness of the inquiry process. Yin (1994) describes this process in case study research as maintaining a case study protocol that details each step in the research process.

For example, Mertens (1991b) began a study of ways to encourage gifted deaf adolescents to enter science careers with a focus on instructional strategies used in science classes. However, emerging patterns in the data suggested the importance of examining administrative practices that facilitated the acquisition of competent interpreters or teachers and staff who were deaf. This change of focus is acceptable and to be expected in qualitative research, but it should be documented.

Confirmability

Guba and Lincoln (1989) identified confirmability as the qualitative parallel to objectivity. Objectivity means that the influence of the researcher's judgment is minimized. Confirmability means that the data and their interpretation are not figments of the researcher's imagination. Qualitative data can be tracked to its source, and the logic that is used to interpret the data should be made explicit. Guba and Lincoln recommend a confirmability audit to attest to the fact that the data can be traced to original sources and that the process of synthesizing data to reach conclusions can be confirmed. Yin (1994) refers to this as providing a "chain of evidence." The confirmability audit can be conducted in conjunction with the dependability audit. Thus, a special education researcher's peers can review field notes, interview transcripts, and so on and determine if the conclusions are supported by the data (Keller, 1993).

Authenticity

Authenticity refers to the presentation of a balanced view of all perspectives, values, and beliefs (Stainback & Stainback, 1988). It answers the question, Has the researcher been fair in presenting views? Among the criteria identified by Guba and Lincoln (1989) to judge the authenticity of investigations conducted within the constructivist paradigm, were the following.

Fairness. Fairness answers the question, To what extent are different constructions and their underlying value structures solicited and honored in the process? To be fair, the researcher must identify the respondents and how information about their constructions was obtained. Conflicts and value differences should be displayed. There should also be open negotiation of the recommendations and agenda for future actions. Total-inclusion research can be judged to be fair if the variety of viewpoints, both for and against (and the conditions under which inclusion would be supported) are included in the report (Keller et al., 1993; Mertens, 1992).

Ontological Authenticity. This is the degree to which the individual's or group's conscious experience of the world became more informed or sophisticated. This can be determined based on member checks with respondents or by means of an audit trail that documents changes in individuals' constructions throughout the process. In the study of increased referrals to a special school, respondents came to understand the discrepancy between policy and practice with regard to referral of students with disabilities to special schools (Mertens, 1990). The policy said that students with disabilities should be educated as much as possible with general education students and that, as a last resort, *before* referral to a special school, they should be provided with educational services in a separate, special education classroom in their home school. Local school staff did not support use of the special education classroom because they perceived it as stigmatizing for the student to go to a separate classroom. They preferred to refer a student to the special school when they had exhausted attempts to integrate a student with a disability in a general education classroom.

Catalytic Authenticity. This is the extent to which action is stimulated by the inquiry process. Techniques for determining this criterion include respondent testimony and examination of actions reported in follow-up studies. Following the completion of the study of increased referrals at the special school, the state department of education representative asked Mertens (1990) to assist them in implementing the recommendations. For example, personnel from the special school began to serve as consultants to the local schools to assist them in retaining and meeting the needs of the students with disabilities prior to referral to the special school.

Emancipatory Paradigm Criteria

Positionality or Standpoint Epistemology. Lincoln (1995) describes the inherent characteristic of all research as being representative of the position or standpoint of the author. Therefore, researchers should acknowledge that all texts are incomplete and represent specific positions in terms of sexuality, ethnicity, and so on. Texts cannot claim to contain all universal truth because all knowledge is contextual; therefore, the researcher must acknowledge the context of the research.

Community. Research takes place within and affects a community (Lincoln, 1995). The researcher should be able to know the community well enough to link the research results to positive action within that community.

Attention to Voice. Lincoln (1995) cites the question that bell hooks (1990) has asked in her writing, Who speaks for whom? Who speaks for those who do not have access to the academy? The researcher must seek out those who are silent and must involve those who are marginalized.

Critical Reflexivity. The researcher must be able to enter into a high-quality awareness to understand the psychological state of others to uncover dialectical relationships (Lincoln, 1995). The researcher needs to have a heightened self-awareness for personal transformation and critical subjectivity.

Reciprocity. The researcher needs to demonstrate that a method of study was used that allowed the researcher to develop a sense of trust and mutuality with the participants in the study (Lincoln, 1995).

Sharing the Perquisites of Privilege. Researchers should be prepared to share in the royalties of books or other publications that result from the research. Lincoln (1995) says, "We owe a debt to the persons whose lives we portray."

In her closing remarks at the annual meeting of the American Educational Research Association, Lincoln (1995) envisioned a different set of criteria for judging the quality of research from what is currently used in most academic settings. She said, "Try to imagine an academic world in which judgments about promotion, tenure, and merit pay were made on the basis of the extent of our involvement with research participants, rather than on our presumed distance."

► *Questions for Critically Analyzing Qualitative Research*

1. Did the researcher maintain sufficient involvement at the site to overcome distortions, uncover people's constructions, and understand the context's culture?

2. Did the researcher avoid premature closure?

3. Did the researcher use peer debriefing?

4. Did the researcher use negative case analysis?

5. Did the researcher prepare a statement of beliefs and share those with the peer debriefer?

6. Did the researcher use member checks?

7. Did the researcher use triangulation?

8. Did the researcher provide sufficient thick description?

9. Did the researcher do a dependability audit?

10. Did the researcher do a confirmability audit?

11. Did the researcher display conflicts and value differences?

12. Did the individuals and groups become more informed or sophisticated about their experiences?

13. Did the evaluation stimulate action?

14. Did the researcher acknowledge the contextual nature of the research?

15. Did the researcher establish links with the community that facilitated action based on the research findings?

16. Did the researcher seek out those who are silent and marginalized?

17. Was the researcher critically reflexive?

18. Did the researcher demonstrate a relationship with the participants based on trust and mutuality?

19. Were arrangements made to share the perquisites of privilege?

■ *Questions and Activities for Discussion and Application*

1. In your opinion, for what types of settings and problems are qualitative research methods appropriate and not appropriate?

2. What are the philosophical assumptions of the constructivist paradigm, and what are the methodological implications of those assumptions? How do they reflect the decision to use qualitative methods?

3. Identify the characteristics of two of the types of qualitative research—that is, ethnography and phenomenology. How are they similar to and different from each other? Give an example in your discipline of an application of each of these approaches.

4. Given the following research problem, explain what the researchers could do to improve the quality of their study. Structure your answer using the following categories:

   a. Credibility

   b. Transferability

   c. Dependability

   d. Confirmability

e. Authenticity

Example: Pull-out programs (e.g., resource rooms or remedial classes) have been criticized for segregating low-achieving students, providing them with a fragmented curriculum, and allowing regular classroom teachers to avoid responsibility for meeting all the students' needs. Pull-in programs have been proposed as one alternative in which the special education or remedial teacher provides instruction in the regular classroom. This study used observations of two pull-in programs to obtain information about implementation, instructional context, and variability among classrooms implementing a pull-in approach. Three pull-out programs taught by the same special and remedial education teachers served as comparison groups (Geilheiser & Meyers, 1992).

5. Brainstorm ideas for a qualitative research study. Choose one idea and briefly explain how you could use each of the qualitative strategies to investigate that topic:

a. Ethnographic research

b. Case study

c. Phenomenology

d. Grounded theory

e. Participative inquiry

f. Clinical research

g. Focus groups

Which of these strategies do you think would be most appropriate for your research topic? Why?

6. Identify one research study for each qualitative research strategy listed in Question 5. Explain your basis for categorizing each study. For each study, do the following:

a. Identify the research problem.

b. Identify the unit of analysis.

c. Describe the data collection methods that were used.

d. Identify the organizing framework for the findings.

e. Summarize the main findings.

f. Use the questions for critical analysis at the end of this chapter to critically analyze each study.

7. In qualitative research, the problem of trust between the researcher and participant is very important. Describe strategies that you can use to build trust. Select

several combinations from the 8-cell table presented below and role play strategies for building trust within that context:

Race/Ethnicity		Gender			
		Researcher		Participant	
		Male	Female	Male	Female
	Dominant culture				
	Minority culture				

a. Add other dimensions to the role play, such as sexual harassment; passive-aggressive behavior; seductive, flirtatious behavior; expectation of deferential behavior, and so on.

b. Create other contexts with other variables, such as presence or absence of a disability, type of disability, and severity of disability, and role-play strategies for gaining trust.

8. In feminist writing about ethnography research, Reinharz (1992) notes that many feminists encourage the development of a close, nurturing relationship between researcher and participants in field settings. What is your opinion of the advantages and disadvantages of such a relationship?

9. What should researchers reveal about their role as the researcher? Should they be complete participants? Should they perform other work in the setting (such as volunteer work)?

10. Judith Stacey (1988, cited in Reinharz, 1992) remarks that fieldwork relations are inherently deceptive and instrumental and feminists ought not relate to women in this way. Reinharz (1992) says that the manipulative nature of the relationship can be reduced by reminding informants of your research intentions, being reciprocally nurturing rather than manipulative, and being motivated by concern for women, not by their exploitation. Where do you stand on this issue?

11. Some ethnographic researchers have reported a dilemma in their fieldwork in that the women they are studying do not seem to be aware of their subordinate position. Is it the researcher's responsibility to raise their level of consciousness? To raise questions about their oppression? Or would this reflect an inappropriate imposition of the values of the researcher as a feminist?

12. Select two qualitative studies from the literature. Compare the authors' handling of the following dimensions:

a. Motivation for conducting the research

b. Data collection strategies

c. Data analysis methods

d. Credibility building/validity

e. Ethics

Answer these questions:

a. How and why do these texts differ? How do they relate to the theoretical readings you are currently doing?

b. Do you think the authors are justified in their methods or presentations? Why? Why not?

c. How will these readings help you make decisions about your own professional work in the field?

d. What do you think are the most important standards to use in comparing these two works?[5]

Notes

1. When qualitative methods are used within the postpositivist paradigm, typically, the researcher establishes predetermined, static questions to guide the research, converts the qualitative data to frequency counts, and so on. However, I focus on the use of qualitative methods within the interpretive/constructivist/emancipatory tradition because of the unique criteria for judging quality associated with such research.

2. The intent of this example is to illustrate how behavioral observations can be used in a qualitative study to provide evidence of attitudinal change. Persons interested in further details about the study (such as the number and characteristics of the participants in the study and the pervasiveness of the attitude changes) are referred to Mertens et al. (1995).

3. Triangulation in qualitative research can be defined as the collection of data on each topic of interest from a variety of data sources and using several data collectors who use several different data collection methods, such as document reviews, interviews, and observations.

4. It should be noted that Yin is basically a postpositivist who does qualitative work and Lincoln and Guba are constructivists in their orientation.

5. I am indebted to an anonymous reviewer for suggesting this line of questioning.

In This Chapter

■ *A rationale for the importance of historical research in education and psychology is discussed.*

■ *Three types of historical research are identified: topical, biographical, and autobiographical.*

■ *Oral history and the narrative study of lives are distinguished, and their place in the sphere of historical research is examined.*

■ *Three sources of historical data are identified: oral history, documents, and artifacts.*

■ *Steps in conducting historical research are described:*

  1. *Types of problems appropriate for historical research and sources that are helpful in the identification of such problems*

  2. *Conducting the literature review, with particular attention to the preliminary and secondary sources most helpful for historical research*

  3. *Identifying historical data, including documents, artifacts, and oral histories*

  4. *Evaluating the quality of historical sources*

■ *Special considerations for conducting biographical research are discussed.*

■ *Questions for evaluating historical and narrative research are provided.*

History and
Narrative Study of Lives

Many of the modern social professions were formed or radically restructured during the Progressive Era (1890-1920). This is true for education in general and the associated profession of vocational guidance in particular. The foundations of these professions, and particularly their ideological underpinnings are, however, not always well understood. . . . In spite of the extensive concern for equality and personal development on the part of progressive educators, professions were often formed and developed in accord with principles that would have the effect of limiting opportunities and access to the occupational structure for the working classes, immigrant groups, people of color, and women.

(Sherman, 1993, pp. 197-198)

Sherman conducted a historical study of vocational choice and examined implications for vocational guidance in today's schools. A summary of this study is presented in Sample Study 8.1.

AUTHOR'S NOTE: I am indebted to Donna Ryan, Stan Schuchman, and Barry Bergen of the Gallaudet University Department of Government and History for their insightful comments on an earlier draft of this chapter.

SAMPLE STUDY 8.1   *Summary of a Historical Research Study*

Research problem: Contradictory perspectives of occupational choice or selection arise between the viewpoints that individuals are free to choose an occupation and that occupational choice is strongly influenced by issues of gender, race, ethnicity, and class.

Research questions: What were the forces that influenced the development of the field of vocational guidance and the notion of vocational choice such that individuals are prepared differentially based on class, gender, and ethnicity, while still maintaining the illusion of equal and free choice? What does vocational choice mean in current psychological or vocational guidance practice?

Method: Historical documents from the Progressive Era were reviewed that related to education, growth of industrial capitalism, and the methods of production, from the 1890s through World War I. Records of business associations such as the National Association of Manufacturers and the National Society for the Promotion of Industrial Education were analyzed. The contribution of one individual, Frank Parsons, was examined in terms of his influence on defining the profession of vocational guidance through reliance on matching an individual's skills and attributes with specific occupations, within appropriate social roles as defined at the time.

Results: Public schooling and vocational guidance were viewed as a way to sort workers into occupations that were appropriate for the new industrial order. A two-tiered system of education was established: a liberal arts program for future-managers and industrial subjects for those slated to be manual workers.

Discussion: Critics and reformers expressed concern about the development of a permanent working class. Current vocational guidance continues to rely on individual assessments of abilities, interests, and values and matching those to industrial requirements, without consideration of the ways in which class, race, ethnicity, or gender affect options.

SOURCE: Based on Sherman (1993).

Importance of Historical and Narrative Research

Some people's view of history is that it is dry as dust; others view it as a fiery debate. How can one area have such a diverse reputation? The controversy arises because of questions such as, Whose history should children study? What has our experience been in America (or in other countries)? Who owns history? Nash (1995) identifies these as the questions that contributed to the "fiery debate" as the National Standards for History were being developed. The National Standards for History were developed through a broad-based national consensus-building process that worked toward reaching agreement on the larger purposes of history in the school curriculum and on the more specific history understandings and thinking processes that all students should have an equal opportunity to acquire over 12 years of precollegiate education (Crabtree & Nash, 1994).

Within the discipline of history, concerns have arisen about the lack of representation of oppressed groups in historical accounts. Scholars who took on the revision of history to represent those voices that had been traditionally overlooked created a movement in history known as *new social history*. Historians are now experiencing what has been termed the *linguistic turn* in their discipline. "In the field of history the term *linguistic turn* denotes the historical analysis of representation as opposed to the pursuit of a discernible, retrievable historical 'reality' " (Canning, 1994, p. 369). The linguistic turn is manifest in the new cultural history[1] based on the French philosophers Derrida and Foucalt. This movement parallels the emancipatory framework within the educational and psychological research communities.

As suggested in the introductory quotation to this chapter, educators and psychologists have not always appreciated the value of historical research. (In fact, one reviewer of my original outline for this book suggested that I leave out the chapter on historical research because she never teaches it anyway.) However, I have included this chapter for three reasons:

1. Educators and psychologists who do not know history cannot fully understand the present.

2. The mood within the historical community closely parallels the changes arising in educational and psychological researchers who are examining the implications of the emancipatory paradigm for their work.

3. Scholars who write about the lives of oppressed people emphasize the importance of an understanding of the historical, cultural, social, and economic conditions surrounding an event.

Tuchman (1994) makes the case that "adequate social science includes a theoretical use of historical information. Any social phenomenon must be understood in its historical context" (p. 306). Reinharz (1992) notes that historical research was especially important for feminists because it draws women out of obscurity and repairs the historical record in which women are largely absent.

Stanfield (1994) recognizes that little work has been published on how to develop an indigenous "ethnic" model for qualitative research. His suggestions for the creation of qualitative research methods indigenous to the experiences of African Americans and other people of color in the United States and elsewhere focused on the importance of a historical perspective. He identifies the following elements for an indigenous-ethnic model for research:

1. It should be based on *oral communication* because so many non-Western cultures within and outside industrial nation-states are oral-communication based.

2. It should be *grounded in holistic* (not fragmented or dichotomized) *notions of human beings* because many non-Westerners view the social, the emotional, and the spiritual as integral parts of a whole person linked to a physical environment.

3. The methodology should incorporate the use of *historical documents, participant observation, and oral history* to allow people of color to articulate holistic explanations about how they construct reality.

He argues that the historical perspective is necessary to develop a logic of inquiry that is grounded in the indigenous experiences of people of color.

Types of Historical and Narrative Research

Historical and narrative research can be topical, biographical, or autobiographical (Gluck, 1979, cited in Reinharz, 1992, p. 126). Topical research focuses on a specific event or phenomenon, such as the history of vocational choice or vocational guidance. Biographical research concerns the life story of an individual other than the narrator-interviewee. Autobiographical history is the life story of the narrator-interviewee.

Oral History and the Narrative Study of Lives

Oral history is an interdisciplinary development involving education, anthropology, history, folklore, biographical literature, psychology, sociology, and ethnography (Yow, 1994). Scholars who conduct oral history research are concerned with the making of meaning and power relationships in the interview situation. Oral history can include taped memoirs, typewritten transcripts, and a research method that involves in-depth interviewing. Different terms are used to describe oral history: *life history, self-report, personal narrative, life story, oral biography, memoir, testament, in-depth interview, recorded memoir, recorded narrative, taped memoirs,* and *life review.* Yow characterizes oral history as involving an interviewer who inspires narrators to begin the act of remembering, jogs their memories, and records and presents the narrators' words through recorded in-depth interviews.

In oral history, the researcher conducts in-depth interviews to determine how things got to be the way they are.[2] The focus is on the *past.* When the same method is used within a research study that is *present centered,* it is termed the *narrative study of lives.* Josselson (1993) describes the development of this approach as follows: "Listening to people talk in their own terms about what had been significant in their lives seemed to us far more valuable than studying preconceived psychometric scales or contrived experiments" (p. ix). She described a strong relationship between oral history and this present-centered use of in-depth interviews; therefore, I have chosen to include this approach in this chapter on historical research methods. The approach has been used by clinical psychologists to study pathological cases, the psychobiography of exemplary and ordinary people, and developmental experiences through the life span.

Sources of Data

To collect data, historical researchers do not go out and design experiments and test the effects of an independent variable on a dependent variable. Their data sources are already in existence and the events have already occurred. Therefore, their data sources include documents, artifacts, and oral histories. Historians do not conduct qualitative research only, because they can use quantitative data sources as well. For example, quantitative data from the census can be used to provide a general context for a period in history. A researcher might examine wages, literacy, education levels, and so on (Tuchman, 1994).

MacDonald (1995) provided a good example of the combination of qualitative and quantitative approaches in her study of southern teachers before and after the Civil War. To provide a general picture of teacher characteristics during this era, she used a data set of 10,000 teachers randomly sampled from the federal censuses for 1860, 1880, 1900, and 1910. (She notes that the data were gathered at the Harvard Graduate School of Education under the direction of the principal investigators Joel Perlmann and Bob Margo, and the sampling methods are described in an article by Perlmann and Margo, 1989, in *Historical Methods.*)

MacDonald's (1995) qualitative data came from sources such as diaries, letters, reminiscences, school reports from Black and non-Black schools, newspapers, and contemporary journal articles. This combination of methods allowed her to tell the teachers' stories within the broader social and economic fabric of schooling and society.

So, how do you do historical-narrative research? How do you find the sources of data mentioned here? Read on . . .

Steps in Conducting Historical-Narrative Research

In some ways, every research study starts as a historical research study because the act of conducting a literature review involves locating and synthesizing information that is already known about a topic. In this sense, historical research is a comfortable and familiar process. However, there are unique twists and turns when the focus of the research is specifically on the historical events and life stories, and these are not familiar territory for most people in education and psychology. The study of how to do historical research is termed *historiography,* and several good texts are available to approach this in general, as well as specific, contexts. Table 8.1 lists a number of historiographic texts that the serious scholar can consult.

Step 1: Define the Problem

Problems appropriate to historical research can be identified through many of the same steps that other research problems are identified. You can be perplexed by current practices or social problems and desire to have a historical understanding of how the conditions developed. For example, the issues of racial, ethnic, gender, or disability-based discrimination all have historical roots, whether your interest is in effective teaching or testing methods or in some other aspect of education and psychology. New facts can be discovered that

TABLE 8.1. Historiographic Texts

General Texts

Barzun, Jacques, & Graff, Henry F. (1992). *The modern researcher* (5th ed.). Boston: Houghton Mifflin.

Bloch, Marc. (1963). *The historian's craft.* New York: Knopf.

Breisach, Ernst. (1994). *Historiography: Ancient, medieval & modern.* Chicago: University of Chicago Press.

Burke, Peter. (1992). *New perspectives on historical writing.* University Park: Pennsylvania State University Press.

Carr, Edward H. (1986). *What is history?* (2nd ed.). London: Macmillan.

Kozicki, Henry. (1993). *Developments in modern historiography.* New York: St. Martin's.

Pok, Attila. (1992). *A selected bibliography of modern historiography.* New York: Greenwood.

Tosh, John. (1991). *The pursuit of history* (2nd ed.). New York: Longman.

Tuchman, Gaye. (1994). Historical social science: Methodologies, methods, and meanings. In N. K. Denzin & Y. S. Lincoln (Eds.), *Handbook of qualitative research* (pp. 306-323). Thousand Oaks, CA: Sage.

Feminist Historiography

Appleby, Joyce Oldham, Hunt, Lynn Avery, & Jacob, Margaret C. (1994). *Telling the truth about history.* New York: Norton.

Benhabib, Seyla. (1995). *Feminist contentions: A philosophical exchange.* New York: Routledge.

Melosh, Barbara. (1993). *Gender and American history since 1890.* London: Routledge.

Purvis, June. (1994). Doing feminist women's history: Researching the lives of women in the Suffragette Movement in Edwardian England. In M. Maynard & J. Purvis (Eds.), *Researching women's lives from a feminist perspective* (pp. 166-189). London: Taylor & Francis.

Scott, Joan Wallach. (1986). Gender: A useful category of historical analysis. *American Historical Review, 91*(5), 1053-1075.

Shapiro, Ann-Louise. (1994). *Feminist revision history.* New Brunswick, NJ: Rutgers University Press.

Walkowitz, J. (1992). *City of dreadful delight: Narratives of sexual danger in Late-Victorian London.* London: Virago.

Ethnic Historiography

Fabre, Genevieve, & O'Meally, Robert G. (1994). *History and memory in African American culture.* New York: Oxford University Press.

Hine, Darlene Clark. (Ed.). (1990). *Black women's history: Theory and practice* (Black women in United States history, Vols. 9-10). Brooklyn, NY: Carlson.

Judy, Ronald A. T. (1993). *(Dis)forming the American canon: African Arabic slave narratives and the vernacular.* Minneapolis: University of Minnesota Press.

White, Deborah Gray. (1987). Mining the forgotten: Manuscript resources for Black women's history. *Journal of American History, 74,* 237-242.

Oral History

Ritchie, Donald A. (1995). *Doing oral history.* New York: Twayne.

Yow, Valerie. (1994). *Recording oral history: A practical guide for social scientists.* Thousand Oaks, CA: Sage.

require a reexamination of old data or a reinterpretation of events using a different theoretical framework. Examples of historical-narrative research topics include the following:

1. *Topical historical research:* What were the forces that influenced the development of the field of vocational guidance and the notion of vocational choice such that individuals are prepared differentially based on class, gender, and ethnicity, while still maintaining the illusion of equal and free choice (Sherman, 1993)?

2. *Topical historical research:* What were the origins of the entrance of Black and White Southern women into the teaching profession before and after the Civil War (MacDonald, 1995)?

3. *Topical historical research:* How has race been constructed and reconstructed between the late 19th century and the 1940s, and what are the implications of that reconstruction for classroom teaching (Banks, 1995)?

4. *Narrative study of lives:* How do adolescent girls understand themselves and their relationships, and how do their understandings change and develop over time (Rogers, Brown, & Tappan, 1994)?

5. *Oral history:* What are the lives of lower-income women like, from birth through old age (Buss, 1985)?

6. *Autobiographical history:* How did a West Indian slave overcome psychological trauma, physical torture, and hardship; how did legal, economic, and social shackles affect her life; and how did she shape her environment to exercise some control over her future (Ferguson, 1993)?

7. *Biographical history:* What were the experiences of Margaret Wise Brown in teaching writing to children at Bank Street (Marcus, 1993)?

Journals as Sources of Research Problems. As with other types of research, you can often find a research problem by reviewing journals and focusing on the "additional research is needed" section of the articles. The following is a partial listing of journals that publish information that might be helpful for a scholar interested in pursuing the formulation of a research problem from a historical-narrative perspective:

American Historical Review
The Annals of the American Academy of Political and Social Science
Comparative Studies in Society and History
Gender & History
History of Education Quarterly
Journal of Interdisciplinary History
Journal of Negro Education
Journal of Southern History
The Narrative Study of Lives (annual book series published by Sage)
Oral History Review

Pedagogica Historica
Radical History Review
Signs: Journal of Women in Culture and Society

"Mucking About" in an Archive or Contacting Professional Organizations. Sometimes, historical researchers do not start with a specific problem in mind. A historian might hear about new opportunities to have access to archival materials (e.g., the Nixon White House tapes or records concerning the Nazi's activities during World War II) and decide that it would be interesting to explore what is in the materials. By reading materials in an archive, a researchable question may emerge. As mentioned in Chapter 2, professional associations can also provide valuable guidance in seeking a research topic. In the case of historical research, you should be aware of the American Historical Association and the Oral History Association.

Step 2: Conduct the Literature Review

You should conduct a review of the literature with two goals: First, you should do background reading to find out what has been published about your topic already. As you struggle to define your research topic, it is important to remember to set limits in terms of geographic region and the time period covered. Local studies and state studies are valid and important parts of historical research, and delimiting a study can be an important step in designing a study that is "do-able."

Second, review literature that is actually the historical data that you seek to analyze (e.g., diaries, letters, etc.) You need to know which preliminary sources (databases) will yield information of a historical nature on your topic to begin your search. You also need to distinguish between primary and secondary sources of information within a historical context.

In historical research, Purvis (1994) suggests the following distinction:

> Although the dividing line between a "primary" and a "secondary" source is somewhat arbitrary, the former is usually regarded as a text that came into being during the period of the past that is being researched while the latter is usually seen as a text that is produced much later than the events being studied, offering an interpretation and conversion of the primary data into an account that may be consulted by others. (p. 168)

Preliminary Sources. You should plan to conduct searches in the standard *databases* for education and psychology, such as ERIC and PsycINFO. In addition, you should search databases such as Historical Abstracts and American History and Life.

Bibliographic indexes can be particularly helpful for locating literature of a historical nature. Examples include the following:

Balay, Robert, & Sheehy, Eugene P. (1992). *Guide to reference books. Supplement to the tenth edition.* Chicago: American Library Association.

Bibliographic index. A cumulative bibliography of bibliographies. (1938-1994). New York: H. W. Wilson.

Norton, Mary Beth, & Gerardi, Pamela (Eds.). (1995). *The American Historical Association's guide to historical literature* (3rd ed.). New York: Oxford University Press.

Sheehy, Eugene P. (1986). *Guide to reference books* (10th ed.). Chicago: American Library Association.

Walford, Albert John, Mullay, Marilyn, & Schlicke, Priscilla. (1993). *Walford's guide to reference material.* London: Library Association Publishing.

Bibliographic services are also available through the American Historical Association (AHA) in Washington, D.C., and the Association for the Bibliography of History in Alexandria, Virginia. The AHA has been providing bibliographic services for its membership by reviewing the monographic literature in the American Historical Review, using a list of books the AHA receives, and reviewing other recently published articles and writings on American history (McCrank et al., 1989).

If you are specifically interested in biography, the *Biography Index* could be useful. This is a reference that was previously published quarterly and contained biographical material that appeared in journals and books. However, it is currently available on-line and has citations from August 1981 to the present. It is published by W. H. Wilson Company in New York. The *Dictionary of American Biography* (American Council of Learned Societies, 1927-1994) consists of 20 volumes of biographies of famous Americans. Harvard University Press published *Notable American Women* (Sicherman & Green, 1980), which contains the biographies of 163 20th-century women in diverse fields.

Step 3: Identify Sources of Historical Facts

Assuming that you have formulated your research questions and done the background reading about your problem, you are now ready to move on to the identification of the primary historical data themselves. As you recall, these include artifacts and documents and oral histories.

Documents and Artifacts. Documents and artifacts can include personal and institutional documents as well as physical objects, such as textbooks, clothes, tools, desks, toys, and weapons, from that historical period. The personal and institutional documents include items such as personal and business correspondence, financial statements, photographs, diaries, manuscript drafts, institutional artifacts, and other unpublished materials. Published archival records include things such as official proceedings of an organization, vital statistics, and official institutional histories (Stanfield, 1993b). Published information also includes censuses, official reports, congressional records, and newspapers. Unpublished archival materials can be found in households, corporations, and private academic and independent research organizations and associations. Public settings include government agencies and repositories, public libraries, public academic institutions, and independent research universities.

The biases in archival materials have been pointed out by a number of historical scholars (Anderson, 1993; Reinharz, 1992; Stanfield, 1993b). Stanfield noted that history written based on this elite bias also reflects the bias of the affluent. Even history written about ordinary people was written from the archives of the affluent class, based on the assumption that ordinary people rarely if ever kept records. However, Blassingame (1972, cited in Stanfield, 1993b) identified voluminous slave autobiographies that have been overlooked (the existence of which had been ignored) by slavery historians for years. Ordinary people do keep records such as personal letters, photo albums, diaries, church records, household bills, and neighborhood newspapers.

Many of the materials related to race and ethnicity and gender are found in private households and libraries because poor people and people of color do not often take their records to local university archives, and the university archives are more interested in famous people's records. A space problem forces archives to be selective, and they generally prefer to house the documents of famous people, not ordinary people (Stanfield, 1993b).

Thus, Stanfield (1993b) recommends seeking out private sources of historical documents when researching the lives of "ordinary people." And when using official archives, keep an open mind. Recognize that history and biography are value-laden activities. Know the literature well to compare what historians have written and what is actually in the archives. Identify gaps and presentations of complex individuals and issues in unidimensional ways. Often, actual review of archival materials results in quite different pictures of individuals and events than is presented in extant historical writings.

Finding Information in Archives. University libraries are a good source of information in that they typically contain collections of rare books, letters, periodicals, personal papers, and so forth. State and local libraries and archives are also accessible for historical research. Local historical societies, state historical societies, and museums can provide a great deal of information.

A number of annotated lists of archives can be helpful in identifying the location of archived information.

The National Historical Publications and Records Commission publishes a *Directory of Archives and Manuscript Repositories in the United States* (1988) that lists the holdings of thousands of repositories in the United States.

A listing of federal documents and libraries can be found in the *National Inventory of Documentary Sources in the United States* (1988).

The Library of Congress compiles the *National Union Catalog,* a register of all books published since 1454 that are held in more than 1,100 North American libraries. Because the *National Union Catalog* is published in book form, many libraries have it in their collections. The *National Union Catalog* is also available on-line, and is called the On-Line Computer Library Center (OCLC). They have other union catalogs that record the location of books in foreign languages, such as Slavic, Hebrew, Japanese, and Chinese.

The Library of Congress also offers assistance in locating source materials in libraries in the United States and throughout the world. It publishes, for sale, bibliographies, guides, and selected lists of materials on a variety of subjects. Through the Library of Congress's National Library Services for the Blind and Physically Handicapped and a network of cooperating regional libraries, the Library of Congress can supply books and magazines recorded on disk or tape with playback equipment at no cost. About 2,500 titles are selected each year for recording or Brailling. The Library of Congress also has an on-line catalog on the World Wide Web that can be accessed at the following address: http://rs7tr0.loc.gov//

The National Endowment for the Humanities supported the development of a home page (H-Net) that provides access to a consortium of discussion list areas of historical research. It can be accessed at this address: http://h-net2.msu.edu/

Of course, you can go directly to the National Archives, the branch of the U.S. government that preserves and makes available for reference and research the permanently valuable records of the U.S. government. Besides well-known documents such as the Declaration of Independence and the Constitution, the National Archives includes 3.2 billion textual documents, 1.6 million cartographic items, 5.2 million still photographs, 9.7 million aerial photographs, 110,000 reels of motion picture film, and 173,000 video and sound recordings—all created by federal government agencies since the creation of the nation. The National Archives and Records Administration operates 14 records centers, 12 regional archives, and 8 presidential libraries in 17 states. (The National Archives opened a center in College Park, Maryland, that provides researchers with access to records through state-of-the-art technology.)

In her study of Black and White teachers before and after the Civil War, MacDonald (1995) used resources from the National Archives such as these:

First Semi-Annual Report of the Superintendent of Schools of the Freedmen's Bureau, January 1, 1866, Bureau of Refugees, Freedmen, and Abandoned Lands (BRFAL), Record Group 105. Washington, DC: National Archives. (On microfilm)

Letter to John Alvord in the *Third Semi-Annual Report of the Superintendent of Schools,* January 1, 1867, BRFAL, Record Group 105. Washington, DC: National Archives. (On microfilm)

Through these materials, she was able to establish the mood of the Southerner elite about who should teach the "Negro" children.

Another national resource is the National Museum of American History at the Smithsonian Institution. The museum provides scholars with access to a collection of rare books relating to science and technology in its Dibner Library and publications such as the international quarterly of the Society for the History of Technology (*Technology and Culture*).

The Genealogical Library of the Daughters of the American Revolution contains over 65,000 books and pamphlets and more than 30,000 manuscripts, much of it available in no other library and almost all of it out of print. The types of material available here are compiled genealogies; state, county, and local histories; published rosters of Revolutionary War soldiers and patriots; abstracts of some Revolutionary War pension files; published vital records; cemetery inscriptions of various county records (e.g., marriages, etc.); published archives of some of the 13 original states; federal census schedules (1850-1880, all states) and federal mortality schedules (a few states); and genealogical periodicals. Regretfully, finances do not permit staff members to do research in person or by mail. Another important source for genealogical information is contained in the Mormon's database in Salt Lake City, Utah.[3]

Copies of documents produced by other government agencies can be obtained by contacting the agency directly through the Freedom of Information Act. Tuchman (1994) suggests calling the agency that has the document and inquiring about the specifics for a document request to that agency under the Freedom of Information Act, because (as you might expect) each agency has some specific requirements. You will save time by finding out exactly what is needed by that agency, and each agency does have an office that handles such requests.

Accessing Historical Materials. Historical materials can be accessed in a variety of formats. Some can be obtained on CD-ROM, others on microfiche, and still others need to be copied in print form. Some cannot be copied, and so you would need to take notes on the contents of those documents. It is important to establish what is available and possible with your source of the information. Stanfield (1993b) emphasized the importance of knowing the legalities of literary heir rights. Even in documents found in private households, the researcher should develop a contractual agreement to protect the rights of access to and use of the materials. In institutions, the archivist usually supplies a contract on behalf of the literary heirs. Typically, access is easier if the researcher can demonstrate an understanding of the literature related to the problem under investigation. Citations can be made in letters to the heirs or archivists. Once a letter has been written, the researcher should follow up with a phone call and make an appointment to discuss the written contract regarding rights of access and use.

Using Archives. In an archive, typically, a register of materials is available that lists what is in the archive. Stanfield (1993b) recommends a careful review of this register, accompanied by an examination of sample files to get a better feel for the materials included. When historians use archives, they record bin, drawer, and call numbers, as well as date and publisher (Tuchman, 1994). It is important to follow the style of historians in recording your sources of information in case you have to return to the source. You will find it easier to reexamine the evidence if you have included the bin, drawer, and call numbers.[4]

Oral Histories and Narrative Studies of Lives. Yow (1994) recognizes that oral history can provide answers to questions that are not available through other means. For example, oral history permits the questioning of witnesses, and thus, description and interpretation comes from a witness of the event rather than through the researcher's efforts. This is not meant to imply that the researcher does not influence the results or that oral history speaks for itself in its entirety. The researcher influences the results of oral history studies by determining which questions to ask and by selection and editing decisions in reporting results.

However, oral history can provide greater insights into the reasons for actions than might otherwise be recorded without an understanding of the motivation for the action. In addition, oral history provides access to information that is not written down (either because of the nature of the events themselves or because of the characteristics of the people involved). People might be more inclined to discuss disagreements and controversies than to create a written record of such events. Life histories in the past have tended to represent only the well-to-do, but oral history makes it possible to record life histories for all socioeconomic levels of the population. Through in-depth interviewing, it is possible to reveal informal, unwritten rules. Reinharz (1992) notes that oral history is especially important for powerless groups because their information is less likely to be included in written records.

Both Yow (1994) and Reinharz (1992) caution researchers about the limitations of oral history. The tendency in oral history is to focus on the individual, personal experience and less on the institutional, national, or international trends that were operating during a person's lifetime. Although it is important to use oral history to break silences, readers must also be aware of sociopolitical problems that are broader than an individual's experience. A second limitation is that oral histories are done with people who *survive*. Therefore, even though oral histories are typically done with older, relatively powerless people, they are not done with the *most* vulnerable—those who did not survive or who are too weak or discouraged to tell their stories. Therefore, in conducting and reading oral histories, the reader should ask how the passage of time and self-selectivity has affected the sample of narrators available.

To overcome the possible bias of obtaining statements only from the most confident and articulate people, Yow (1994) recommends this:

> Bear with the inarticulate: Try to get them to talk when you know that they have been directly involved in the event you are studying. In your own sample, you will know the individuals you must seek out, no matter how laconic they may be. But if they refuse to talk except in monosyllables and your good interviewing techniques are of no avail, do not be discouraged. Knowing that you have done your best to interview this key witness, turn to the next narrator and try to get the information from other witnesses and written records. (p. 48)

Ritchie (1995) identifies another caution associated with doing oral history work that might be of particular interest to psychologists. He raised the question, "Isn't oral history limited by the fallibility of human memory?" (p. 11). He suggests that oral history re-searchers keep in mind that people tend to remember events that had importance for them personally and to forget those activities that were more mundane or routine. The human memory does not work like a camera; rather, memory is selective and constructed by the person. Thus, it should not be surprising that no two individuals will give the exact same account of an event, especially when that event occurred many years in the past.

Assuming that you have gone through the previously outlined steps of identifying a topic and reading everything that has been published on that topic, how do you access data for an oral history study? Well, of course, you need people to interview and a list of topics (an interview guide) to use to guide the conversation. Yow (1994) suggests that you start with names from the published and unpublished documents that you have reviewed. Find out addresses for these individuals through their university affiliations or directory assistance if you have geographic locations for the people. Send a letter to the individuals and explain the general nature of your project. Ask about their willingness to talk with you further. Include your phone number in case they have any questions, but follow up with a phone call to determine their willingness to cooperate with you. These first contacts should not be to obtain substantive data about your topic; rather, they are informal interviews to determine the person's willingness to participate and to get ideas for additional actions on your part. Yow suggests asking questions such as these:

- If you were writing this study what would you include?
- Who would you recommend that I interview?
- If you were writing this history, what would you consider important?
- Who was present at the event?
- Who was influential in making this event happen?
- Who was affected by this?

The sampling techniques commonly used in oral histories are the same as those for most qualitative research studies: snowball sampling, purposive sampling, universal sam-pling, and saturation. These strategies are discussed in detail in Chapter 10. I have included one excerpt from an oral history project to give you the flavor of sampling within the context of this approach to research. The researchers conducted a study of child workers in a mill village before World War I:

> For the mill village project, my co-researchers and I visited the ministers of the two churches and asked who the oldest members were. We wrote to these members. In addition, we put an advertisement in the local newspaper but got a poor response; nevertheless, other researchers have had better luck with this method. . . . I sought out every person mentioned to me as a worker in the mill early in the century. . . . At that point, the narrators were in their 70s and 80s, and I contacted all living persons who had been part of that history and still resided in that town. The number was so small that it was feasible to contact all

survivors. In fact, the narrators finally numbered 30 men and women who were able and willing to talk to us. (Yow, 1994, p. 45-48)

A tentative list of narrators can then be drawn up and a letter prepared to introduce yourself and your study to those people you desire to interview. Yow says that the initial contact is almost always better done through a letter, with a follow-up phone call. She does recognize that some people might distrust anything in print or resist such an invitation. In such circumstances, it would be to your advantage to identify someone they trust to explain the project to them as a first method of contact. Keeping index cards with each person's name, address, and so on as well as his or her response to your contacts will be useful.

You should prioritize the names on your list for interviewing. Ritchie (1995) suggests starting with the oldest and most significant individuals first. Begin with a few well-conducted, in-depth interviews. Once you have fully processed them, interview younger or secondary individuals.

According to the *Oral History Evaluation Guidelines* (Oral History Association, 1992), interviewees must be informed of the purpose, procedures, and potential use of the oral history project, and then, they should be asked to sign a legal release permitting use of the data collected within the specified conditions. A sample legal release form can be found in Ritchie's (1995) *Doing Oral History*. The interviewee maintains the right to refuse to discuss certain subjects, to seal portions of the interview, or to choose to remain anonymous. The interviewee should also be made aware of any arrangements that the researcher has made to deposit the interviews in a repository such as an archive or library for use by other researchers. The responsibility for making data available through preservation in archives in historical research contrasts with the situation in education and psychology in which the data are more typically viewed as belonging to the individual researcher. Because of the importance of conducting research in an ethical manner, researchers interested in using the oral history approach should become familiar with the full text of the *Oral History Evaluation Guidelines* and *Oral History and the Law* (Neuenschwander, 1993).[5]

The actual process of conducting the interview is roughly parallel to that outlined in Chapter 5 on survey research, so I will not repeat that here.

Step 4: Synthesize and Evaluate Historical Data

General Historical Documents. Once you have identified a list of references that you think might be relevant to your research problem, Tuchman (1994) suggests that you try to determine if the scholarship meets acceptable standards. One way to determine the acceptability of a source is to check how frequently that source is cited. This can be done by using a citation index such as the *Social Science Citation Index* or the *Arts and the Humanities Citation Index.*

In theory, the more times your source is cited, the greater contribution that source has made to the literature. However, Tuchman notes two caveats to this test: First, some sources may be frequently cited because other authors believe they are wrong and thus cite them as a classic example of a common misinterpretation. Second, few citations may result from a highly specialized topic. Thus, Tuchman suggests asking yourself four questions to establish a source's utility for you:

1. Why is the author making this argument?
2. Do other scholars dispute this argument?
3. Why were these particular materials chosen but not others?
4. Do the author's questions suggest other issues relevant to the project at hand?

To answer these questions, Tuchman suggests that you read book reviews of the work in scholarly journals of the time. You can use the *Social Science Citation Index* to locate reviews. Purvis (1994) warns that even book reviewers who wrote at the time of the book's publication can have biases that need to be explored before accepting their word as a final assessment of a document's worth.

Historical Materials in General. Stanfield (1993b) raises the issues of validity and reliability in his discussion of the quality of historical data. He defined validity in this context as the adequacy of the collected data for making theoretical statements that are isomorphic with empirical reality. In other words, what are the relationships between constructs that can be stated and supported by empirical evidence? Reliability asks, Can this be replicated under similar empirical conditions? Researchers need to be mindful of the ways in which a social setting can potentially limit what or who he or she sees. Stanfield depicts internal validity problems in the form of dilemmas for researchers:

1. The single-case dilemma arises when one personal letter or diary entry suggests an event but no additional evidence can be found to corroborate that event.
2. The historical-fame dilemma arises when a person becomes aware at some point of his or her historical fame and becomes more guarded in the content of printed documents produced.
3. A dilemma arises over destroyed and forged documents. What was destroyed? Why?
4. Researchers can be misled into overgeneralizing characteristics evidenced at one point in life, without recognizing that people change as they get older.

External validity questions can be resolved by checking with other sources. Triangulation can be used to check with other sources, or consistency can be sought within a source.

Tuchman (1994) also suggests that the researcher ask questions of materials that have been archived:

■ Who saved the materials and why?
■ Who sorted them and how?

■ What was the nature of the organizational system for filing?

Notes Specific to Personal Documents. Diaries, journals, and letters are examples of personal documents often used in historical research. Historical researchers caution that these must be read and interpreted in light of the conditions of the day. Tuchman (1994) suggests that researchers interrogate personal documents with such questions as the following:

■ What could be written?
■ How could it be expressed?
■ Who would be reading it at the time?
■ What were the characteristics of the writer?
■ How should you view what was written in terms of its social location?

Tuchman indicates that it was common practice for teachers to read students' journals, thus influencing what students would be willing to write and how they would write it.

Purvis (1994) identifies a similar source of bias in letters written by women in prison during the Suffragette Movement. The prisoners were encouraged to write letters so that they could maintain connections with respectable friends. All the letters were read by prison authorities and censored if they found any of the material objectionable. Consequently, one might be a bit skeptical when the women's censored letters said that all was well, especially when those that were smuggled out of prison painted a very different picture. In addition, a number of women purposely wrote their letters with the intention of getting them published on the outside. The leaders of the movement tended to write such letters, including praise for their supporters and suggesting further direction for political activities.

Oral History Issues. Oral histories are sometimes criticized because they represent retrospective evidence; that is, the witness is recalling events that happened a long time ago. To determine the worth of evidence from oral history, Yow (1994) suggests bearing in mind research about how memory functions:

> Beginning in their 40s and continuing through the rest of their lives, people reminisce. Memories of childhood, adolescence and early adulthood may be more easily recalled than those from middle and late years. If the event or situation was significant to the individual, it will likely be remembered in some detail, especially its associated feelings. However, the interpretation may reflect current circumstances and needs. (p. 21)

Recognizing the faults of human memory, researchers should be concerned with two aspects of the data: consistency in the testimony (reliability) and accuracy (validity) in relating factual information. The researcher can check out inconsistencies within the testimony by asking for clarification from the narrator. Accuracy can be checked by consulting other sources and comparing accounts.

The quality of the evidence provided by a witness can be determined by asking the following questions:

- What motive did the witness have for saying this?
- For whom was the interview transcript intended?
- How informed was this witness about the event?
- What prior assumptions did the witness bring to the observation?
- What kind of details were omitted?

The second point is raised within the context of oral history but applies to any type of historical writing. Researchers debate the amount of involvement that the interviewer should have in the interview process and that the writer should have in presenting the results. Some interviewers use only very open-ended probes such as "Tell me about your childhood," in an effort to avoid biasing the responses of the narrator. Others use a more direct approach, inquiring specifically about areas that might not be brought up otherwise. In writing oral histories, some authors use only the words of the narrators; others include their own questions and probes as part of the text, and still others add contextual and interpretive information as bridges between narrator comments. A variety of styles can be used. Reinharz (1992) comments as follows:

> In my view, feminist oral historians need not silence themselves to let other women be heard. The refusal to analyze transcripts does not produce a kind of purity in which women speak for themselves in an unmediated way. After all, the oral historian already had a role in producing the oral history and preparing it for publication. Since any involvement at all by the oral historian is a de facto interpretation, feminist researchers should be interested in providing an analysis so that the reader has a sense of the perspective used. (pp. 137-138)

Special Notes on Biographical Research

Biographies are life histories that contain more than a listing of chronological events in a person's life and more than just anecdotal stories about that person. Biographies should help the reader understand the way the individual sees (or saw) herself or himself—"the inner struggles and motivation, the way psychological makeup influenced the subject's interpersonal relationships, the interpretation the subject gave to life's events" (Yow, 1994, p. 167).

Biographies generally attempt to unite an individual story with the tenor of the times in which a person lived. Tuchman's (1978) *A Distant Mirror* provides one example in which the history of the 14th century in Europe is told largely through the biography of a single individual, Enguerrand de Coucy VII. Tuchman explains her rationale for choosing this individual:

> The fifty years that followed the Black Death of 1348-50 are the core of what seems to me a coherent historical period extending approximately from 1300 to 1450 plus a few years. To narrow the focus to a manageable area, I have chosen a particular person's life as the vehicle of my narrative. . . . The person in question is not a king or queen, because everything about such persons is *ipso facto* exceptional, and. . . . not a commoner, because commoners' lives in most cases did not take the wide range that I wanted . . . nor a woman, because any medieval woman whose life was adequately documented would be atypical. (p. *xvi*)

Tuchman (1978) provides insights into the difficulty of doing biographical research in her discussion of contradictions with regard to dates, numbers, and hard facts. During the Middle Ages, there was no standard calendar, thus confusing not only contemporary writers but also the people who lived during that time. Writers of the time tended to exaggerate the numbers of people in armies, battles, plagues, and so forth because they viewed the use of numbers as a literary device with which they could amaze their readers. Discrepancies of supposed facts were the result of oral transmission of information or the misreading of available documents. Tuchman views contradictions as part of life and thus not merely a matter of conflicting evidence. She also recognizes that historians' prejudices and points of view influence the selection of materials reported in historical documents.

Some biographies are based on oral histories. When this is the case, it is important to get an agreement with the person as to the nature, duration, and control of the work. Writing a biography often involves extensive interviewing that could stretch over years. Establish a tentative work schedule that indicates the time and place and the nature of questions. Get a written contract with the individual that specifies access to other information and editorial rights to the final manuscript. In addition, it is important to point out that you are not going to include only positive things about the person. A biography that creates a "plaster saint" of an individual lacks credibility. It is important to be sensitive to the individual's feelings and to family members. When in doubt about the effect of including controversial information, seek advice from a trusted informant.

Yow (1994) suggests starting the interview process with some general questions:

- What are the most important events in your life?
- Which persons were significant in your life?
- Who knew you well? Shared your joys and sorrows?
- Are there letters, photographs, or newspaper clippings that would be useful?

Biographers for women should be aware of specific challenges presented because of the social influences of gender in a historical context. In *Notable American Women*

(Sicherman & Green, 1980), a historical text of women's biographies noted earlier in this chapter, the authors stated that they were unable to include all the background information about each woman that they wanted. Even information about birth dates was often unattainable. Reinharz (1994) explores a number of reasons for this difficulty:

1. Women's lives were not viewed as significant; therefore, careful records were not kept.

2. Women were less likely to hold public offices; therefore, information about their lives would be less likely to be included in public records.

3. Many famous women, such as Elizabeth Cady Stanton and Alice Fletcher, have destroyed their primary documents.

4. Name changing is common for women, primarily due to marriage, but also many women used pseudonyms to disguise their gender for their public writing.

Despite these challenges, Reinharz suggests that writing feminist biographies is a rewarding experience for the writer and for readers, because it represents one way to add to our knowledge of the past and our understanding of the present.

▶ Questions for Critically Analyzing Historical-Narrative Research

Yow (1994) provides a comprehensive list of questions for evaluating oral history research studies. Many of her questions parallel those found in earlier chapters concerning clarity of purpose of the study and so on. Consequently, the questions presented here focus on the historical aspect of the study rather than on the introduction, literature review, interview process, or ethics with the narrator (that last topic is discussed in Chapter 10). Although the following list is a partial adaptation of Yow's criteria, readers interested in conducting oral history studies are referred to Yow's complete list of criteria in *Recording Oral History.* Readers should also be aware of the American Historical Association's *Statement on Standards of Professional Conduct* (1992).

The following questions can be used to assist you in critically evaluating historical-narrative research:

1. To what extent does the study add fresh information, fill gaps in the existing record, and/or provide fresh insights and perspectives?

2. To what extent is the information reliable and valid?

3. Is it eyewitness or hearsay evidence?

4. How well and in what manner does it meet internal and external tests of corroboration and explication of contradictions?

5. What is the relationship between information obtained from primary sources (e.g., interviews, letters, diaries, etc.) and existing documentation and historiography?

6. Are the scope, volume, and representativeness of the data used appropriate and sufficient to the purpose? If interviews were used, is there enough testimony to validate the evidence without passing the point of diminishing returns?

▶ For Oral History-Narrative Studies[6]

7. In what ways did the interviewing conditions contribute to or distract from the quality of the data? For example, was proper concern given to the narrator's health, memory, mental alertness, ability to communicate, and so on. How were disruptions, interruptions, equipment problems, and extraneous participants handled?

8. Did the interviewer do the following?

   a. Thoroughly explore pertinent lines of thought.

   b. Make an effort to identify sources of information.

   c. Employ critical challenges when needed.

   d. Allow biases to interfere with or influence the responses of the interviewee.

■ Questions and Activities for Discussion and Application

1. Brainstorm ideas for historical-narrative research. Choose one idea and briefly explain how you could use each of the types of historical research to investigate that topic:

   a. Topical

   b. Biographical

   c. Autobiographical

   d. Oral history

   e. Narrative study of lives

   Which of these strategies do you think would be most appropriate for your research topic? Why?

2. Through a search of the literature, identify one research study for each type of historical-narrative research strategy listed in Question 1. Explain your basis for categorizing each study. For each study do the following:

    a. Identify the research problem.

    b. Identify the data collection methods that were used.

    c. Describe the organizing framework for the findings.

    d. Summarize the main findings.

    e. Use the questions for critical analysis at the end of this chapter to critically analyze each study.

3. Choose one topic for a historical-narrative research study. Conduct a literature review to identify at least three secondary sources that discuss your topic. Formulate a researchable historical-narrative question for your topic based on your literature review. Identify sources that you would search for primary data on that topic.

4. Choose a document from a federal agency that you would like to read related to a historical or current issue. Contact the agency and determine its procedures for obtaining the document through the Freedom of Information Act. Follow through on your request.

5. Role-play the following scenarios:

    a. You want to conduct an oral history project on a specific topic. Role-play your introductory interview with a prospective narrator.

    b. You want to conduct a biographical study. Role-play your interaction with that person—assuming that he or she is still alive. How would you convince him or her that you are the right person to write a biography and that his or her biography is worth telling (should that person not think so)?

    c. You come across one piece of information in a letter suggesting that an important person you are researching stole votes to get passage of a crucial piece of legislation. You cannot find any other written record to corroborate the letter. Role-play an interaction with a trusted confidant, discussing your appropriate action in this situation.

Notes

1. For further reading in cultural history, see Chartier (1988).

2. This is not meant to imply that historians rely only on oral data. They avail themselves of information from other sources as well.

3. Contact the Historical Department, Church of Jesus Christ of the Latter-Day Saints, 50 East North Temple, Salt Lake City, UT 84150.

4. Historians tend to use *The Chicago Manual of Style* (University of Chicago Press, 1993) rather than the American Psychological Association's style (1994) that is widely used in education and psychology.

5. Both of these documents are available from the Oral History Association, P.O. Box 3968, Albuquerque, NM 87290-3968. For those who are interested in conducting oral history as a classroom project, the Oral History Association has a guide for teachers who want to use oral history as a teaching tool with their students (Lanham & Mehaffy, 1988).

6. The reader is referred to the *Oral History Evaluation Guidelines* (Oral History Association, 1992) for a more comprehensive listing.

In This Chapter

■ *Evaluation is defined and distinguished from research in terms of purpose, method, and use.*

■ *The history of evaluation and current theoretical models are explained, including objectives-based evaluation, discrepancy evaluation, the CIPP model, responsive evaluation, theory-based evaluation, participatory evaluation, developmental evaluation, and empowerment evaluation.*

■ *Steps for planning an evaluation are described, including a description of what is to be evaluated, the purpose of the evaluation, the stakeholders in the evaluation, constraints affecting the evaluation, the evaluation questions, selection of an evaluation model, data collection specification, analysis and interpretation strategies, utilization, management of the evaluation, and meta-evaluation plans.*

■ *Questions to guide critical analysis of evaluation studies are provided, with special reference to The Program Evaluation Standards: How to Assess Evaluations of Educational Programs (Joint Committee on Standards for Educational Evaluation, 1994).*

9

Evaluation

In response to the overwhelming problem of alcohol and other drug abuse, and the disproportionate number of alcohol-related illnesses and fatalities incurred by young people of color, the University of New Mexico School of Medicine implemented a primary prevention, empowering education program for youths, in partnership with schools and communities throughout New Mexico. Started in 1982, the Alcohol Substance Abuse Prevention (ASAP) Program, alternatively called the Adolescent Social Action Program, was created to help youths address their risky environments.

(Wallerstein & Martinez, 1994, p. 131)

Evaluation specialists were called in to determine the effectiveness of the ASAP program mentioned above. A summary of this study is presented in Sample Study 9.1.

Defining Evaluation

Evaluators have not been immune to the generally contentious spirit prevailing in the research community. This is partially because evaluations are typically conducted on programs designed to "help" oppressed and troubled people. The direct relationship between the evaluation of social and educational programs and access to resources sets the

SAMPLE STUDY 9.1 *Summary of an Evaluation Study*

Evaluation problem: A high rate of alcohol and other drug abuse resulted in a disproportionate number of alcohol-related illnesses and fatalities incurred by young
people of color in New Mexico. A substance abuse prevention program was
initiated to address this problem, but the program staff did not know how effective
the program was.

Evaluation questions: What were the changes in the youths' abilities to engage in
dialogue? How did the youths change in their critical thinking ability to perceive
the social nature of the problems, their personal links to society, and their level
of action to promote changes?

Method: An experimental design was used that included random assignment of a
volunteer pool of students with a pretest, posttest, and 8-month follow-up.
Qualitative methods were used to collect data from two groups participating in
the Alcohol Substance Abuse Prevention (ASAP) program.

Setting: Two high school sites were used: a large semiurban high school with
1,700 students, 70% Hispanic, and a smaller rural reservation school with 450
students.

Treatment: ASAP brought middle and high school students from high-risk,
predominantly minority communities into a university hospital and a county
detention center to interview patients and jail residents who had experienced
consequences of drug-, tobacco-, and alcohol-related abuse, interpersonal
violence, and unprotected sexuality. Over a 6-week period, facilitators led
discussions with the students about how the patient and jail resident stories
related to the students' own lives.

Data collection: Data were collected by means of pre- and postinterviews,
participant observation of all hospital and jail sessions, and supplementary
interviews with school personnel and the comparison students.

Results: In support of Freire's (1971) dialogical theory, the data revealed that dialogue
was a way to establish connections, disclose personal feelings, and adopt a
caring stance, a precursor to social responsibility. The youths experienced
changes on emotional, critical thinking, and action levels.

Discussion: "Participatory dialogue from the program started the three-stage process
of self-identity change. . . . In the first stage, youth developed an action orientation of caring about the problem, about their own actions, and about each other.
In the second stage, youth began to act for individual changes, expressing an
ability to help family and friends. In the third stage, youth reached an understanding of social responsibility, and the possibility for social actions" (Wallerstein & Martinez, 1994, p. 135).

SOURCE: Based on Wallerstein and Martinez (1994).

stage for conflict. Ernie House (1993) captures this spirit in his description of the evolution of evaluation:

> Gradually, evaluators recognized that there were different interests to be served in an evaluation and that some of these interests might conflict with one another. The result was pluralist conceptions of evaluation in which multiple methods, measures, criteria, perspectives, audiences, and interests were recognized. Conceptually, evaluation moved from monolithic to pluralist conceptions, reflecting the pluralism that had emerged in the larger society. How to synthesize, resolve, and adjudicate all these multiple multiples remains a formidable question, as indeed it does for the larger society. Evaluation, which was invented to solve social problems, was ultimately afflicted with many of the problems it was meant to solve. (p. 11)

Given the tone of House's words, it should come as no surprise that even the definition of evaluation has been contested. Although many definitions of evaluation have been proposed, one that seems to persist over time is this:

> Evaluation is the systematic investigation of the merit or worth of an object (program) for the purpose of reducing uncertainty in decision making.

Alternative definitions tend to emphasize different aspects of the evaluation process. For example, Hadley and Mitchell (1995) define evaluation as "applied research carried out to make or support decisions regarding one or more service programs" (p. 48). Shadish (1994) calls for an expansion of the definition in terms of the purposes for which evaluations are done. His definition of evaluation included the "use of feasible practices to construct knowledge of the value of the evaluand[1] that can be used to ameliorate the problems to which the evaluand is relevant" (p. 352). And Fetterman (1995) writes that the definition of evaluation should include the idea of program improvement and emancipatory facets, such as illumination and liberation.

Even the part of the definition that refers to the purpose of the evaluation has been discussed and criticized. Sometimes, evaluations are done, but no big decisions are made based on the results. Patton (1986) notes that evaluations can be used to reduce uncertainty about decisions that have to be made but that many other factors influence program decisions, such as availability of resources and the political climate.

At any rate, these definitions contain some jargon from the evaluation community that requires explanation for you to really understand what evaluation is and how it is different from research. There is much overlap between the world of research and evaluation, yet evaluation occupies some unique territory (Mertens, 1995). Some terms with special meanings in evaluation are defined in the box labeled "Definition of Terms in Evaluation Parlance." A more comprehensive listing of terms and their meanings can be found in Scriven's (1991) *Evaluation Thesaurus* (4th ed.).

Evaluations can be conducted on social and educational policies, programs, products, or personnel. For purposes of this chapter, I focus on the evaluation of social and educational

■ DEFINITION OF TERMS IN EVALUATION PARLANCE

When evaluators talk about the *evaluand* or object of the evaluation, they are talking about what it is that will be evaluated. This can include a social or educational program, a product, a policy, or personnel. Examples of the kinds of programs that are evaluated include enrichment programs for deaf, gifted adolescents; drug and alcohol abuse programs for the homeless; and management programs for high-level radioactive waste (Mertens, 1994).

Merit refers to the excellence of an object as assessed by its intrinsic qualities or performance; *worth* refers to the value of an object in relation to a purpose. So merit might be assessed by asking, How well does your program perform? And worth might be assessed by asking, Is what your program does important? For example, a university might establish an excellent program in physics, and it might have data that indicates that students who complete the program are very knowledgeable about physics. This program would have merit. However, if the university decides that it is not in line with its mission to produce competent physicists, the program would not have worth. In other words, the program may do what it does very well (merit), but what it does is not considered important to that organization at this time (worth).

Formative evaluations are conducted primarily for the purposes of program improvement. Typically, formative evaluations are conducted during the development and implementation of the program and are reported to in-house staff who can use the information to improve the program. A *summative evaluation* is an evaluation to make decisions about the continuation, revision, elimination, or merger of a program. Typically, it is done on a program that has stabilized and is often reported to an external agency.

Internal evaluators work within the organization that operates the program. *External evaluators are* "experts" brought in from outside the organization for the express purpose of conducting or assisting with the evaluation. ■

programs. References for individuals interested in personnel evaluation are provided in Table 9.1

Greene (1994) writes about the commonalities that demarcate evaluation contexts and distinguish program evaluation from other forms of social inquiry (such as research). She argues, based on the writings of Patton (1987), Cronbach and associates (1980), and Weiss (1987), that what distinguishes evaluation from other forms of social inquiry is its political inherency; that is, in evaluation, politics and science are inherently intertwined. Evaluations are conducted on the merit and worth of programs in the public domain, which are themselves responses to prioritized individual and community needs that resulted from political decisions. Thus, program evaluation "is integrally intertwined with political decision making about societal priorities, resource allocation, and power" (Greene, 1994, p. 531).

In addition to conducting inquiry about a politically defined evaluand, the evaluators work within a political context in that they must respond to the concerns and interests of selected members of the setting being evaluated (often termed the *stakeholders*). These include the program funders, the administrators, staff members, and recipients of the

Books	Journals
TABLE 9.1 References for Personnel Evaluation	
Howard, Ann. (Ed.). (1995). *The changing nature of work.* San Francisco, CA: Jossey-Bass.	*Counselor Education and Supervision*
	Journal of Counseling Psychology
Joint Committee on Standards for Educational Evaluation. (1988). *The personnel evaluation standards.* Newbury Park, CA: Sage.	*Educational Leadership*
	Journal of Occupational and Organizational Psychology
Millman, J., & Darling-Hammond, L. (Eds.). (1990). *The new handbook of teacher evaluation.* Newbury Park, CA: Sage.	*Journal of Personnel Evaluation in Education*
	Journal of Applied Psychology
	Personnel Psychology
	Phi Delta Kappan

services. These are the audiences that the evaluators serve in the planning, conduct, and use of the evaluation study, compared with the scholarly, academic audience of the researcher.

Thus, in the development of questions, methods, and the criteria to be used for judging merit and worth, the evaluator works within a pluralistic environment. Greene (1994) states,

> Yet neither these diverse criteria for program effectiveness nor different stake-holders' widely divergent evaluation questions can be equally well addressed by the same evaluation methodology. In this respect, it is the fundamental political nature of program evaluation contexts, intertwined with the predispositions and beliefs of the evaluator, that shape the contours of the evaluation methodologies and guide the selection of a specific evaluation approach for a given context. Different evaluation methodologies are expressly oriented around the information needs of different audiences. (p. 531)

This ties in (again) with the quotation that appeared earlier in this chapter. You might be wondering, what is the time period referenced in House's (1993) remark that "gradually, evaluators recognized. . ." When did evaluators think differently, and what did they think? I now present you with a brief history of evaluation that provides the context for the current debate about theories and methods in evaluation.

History and Current Models of Evaluation

The origins of evaluation could be traced back to the 1800s when the government first asked for external inspectors to evaluate public programs such as prisons, education, hospitals, and orphanages (Madaus, Stufflebeam, & Scriven, 1983). However, most writers peg the beginning of the profession of evaluation as it is now known in the 1960s with the passage of Great Society legislation (e.g., Head Start programs) that mandated evaluations as a part of the program. The history of evaluation roughly parallels the paradigmatic framework presented in Chapter 1. However, evaluation is a relatively "young" profession, and thus, the transformations have occurred in a somewhat compressed time frame.

Postpositivist Paradigm

Evaluation in both education and psychology began in the positivist/postpositivist paradigm. In education, evaluation emerged from a tradition of testing to assess student outcomes and progressed through an era of specification of objectives and measurement to determine if the objectives had been obtained. Ralph Tyler (cited in Madaus et al., 1983) developed the objectives-based model for evaluation, and Malcom Provus (cited in Madaus et al., 1983) developed the discrepancy evaluation model. In psychology, the early years of evaluation were dominated by the work of Donald Campbell (see Shadish, Cook, & Leviton, 1991) in quasi-experimental design (a topic that was discussed extensively in Chapter 3 of this book). Contemporary evaluators have not abandoned the use of testing, objectives, and quasi-experimental designs, but they have modified and extended these strategies and added new approaches in the ensuing years. When evaluators discovered that using "objective social science methods" was not enough to ensure that their work would have an effect on public policy and social program decisions, they shifted their focus to more decision-based models of evaluation.

As evaluators gained experience with trying to improve social programs, other models of evaluation were developed that tried to address some of the shortcomings of traditional educational assessment or experimental designs. Stufflebeam (1983) was instrumental in pushing the definition of evaluation beyond the achievement of objectives to include the idea that it was a process of providing information for decision making. From his efforts with the Ohio State Evaluation Center and under the auspices of Phi Delta Kappa, Stufflebeam worked with other pioneers in the field of evaluation (including Egon Guba) to develop the CIPP model of evaluation:

C	=	Context
I	=	Input
P	=	Process
P	=	Product

Thus, the CIPP model tries to incorporate many aspects of the program that were not considered under earlier models. The components of the model can be explained by the nature of the evaluation questions asked for each component.

Component	Evaluation Questions
Context	What are the program's goals? Do they reflect the needs of the participants?

Input   What means are required to achieve a given set of goals, in terms of schedules, staffing, budget, and the like?

Process   How were the participants informed of the process? How were the resources allocated? How were the materials adapted?

Product   What is the evidence of outcomes? Should we terminate, continue, or revise this program? Should we decrease or increase funds? Should we merge it with another program?

The context and input phases represent a needs assessment function that evaluation sometimes plays to determine what is needed in terms of goals and resources for a program. For more recent thinking on needs assessment, the reader is referred to Witkin and Altschuld's work (1995).

Additional contributions to postpositivist approaches to evaluation can be found in the extensions of Donald Campbell's work explicated in the current writings of Chen and Rossi on *theory-based evaluation* (Chen, 1990a, 1990b, 1994; Chen & Rossi, 1992). Theory-based evaluation is defined as an approach in which the evaluator constructs a model of how the program works using models based on stakeholders' theories, available social science theory, or both to guide question formation and data gathering.

Chen and Rossi (1992) view theory-based evaluation as a way to mitigate the problems encountered in a more simplistic notion of quasi-experimental design when applied in an evaluation setting. The role of the evaluator is to bring a theoretical framework from existing social science theory to the evaluation setting. This would add insights to the structure of the program and its effectiveness that might not be available to the stakeholders in the setting. They warn against uncritically accepting the stakeholders' viewpoints as the basis for understanding the effectiveness of the program. They acknowledge that qualitative methods can be used during the program conceptualization and monitoring, but they advocate the use of randomized experiments for assessing program impact. Because theory-based evaluation, as it is conceptualized by Chen and Rossi, is guided by a preference to use structural modeling methods, the kinds of question formulated for the evaluation are those that fit neatly into causal modeling (Shadish et al., 1991).

Interpretive/Constructivist Paradigm

Stake (1983) combines some of the elements of the CIPP Model and discrepancy evaluation in his model of responsive evaluation. He includes the idea that evaluation involves comparing an observed value compared with some standard. The standard is to be defined by the expectations and criteria of different people for the program and the observed values is to be based on those values actually held by the program. The evaluator's job is to make a comprehensive statement of what the observed program values are with useful references to the dissatisfaction and satisfaction of appropriately selected people. He extended his work in the direction of case study methodology, thus clearing the way for the introduction of qualitative methods in evaluation inquiry.

Stake's work in responsive evaluation led the way to the introduction of a new paradigm within the evaluation community. Guba and Lincoln (1989) acknowledge the foundation provided by Stake's work in responsive evaluation in their development of what they termed *fourth-generation evaluation.* They conceptualized the four generations this way:

First generation: Measurement—testing of students
Second generation: Description—objectives and tests (Tyler's work, cited in Madaus et al., 1983)
Third generation: Judgment—the decision-based models, such as Stake (1983), Scriven (1967), and Stufflebeam (1983)
Fourth generation: Constructivist, heuristic evaluation

Guba and Lincoln depict the stages of evaluation as generations, with the more recent replacing those that came earlier. It is my perception that the evaluation community does not generally share this depiction, in that many of the methods and models that were developed in evaluation's earlier days continue to have influence on theory and practice.

Theorists such as Guba and Lincoln, Patton, Stake, and House were influential in bringing the interpretivist-constructivist paradigm, along with qualitative methods into evaluation. Greene (1994) notes that qualitative methods were initially contested on both practical and methodological grounds. However, she describes the current situation as a "détente," "signaling the important acceptance of these alternative evaluation methodologies, at least among many evaluation theorists and methodologists" (p. 535). Greene does acknowledge that this acceptance is not universal among all the members of the evaluation community.

Emancipatory Paradigm

Although interpretive/constructivist qualitative evaluators recognize the importance that values play in the inquiry process, this paradigm does not justify any particular set of values. House (1993), Sirotnik (1990), and Sirotnik and Oakes (1990) raise the question of what social justice and fairness mean in program evaluation. An emerging movement within evaluation is beginning to focus on the meaning of social justice and fairness within evaluation, with the consequent opening of the door to the emancipatory paradigm of social inquiry for evaluators. As Greene (1994) recognizes, "What importantly distinguishes one evaluation methodology from another is not methods, but rather whose questions are addressed and which values are promoted" (p. 533).

Perhaps more contentious than the interpretive/constructivist paradigm for researchers is the problem that the emancipatory paradigm poses for the evaluation community. The problem is framed as a split within the evaluation community between

those who wish to use evaluation as a way to promote a favored political agenda and those who wish evaluation to be objective and scientific. . . . These are critical concerns that the field must address, for if we cannot be trusted to be neutral on program topics and objective, to the best of our abilities, then what reason is there for our services? (M. F. Smith, 1994, p. 226).

One response to this concern was voiced by the authors of the African Development Foundation's (ADF) *Participatory Evaluation Handbook:*

> Moreover, most evaluation methodologies insist that there be a certain "distance" between evaluator and grantee. Objectivity, it is called. ADF defines objectivity a bit differently than is the tradition. "Distance" in participatory evaluation as practiced by the RE (Resident Evaluator) Network, is not equated with a lack of rapport. Rather, participatory methodology encourages *grantees to develop a "distance" from problems encountered* in order to better assess the appropriate next steps to be taken. "Distance," in participatory evaluation process, means not tying the grantee's sense of self-worth to the shortcomings of the projects. "Distance" means reflection and objectivity aimed at improvement of the situation; not indictment of those involved with the project. Thus, "distance" and rapport are compatible concepts in participatory evaluation methodology. (Owano & Jones, 1995, p. 3)

Proponents of an emancipatory approach to evaluation argue that working within this paradigm can lead to more appropriate interventions and more judicious distribution of resources. The emancipatory paradigm in evaluation follows the same principles outlined in Chapter 1 for research. Within the field of evaluation, three approaches have begun to explicitly address issues of power and representativeness of traditionally silenced groups: empowerment evaluation, developmental evaluation, and participatory evaluation.

Empowerment Evaluation

Empowerment evaluation is a model for evaluation developed by Fetterman (1994, 1995) that uses evaluation concepts and techniques to foster improvement and self-determination. In keeping with the definition of evaluation as a determination of merit and worth, value determination and plans for improvement are conducted by the group with the assistance of a trained evaluator. Because program participants conduct their own evaluation, Fetterman (1994) views empowerment evaluation as a means to foster self-determination, generate illumination, actualize liberation, and institutionalize systematic evaluation.

Stufflebeam (1994) criticizes empowerment evaluation on the basis that it would produce public relations exercises, or worse, rather than objective evaluation findings. Fetterman states that the process of conducting an empowerment evaluation requires appropriate involvement of stakeholders, meaning that the entire group is responsible for conducting the evaluation. Thus, the group serves as a check on its own members and can moderate the biases and agendas of individual members. Because the process is an open one, it is less likely that illicit or ineffective activity will be covered up. Fetterman (1995) states,

> It provides an infrastructure and network to combat institutional injustices. . . .
> It also provides an opportunity and a forum to challenge authority and manage-

rial facades by providing data about actual program operations—from the ground up. The approach is particularly valuable for disenfranchised people and programs to ensure that their voice is heard and that real problems are addressed. (p. 183)

Empowerment evaluation is designed to be responsive to rapid and unexpected changes in program design and operation. However, empowerment evaluation, as conceptualized by Fetterman (1994), does not explicitly address the issues of power related to sexism, racism, or oppression of people with disabilities (Whitmore, 1996). Developmental evaluation emerged as another version of an emancipatory evaluation approach that explicitly addressed involvement of ethnic-racial minorities in the evaluation process.

Developmental Evaluation

Developmental evaluation evolved from the work of Stockdill, Duhon-Sells, Olsen, and Patton (1992) and Patton (1994) in which they explored ways to actively involve people of color in the evaluation process of a multicultural education project. Stockdill's reflections capture the impetus for the emergence of the developmental evaluation model:

> My training taught me that carefully developed data-collection instruments could obtain the needed information validly and reliably. Now I am learning that my white female culture got in the way, and that I was isolated from critical pieces of information. For example, it was only through visits to Cambodian families' homes that the Cambodian staff member could determine their concerns about their children's education. It was only through telephone calls by African American parents to other African American parents that we learned of the racism experienced by their children. It was only because of the cultural sensitivity of Saint Paul American Indians in Unity that eighteen of twenty Indian parents attended a meeting and shared the depth of their frustration about the failure of schools to educate their children. (Stockdill et al., 1992, p. 28)

The struggle to meaningfully evaluate programs of this nature led to the emergence of the developmental approach to evaluation. Patton (1994) describes developmental programs as those that are fluid, constantly searching for ways to be responsive to an ever-changing set of conditions: "Developmental programming calls for developmental evaluation in which the evaluator becomes part of a design team helping to monitor what's happening, both processes and outcomes, in an evolving, rapidly changing environment of constant feedback and change" (p. 313).

Patton (1994) says that the developmental approach to evaluation is not a model but is a relationship founded on the shared purpose of developing a program. The evaluator brings the expertise of evaluation logic, knowledge of effective programming, and inquiry methods. The evaluator serves as a member of the team in which all team members make evaluation judgments together and decide how to apply the implications of the results to the next stage of the project. He defined developmental evaluation this way:

Developmental evaluation: Evaluation processes and activities that support program, project, product, personnel, and/or organizational development (usually the latter). The evaluator is part of a team whose members collaborate to conceptualize, design, and test new approaches in a long-term, ongoing process of continuous improvement, adaptation, and intentional change. The evaluator's primary function in the team is to elucidate team discussions with evaluative data and logic, and to facilitate data-based decision-making in the developmental process. (p. 317)

Patton recognizes that this conceptualization of evaluation might be problematic for others in the evaluation community who view evaluation as a process of rendering judgment about whether or not a program's goals have been met. He argues that this is one option for evaluators who wish to be valuable partners in the design process of programs for which the goals are emergent and changing and for which the purpose is learning, innovation, and change.

Participatory Evaluation

A third evaluation approach evolving within the emancipatory paradigm is participatory evaluation (akin to participatory action research described in Chapter 7). Participatory evaluation means that evaluation is a participatory process that involves the stakeholders in the various tasks of the evaluation so that the results are fully comprehensible to project participants (Cousins & Earl, 1995; Mertens, Berkeley, & Lopez, 1995; Owano & Jones, 1995). The question of who is invited to participate in the process and the nature of their participation determines the extent to which participatory evaluation exemplifies the principles of the emancipatory paradigm. For example, Cousins and Earl (1995) explicitly acknowledge that participatory evaluation, as they conceptualize it, does not have as a goal the empowerment of individuals or groups or the rectification of societal inequities. Rather, they seek to enhance the use of evaluation data for practical problem solving within the contemporary organizational context.

Nevertheless, the basic processes involved in the conduct of participatory evaluation provide a first step toward an emancipatory perspective in evaluation in that the professional evaluator works as a facilitator of the evaluation process but shares control and involvement in all phases of the research act with practitioners. In participatory evaluation, the evaluator helps to train key organizational personnel in the technical skills vital to the successful completion of the evaluation project. These key organizational personnel—often administrators, counselors, or teachers—are taught sufficient technical knowledge and research skills to enable them to take on the coordinating role of continuing and new projects, with consultation with a professional evaluator as necessary.

The project participants are coplanners of the evaluation who complete the following tasks:

1. Discuss the evaluation questions that need to be addressed to determine if the project is making progress

2. Help define and identify sources of data required to answer evaluation questions

3. Are involved in the data collection and analysis and in report preparation

The main goal of participatory evaluation is to provide information for project decision makers and participants who will monitor the progress of, or improve, their project (Owano & Jones, 1995).

Whitmore (1996) notes that not all evaluations that use the label of participatory evaluation are truly emancipatory. Emancipatory program evaluation requires that the investigator is explicitly concerned with gender, class, race, ethnicity, sexual orientation, and different abilities and the consequent meaning of these characteristics for access to power. For evaluators interested in empowerment of less powerful constituencies that results from a critical analysis of dominant institutions, suggested sources include Brunner and Guzman (1989); Ellis, Reid, and Barnsley (1990); Mertens, Farley, Madison, and Singleton (1994); Mertens (1996); Truman (1995); and Whitmore (1991).

Steps in Conducting Evaluations

A general outline for steps in conducting evaluations is presented here. However, for the student who is seriously considering conducting an evaluation study, the following list of resources is provided:

Books and Monographs

Guba, Egon G., & Lincoln, Yvonna S. (1989). *Fourth generation evaluation.* Newbury Park, CA: Sage.

Hadley, Robert G., & Mitchell, Lynda K. (1995). *Counseling research and program evaluation.* Pacific Grove, CA: Brooks/Cole.

Madison, Anna-Marie (Ed.). (1992). *Minority issues in program evaluation* (New Directions for Program Evaluation, Vol. 53). San Francisco, CA: Jossey-Bass.

Patton, Michael Q. (1990). *Qualitative evaluation and research methods.* Newbury Park, CA: Sage.

Popham, W. James. (1988). *Educational evaluation.* Englewood Cliffs, NJ: Prentice Hall.

Posavac, Emil J., & Carey, Raymond G. (1992). *Program evaluation: Methods and case studies.* Englewood Cliffs, NJ: Prentice Hall.

Rossi, Peter H., & Freeman, Howard E. (1993). *Evaluation: A systematic approach.* Newbury Park, CA: Sage.

Scriven, Michael. (1991). *Evaluation thesaurus* (4th ed.). Newbury Park, CA: Sage.

Shadish, William R., Jr., Cook, Thomas D., & Leviton, Laura C. (1991). *Foundations of program evaluation.* Newbury Park, CA: Sage.

Worthen, Blaine R., Sanders, James R., & Fitzpatrick, Jody. (1997). *Program evaluation.* New York: Addison Wesley, Longman.

Evaluation Journals
Educational Evaluation and Policy Analysis
Evaluation Practice
Evaluation Review
Evaluation and Program Planning
Evaluation and the Health Professions
Evaluation and Educational Policy
Studies in Educational Evaluation

Professional Associations
The American Evaluation Association is the primary professional organization for practicing evaluators. (Other countries also have professional organizations, such as the Canadian Evaluation Association and the Australian Evaluation Association.) The American Evaluation Association publishes a journal (*Evaluation Practice*) and one monograph series (*New Directions for Program Evaluation*).

In some respects, the steps for conducting the evaluation parallel those used to conduct any research project. However, variations occur in terms of the process of inquiry because this is an *evaluation* study and because of factors such as the status of the program being evaluated and the model of evaluation that you choose to use. The steps are listed in the box labeled "Steps for Planning an Evaluation Study" and are further explained in the next section.

What follows is a general description of the steps for focusing and planning an evaluation. I have integrated ideas from all three paradigms, drawing on the work of Brinkerhoff, Brethower, Hluchyji, and Nowakowski (1983); Guba and Lincoln (1989); Madison (1992); Rossi and Freeman (1993); Shadish et al. (1991); Stockdill et al. (1992); and Worthen, Sanders, and Fitzpatrick (1996).

Before launching into the focusing stage, I want to acknowledge that all evaluators would not necessarily move through the process in exactly the same way. Nevertheless, if these steps are viewed as a nonlinear, iterative framework for planning an evaluation, they should provide a helpful guide to that end for all evaluators, no matter what their orientation. Furthermore, my remarks are probably biased toward the perspective of an external evaluator because that has been my experience for the last 15 years or so; however, I did work as an internal evaluator for about 8 years prior to assuming the external status. I attempt to write information that would be pertinent and helpful to both internal and external evaluators.

Focusing Stage

During the focusing stage, the evaluator(s) need to determine what is being evaluated, the purpose of the evaluation, the stakeholders in the evaluation, and the constraints within which the evaluation will take place. In one sense, the evaluator is stuck with a "which came first, the chicken or the egg" dilemma, even in the first stage of the evaluation, in that just

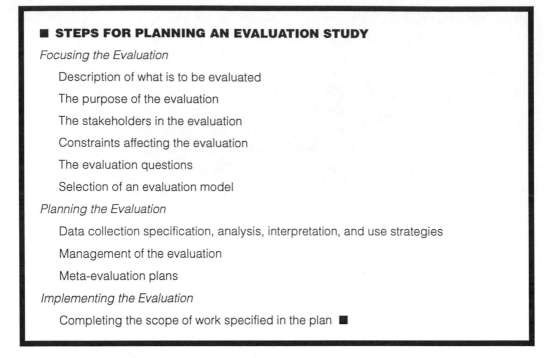

■ **STEPS FOR PLANNING AN EVALUATION STUDY**

Focusing the Evaluation

    Description of what is to be evaluated

    The purpose of the evaluation

    The stakeholders in the evaluation

    Constraints affecting the evaluation

    The evaluation questions

    Selection of an evaluation model

Planning the Evaluation

    Data collection specification, analysis, interpretation, and use strategies

    Management of the evaluation

    Meta-evaluation plans

Implementing the Evaluation

    Completing the scope of work specified in the plan ■

learning about what is to be evaluated implies contact with at least one group of stakeholders. Typically, the evaluator is contacted to perform an evaluation by some individual or agency that represents one group of stakeholders in the program. Often, this first contact is initiated by a program director, policymaker, or funding group. When listening to the description of the evaluand, purpose, stakeholders, and constraints within this initial context, the evaluator can gain valuable information by asking the right kinds of questions. These questions can provide a sufficient knowledge base to direct further planning efforts and to alert the initial contact person(s) of things that might not have been thought of, such as theoretical perspectives (Chen, 1990b) or groups that need to be included because they will be affected by the program (Harding, 1993; Mertens, 1995).

Description of the Evaluand

The evaluand, you recall, is what is being evaluated—a substance abuse prevention program, a multicultural education program, or a state agency policy. The evaluator needs to determine the status of the evaluand: Is it a developing, new, or firmly established program? If it is developing, it is possible that the evaluator will be asked to play a role in the evolution of the evaluand. Thus, an evaluator who is using the developmental evaluation model (Patton, 1994) might find that a considerable amount of time is spent collaboratively designing the evaluand. If it is new or firmly established, the program is probably described in printed documents. It is always a good idea to ask for whatever printed documents are available about the program in advance of your meeting with the initial stakeholder(s), if possible. Reading documents such as an annual report, accreditation agency report, previous evaluation reports, or a proposal can give you a good background about the evaluand and the context within which it functions. Questions to start with include the following:

▶ Is there a written description of what is to be evaluated?

▶ What is the status of the evaluand? Relatively stable and mature? New? Developing? How long has the program been around?

▶ In what context will (or does) the evaluand function?

▶ Who is the evaluand designed to serve?

▶ How does it (the evaluand) work? Or how is it supposed to work?

▶ What is it supposed to do?

▶ What resources are being put into the evaluand (e.g., financial, time, staff, materials, etc.)?

▶ What are the processes that make up the evaluand?

▶ What outputs are expected? Or occur?

▶ Why do you want to evaluate it?

▶ Whose description of the evaluand is available to you at the start of the evaluation?

▶ Whose description of the evaluand is needed to get a full understanding of the program to be evaluated?

You should read available documents and hold initial discussions with the conscious realization that things are not always being played out exactly as they are portrayed on paper or in conversation. Therefore, it would behoove you to alert the client to the fact that you will want to observe the program in action (in its development, implementation, etc.) to get a more accurate picture of what is being evaluated. You should also let the client know that you are aware that programs are generally not static (i.e., you will expect changes in the program throughout the duration of the evaluation) and that multisite programs will probably not be implemented in exactly the same way from site to site.

You should be aware that different individuals with different relationships with the program may view the program quite differently. Explain to your client that this often happens in evaluations and that you want to build in a mechanism to discover diverse views about the program and to explore these diversities within a public context. In this way, you can increase the chances that the program you think you are evaluating is the one that is actually functioning or developing. Without this assurance, you may find at the end of the evaluation that your results are challenged because you did not adequately represent different perceptions of the program.

Part of the description of the evaluand should include ascertaining diverse views of the program's purpose. Stockdill et al. (1992) describe one step in a developmental evaluation as helping program staff members, advisory committees, and partnership teams make "claims" statements regarding the multicultural program. The claims represent the participants' perceptions of what would change as a result of the program activities. The evaluators lead the meeting by asking the stakeholders to comment on what they were committed to changing—and ask them to voice their real expectations for change. In this way, they hope to increase the ownership by those responsible for the program activities for the intended changes. The following is an example of a claims statement that was generated by the group in this study:

> School staff interact with students, families, and communities with cultural awareness, warmth, and sensitivity—on the phone, in person, and in written communication. They use proper pronunciation of names, arrange children's seating to provide for integrated classroom environments, avoid racial jokes and innuendo, and confront prejudice when expressed by children or adults. (p. 30)

Purpose of the Evaluation

As you discuss the evaluand, the purpose of the evaluation may begin to emerge. However, it is important to directly address this issue, within the context of what stimulated the need for the evaluation and the intended use of the evaluation results. The purpose of the evaluation needs to be distinguished from the purpose of the program. The sample claims statement presented previously exemplifies a partial statement of purpose for the program. Scriven (1967) identifies formative and summative purposes for evaluation. More recently, Patton (1994) has added a developmental purpose for evaluations.

Formative evaluations are conducted during the operation of a program to provide information useful in improving the program. Summative evaluations are conducted at the end of a program to provide judgments about the program's worth or merit. Developmental evaluations are typically designed to provide systematic data in a fluid, dynamic, changing context of program development. Although summative evaluations tend to focus more on program impact, formative and developmental evaluations can include program impact data that is viewed as a barometer for program changes.

Patton distinguishes between the purposes in a formative and developmental evaluation:

> Formative evaluation typically assumes that ultimate goals are known, and that the issue is how best to reach them. By contrast, developmental evaluation is preformative in the sense that it is *part of the process of developing goals* and implementation strategies. Developmental evaluation brings the logic and tools of evaluation into the early stages of community, organization, and program development. (cited in Stockdill et al. 1992, p. 26)

Questions can be asked to determine the purposes of the evaluation; the questions should be asked with an understanding of diversity of viewpoints and the necessity of representation of appropriate people in the discussions. Possible questions include these:

▶ What is the purpose of the evaluation?

▶ What events triggered the need for the evaluation?

▶ What is the intended use of the evaluation findings?

▶ Who will use the findings and for what purpose?

▶ Whose views should be represented in the statement of evaluation purpose?

Worthen et al. (1996) identify a number of possible purposes for evaluations:

■ To decide whether to adopt a new program or product

■ To determine whether to continue, modify, expand, or terminate an existing program

■ To examine the extent to which the operation of an endeavor is congruent with its design

■ To judge the overall value of a program and its relative value and cost compared with that of competing programs

■ To help evaluation sponsors, clients, participants, and stakeholders determine whether identified problems are being solved

They also warn against a number of purposes for evaluation that are indicative of *not* conducting an evaluation. The evaluator should be on the alert for evaluations conducted without a clear commitment to use the results, for which decisions have already been made and the decision maker is looking for justification or cases in which the evaluation is looked at only as a public relations activity. Of course, decision makers are unlikely to characterize the purpose of the evaluation in such blunt terms, so the evaluator must be aware of establishing a clear purpose with intentions for use prior to commencing on the evaluation proper.

The purpose of the evaluation is also something that may change as the project evolves. Wallerstein and Martinez (1994) developed an empowerment evaluation model to evaluate an adolescent substance abuse prevention program. In the initial stages of the evaluation, they viewed the purpose as documenting the processes and conditions necessary for a Freirean program to promote community change. (A Freirean program is one based on the teachings of Paulo Freire in which empowerment is viewed as establishing a connection with others to gain control over your own life in the context of improving the life of the community.) As the evaluation continued, the purpose shifted to focusing on analyzing how individual actors engaged in the larger change process. The areas of change included three that were predicted from the Freirean theory:

1. Changes in the youths' abilities to engage in dialogue

2. Changes in their critical thinking ability to perceive the social nature of the problems and their personal links to society

3. Changes in the youths' level of actions to promote changes

The evaluators also found that two other areas of change emerged from the study that had not been predicted from the theory:

4. Changes in the youths' emotions related to connectedness with others and self-disclosure

5. Changes in self-identity

Identification of Stakeholders

Of course, by now, you should know who the primary players in the program are. However, you should ask specific questions to ascertain whether all of the appropriate stakeholders have been identified. It is not uncommon in evaluations to address the concerns of the funding agency, the policymakers, or the program managers. However, this does not really cover all the people who are or will be affected by the program. Therefore, it is incumbent on you as the evaluator to raise questions about who should be involved in the evaluation process and to raise the consciousness of the powerful people to include those who have less power. You can ask such questions as these:

▶ Who is involved in the administration and implementation of the program?

▶ Who are the intended beneficiaries?

▶ Who has been excluded as being eligible for participation in the program?

▶ Who stands to gain or lose from the evaluation results?

▶ Which individuals and groups have power in this setting? Which do not?

▶ Did the program planning and evaluation planning involve those with marginalized lives?

▶ Who is representative of the people with the least power?

▶ What opportunities exist for mutual sharing between the evaluators and those without power?

▶ What opportunities exist for the people without power to criticize the evaluation and influence future directions?

▶ Is there appropriate representation on the basis of gender, ethnicity, disability, and income levels?

▶ Who controls what the evaluation is about and how it will be carried out?

▶ Who has access to the program resources?

▶ What are the dominant cultural values and assumptions in the program?

▶ Who are the supporters of the program? Who are its opponents?

Possible stakeholders in evaluations include the following:

- Sponsors and funders
- Governing and advisory boards
- State- and federal-level agency representatives
- Policymakers
- Administrators (at various levels)
- Staff members (regular education teachers, special education teachers, resource personnel, psychologists, etc.)
- Service recipients (clients, students, etc.)
- Parents of service recipients
- Grassroots organization representatives in the community
- Public community representatives

This list is not meant to be exhaustive but, rather, to give you an idea that the breadth of the impact of an evaluation can extend far beyond the individuals with whom you first discuss the evaluation project.

Guba and Lincoln (1989) suggest several strategies for identifying stakeholders. The most obvious is to ask the person who represents your first contact with the program for nominations. Then each stakeholder who is added to the list can be shown the list and asked to nominate others that seem appropriate. Advertisements can be put in local newspapers. Every effort should be made to represent diversity of opinion within stakeholder groups (e.g., parents who support *and* those who oppose the program.)

Constraints of the Evaluation

Evaluations occur within specific constraints:

Money: We have budgeted so much money for the evaluation.

Time: We need the results of the evaluation before the Board meets 6 months from now.

Personnel: The teachers will be given 4 hours per week release time to assist with data collection.

Existing data: Program records are on disk, and they contain information about all recipients and their characteristics.

Politics: If this program was reduced, it would free up additional funds to respond to other needs.

Politics are integrally involved in the evaluation process. Therefore, the evaluator must be aware at the start, and sensitive throughout the process, of who supports or opposes the program; who would gain or lose if the program was continued, modified, reduced, or eliminated; who sanctions the evaluation and who refuses to cooperate; who controls access to information; and who needs to be kept informed as the evaluation progresses.

This would be a good time in the evaluation planning to bring up the issue of communication lines and mechanisms so that you are sure there is a formalized understanding of who needs to be informed of what and by what means.

Also, it is important to note that people move in and out of programs, so it is not safe to assume that the understandings engendered by your initial efforts will be shared by those who enter the program later (Mertens et al., 1995; Stockdill et al., 1992). You will need to orient those who enter the program later about the purpose, process, and so on of the evaluation. If you do not do it yourself, you might establish a mechanism to have other knowledgeable participants take on the task of orienting newcomers.

It is usually a good idea at this point to prepare a synthesis of your current understanding of a program, in terms of the evaluand, purpose of the evaluation, stakeholders, and constraints. You can then share this synthesis with the stakeholder groups, characterize it as your current understanding, and ask for their feedback.

Evaluation Questions

Evaluation questions can be derived from the statement of purpose for the evaluation, expanded on by holding brainstorming sessions with stakeholder groups, borrowed from previous evaluation studies, or generated by a theoretical framework that is relevant to the study. The U.S. General Accounting Office examined categories of evaluation questions that would provide useful information for Congress (Shipman, MacColl, Vaurio, & Chennareddy, 1995). I share these with you as they seem to have generic relevance for evaluators in local settings as well:

1. *Descriptive questions*—those that tell what the program is and what it does:
   a. What activities does the program support?
   b. Toward what end or purpose?
   c. Who performs these activities?
   d. How extensive and costly are the activities, and whom do they reach?
   e. Are conditions, activities, purposes, and clients fairly similar throughout the program, or is there substantial variation across program components, providers, or subgroups of clients?

2. *Implementation questions*—those that tell about how and to what extent activities have been implemented as intended and whether they are targeted to appropriate populations or problems:
   a. Are mandated or authorized activities actually being carried out?
   b. Are the activities in accordance with the purpose of the law and implementing regulations?
   c. Do they conform to the intended program model or to professional standards of practice, if applicable?
   d. Are program resources efficiently managed and expended?

3. *Impact questions*—those that illuminate the program effects:

   a. Is the program achieving its intended purposes or outcomes? What is the aggregate impact of the program? How did impact or outcomes vary across participants and approaches? How did impact vary across providers; specifically, did the program support providers whose performance was consistently weak?

   b. What other important effects relate to the program (side effects)? What unforeseen effects came from the program (either positive or negative) on problems or clients it was designed to address? Did the program have an effect on other programs aimed at a similar problem or population?

   c. How does this program compare with an alternative strategy for achieving the same ends? Are the effects gained through the program worth its financial and other costs? Taking both costs and effects into account, is the current program superior to alternative strategies for achieving the same goals?

If evaluation questions are prepared within the emancipatory framework, they exemplify an understanding of the power relationships that need to be addressed (Mertens, 1995). Examples of evaluation questions from this perspective might include the following:

▶ How can we teach and counsel students and clients so that they do not continue to be oppressed?

▶ Are the resources equitably distributed?

▶ How has the institution or agency been unresponsive in meeting the needs of people with disabilities?

The focus of these questions is to place the problem in an unresponsive system with power inequities rather than in the individual without power.

No matter what the initial evaluation questions, the evaluator should always be sensitive to emerging issues that necessitate a revision of these questions. This might be especially important in developmental evaluations.

Selection of an Evaluation Model

Evaluators carry an inclination, based on their worldview, to use specific models in their evaluation work. However, the needs of the evaluation will determine the appropriateness and feasibility of using a specific model. At this point, evaluators must ask themselves, Can I conduct this evaluation using the model that seems most appropriate to me, given my view of the world? Can I modify, adjust, adapt my way of thinking to be responsive to the needs of this client in this setting? Can I use my way of thinking to help the client think about the problem in ways that are new and different and, ideally, more constructive and productive? I suspect that older, more experienced evaluators can make choices based on compatibility with their worldviews more readily than newer, less experienced evaluators. Perhaps newer evaluators would find it easier to adjust their model selection to the needs of the client. Patton (1988) declares himself to be a pragmatist in his choice of models and methods, asserting that sensible methods decisions should be based on the purpose of the inquiry, the questions being investigated, and the resources available.

The reader should review the major models of evaluation as they are presented earlier in this chapter. If one model seems to address the needs of the evaluation more than another, consider if that is a model that aligns with your worldview. If you think that you can "enlighten" a client to a different approach to evaluation, give it a try. One of the roles that evaluators fulfill is educating the client about evaluation. Just as the implicit or explicit model that you entered the situation with influenced your decisions up to this point, the model that you choose to operationalize influences your next steps in planning the evaluation.

Planning the Evaluation

Data Collection Decisions

Data collection decisions basically answer these questions: What data collection strategies will you use? Who will collect the data? From whom will you collect the information (sampling)? When will you collect the information? Where will you collect it? How will the information be returned to you?

Your basic choices for data collection strategies are the same as those outlined in Chapters 10 (sampling) and 11 (data collection) in this text, as well as those discussed in Chapter 5 on survey research and Chapter 7 for qualitative methods. Your major concern is choosing data collection strategies that provide answers to your evaluation questions within the constraints of the evaluation study and that satisfy the information needs of your stakeholders. The constraints of data collection in public institutions and agencies sometimes include specific policies about who can have access to information. When the data collection plan is being developed, the evaluator should inquire into such possible constraints. Stakeholders should participate in the development of the data collection plan and should reach agreement that the data collected using this plan will satisfy their information needs. Of course, you need to stay flexible and responsive to emerging data collection needs.

Analysis, Interpretation, and Use

Issues related to analysis, interpretation, and use planning are directly affected by your data collection choices. These topics are discussed in Chapter 12 of this text. Nevertheless, as a part of the evaluation plan, the steps that you will take for analysis, interpretation, and use of the evaluation data should be specified. Your model of evaluation will determine how interactive and iterative the analysis and interpretation phases are. For example, in developmental or interpretive/constructivist evaluations, you would expect to have fairly constant interaction with the stakeholder groups. You would share preliminary results and consult on the use of the findings for the purpose of program modification, as well as for directions for further data collection and analysis. If you are functioning within a more traditional postpositivist model, you would be less likely to have such a high level of interaction with your stakeholder groups. Rather, you would attempt to maintain distance so that your presence did not unduly influence the effects of the program.

In terms of interpretation, evaluators have emphasized the development of a standard for use in making judgments about a program's merit or worth. For example, if a program is designed to reduce the dropout rate of high school students, is a 50% reduction considered successful? How about a 25% reduction? Such standards are appropriate for studies that focus on impact evaluation, although process-oriented standards could be established in terms of number of clients served or number of participants at a workshop.

Management of the Evaluation

The management plan for the evaluation should include a personnel plan as well as a budget. The personnel plan specifies the tasks that will be done, how, when, and by whom. The cost plan specifies the costs of the evaluation in categories such as personnel, travel, supplies, and consultants. Together, these two parts of the management plan can be used as the basis of a formal contract between the evaluator and the sponsoring agency.

Meta-Evaluation Plan

The meta-evaluation plan specifies how the evaluation will be evaluated. Typically, the meta-evaluation specifies when reviews of the evaluation will be conducted, by whom, and with reference to what standards. In evaluation work, three time points often seem appropriate for meta-evaluation to occur: (a) after the preliminary planning is finished, (b) during the implementation of the evaluation, and (c) after the evaluation is completed. The meta-evaluation can be accomplished by asking a person outside of the setting to review the evaluation planning documents, the progress reports, and the final report. It can also involve feedback from the stakeholder groups. One source of standards that the evaluation can be measured against is *The Program Evaluation Standards: How to Assess Evaluations of Educational Programs* (Joint Committee on Standards for Educational Evaluation, 1994). These standards are discussed in the next section.

Standards for Critically Evaluating Evaluations

The *Program Evaluation Standards* (referred to above and hereafter referred to as the *Standards*) were developed by a joint committee that was initiated by the efforts of 3 organizations: the American Educational Research Association, the American Psychological Association, and the National Council on Measurement in Education. Representatives of these 3 organizations were joined by members of 12 other professional organizations (e.g., American Association of School Administrators, Association for Assessment in Counseling, and the National Education Association) to develop a set of standards that would guide the evaluation of educational and training programs, projects, and materials in a variety of settings. The *Standards* have not yet been adopted as the official standards for any of these organizations, and they have been criticized for not sufficiently addressing the complexities of conducting interpretive/constructivist and emancipatory evaluations (Fetterman, 1995; Lincoln, 1995). Nevertheless, they do provide one comprehensive (albeit not all-encompassing) framework for examining the quality of an evaluation.

The *Standards* are organized according to four main attributes of evaluations:

Utility: These standards are intended to ensure that an evaluation will serve the information needs of intended users.

Feasibility: These standards are intended to ensure that an evaluation will be realistic, prudent, diplomatic, and frugal.

Propriety: These standards are intended to ensure that an evaluation will be conducted legally, ethically, and with due regard for the welfare of those involved in the evaluation, as well as those affected by its results.

Accuracy: These standards are intended to ensure that an evaluation will reveal and convey technically adequate information about the features that determine worth or merit of the program being evaluated.

Each of the main attributes is defined by standards relevant to that attribute. The box labeled "A Summary of *The Program Evaluation Standards*" contains a summary of the standards organized by attribute. Guidelines and illustrative cases are included in *The Program Evaluation Standards* text itself. The illustrative cases are drawn from a variety of educational settings, including schools, universities, the medical and health care field, the military, business and industry, the government, and law.

Mertens (1995) and Kirkhart (1995) recognize that concerns about diversity and multiculturalism have pervasive implications for the quality of evaluation work. Sanders (1994) attempts to analyze the *Standards* in terms of their implications for social justice; however, Kirkhart (1995) proposes specific consideration of what she terms "multicultural validity," which she defined as "the vehicle for organizing concerns about pluralism and diversity in evaluation, and as a way to reflect upon the cultural boundaries of our work" (p. 1). She outlines three types of validity traditionally discussed in the inquiry process but addresses them from the perspective of multicultural validity. She then identifies threats specifically relevant to multicultural validity. The traditional types of validity are defined and discussed below:

1. *Methodological validity* concerns the soundness or trustworthiness of understandings warranted by our methods of inquiry, particularly with reference to the measurement instruments, procedures, and logic of inquiry.

2. *Interpersonal validity* refers to the soundness or trustworthiness of understandings emanating from personal interactions.

3. *Consequential validity* refers to the soundness of change exerted on systems by evaluation and the extent to which those changes are just.

■ A SUMMARY OF THE PROGRAM EVALUATION STANDARDS

Utility

The utility standards are intended to ensure that an evaluation will serve the information needs of intended users.

U1   Stakeholder identification: Persons involved in or affected by the evaluation should be identified so that their needs can be addressed.

U2   Evaluator credibility: The persons conducting the evaluation should be both trustworthy and competent to perform the evaluation so that the evaluation findings achieve maximum credibility and acceptance.

U3   Information scope and selection: Information collected should be broadly selected to address pertinent questions about the program and be responsive to the needs and interests of clients and other specified stakeholders.

U4   Values identification: The perspectives, procedures, and rationale used to interpret the findings should be carefully described so that the bases for value judgments are clear.

U5   Report clarity: Evaluation reports should clearly describe the program being evaluated, including its context, and the purposes, procedures, and findings of the evaluation so that essential information is provided and easily understood.

U6   Report timeliness and dissemination: Significant interim findings and evaluation reports should be disseminated to intended users so that they can be used in a timely fashion.

U7   Evaluation impact: Evaluations should be planned, conducted, and reported in ways that encourage follow through by stakeholders so that the likelihood that the evaluation will be used is increased.

Feasibility

The feasibility standards are intended to ensure that an evaluation will be realistic, prudent, diplomatic, and frugal.

F1   Practical procedures: The evaluation procedures should be practical, to keep disruption to a minimum while needed information is obtained.

F2   Political viability: The evaluation should be planned and conducted with anticipation of the different positions of various interest groups so that their cooperation may be obtained and so that possible attempts by any of these groups to curtail evaluation operations or to bias or misapply the results can be averted or counteracted.

F3   Cost-effectiveness: The evaluation should be efficient and produce information of sufficient value so that the resources expended can be justified.

Propriety

The propriety standards are intended to ensure that an evaluation will be conducted legally, ethically, and with due regard for the welfare of those involved in the evaluation as well as of those affected by the results.

continued ➡

P1   Service orientation: Evaluations should be designed to assist organizations to address and effectively serve the needs of the full range of targeted participants.

P2   Formal agreements: Obligations of the formal parties to an evaluation (what is to be done, how, by whom, when) should be agreed to in writing so that these parties are obligated to adhere to all conditions of the agreement or formally to renegotiate it.

P3   Rights of human subjects: Evaluations should be designed and conducted to respect and protect the rights and welfare of human subjects.

P4   Human interactions: Evaluators should respect human dignity and worth in their interactions with other persons associated with an evaluation so that participants are not threatened or harmed.

P5   Complete and fair assessment: The evaluation should be complete and fair in its examination and recording of strengths and weaknesses of the program being evaluated so that strengths can be built on and problem areas addressed.

P6   Disclosure of findings: The formal parties to an evaluation should ensure that the full set of evaluation findings along with pertinent limitations are made accessible to the persons affected by the evaluation and to any others with expressed legal rights to receive the results.

P7   Conflict of interest: Conflict of interest should be dealt with openly and honestly so that it does not compromise the evaluation processes and results.

P8   Fiscal responsibility: The evaluator's allocation and expenditure of resources should reflect sound accountability procedures and otherwise be prudent and ethically responsible so that expenditures are accounted for and appropriate.

Accuracy

The accuracy standards are intended to ensure that an evaluation will reveal and convey technically adequate information about the features that determine worth or merit of the program being evaluated.

A1   Program documentation: The program being evaluated should be described and documented clearly and accurately so that the program is clearly identified.

A2   Context analysis: The context in which the program exists should be examined in enough detail so that its likely influences on the program can be identified.

The specific threats to *multicultural validity* were identified as these:

1. It takes time to reflect multicultural perspectives soundly. Many evaluations are conducted in compressed time frames and on limited budgets, thus constraining the ability of the evaluator to be sensitive to the complexity of multicultural dimensions.

2. Cultural sophistication needs to be demonstrated on cognitive, affective, and skill dimensions. The evaluator needs to be able to have positive interpersonal connec-

A3   Described purposes and procedures: The purposes and procedures of the evaluation should be monitored and described in enough detail so that they can be identified and assessed.

A4   Defensible information sources: The sources of information used in a program evaluation should be described in enough detail so that the adequacy of the information can be assessed.

A5   Valid information: The information-gathering procedures should be chosen or developed and then implemented so that they will ensure that the interpretation arrived at is valid for the intended use.

A6   Reliable information: The information-gathering procedures should be chosen or developed and then implemented so that they will ensure that the information obtained is sufficiently reliable for the intended use.

A7   Systematic information: The information collected, processed, and reported in an evaluation should be systematically reviewed, and any errors found should be corrected.

A8   Analysis of quantitative information: Quantitative information in an evaluation should be appropriately and systematically analyzed so that evaluation questions are effectively answered.

A9   Analysis of qualitative information: Qualitative information in an evaluation should be appropriately and systematically analyzed so that evaluation questions are effectively answered.

A10   Justified conclusions: The conclusions reached in an evaluation should be explicitly justified so that stakeholders can assess them.

A11   Impartial reporting: Reporting procedures should guard against distortion caused by personal feelings and biases of any party to the evaluation so that evaluation reports fairly reflect the evaluation findings.

A12   Meta-evaluation: The evaluation itself should be formatively and summatively evaluated against these and other pertinent standards so that its conduct is appropriately guided and, on completion, stakeholders can closely examine its strengths and weaknesses.

tions, conceptualize and facilitate culturally congruent change, and make appropriate cultural assumptions in the design and implementation of the evaluation.

3. The evaluator must avoid cultural arrogance that is reflected in premature cognitive commitments to a particular cultural understanding as well as to any given model of evaluation.

▶ *Questions for Critically Analyzing Evaluation Studies*

These questions are designed to parallel the *Standards* and to address issues raised by the construct of multicultural validity as it was described by Kirkhart (1995).

▶ *Utility*

1. *Stakeholder identification.* Were the people involved in or affected by the evaluation identified?

2. *Evaluator credibility.* Is the evaluator perceived to be trustworthy and competent to perform the evaluation?

3. *Information scope and selection.* Was the information collected broadly selected to address pertinent questions about the program and responsive to the needs and interests of clients and other important stakeholders?

4. *Values identification.* Were the perspectives, procedures, and rationale used to interpret the findings carefully described, providing a basis for value judgments that was clear?

5. *Report clarity.* Did the evaluation reports clearly describe the program being evaluated, including its context and the purposes, procedures, and findings of the evaluation, so that essential information was provided and easily understood?

6. *Report timeliness and dissemination.* Were significant interim findings and evaluation reports disseminated to intended users so that they could be used in a timely fashion?

7. *Evaluation impact.* Was the evaluation planned, conducted, and reported in ways that encouraged follow through by stakeholders so that the likelihood that the evaluation was used was increased?

▶ *Feasibility*

1. *Practical procedures.* What evidence is there that the evaluation was conducted in a practical way, keeping disruption to a minimum?

2. *Political viability.* What evidence is there that the evaluation was planned and conducted with anticipation of the different positions of various interest groups? What evidence is there that the cooperation of the various interest groups was obtained? What evidence is there that possible attempts by any of these groups to curtail evaluation operations or to bias or misapply the results were averted or counteracted?

3. *Cost-effectiveness.* What evidence is there that the evaluation was conducted in an efficient manner and produced information of sufficient value to justify the resources expended?

▶ Propriety

1. *Service orientation.* What evidence is there that the evaluation was designed to assist organizations to address and effectively serve the needs of the full range of targeted participants?

2. *Formal agreements.* What evidence is there that a formal agreement for the evaluation work was agreed to by formal parties?

3. *Rights of human subjects.* What evidence is there that the rights and welfare of the people participating in the evaluation were respected and protected?

4. *Human interactions.* What evidence is there that the evaluators respected the dignity and worth of the people associated with the evaluation?

5. *Complete and fair assessment.* What evidence is there that the evaluation was complete and fair in its examination and recording of strengths and weaknesses of the program being evaluated?

6. *Disclosure of findings.* What evidence is there that the full set of evaluation findings along with pertinent limitations were made accessible to the persons affected by the evaluation and any others with expressed legal rights to receive the results?

7. *Conflict of interest.* What evidence is there that any conflict of interest was dealt with openly and honestly so that it did not compromise the evaluation processes and results?

8. *Fiscal responsibility.* What evidence is there that the evaluator's allocation and expenditure of resources reflected sound accountability procedures and that expenditures were accounted for and appropriate?

▶ Accuracy

1. *Program documentation.* What evidence is there that the program being evaluated was described and documented clearly and accurately?

2. *Context analysis.* What evidence is there that the context in which the program exists was examined in enough detail so that its likely influences on the program could be identified?

3. *Described purposes and procedures.* What evidence is there that the procedures of the evaluation were monitored and described in enough detail to be identified and assessed?

4. *Defensible information sources.* What evidence is there that the sources of information used in a program evaluation were described in enough detail so that the adequacy of the information could be assessed?

5. *Valid information.* What evidence is there that the information-gathering procedures could ensure validity of the interpretations for their intended uses?

6. *Reliable information.* What evidence is there that the information-gathering procedures could ensure that the information obtained was sufficiently reliable for the intended use?

7. *Systematic information.* What evidence is there that the information was collected, processed, and reported in a way that allowed for systematic review and correction of errors?

8. *Analysis of quantitative information.* What evidence is there that the quantitative information was appropriately and systematically analyzed so that evaluation questions could be effectively answered?

9. *Analysis of qualitative information.* What evidence is there that the qualitative information was appropriately and systematically analyzed so that evaluation questions could be effectively answered?

10. *Justified conclusions.* What evidence is there that the conclusions reached in the evaluation could be explicitly justified?

11. *Impartial reporting.* What evidence is there that the reporting procedures guarded against distortion caused by personal feelings and biases of any party to the evaluation?

12. *Meta-evaluation.* What evidence is there that the evaluation itself was formatively and summatively evaluated against these and other pertinent standards? Can stakeholders closely examine the evaluation's strengths and weaknesses?

▶ Methodological Validity

1. *Face validity.* Do the items on the measurement instrument appear relevant to the life experiences of persons in a particular cultural context?

2. *Content validity.* Do the measurement items or tools have content relevance?

3. *Criterion-related validity.* Have the measures selected been validated against external criteria that are themselves culturally relevant?

4. *Construct validity.* Are the constructs that are used developed within an appropriate cultural context?

5. *Generalization.* Have threats to generalization of causal connections been considered in terms of connections across persons and settings, nonidentical treatments, and other measures of effects?

▶ Interpersonal Validity

1. *Personal influences.* What are the influences of personal characteristics or circumstances, such as social class, gender, race and ethnicity, language, disability, or sexual orientation in shaping interpersonal interactions, including interactions

between evaluators, clients, program providers, and consumers, and other stake-holders?

2. *Beliefs and values.* What are the influences of the beliefs and values of the evaluator and other key players in filtering the information received and shaping interpretations?

▶ *Consequential Validity*

1. *Catalyst for change.* What evidence is there that the evaluation was conceptualized as a catalyst for change (e.g., shift the power relationships among cultural groups or subgroups)?

2. *Unintended effects.* What evidence is there of sensitivity to unintended (positive or negative) effects on culturally different segments of the population?

▶ *Multicultural Validity*

1. *Time.* Were the time and budget allocated to the evaluation sufficient to allow a culturally sensitive perspective to emerge?

2. *Cultural sophistication.* Did the evaluator demonstrate cultural sophistication on the cognitive, affective, and skill dimensions? Was the evaluator able to have positive interpersonal connections, conceptualize and facilitate culturally congruent change, and make appropriate cultural assumptions in the design and implementation of the evaluation?

3. *Avoidance of arrogant complacency.* What evidence is there that the evaluator has been willing to relinquish premature cognitive commitments and to be reflexive?

■ Questions and Activities for Discussion and Application

1. Review the definitions of evaluation presented at the beginning of this chapter. Locate a published evaluation study. Explain why that study should or should not be classified as an evaluation study (as opposed to research study) based on the definition of evaluation. What do you derive from this exercise in terms of the difference between evaluation and research?

2. Review the historical and current models of evaluation presented in this chapter. Select three models (one from each paradigm, perhaps). For each model, determine the theorist's viewpoint regarding the following:

   a. The purpose(s) of evaluation

   b. The role of the evaluator in making valuing judgments

   c. The role of the evaluator in making causal claims

    d. The role of the evaluator in accommodating to the political setting

    e. The role of the evaluator in providing information for decision making

    f. The perception of the theorist as to who is the primary audience for the evaluation

    g. The perception of the theorist as to the appropriate role of stakeholders in the evaluation

    h. The perception of the theorist as to the role of other parties affected by or interested in the evaluation

    i. The most appropriate way to train an evaluator based on that theoretical perspective

3. Find a published evaluation study. On the basis of information given in the article, create an "evaluation plan" (in retrospect) using the guidelines for planning provided in this chapter. Your plan should include the following:

    a. Description of what is to be evaluated

    b. The purpose of the evaluation

    c. The stakeholders in the evaluation

    d. Constraints affecting the evaluation

    e. The evaluation questions

    f. Description of the evaluation model

    g. Data collection specifications

    h. Analysis, interpretation, and use strategies

    i. Management plan

    j. Meta-evaluation plans

    If you are unable to locate information from the published article that would provide a complete "retrospective plan," make a note of the missing elements. *Add* a section to your plan indicating what you think would have been good to include to make a complete plan. This will require some creative thinking on your part.

4. Find a published evaluation study. Critically analyze the study using the questions for critical evaluation of evaluation studies listed in this chapter. Summarize the strengths and weaknesses of the study. Suggest possible changes that might strengthen the study.

5. Find a second published evaluation study that exemplifies a different evaluation model or paradigm. Critically analyze it using the questions for critical evalu-

ation of evaluation studies listed in this chapter. Suggest possible changes that might strengthen the study.

6. Contrast the types of strengths and weaknesses that emerge from the two studies that were conducted from a different evaluation model or paradigm. How did the differences in the studies affect your use of the evaluation standards that were presented in this chapter (the *Standards* and Kirkhart's, 1995, multicultural validity standards)?

7. The joint committee that developed the *Standards* invited people conducting evaluations to communicate with them about their experiences in using the *Standards* to be used in the revisions of future editions of the *Standards*. Compose a letter to the Joint Committee on Standards for Educational Evaluation summarizing your experiences with the *Standards*.[2] In the letter address the following issues:

   a. Describe the way that you used the *Standards* (e.g., to conduct a class exercise in critiquing an evaluation study)

   b. Provide a summary of the evaluation study itself

   c. Describe problems that arose in applying the individual standards

   d. Describe conflicts found among the *Standards* and how they were resolved

   e. Describe flaws found in the *Standards* and suggest improvements or refinements

   f. Identify important areas that should be, but are not, covered by the *Standards*.

8. Because the *Standards* were developed within the context of educational evaluations, there has been some discussion about their applicability to evaluations in other settings. Review an evaluation study based in another type of program (e.g., drug abuse, clinical services). Critically comment on the usefulness of the *Standards* within this context. Use the points presented in Question 7 above to structure your response.

9. Stufflebeam (1994) published an article in *Evaluation Practice* that was critical of empowerment evaluation in terms of its responsiveness to the *Standards*. Fetterman (1995) wrote a response to Stufflebeam's critique in which he characterized Stufflebeam's position as "data free." Fetterman then outlined how empowerment evaluation could use and extend our understanding of the *Standards*. The following quotation gives you a flavor of the discussion:

   Myth: Empowerment Evaluation may violate the *standards*. Empowerment evaluation is consistent with the spirit of the *standards* and is designed to institutionalize evaluation. Dr. Stufflebeam's critique of empowerment was an opportunity to highlight and promote the Joint Committee's Program Evaluation Standards. Unfortunately, it also illustrated how the *standards*, developed for educational evaluation, can be inappropriately implemented, resulting in misevaluation.

First, an evaluation or in this case an entire evaluation approach was condemned without significant input from participants concerning the construction or orchestration of the effort. In addition, no data are cited or specific examples given. Instead, significant and faulty assumptions are made, permeating the entire discussion, and the approach is publicly condemned—in the name of the *standards*" (Fetterman, 1995, p. 185).

If possible, read both Stufflebeam and Fetterman's articles, and discuss the implications of the emancipatory paradigm for the use of the *Standards*.

10. Brainstorm ideas for an evaluation study. Working in a small group, design an evaluation plan following the steps outlined in this chapter. Include in your plan all the components listed in Chapter 3. Critique your plan using the questions for critical analysis listed in this chapter.

Notes

1. See the box labeled "Definition of Terms in Evaluation Parlance" for an explanation of this term.

2. The Joint Committee on Standards for Educational Evaluation has developed a package of information consisting of a letter of acknowledgment, information about the review and update process, and a supply of feedback forms with directions for their use. The package can be ordered from the joint committee. Consider requesting the package and sending your comments to the joint committee. The package request should be sent to the Joint Committee on Standards for Educational Evaluation, The Evaluation Center, Western Michigan University, Kalamazoo, Michigan 49008-5178.

In This Chapter

■ *The viewpoints of researchers who work within the postpositivist, interpretive/constructivist, and emancipatory paradigms are contrasted in relation to sampling strategies and generalizability.*

■ *Challenges in the definition of specific populations are described in terms of conceptual and operational definitions, identifying who is a minority or a disabled person, heterogeneity within populations, and cultural issues.*

■ *Strategies for designing and selecting samples are provided, including probability-based, theoretical-purposive, and convenience sampling.*

■ *Sampling bias, access issues, sample size, and external validity are discussed.*

■ *Ethical standards for the protection of study participants are described in terms of an institutional review board's requirements.*

■ *Questions to guide critical analysis of sampling definition, selection, and ethics are provided.*

10

Sampling:
Definition, Selection, and Ethics

When Ann Landers, the advice columnist, asked people to write in and answer the question, "If you had it to do over again, would you have children?," 70% of the nearly 10,000 respondents said that they would not have children if they could make the choice to be a parent again. However, when a statistically designed opinion poll on the same issue a few months later was conducted, it was reported that 91% of parents said that they would have children again! (Moore & McCabe, 1993, p. 248).

Sampling Strategies: Alternative Paradigms

The decisions that a researcher makes regarding from whom data will be collected constitute the subject of this chapter on sampling. Sampling refers to the method used to select a given number of people (or things) from a population. As can easily be deduced from the example that introduced this chapter, the strategy for selecting your sample influences the quality of your data and the inferences that you can make from it. The issues surrounding from whom you collect data are what sampling is all about. Within all approaches to research, researchers use sampling for very practical reasons. In most research studies, it is just not feasible to collect data from every individual in a setting or population.

Sampling is one area in which great divergence can be witnessed when comparing the various research paradigms. In general, researchers who function within the postpositivist paradigm see the ideal sampling strategy as some form of probability sampling. Henry (1990) describes probability sampling as follows:

> Probability samples are selected in such a way that every member of the population actually has a possibility of being included in the sample. . . . Probability samples can be rigorously analyzed to determine possible bias and likely error. There is no such advantage for nonprobability samples. (p. 17)

Researchers within the interpretive/constructivist paradigm tend to use a theoretical or purposive approach to sampling. Their sampling activities begin with an identification of "groups, settings, and individuals where (and for whom) the processes being studied are most likely to occur" (Denzin & Lincoln, 1994, p. 202). As Morse (1994) explains,

> Data collection and sampling are dictated by and become directed entirely toward the emergent model. The researcher seeks indices of saturation, such as repetition in the information obtained and confirmation of previously collected data. Using theoretical sampling, he or she looks for negative cases to enrich the emergent model and to explain all variations and diverse patterns. (p. 230)

Researchers within the emancipatory paradigm could choose either a probability or theoretical-purposive approach to sampling, depending on their choice of quantitative or qualitative methods. However, they would function with a distinctive consciousness of representing the populations that have traditionally been underrepresented in research.

Despite the contrasting views of sampling evidenced within the various paradigms, issues of common concern exist. All sampling decisions must be made within the constraints of ethics and feasibility. Although randomized, probability samples are set forth as the ideal in the postpositivist paradigm, they are not commonly used in educational and psychological research. Thus, in practice, the postpositivist and interpretive/constructivist paradigms are more similar than different in that both use nonrandom samples. Sometimes, the use of convenience samples (discussed at greater length later in this chapter) means that less care is taken by those in both paradigms. All researchers should make conscious choices in the design of their samples rather than accepting whatever sample presents itself as most convenient.

External Validity (Generalizability) or Transferability

As you will recall from Chapter 3, *external validity* refers to the ability of the researcher (and user of the research results) to extend the findings of a particular study beyond the specific individuals and setting in which that study occurred. Within the postpositivist paradigm, the external validity depends on the design and execution of the sampling strategy.

Henry (1990) talks about *generalizability* in terms of the *target population,* which he defines as the group to whom we want to generalize findings.

In the constructivist paradigm, every instance of a case or process is viewed as both an exemplar of a general class of phenomena and particular and unique in its own way (Denzin & Lincoln, 1994). The researcher's task is to provide sufficient "thick description" about the case so that the readers can understand the contextual variables operating in that setting (Guba & Lincoln, 1989). The burden of generalizability then lies with the readers, who are assumed to be able to generalize subjectively from the case in question to their own personal experiences (Stake, 1994). Guba and Lincoln (1989) label this type of generalizability *transferability.*

Defining the Population and Sample

Research constructs such as *ethnic minority* or *deaf student* can be defined in two ways. Conceptual definitions are those that use other constructs to explain the meaning, and operational definitions are those that specify how the construct will be measured.

Researchers often begin their work with a conceptual idea of the group of people they want to study, such as working mothers, drug abusers, students with disabilities, and so on. Through a review of the literature, they should formulate a formal, conceptual definition of the group they want to study. For example, the target population might be first-grade students in the United States.

An operational definition of the sample in the postpositivist paradigm is called the *experimentally accessible population,* defined as the list of people who fit the conceptual definition. For example, the experimentally accessible population might be all the first-grade students in your school district. You would next need to obtain a list of all the students in that school district. This would be called your *sampling frame,* examples include (a) the student enrollment, (b) a list of clients who receive services at a clinic, (c) professional association membership directories, or (d) city phone directories. The researcher should ask if the lists are complete and up-to-date and who has been left off the list? For example, lists of clients at a community mental health clinic eliminate those who need services but have not sought them. Telephone directories eliminate people with unlisted or newly assigned numbers. In the postpositivist view, generalizability is in part a function of the match between the conceptual and operational definitions of the sample. If the lists are not accurate, systematic error can occur because of differences between the true population and the study population (Henry, 1990). When the accessible population represents the target population, this establishes *population validity.*

The researcher must also acknowledge that the intended sample might differ from the obtained sample. The issue of response rate was addressed in Chapter 5 on survey research, along with strategies such as follow-up on nonrespondents and comparison of respondents and nonrespondents on key variables. The size and effect of nonresponse or attrition should be reported and explained in all approaches to research to address the effect of people not responding, choosing not to participate, being inaccessible, or dropping out of the study. This effect represents a threat to the internal and external validity (or credibility and transferability) of the study. You may recall the related discussion of this issue in the section on experimental mortality in Chapter 3 and the discussion of credibility and transferability in Chapter 7. A researcher can use statistical processes (described in Chapter 12) to identify the plausibility of fit between the obtained sample and the group from which it was drawn when the design of the study permits it.

Identification of Sample Members

It might seem easy to know who is a member of your sample and who is not; however, complexities arise because of the ambiguity or inadequacy of the categories typically used by researchers. Examples of errors in identification of sample members can readily be found in research with ethnic minorities and persons with disabilities. Two examples are presented here and the reader is referred to Chapter 4 on causal comparative and correlational research to review the complexities associated with this issue.

Identification of African American and Latino Populations

Investigators who examine racial groups and differences between such groups frequently do so without a clear sense of what race means in a research context (Davis, 1992). Researchers who use categorization and assume homogeneity of condition are avoiding the complexities of participants' experiences and social locations. Selection of samples on the basis of race should be done with attention to within-group variation and to the influence of particular contexts. Race as a biogenetic variable should not serve as a proxy variable for actual causal variables, such as poverty, unemployment, or family structure.

Race is sometimes used as a substitute for ethnicity, which is usually defined in terms of a common origin or culture resulting from shared activities and identity based on some mixture of language, religion, race, and ancestry (Yinger, 1985, cited in Ragin & Hein, 1993). Ragin and Hein suggest that the profoundly contextual nature of ethnicity must be taken into account in the study of ethnic and race relations.

Heterogeneity has been recognized as a factor that contributes to difficulty in classifying people as African American or Latino (Massey, Zambrana, & Bell, 1995; Stanfield, 1993a). In reference to African American populations, Stanfield (1993a) writes,

> Identity questions—such as "What is a white person?" or "What is a Black person?"—become problematic when one considers the extensiveness of ethnic mixing that has occurred in the United States in reciprocal acculturation and cultural assimilation processes, if not in miscegenation experiences. (p. 21)

Thus, he recognizes that many people are not pure racially. In addition, some African American people have skin color that is light enough to "pass" for White.

In Massey et al.'s (1995) exploration of the meaning of the term *Latino,* they concluded that Latino does not exist apart from classifications created by the federal statisticians to provide data on people of Mexican, Cuban, Puerto Rican, Dominican, Colombian, Salvadoran, and other extractions. Also, *Hispanic* is a label that has been used to include all those who can trace their origins to an area originally colonized by Spain.

These two labels obscure important national diversity within this population. The varied origins and immigration histories of groups termed Latino must be considered in definition of the samples, or, the writers warn, the research is not likely to be productive.

People With Disabilities

In the federal legislation "Individuals With Disabilities Education Act" (IDEA; 34 *CFR*, pts. 300-399, July 1, 1987), categories of disabilities are defined:

- Mental retardation
- Hearing impairments
- Speech or language impairments
- Visual impairments
- Serious emotional disturbance
- Orthopedic impairments
- Other health impairments
- Specific learning disabilities
- Multiple disabilities
- Deaf-blindness
- Autism
- Traumatic brain injury

Mertens and McLaughlin (1995) present an operational and conceptual definition for each of these disability categories. The conceptual definitions can be found in the IDEA. The "translation" of this conceptual definition into an operational definition is fraught with difficulty. You can imagine the diversity of individuals who would be included in a category such as serious emotional disturbance that is defined in the federal legislation as individuals who are unable to build or maintain satisfactory interpersonal relationships, exhibit inappropriate types of behaviors or feelings, have a generally pervasive mood of unhappiness or depression, or have been diagnosed with schizophrenia. Psychologists have struggled for years with finding ways to accurately classify people with such characteristics.

The difference between conceptual and operational definitions can be further illustrated by examining federal regulations concerning learning disabilities. The following conceptual definition of learning disability is included in the IDEA legislation:

> "Specific learning disability" means a disorder in one or more of the basic psychological processes involved in understanding or in using language, spoken or written, which may manifest itself in an imperfect ability to listen, think, speak, read, write, spell, or to do mathematical calculations. The term includes such conditions as perceptual impairments, brain injury, minimal brain disfunction, dyslexia, and developmental aphasia. The term does not include children who

have learning problems which are primarily the result of visual, hearing, or motor impairments, mental retardation, emotional disturbance or environmental, cultural, or economic disadvantage. (34 *Code of Federal Regulations* 300.5 (a))

The federal government addressed the issue of an operational definition of learning disability as "an ability achievement discrepancy, existing in spite of the provision of age appropriate instruction, not caused primarily by other conditions" (U.S. Department of Health, Education, and Welfare, 1977, Section 121a.541). (The other conditions referred to in the operational definition are those listed in the previously presented conceptual definition.)

Nevertheless, researchers have found that use of current operational definitions results in the misclassification of many students. For example, 85% of normal children could be classified as learning disabled (LD), 88% of low-functioning students could be classified as LD, and 4% of LD students did not meet the criteria for such a placement (Ysseldyke, Algozzine, & Epps, 1983). Thus, the researcher must be wary when conceptually and operationally defining the population.

Cultural issues also come into play in the definition of people with disabilities. For example, people who are deaf use a capital "D" in writing the word *Deaf* when a person is considered to be culturally Deaf. This designation as culturally Deaf is made less on the basis of one's level of hearing loss and more on the basis of one's identification with the Deaf community and choice of American Sign Language as one's preferred mode of communication.

Sampling Strategies

As mentioned previously, the strategy chosen for selecting samples vary based on the logistics, ethics, and paradigm of the researcher. Henry (1990) divides sampling strategies into probabilistic and nonprobabilistic. Persons working in the interpretive/ constructivist paradigm rarely use the term *nonprobabilistic* but prefer the terms *theoretical* or *purposive* to describe their sampling strategies (Morse, 1994).

A third category of sampling that is often used, but not endorsed by proponents of any of the major paradigms, is *convenience sampling*.

Probability-Based Sampling

Henry (1990) and Conley and Fink (1992) make a case for the use of probability-based sampling because mathematically it is possible to analyze the possible bias and likely error. *Sampling error* is defined as the difference between the sample and the population, and can be estimated for random samples. *Random samples* are those in which every member of the population has a known, nonzero probability of being included in the sample. *Random* means that the selection of each unit is independent of the selection of any other unit. Random selection can be done in a variety of ways, including using a lottery procedure drawing well-mixed numbers, extracting a set of numbers from a list of random numbers, or producing a computer-generated list of random numbers.

If the sample has been drawn in such a way that makes it probable that the sample is approximately the same as the population on the variables to be studied, it is deemed to be *representative* of the population.

Researchers can choose from five strategies for probability-based sampling.

Simple Random Sampling

Simple random sampling means that each member of the population has an equal and independent chance of being selected. The researcher can choose a simple random sample by assigning a number to every member of the population, using a table of random numbers, randomly selecting a row or column in that table, and taking all the numbers that correspond to the sampling units in that row or column. Or the researcher could put all the names in a hat and pull them out at random. Computers could also be used to generate a random list of numbers that correspond to the numbers of the members of the population.

This sampling strategy requires a complete list of the population. Its advantages are the simplicity of the process and its compatibility with the assumptions of many statistical tests (described further in Chapter 12). Disadvantages are that a complete list of the population might not be available or that the subpopulations of interest might not be equally represented in the population.

In telephone survey research in which a complete listing of the population is not available, the researcher can use a different type of simple random sampling known as random digit dialing (RDD). RDD involves the generation of random telephone numbers that are then used to contact people for interviews. This eliminates the problems of out-of-date directories and unlisted numbers. If the target population is households in a given geographic area, the researcher can obtain a list of the residential exchanges for that area, thus eliminating wasted calls to business establishments.

Systematic Sampling

For systematic sampling, the researcher will take every *n*th name off the population list. The procedure involves estimating the needed sample size and dividing the number of names on the list by the estimated sample size. For example, if you had a population of 1,000 and you estimated that you needed a sample size of 100, you would divide 1,000 by 100 and determine that you need to choose every 10th name on the population list. You then randomly pick a place to start on the list that is less than *n* and take every 10th name past your starting point.

The advantage of this sampling strategy is that you do not need to have an exact list of all the sampling units. It is sufficient to have knowledge of how many people (or things) are in the accessible population and to have a physical representation for each person in that group. For example, a researcher could sample files or invoices in this manner. Henry (1990) notes that the systematic sampling strategy can be used to accomplish de facto stratified sampling. Stratified sampling is discussed next, but the basic concept is sampling from previously established groups (e.g., different hospitals or schools). If the files or invoices are arranged by group, the systematic sampling strategy can result in de facto stratification by group (i.e., in this example, location of services).

One caution should be noted in the use of systematic sampling. If the files or invoices are arranged in a specific pattern, that could result in choosing a biased sample. For example, if the files are kept in alphabetical order by year and the number *n* results in choosing only individuals or cases whose last names begin with the letter A, this could be biasing.

Stratified Sampling

This type of sampling is used when there are subgroups (or *stratum*) of different sizes that you wish to investigate. For example, if you want to study gender differences in a special education population, you need to stratify on the basis of gender because boys are known to be more frequently represented in special education than girls. The researcher then needs to decide if he or she will sample each subpopulation proportionately or disproportionately to their representation in the population.

Proportional stratified sampling means that the sampling fraction is the same for each stratum. Thus, the sample size for each stratum will be different when using this strategy. This type of stratification will result in greater precision and reduction of the sampling error, especially when the variance between or among the stratified groups is large. The disadvantage of this approach is that information must be available on the stratifying variable for every member of the accessible population.

Disproportional stratified sampling is used when there are big differences in the sizes of the subgroups, as mentioned previously in gender differences in special education. Disproportional sampling requires the use of different fractions of each subgroup, and thus requires the use of weighting in the analysis of results to adjust for the selection bias. The advantage of disproportional sampling is that the variability is reduced within the smaller subgroup by having a larger number of observations for the group. The major disadvantage of this strategy is that weights must be used in the subsequent analyses; however, most statistical programs are set up to use weights in the calculation of population estimates and standard errors.

Cluster Sampling

Cluster sampling is used with naturally occurring groups of individuals—for example, city blocks or classrooms in a school. The researcher would randomly choose the city blocks and then attempt to study all (or a random sample of) the households in those blocks. This approach is useful when a full listing of individuals in the population is not available but a listing of clusters is. For example, individual schools maintain a list of students by grade, but no state or national list is kept. Cluster sampling is also useful when site visits are needed to collect data; the researcher can save time and money by collecting data at a limited number of sites.

The disadvantage of cluster sampling is apparent in the analysis phase of the research. In the calculations of sampling error, the number used for the sample size is the number of clusters, and the means for each cluster replaces the sample mean. This reduction in sample size results in a larger standard error and thus less precision in estimates of effect.

Multistage Sampling

This method consists of a combination of sampling strategies. For example, the researcher could use cluster sampling to randomly select classrooms and then use simple random sampling to select a sample within each classroom. The calculations of statistics for multistage sampling become quite complex, and the reader is referred to Henry's (1990) discussion of this topic. Henry does note that too few strata would yield unreliable extremes of the sampling variable. Hess (1985) suggests that roughly between 30 and 50 strata work well for multistage samples using regression analysis.

Example of Sampling in a Quantitative Study

Auchter and Skaggs (1994) investigated the relationship between 1993 graduating high school seniors' letter grades earned, courses taken, and course-taking patterns and the seniors' passing rates on the tests of general educational development (GED tests). Their goal was to gain knowledge about the essential academic skills and knowledge associated with a high school education by obtaining information related to the current curricula and by evaluating the influence of the curricula on achievement. They used a two-stage, stratified random sample of graduating high school seniors to represent the national population of the graduating seniors.

> Eligible schools were stratified according to five geographic regions (Northeast, South and Atlantic, East North Central, Central, and West), and the nature of the school (public or nonpublic). For public schools, school districts were also grouped according to five socioeconomic strata, defined as the poverty-level ratio as measured by the U.S. Bureau of the Census. A random sample of approximately 30 students was selected from the eligible population of each selected school. Each student was administered only one of the five subject area GED tests. . . . Except for the writing skills test, sample sizes ranged from 2,565 to 2,795. The writing skills test sample was much smaller because although all students took both the multiple-choice portion of the test and the essay, some of the essay topics were field-test topics and failed the topic evaluation process. For this study, only students who had scores for both parts of the test were used. (p. 4)

Purposeful or Theoretical Sampling

As mentioned previously, researchers working within the interpretive/constructivist paradigm typically select their samples with the goal of identifying information-rich cases that will allow them to study a case in-depth. Although the goal is not generalization from a sample to the population, it is important that the researcher make clear the sampling strategy and its associated logic to the reader. Patton (1990) identifies the following sampling strategies that can be used in interpretive/constructivist research study.

Extreme or Deviant Cases. The criterion for selection of cases might be to choose individuals or sites that are unusual or special in some way. For example, the researcher might choose to study a school with a low record of violence compared with one that has a high record of violence. The researcher might choose to study highly successful programs and compare them with programs that have failed. Study of extreme cases might yield information that would be relevant to improving more "typical" cases. The researcher makes the assumption that studying the unusual will illuminate the ordinary. The criterion for selection then becomes the researcher's and users' beliefs about which cases they could learn the most from. Psychologists have used this sampling strategy to study deviant behaviors in specific extreme cases.

Intensity Sampling. Intensity sampling is somewhat similar to the extreme-case strategy, except there is less emphasis on extreme. The researcher wants to identify sites or individuals in which the phenomenon of interest is strongly represented. Critics of the extreme- or deviant-case strategy might suggest that the cases are so unusual that it distorts the situation beyond applicability to typical cases. Thus, the researcher would look for rich cases that are not necessarily extreme. Intensity sampling requires knowledge on the part of the researcher as to which sites or individuals meet the specified criterion. This knowledge can be gained by exploratory fieldwork.

Maximum-Variation Sampling. Sites or individuals can be chosen based on the criterion of maximizing variation within the sample. For example, the researcher can identify sites located in isolated rural areas, urban centers, and suburban neighborhoods to study the effect of total inclusion of students with disabilities. The results would indicate what is unique about each situation (e.g., ability to attract and retain qualified personnel) as well as what is common across these diverse settings (e.g., increase in interaction between students with and without disabilities).

Homogeneous Samples. In contrast to maximum variation sampling, homogeneous sampling involves identification of cases or individuals that are strongly homogeneous. In using this strategy, the researcher seeks to describe the experiences of subgroups of people who share similar characteristics. For example, parents of deaf children aged 6 through 7 represent a group of parents who have had similar experiences with preschool services for deaf children.

Homogeneous sampling is the recommended strategy for focus group studies. Researchers who use focus groups have found that groups made up of heterogeneous people often result in representatives of the "dominant" group monopolizing the focus group discussion. For example, combining parents of children with disabilities in the same focus group with program administrators could result in the parents' feeling intimidated.

Typical-Case Sampling. If the researcher's goal is to describe a typical case in which a program has been implemented, this is the sampling strategy of choice. Typical cases can be identified by recommendations of knowledgeable individuals or by review of extant demographic or programmatic data that suggest that this case is indeed "average."

Stratified Purposeful Sampling. This is a combination of sampling strategies such that subgroups are chosen based on specified criteria, and a sample of cases is then selected within those strata. For example, the cases might be divided into highly successful, average, and failing, and the specific cases can be selected from each subgroup.

Critical-Case Sampling. Patton (1990) describes critical cases as those

> that can make a point quite dramatically or are, for some reason, particularly important in the scheme of things. A clue to the existence of a critical case is a statement to the effect that "if it happens there, it will happen anywhere" or vice versa, "if it doesn't happen there, it won't happen anywhere." (p. 174)

For example, if total inclusion is planned for children with disabilities, the researcher might identify a community in which the parents are highly satisfied with the education of their children in a separate school for children with disabilities. If a program of inclusion can be deemed to be successful in that community, it suggests that it would be possible to see that program succeed in other communities in which the parents are not so satisfied with the separate education of their children with disabilities.

Snowball (or Chain) Sampling. Snowball sampling is used to help the researcher find out who has the information that is important to the study. The researcher starts with key informants who are viewed as knowledgeable about the program or community. The researcher asks the key informants to recommend other people to whom he or she should talk based on their knowledge of who should know a lot about the program in question. Although the researcher starts with a relatively short list of informants, the list grows (like a snowball) as names are added through the referral of informants.

Criterion Sampling. The researcher must set up a criterion and then identify cases that meet that criterion. For example, a huge increase in referrals from a regular elementary school to a special residential school for students with disabilities might lead the researcher to set up a criterion of "cases that have been referred to the special school within the last 6 months." Thus, the researcher could determine reasons for the sudden increase in referrals (e.g., Did a staff member recently leave the regular elementary school? Did the special school recently obtain staff with expertise that it did not previously have?).

Theory-Based or Operational Construct Sampling. Sometimes, a researcher will start a study with the desire to study the meaning of a theoretical construct such as creativity or anxiety. Such a theoretical construct must be operationally defined (as discussed previously in regard to the experimentally accessible population). If a researcher operationalizes the theoretical construct of anxiety in terms of social stresses that create anxiety, sample selection might focus on individuals who "theoretically" should exemplify that construct. This might be a group of people who have recently become unemployed or homeless.

Confirming and Disconfirming Cases. You will recall that in the grounded theory approach (discussed in Chapter 7 on qualitative methods), the researcher is interested in emerging theory that is always being tested against data that is systematically collected. The "constant comparative method" requires the researcher to seek verification for hypotheses that emerge throughout the study. The application of the criterion to seek "negative cases" suggests that the researcher should consciously sample cases that fit (*confirming*) and do not fit (*disconfirming*) the theory that is emerging.

Opportunistic Sampling. When working within the interpretive/constructivist paradigm, researchers seldom establish the final definition and selection of sample members prior to the beginning of the study. When opportunities present themselves to the researcher during the course of the study, the researcher should make a decision on the spot as to the relevance of the activity or individual in terms of the emerging theory. Thus, opportunistic sampling involves decisions made regarding sampling during the course of the study.

Purposeful Random Sampling. In interpretive/constructivist work, samples tend to be relatively small because of the depth of information that is sought from each site or individual. Nevertheless, random sampling strategies can be used to choose those who will be included in a very small sample. For example, in a study of sexual abuse at a residential school for deaf students, I randomly selected the students to be interviewed. The result was not a statistically representative sample but a purposeful random sampling that could be defended on the grounds that the cases that were selected were not based on recommendations of administrators at the school who might have handpicked a group of students who would put the school in a "good light."

Sampling Politically Important Cases. The rationale for sampling politically important cases rests on the perceived credibility of the study by the persons expected to use the results. For example, if a program has been implemented in a number of regions, a random sample might (by chance) omit the region in which the legislator who controls funds for the program resides. It would be "politically expedient" for the legislator to have information that came directly from that region. Therefore, the researcher might choose purposively to include that region in the sample to increase the perceived usefulness of the study results. Henry (1990) agrees that "sampling for studies where the results are to be used in the political environment may require an additional layer of concern for political credibility beyond scientific concerns for validity" (p. 15).

Examples of Qualitative Research Sampling

In her discussion of oral history, Yow (1994) describes using a variety of sampling strategies. In a study of child workers in a mill village before World War I, she asked the ministers of the two village churches who the oldest members were. In a study of a World War II industrial town, she read the company newsletter to identify names and then checked the city directory to see who still lived there. Using the names of a few superintendents and workers identified by this means, she used snowball sampling, asking those initially identified to name employees who still lived in the vicinity and were well enough to participate. Then Yow and her colleagues asked those employees who they thought the researchers should talk with. This provided the researchers with a tentative list of narrators (people to interview).

They then made decisions as to who to interview based on which narrators were involved in pivotal events and who had lived in the community longest.

Yow adapted the stratified sampling design discussed under quantitative sampling strategies in her study of a psychiatric hospital. She wanted to interview narrators at every level in the workforce: grounds workers, housekeepers, maintenance people, psychiatrists, mental health workers, social workers, nurses, occupational therapists, cooks, carpenters, the administrative director, and members of the board of trustees. She combined this stratified approach with purposive sampling by deliberately seeking a variety of opinions on controversial topics and a variety of levels of allegiance to the formal organization. She interviewed people who no longer worked in the hospital, people who were for and against the union, people known to be favored by the administration, and those reported to be dissatisfied with the way things were going.

Convenience Sampling

Convenience sampling means that the persons participating in the study were chosen because they were readily available (Henry, 1990; Patton, 1990). Although this might be the least desirable sampling strategy, it is probably the most commonly used. Much psychological research has been conducted using undergraduate students in psychology classes because they are available. When such a convenience sample is used, the researcher must acknowledge the limitations of the sample and not attempt to generalize the results beyond the given population pool. The cost of convenience sampling is illustrated in the example that introduced this chapter. It appears that parents who were unhappy about having been parents were much more likely to volunteer their views than parents who were happy being parents. (The "happy" parents were probably either too busy to respond, or they don't read Ann Landers because they don't need any advice.)

It should be noted, however, that because of ethical concerns, all samples are in the end "volunteers." In addition, reality constraints such as access and cost must be considered in all sampling decisions. Luanna Ross's (1992) description of her sampling strategy in a study of Native American women in prison exemplifies the constraints sometimes encountered and how this researcher worked around them (see the box labeled "Example of Constraints in Sampling Procedures").

Sampling Bias

Henry (1990) identifies three sources of bias related to sampling design:

1. Nonsampling bias, which includes systematic error due to differences among the true population and the study population and measurement error (discussed in the next chapter)

2. Sampling bias, which includes systematic error from sampling approaches that overrepresent a portion of the study population

3. Sampling variability, which is related to sample size and sample homogeneity

---

■ EXAMPLE OF CONSTRAINTS IN SAMPLING PROCEDURES

"A series of constraints were encountered during the initial phase of sample selection. I originally planned on using a snowball technique, starting with my cousin and spinning off from there. After my first interview, which was with my cousin, the treatment specialist presented me with a list of incarcerated mothers, Indian and white, whom she thought I should interview. I wondered who she left off the list and why, and I felt too intimidated to suggest a different technique. Also, she said that I would not be allowed, for my own safety, to interview dangerous offenders with the exception of one woman because the treatment specialist thought she would 'be interesting.' I took the list and started interviewing women from my reservation whom I had known for several decades.

"Next, feeling constrained by the situation, I followed the treatment specialist's instructions and went down the list of women. After several weeks, however, I became familiar with women in the halls and would request that the guards send them to me to be interviewed, although they were not on the list. For example, one young pregnant woman seemed appealing given her age and pregnancy; and, from other prisoners, I heard about and then interviewed an Indian woman who was confined in an isolation cell in the general-population building. When the staff discovered this, nothing was said and I continued the process. Thus, I purposefully chose women I wanted to interview. I knew that I wanted a sample that would elicit data regarding variations: for instance, different races, mothers with children of various ages, and prisoners confined in different units." ■

SOURCE: Ross (1992, pp. 79-80).

Henry (1990) criticizes "nonprobability-based" sampling strategies primarily on the basis of sampling bias that might occur:

> Because of the subjective nature of the selection process, nonprobability samples add uncertainty when the sample is used to represent the population as a whole. Confounding variables can influence the study results. The accuracy and precision of statements about the population can only be determined by subjective judgment. The selection procedure does not provide rules or methods for inferring sample results to the population, in contrast to probability sampling. ... Therefore, there is a risk that the findings are not valid because of bias in the selection process. (p. 24)

In the interpretive/constructivist spirit, Guba and Lincoln (1989) reject the notion that it is possible to reach a "generalizable" conclusion because of a particular sampling strategy. They argue that research and evaluation results are limited by context and time and that "one cannot determine that this curriculum (as an example) will *fit* into and *work* in a given setting without trying it in that setting" (p. 61). They continue with their views on sampling within this paradigmatic framework:

First, respondents who will enter into the hermeneutic process must be selected. But such sampling is not carried out for the sake of drawing a group that is representative of some population to which the findings are to be generalized. Nor is the sample selected in ways that satisfy statistical requirements of randomness. The sample is selected to serve a different purpose, hence the term "purposive sampling" is used to describe the process. . . . For the constructivist, maximum variation sampling that provides the *broadest scope of information* (the broadest base for achieving local understanding) is the sampling mode of choice. (pp. 177-178)

They go on to describe a sampling process that is not preordained but allowed to evolve with the emergence of issues in the research.

Access Issues

Accessibility to a sample or population is an important factor to consider when making decisions about sampling designs. For some populations, such as illegal drug users or homeless people, it might not be possible to obtain a complete listing of the members of the population, thus making it difficult to use the probability-based sampling strategies (Hedrick, Bickman, & Rog, 1993; Henry, 1990). The likelihood of a population's being accessible or willing to respond to mail or phone surveys should also be considered. The populations just mentioned might not be accessible by these means because of residential transience or for financial reasons.

Access in Educational Settings

Maruyama and Deno (1992) address the issues involved in accessing samples in educational settings. They recognized that it can be a long process to finally reach agreement with the appropriate persons that the research will be allowed to take place and who will participate in the research itself as sample members. Identification of the "appropriate persons" who have the power to grant access is a complex issue in itself. The appropriate point of entry depends partially on the scope of the study that you plan. If you are interested in using only a few classrooms, you might start with teachers to determine their willingness to support your request to administrators. On the other hand, school-level research might start at the principal level and district-level research with the superintendent. Whichever level you start with should be viewed as only a starting point, because each school district has specific procedures for requesting access to its students and staff for research purposes. Early contacts can be helpful to "test the waters" and cultivate advocates for your later, more formal requests.

Researchers should be aware of complications from real life that can present obstacles to sampling as it is ideally conceived. For example, some educators might resist participating in research because they view research as a risky operation that can produce results that will damage their reputations. Also, some schools receive requests for a variety of different research projects, and thus, the effect of the treatment you design might be compromised because of interactions with another experimental treatment. Staff changes or district reorganizations can result in schools pulling out of projects after you think you have your sample defined.

Assuming that you can reach agreement on particular schools or classrooms, you must obtain consent from the individuals (students or parents or staff members) who will be asked to provide data in the study. This issue will be discussed further in the section of this chapter on ethics. However, it does have implications for the type of sampling design that is feasible.

School systems will rarely allow a researcher to take all student participants and randomly assign them to conditions. It is not that school systems are mean-spirited; they have the students' best interests at heart. For example, teachers will often recommend a student with disabilities when they feel that the student is ready to enter a mainstream environment and the environment has been suitably adapted for the student's special needs. Randomly selecting students for assignment to mainstream classrooms could result in educationally unsound and ethically indefensible decisions.

More frequently, researchers need to adjust their sampling plans to allow for working with intact groups—for example, administering a treatment to an entire class of students. This, of course, presents challenges that were discussed in Chapter 3 related to differential selection as a threat to internal validity in quasi-experimental designs, as well as having implications for statistical analysis discussed in Chapter 12.

Researchers who wish to use stratified sampling should also be aware of the complexities of subdividing the sample on the basis of gender, race or ethnicity, disability, or ability levels within a school setting. First, there are the logistical and ethical obstacles to using stratification. It might not be feasible, educationally sound, or ethical to divide students by demographic categories as would be called for in a stratified sampling design. Second, there are definitional problems in that schools might not use the same definition to "label" students as you have in mind. Also, if you are using more than one site, definitions might vary by site.

Mertens and McLaughlin (1995) describe issues that complicate sampling with special education populations. First, the researcher needs to be aware of the heterogeneity within any special education category and variables that might be uniquely associated with any particular group of people with disabilities. For example, in the area of deafness, characteristics that are important include things such as when the person became deaf, whether the parents are hearing or deaf, and what his or her preferred mode of communication is. Second, some disability conditions occur with a low frequency, and thus sampling becomes problematic because of the low incidence of individuals within any one setting. This has implications for variability across contexts as well as for adequate sample size. Sample size then has implications for sampling bias and error.

Third, researchers commonly seek comparison groups to include in their samples. Selecting an appropriate comparison group for special education populations can be tricky. DeStefano and Wagner (1991) discuss the following options:

1. *Selecting individuals from the general population.* It is important to remember that people with disabilities differ from nondisabled peers in important ways; for example, the disabled population contains more males, African Americans, urban dwellers, people with lower incomes, and single-parent households (Marder & Cox, 1990).

2. *Comparisons across disability categories.* You should be aware of the heterogeneity within categories, as well as variations on variables, such as IQ between categories.

3. *Cross-unit comparisons that involve the comparison of students with disabilities in one school or school district with students in another school or school district.* Of course, contextual variation is a problem here.

4. *Longitudinal studies that allow comparisons with one group at two or more points in time.* Variation in results could be attributable to historical factors (as discussed in Chapter 3 regarding threats to internal validity).

Courts in New York and Texas have imposed limits on research with people who are mentally ill (Burd, 1995). In New York, researchers are barred from conducting experiments with mentally ill patients in the state's psychiatric hospital without first obtaining their informed consent. In addition, research with children in the hospital is prohibited unless it offers health benefits to these patients. This raises a conflict: How can people be declared involuntarily mentally incompetent (which is the basis for placement in the state psychiatric hospital) and execute legal documents subjecting themselves to experiments? Such issues are currently being debated in several state court systems. Howe and Miramontes (1991) present a framework for ethical deliberation in special education, more generally.

Access to Records

Although much of the discussion of sampling has implied that the sample consists of people, I do not want to ignore a source of data that is frequently used in educational and psychological research—for example, extant records. The researcher needs to be concerned with the accessibility of the records for research purposes. Hedrick et al. (1993) suggest that researchers sample the desired records on a pilot basis to ensure that the records contain the information required for the study and that they are appropriately organized for the research study. For example, records might be kept only at a local level and not centralized at any one location, making data collection problematic. In addition, the records may or may not contain all the information that the researcher needs for the study.

The researcher must also be able to demonstrate how the confidentiality of the records will be protected. In most organizations, the records contain the names of the clients or students, and thus, the organization might not be willing to provide the researcher access to the records themselves. The researcher can then consider the feasibility and appropriateness of alternative means of achieving access to the archival information, such as asking the agency to provide the records with identifying information deleted, asking if an employee of the agency could be paid to code the information from the records without names, or determining if it is possible to obtain a computer printout with codes in place of personal identification information.

Sample Size

The optimum sample size is directly related to the type of research you are undertaking. For different types of research, "rules of thumb" can be used to determine the appropriate sample size. It should be noted that there are some research methodologists who feel that rules of thumb are never appropriate as a basis for making sample size decisions (e.g., Krathwohl, 1993). Nevertheless, I present these as guides to new researchers who need some kind of "ballpark feel" for sample sizes.[1] In some cases, your sample size will be determined by very practical constraints, such as how many people are participating in a program or are in a classroom. (This is often, but not always, the case in evaluation studies.) When you are conducting quantitative experimental research and you have the freedom to choose a sample size, there are formulas that can guide you in those decisions. So let's take a look at sample size from these different perspectives: rules of thumb and formulaic determination.

Rules of Thumb

Quantitative Research Rules of Thumb

Borg and Gall (1989) recommend the following sample sizes for these different kinds of research:

Type of Research	Recommended Sample Size
Correlational	About 30 observations
Multiple regression	At least 15 observations per variable
Survey research	100 observations for each major subgroup; 20 to 50 for minor subgroups
Causal-comparative, experimental, or quasi-experimental	About 15 observations per group

A more complex rule-of-thumb table can be found in Cohen (1992). He provides suggested sample sizes for eight different statistical tests (e.g., t test, correlation, chi-square) based on small, medium, and large effect sizes at power $= .80$,[2] for $\alpha = .01, .05,$ and $.10$. Further explanation of these concepts are presented in a subsequent section of this chapter.

Qualitative Research Rules of Thumb

The sample size decisions are a bit more dynamic in qualitative research than in quantitative research in that the number of observations is not determined in the former type of research prior to data collection. Rather, a researcher makes a decision as to the adequacy of the observations on the basis of having identified the salient issues and finding that the themes and examples are repeating instead of extending. Thus, sample size is integrally related to length of time "in the field." Nevertheless, rules of thumb for sample sizes in qualitative research can give you an estimate of the number of observations needed for different kinds of qualitative research. I return to the types of research discussed in Chapter 7 for the suggestions listed below:

Type of Research	Recommended Sample Size
Ethnography	Approximately 30 to 50 interviews[3]
Case studies	Can be only 1 case or can be multiple cases
Phenomenology	Approximately 6 participants
Grounded theory	Approximately 30 to 50 interviews
Participative inquiry	Small "working team"; whole communities for meetings; samples for surveys (see quantitative rules of thumb)
Clinical research	Can focus in-depth on 1 client
Focus groups	7 to 10 people per group; 4 groups for each major audience[4]

Stake (1995) provides good direction in his comments regarding choosing the sample for case study research:

> The first criterion should be to maximize what we can learn. Given our purposes, which cases are likely to lead us to understandings, to assertions, perhaps even to modifying of generalizations? Our time and access for fieldwork are almost always limited. If we can, we need to pick cases which are easy to get to and hospitable to our inquiry, perhaps for which a prospective informant can be identified and with actors (the people studied) willing to comment on certain draft materials. Of course we need to carefully consider the uniqueness and contexts of the alternative selections, for these may aid or restrict our learning. But many of us case-workers feel that good instrumental case study does not depend on being able to defend the typicality of the [case]. (p. 4)

Stake (1994) says that once the case itself (or cases) is (are) chosen, the researcher should follow a similar logic for selecting persons, places, and events to observe within the case. Choices should be made based on a desire to represent variety but not necessarily representativeness. Decisions should be weighted by considerations of access and hospitality and by time constraints.

In historical studies, Yow (1994) notes the same criteria for sufficient sample size as noted earlier; that is, when you have heard the same story for the 20th time and you are not getting any new information, you probably have heard enough. She provided a few guidelines for different types of historical research. For example, for a family history, you might want to record the life story of every family member. For a biography, you might want to talk to the individual's associates, relatives, friends, and critics. For studies in which there are few survivors, universal sampling is recommended—that is, interviewing all who are able to participate meaningfully.

Formulaic Determinations of Sample Size

Lipsey (1990) and Cohen (1988) have written excellent texts that describe the logic and procedure for selection of sample size when the researcher is conducting a quantitative study of treatment effectiveness. Lipsey (1990) frames his discussion around the concept of *design sensitivity,* which he defines as follows: "Design sensitivity . . . results in data that are likely to yield statistical significance if, in fact, the treatment under investigation is effective" (p. 10). In other words, how big does your sample have to be to obtain statistically significant results, if the treatment is indeed effective? He continues: "Sensitivity refers to the likelihood that an effect, if present, will be detected" (p. 12).

So what does sample size have to do with detecting statistically significant differences? Our ability to detect statistically significant differences is determined in part by the amount of variability on our dependent measure within the sample:

Less variability = greater sensitivity
More variability = less sensitivity

And sample size has a direct relationship with variability:

Larger sample sizes = less variability
Smaller sample sizes = more variability

If you put the logic of these two statements together, you realize that it is easier to obtain statistical significance if you have a larger sample. However, there is one sticking point:

Larger samples = more costly
Smaller samples = less costly

So, as a researcher, you want to know what is the smallest sample you can use that will take into account the variability in the dependent measure and still be *sensitive* enough to detect a statistically significant difference, if there is one.

Another important concept that enters the discussion of sample size calculation is the *power* of a statistical test, defined as "its ability to detect deviations from the null hypothesis"

(Moore & McCabe, 1993, p. 511). Lipsey defines *power* as "the probability that statistical significance will be attained *given* that there really is a treatment effect" (p. 20). Thus, power in one sense is the quantification of the sensitivity. Sensitivity or power in statistical language is described in terms of probability of finding a difference when there really is one there. I digress for a moment to explain a few terms to finish the explanation of statistical power.

If we claim that we *do* have a real difference, but we really *do not,* this is called *Type I error.* Usually, researchers establish a level of Type I error that they are willing to live with, and this is called an *alpha level* (α). For example, if researchers are willing to live with a .05 probability that they might say there is a statistically significant difference when there is not, they have established an alpha level of .05. If we claim that we *do not* have a real difference, but we really *do,* this is a *Type II error* (or β). Perhaps a graphic display will help:

Your Claim	Statistical Significance?		Type of Error
	Really	Really not	
Yes, a difference		X	Type I (alpha)
No difference	X		Type II (beta)

All this explanation was necessary because the *power of a statistical test* can be defined as $1 - \beta$ (Krathwohl, 1993).

There are tables you can use to estimate sample sizes that are based on the establishment of your acceptable *alpha* and *beta* levels and the estimated effect size you expect to find between the treatment and comparison groups. (The effect size is the difference between the two group means in terms of their common standard deviation.) Lipsey (1990) presents such a table for studies that involve experimental and control group comparisons; Shaver (1992) provides a similar table for correlational research; and (as previously mentioned) Cohen (1992) provides a more comprehensive table of sample sizes for eight different statistical procedures.

Now, this section has the title "Formulaic Determinations of Sample Size," so you are probably wondering where are the formulas. I am going to provide you with one formula to give an idea of how the formulas work. However, you should be aware of a number of caveats in regard to the use of such a formula. Moore and McCabe (1993) identify the following assumptions that underlie the use of simplistic formulas such as the one presented here:

1. The data must be from a simple random sample. If data are not from a simple random sample, the researcher must be able to plausibly think of the data as independent observations from a population.

2. The formula is not correct for any sampling designs that are more complex than a simple random sample.

3. There are no correct methods for data that are haphazardly collected with bias of unknown size.

4. Outliers can have a large effect on the confidence interval; therefore, extreme values should be corrected or removed before conducting the analysis.

5. Small sample sizes and nonnormality in the population can change the confidence level.

Given those caveats, Borg and Gall (1989) present the following formula for estimating the size of sample needed:

$$N = \frac{2s^2 \times t^2}{D}$$

where:

$N =$ number of people needed in each group
$s =$ standard deviation of your dependent variable
$t =$ t-test value needed to get your desired *alpha* level
$D =$ estimated difference between experimental and control groups

Now, you may be wondering, where do I get the standard deviation or effect size without having already done the research. Good question. You could rely on estimates of s and D that are available from previous research reported in the literature, or you could conduct pilot work to obtain your own estimates. Lipsey (1990) also suggests the possibility of establishing an acceptable effect size based on discussions with program leaders to determine what would be a meaningful result. The t-test value can be obtained from a table in any statistics book once you have established your desired *alpha* level.

You may also be wondering what to do in case your sampling strategy does not fit all of the caveats presented previously. In actuality, the preferred method for calculating estimated sample size is by using any of the various statistical programs that are now available for estimating power or sample size. These allow you to personalize the estimation process to your exact needs as well as to play with the estimates of sample size to weigh the differential effects on precision and cost.

You should be aware of the important implications of this discussion of sample size. As Lipsey (1990) and Hedrick et al. (1993) point out, much educational and psychological research is doomed to failure before any data is collected because of insufficient power to detect the effects of an intervention. Hedrick et al. also point out that increasing sample size is not the only route to increasing statistical power. Other alternatives include improving the delivery of the treatment, selecting other statistical tests, or raising the *alpha* level. Of course, sample size is also influenced by the willingness of the chosen people to participate in the study. That is our next topic: ethics in research.

Ethics and Protection of Study Participants

Most novice researchers encounter serious questions about the ethics of their planned research within the context of their institutions' institutional review boards (IRB) or human subjects committees. An IRB is a committee mandated by the National Research Act, Public Law 93-348. Every university or other organization that conducts biomedical or behavioral research involving human subjects is required to have an IRB if federal funding is used for research involving human subjects. The federal regulations are included in Title 45 *Code of Federal Regulations* Part 46. You can obtain a copy of these regulations from any university's research office, a reference librarian, or from the Office for Protection From Research Risk in the National Institutes of Health (located in Bethesda, Maryland).

You should always contact your own institution's IRB to find out its policies and procedures early in your research planning process. Sometimes, review by the IRB can occur in stages if you are planning to conduct pilot work or obtain funding from an external agency. In any case, you should be prepared to submit your research proposal in the appropriate format to the IRB well in advance of the time that you actually plan to start data collection. The IRB committee members need time to read and discuss your proposal, and they might have questions that will require some revision of your planned procedures. Lead time, an open mind, and a cooperative attitude help.

IRBs need to approve all research that is conducted that involves human subjects (with a few exceptions that will be discussed soon). If you are planning to conduct pilot testing as a part of your study, you should contact your IRB to determine its policy with regard to that. Sieber (1992) found that, generally, IRBs do not review proposals for pilot testing if it just involves fine-tuning an instrument or a research procedure. However, they do review pilot testing that is conducted as an exploratory study to determine if additional research is necessary. Because pilot testing is an important part of many surveys and qualitative studies, it is important that you are aware of this requirement.

Certain exemptions to IRB approval are relevant to research conducted with school children. Even if you think your research might fall into one of the exempt categories, you should contact your IRB because most institutions still require an abbreviated review to establish the legitimacy of the exemption. Some of the exemptions include the following:

1. Research that is conducted in established or commonly accepted educational settings, involving normal education practices, such as instructional strategies or classroom management techniques.

2. Research that involves the use of educational tests if unique identifiers are not attached to the test results.

You need to give the IRB a research protocol that may be a summary of your actual proposal with specific ethical issues addressed in greater detail. For the exact specifications at your institution, again, check with your IRB. For a general sense of what the IRB might want to see in a research protocol, see the box labeled "Checklist for Research Protocol." The first three items on the protocol checklist parallel closely what you would put into your

■ CHECKLIST FOR RESEARCH PROTOCOL

1. Cover Page, including

  - Name and department of the principal investigator (PI)
  - The PI's faculty rank or student status
  - PI's home and office phone number and address
  - The project title
  - The type of research (e.g., faculty research, externally funded project, student-directed research[a])
  - Intended project starting and ending dates
  - Your qualifications in a paragraph or two (or in an attached curriculum vitae or within the description of the methodology)
  - Signature of the PI
  - If PI is a student, signature of the adviser

2. A description of the research

  - The purpose of the research and the hypotheses
  - The literature review (in a summary form)
  - The research method, design, and mode of analysis
  - A realistic statement of the value of the research (specifically addressing what value it will have for the participants and their community, the research institution, the funder, or science)
  - The location of the research (e.g., the exact laboratory, community, institution, etc.), why that setting was chosen, and how the researcher happens to have access to it
  - Duration of time for the project and how that time frame relates to the project (e.g., in terms of the school calendar, etc.)

3. A description of the research participants

  - Demographic characteristics: for example, ethnic background, sex, age, and state of health
  - Rationale for the choice of this population
  - Source from which the research participants will be obtained
  - A statement of the selection criteria
  - If vulnerable populations are included (e.g., children, mentally disabled, drug abusers), the rationale for their use should be stated
  - If the participants are coming from an institutional setting (e.g., school, clinic, hospital, club), written permission of the person in charge must be attached to your protocol
  - The expected number of participants should be provided

4. A discussion of the possible risks

  - Inconveniences or discomforts, especially to the participants, and an estimate of the likelihood and magnitude of harm
  - What will be done to allay each actual risk or unwarranted worry
  - Any alternative methods that were considered and why they were rejected
  - A justification if unique identifiers will be collected

5. Discussion of inducements and benefits to the research participants and others

6. Freedom of research participants to withdraw at any time with no adverse consequences

7. Source and amount of compensation in the event of injury (if any, although this is not usually offered to participants in educational and psychological research studies)

8. Analysis of risks and benefits (and a description of how the benefits will substantially outweigh the risks)

9. The informed consent procedure should be described
   - How, where, and by whom the informed consent will be negotiated
   - How debriefing will be conducted
   - Procedures for obtaining children's consent and parental or guardian permission for the research
   - The actual consent form should be attached to your protocol
   - If oral consent is planned, provide a description of the information that will be presented
   - Attach a copy of the information to be used in debriefing

10. A copy of the consent form itself should be attached. It should include the following:
    - An explanation of the research purpose, duration, and procedures; if deception is to be used, the researcher should explain that not all of the details can be provided at this time but that a full explanation will be given later
    - A description of any foreseeable risk or discomfort
    - A description of alternative ways people can obtain the services (e.g., educational intervention or counseling) (if they choose not to participate in the research)
    - A description of how confidentiality or anonymity will be ensured
    - A statement as to whether compensation or treatment for harm or injury is available (if the research involves more than minimal risk)
    - The name of a person to contact for answers to additional questions
    - A statement that participation is voluntary, that refusal will not result in any penalty, and that the person is free to withdraw at any time (Note: The person must be given a copy of the consent form)

11. Any additional attachments (e.g., letters of permission, interview or survey questions, materials to be presented to the participants, tests, or other items connected with the research) ■

SOURCE: Adapted from Sieber (1992).
a. If the research is student-directed research, include the name of the faculty adviser and indicate if the research is for a thesis or dissertation or for a course requirement (include course number and faculty name).

■ EXAMPLE OF A CONSENT FORM

Project   Title: Support Services for Parents of Children Who Are Deaf or
                         Hard of Hearing

Principal Investigator: Kathryn Meadow-Orlans, Senior Research Scientist, Center for
                         Studies in Education and Human Development,
                         Gallaudet University, Washington DC 20002-3695
Phone: 202 651-XXXX (V or TDD)
E-mail: KMEADOWORLAN@XXXXX.XXXXX

Thank you for volunteering to participate in a group interview as a follow-up to the Gallaudet National Survey for Parents. Your signature on this consent form shows that you have been informed about the conditions, risks, and safeguards of this project.

1. Your participation is voluntary. You can withdraw from the study at any time, for any reason, without penalty.

2. There is no more than minimal risk to individuals who participate in this research, and complete confidentiality is ensured. Your name will not be used. Instead, you will be given a code number in order to guarantee your anonymity. The typed transcript of the interview will show this code number rather than your name. Your comments will be entered on a computer, and any identifying information will be changed for any written reports. Only the project investigators and their research assistants will have access to the transcript.

3. Questions about risk to you because of participation in this study may be addressed to the researcher at the phone number or e-mail listed at the top of this page or to Dr. Carolyn Corbett, Chairperson, Gallaudet University Institutional Review Board for Protection of Human Subjects (IRB) at (202) 651-XXXX (V or TDD).

4. To cover possible incidental expenses that you might have related to your participation, you will be paid an honorarium of $50. In addition, you have our deep appreciation. We believe that this study will help to improve support services for parents and for children who are deaf and hard of hearing.

****

I have read the information provided and agree to participate in the interview for parents.

_____   _____
          signature   date

_____
          print name

research proposal itself, although the IRB usually asks for a shorter version. Items 4 through 10 on the checklist really zero in on the issues specific to ethical practice in research. You will notice that Item 10 concerns a consent form that you should have your study participants sign. The box labeled "Example of a Consent Form" shows a sample consent form.

Confidentiality means that the privacy of individuals will be protected in that the data they provide will be handled and reported in such a way that it cannot be associated with them personally. *Anonymity* means that no uniquely identifying information is attached to the data, and thus, no one, not even the researcher, can trace the data back to the individual providing it. As discussed under "Access to Records" earlier in this chapter, it is sometimes possible to obtain data within the context of anonymity by having someone other than the researcher draw the sample and delete unique identifying information. Sieber (1992) also suggests the possibility of having a respondent in a mail survey return the questionnaire *and* to mail *separately* a postcard with his or her name on it. Thus, the researcher would be able to check off those who had responded and to send a second mailing to those who had not.

However, in many instances, this is not feasible, and the researcher must arrange to respect the privacy and confidentiality of the individuals in the research study. This can be done by coding the data obtained and keeping a separate file with the code linked to unique identifying information. The separate file can then be destroyed once the necessary data collection has been completed.

Federal legal requirements concerning confidentiality include the following:

1. The Buckley Amendment, which prohibits access to children's school records without parental consent.

2. The Hatch Act, which prohibits asking children questions about religion, sex, or family life without parental permission

3. The National Research Act, which requires parental permission for research on children

There are two circumstances in which the IRB can choose *not* to require parental permission:

1. If the research involves only minimal risk (i.e., no greater risk than in everyday life), parental permission can be waived.

2. If the parent cannot be counted on to act in the best interests of the child, parental permission can be waived. This circumstance usually involves parents who have been abusive or neglectful.

As a part of the confidentiality issue, the research participants should also be informed that the researcher is required by law to inform the appropriate authorities if they learn of any behaviors that might be injurious to the participants themselves or that cause reasonable suspicion that a child, elder, or dependent adult has been abused. In Luanna Ross's (1995) study of Native American women in prison, for example, she told her participants that she was required to report to the warden if they revealed involvement in illicit activities, such as drug usage or escape plans.

▶ *Questions for Critically Analyzing Sampling Strategies*

All of these questions might not be equally important for research conducted within the different paradigms. For example, an affirmative answer to the question about generalizability or transferability might not be as important to a researcher in the interpretive/constructivist or emancipatory paradigms. Nevertheless, an answer to the question is still possible and informative.

1. What is the population of interest? How was the sample chosen—probability, purposeful, convenience sampling? What are the strengths and weaknesses of the sampling strategy?

2. What are the characteristics of the sample? To whom can you generalize or transfer the results? Is adequate information given about the characteristics of the sample?

3. How large is the population? How large is the sample? What is the effect of the sample size on the interpretation of the data?

4. Is the sample selected related to the target population?

5. Who dropped out during the research? Were they different from those who completed the study?

6. In qualitative research, was thick description used to portray the sample?

7. In qualitative research, what is the effect of using purposive sampling on the transferability to other situations?

8. Are female participants excluded, even when the research question affects both sexes? Are male subjects excluded, even when the research affects both sexes?

9. Does the researcher report the sample composition by gender and other background characteristics, such as race or ethnicity and class?

10. How does the researcher deal with the heterogeneity of the population? Are reified stereotypes avoided and adequate opportunities provided to differentiate effects within race/gender/disability group by other pertinent characteristics (e.g., economic level)?

(Items 11 through 14 are adapted from Lincoln's, 1995, address to the AERA, *Standards for Qualitative Inquiry.*)

11. Did the researcher objectify the human beings who participated in the research study?

12. Did the researcher know the community well enough to make recommendations that will be found to be truly useful for community members?

13. Did the researcher adequately acknowledge the limitations of the research in terms of contextual factors that affect its generalizability or transferability?

14. Whose voices were represented in the research study? Who spoke for those who do not have access to the researchers? Did the researchers seek out those who are silent? To what extent are alternative voices heard?

15. If deception was used in the research, did the researcher consider the following issues (adapted from Sieber, 1992):

    a. Could participant observation, interviews, or a simulation method have been used to produce valid and informative results?

    b. Could the people have been told in advance that deception would occur, so they could then consent to waive their right to be informed?

    c. How are the privacy and confidentiality of the participants' ensured?

    d. If you are studying bad behavior, have the people agreed to participate in the study? Can you run a pilot group in which you honestly inform people of the type of behavior you are studying and determine if they would agree to participate?

    e. If studying bad behavior, is the behavior induced? How strongly?

    f. How will debriefing, dehoaxing, and desensitizing (removing any undesirable emotional consequences of the research) be handled?

    g. Is the study important enough and well designed enough to justify deception?

■ Questions and Activities for Discussion and Application

1. Using some of the research studies you previously identified through literature searches, read through the section on sample selection and participant characteristics. Try to identify the different types of sampling discussed in this chapter. Justify your choice of a "label" for the type of sampling used in the studies, based on evidence presented in the article. Be sure to look at studies that exemplify the three major paradigms discussed in this book.

2. What is your opinion of a researcher's ability to generalize results? Is it possible? Under what conditions? What do you think of the alternative concept of transferability?

3. How do you think researchers can address the issues of heterogeneity within different populations? Find examples of research studies with women, ethnic minorities, and people with disabilities. How did the researchers address heterogeneity in their studies? What suggestions do you have for improving the way this issue is addressed?

4. Select a research problem of your own (or in a group in your class). Discuss how you could use the different sampling strategies described in this chapter. Provide

examples for all of the different types of probability-based, theoretical-purposive, and convenience sampling strategies. What is the effect of the sampling strategy on the way you view your research problem? Do you find yourself modifying the research problem to accommodate the different sampling requirements?

5. Reexamine the research studies that you are using for these exercises. This time, critique studies in terms of their sampling bias. How did the researchers address this issue?

6. Compare a number of studies' sample sizes. What justification do the researchers provide for their choice of sample size?

7. Think of a simplistic experimental design that would have two groups and allow simple random sampling. Using numbers available in published literature, use the formula for calculating sample size in the chapter. Calculate the sample size needed for different levels of confidence in the results.

8. Identify a computer program that allows you to conduct a power analysis of different sample sizes. Play with the program with a hypothetical example or use a published research study to determine what the effect of having had a different sample size would have been.

9. Contact your institution's IRB. Review its requirements in terms of review of proposals and format of prospectus. Write a sample research prospectus that you think would satisfy your institution's IRB. (A smaller "bite" of the same apple: Write an informed consent form that you could use for a sample study. Variations on a theme: Write the informed consent form for an adult, for a parent of a child, for an adult with limited mental abilities.)

10. The question of whether or not researchers should be allowed to use deception in their research has been hotly debated in the research community and in the wider society. Sieber (1992) summarizes her stance as follows: "I can only hope that I have brought all readers to recognize two things: (a) Some important forms of behavior vanish under obvious scrutiny; concealment or deception is sometimes necessary in research, and (b) the more objectionable forms of deception are unnecessary" (p. 70). What is your opinion? Should deception be allowed in research? If so, under what conditions? What do you think of the conditions permitted by the various professional associations cited in this chapter (e.g., with debriefing, dehoaxing, informed consent)?

11. Identify a research study and use the questions for critical analysis to thoroughly critique its sampling section and its ethical integrity.

Notes

1. I am in good company: Cohen (1992) also published a "rule-of-thumb" guide for researchers who might find the formulaic approach too complicated. His rule-of-thumb guide is much more comprehensive than that presented here and could actually serve as a basis for decisions about sample size.

2. He chose power = .80 because smaller values would incur too great a risk of Type II error; larger values might lead to excessive cost in trying to select a larger sample.

3. The suggested sample sizes for ethnography, phenomenology, and grounded theory are from Morse's (1994) example of a comparison of strategies in the conduct of a hypothetical project.

4. Krueger (1988).

In This Chapter

■ Operationalizing concepts is explained as the basis for making decisions about data collection.

■ Standards for judging the quality of data collection are discussed from the vantage point of various paradigms:
  - Reliability and dependability
  - Validity and credibility
  - Objectivity and confirmability
  - Avoidance of bias based on gender, race and ethnicity, or disability

■ Specific topics related to quantitative measures are discussed:
  - Standardized and nonstandardized testing
  - Norm-referenced and criterion-referenced testing
  - Individual and group tests; speed and power tests
  - Performance and portfolio assessment
  - Curriculum-based assessment
  - Secondary sources of data

■ Selection and development of data collection instruments are described in terms of the following:
  - Sources of previously developed instruments
  - Steps in the development of your own instrument

■ Qualitative approaches to data collection are described:
  - Observation
  - Interviews (individual and focus groups)
  - Records and document review
  - Questions for critically analyzing data collection in research are provided.

11

Data Collection

Did deaf and hearing students increase their interactions with each other as a result of being included in the same classroom? Did the social interaction skills of all the students change as a result of training in how to work together? What concerns did the teachers and parents of the students express related to the inclusion of deaf and hearing students in the same classroom? What communication problems arose? How were these resolved? What was the cost of the intervention? What changes in school achievement were observed at the end of the school year?

The common theme of all of these questions is the need for information. We acquire information about people and things through collecting data. Data collection is the vehicle through which researchers collect information to answer their research questions and defend their conclusions and recommendations based on the findings from the research. The collection of data allows researchers to anchor what they wish to discuss in the empirical world.

In education and psychology, data is often collected to make decisions about individuals regarding diagnoses, treatment, or school placement. Data collection for individual decision making is sometimes called *psychological* or *educational* assessment. Although much of what you know about psychological and educational assessment will transfer into the research setting, you should be aware that the use of data for such decisions differs from the use made for research purposes.

Options for data collection in research include tests, mail surveys, checklists, observations, records and document reviews, and interviews (personal and telephone). Hedrick, Bickman, and Rog (1993) divided the information sources into primary—people (surveys and interviews), observation of events, physical documents (products such as student portfolios), and assessments (tests)—and secondary—administrative records, prior research studies, extant databases (e.g., the National Assessment of Educational Progress), and various forms of documentary evidence (e.g., evaluation reports). I first describe standards for judging the quality of data collection in research from various paradigmatic perspectives, and then I address more conceptual and procedural issues for quantitative and qualitative data collection strategies.

Operationalizing Concepts

The purpose of data collection is to learn something about people or things. The focus is on the particular attribute or quality of the person or setting. For example, quality of life is a subjective concept that needs to be operationalized in order to study it. Vickrey (1993) was interested in the perceptions of individuals who had undergone surgery for epilepsy about their quality of life. This measurement challenge is of interest to psychologists and educators alike because it has relevance for individuals' psychological well-being, and people with epilepsy are included in the federal definition of individuals with disabilities. Vickrey recognized the need for a conceptual model that would include the complex dimensions associated with "quality of life." The model measured physical, mental, social, and general health and included specific reference to memory problems and cognitive functioning.

In the initial stages of planning data collection, the challenge to the researcher is twofold: First, the attributes of interest must be identified; second, a decision must be made about how to collect data about those attributes. Building on the work that you did during your review of the literature, you should have formulated research questions or hypotheses that can guide you in the identification and operationalizing of the attributes. How can the researcher decide what to include in data collection? Previous experiences with the research topic is an important preliminary guide. The literature review is the central information base for identifying what attributes to include and how to collect data about them. The process of determining what to collect data about and how to do it is often referred to as *operationalizing*. That is, through these steps, the researcher identifies the strategies that will make it possible to test the concepts and theories posed through the research question.

In Vickrey's (1993) study of the quality of life for epilepsy patients following surgery, for example, she operationalized the concept "health-related quality of life" through data collection with the Epilepsy Surgery Inventory (ESI)—a 55-item, self-report measure.

Standards for Judging Quality of Data Collection

The way that the researcher chooses to operationalize the attributes is crucial in that this determines the inferences that can be made from the data. Beyond conceptual relevance and appropriateness, the researcher needs to consider the quality of the data collection strategy. The researcher must establish indicators that provide evidence that the information generated in the research is trustworthy and believable. Three standards have emerged from the postpositivist paradigm for judging the quality of quantitative research measurement: reliability, validity, and objectivity. The parallel criteria from the interpretive/constructivist paradigm collection of qualitative data are dependability, credibility, and confirmability. These last three criteria are discussed only briefly in this chapter because they were discussed in more depth in Chapter 7. Although both qualitative and quantitative researchers have traditionally expressed concern for avoidance of bias based on gender, race and ethnicity, or disability, in the emancipatory paradigm, bias related to these sources is explicitly recognized as a central tenet of research. Therefore, this category of quality for data collection is discussed within that context. You can use the outline of the standards for judging quality of data collection in research presented in the box labeled "Standards for Judging Quality of Data Collection" to guide you through this section of this chapter.

Postpositivist: Reliability

To be useful, data collection instruments must be consistent. When we measure a particular attribute, we are concerned about the accurate estimate of the target attribute. If you measured students' ability to handle interpersonal conflict one day and, without additional instruction or intervention, gave them the same instrument the next day, you would expect that their scores on the instrument would be about the same. Ability to handle interpersonal conflict, like most attributes, does not vary across time without some intervention. In this example, if the students' scores changed, their performance must have been influenced by something other than their ability to handle interpersonal conflicts. These other influences cause error; the extent to which measurement instruments are free from error indicates their reliability. The more reliable the measurement, the closer the researcher can arrive at a true estimate of the attribute addressed by the measure.

The purpose of measurement is to get an accurate estimate of a particular attribute. Accuracy is achieved by minimizing sources of error as much as possible and obtaining an estimate of how much error remains. Two types of error can influence performance on a measurement instrument: systematic and unsystematic. Systematic errors inflate or deflate performance in a fixed way and thus do not affect a measures' reliability. (They do, however, affect validity.) In the previous example, additional instruction based on systematic desensitization could be thought of as a systematic influence on performance. The effect of a systematic error on performance is constant and therefore can be predicted.

Unsystematic errors, however, are a concern for researchers. These vary at random from situation to situation and therefore cannot be predicted. Unsystematic errors are produced by factors that fall into three categories:

■ Standards for Judging Quality of Data Collection

Reliability-Dependability

    Postpositivist reliability

        Repeated measures

            • Coefficient of stability (test-retest)

            • Coefficient of equivalence (parallel forms)

        Internal consistency

            • Method of rational equivalence

        Reliability with observers

            • Interrater reliability

            • Intrarater reliability

    Interpretive/constructivist

        Dependability

Validity-Confirmability

        Postpositivist validity

            • Construct validity

            • Content validity

            • Predictive validity

            • Concurrent validity

            • Consequential validity

        Interpretive/constructivist

        Credibility

Objectivity-Confirmability

    Postpositivist—objectivity

    Interpretive/constructivist—confirmability

Avoidance of Bias Based on Gender, Race and Ethnicity, or Disability

    Emancipatory paradigm ■

---

1. Those within the person being measured (e.g., motivation or alertness)

2. The conditions of the administration of the measurement (e.g., providing different instructions, changing the environment, or allowing more time)

3. Changes in the measurement instrument or tasks (e.g., changes in the items on the instrument or the behaviors being sampled)

Typically, reliability is calculated using a statistic that compares performances by the same individuals at different times or on different parts of the instrument. The reliability coefficient is interpreted much like a correlation coefficient. As you will recall from Chapter 4, correlation coefficients range from .00 to ± 1.00, with 1.00 indicating perfect reliability, which is rarely accomplished for any measure. The closer to 1.00, the more reliable the instrument. Most reliability coefficients range from .75 to .95. The important thing to remember is that anything less than 1.00 indicates the presence of error. The researcher's task is to identify the potential sources of such error and make them public.

How is reliability determined? Researchers can use several approaches to determine the reliability of a particular data collection instrument. Two of the most common approaches involve the use of repeated measures (e.g., test-retest and parallel forms) and calculation of internal consistency (e.g., coefficient alpha or Kuder-Richardson formulas). If observational data are collected within a quantitative study, the consistency between observers and within an observer must be addressed. For a more thorough review, the reader should consult a text on measurement such as Anastasi (1988), DeVellis (1991), or Linn (1989).

Before I explain the specific ways to determine the reliability of a data collection instrument, it is important for you to know that the reliability reported in the test manual or published literature does not follow the test or instrument. Reliability should be calculated after every use. You may well find that your obtained reliability will be lower than the published ones because of differences in groups, settings, and so on. This caveat should also be kept in mind for validity claims.

Repeated Measures Reliability

Two types of repeated measures reliability are described.

Coefficient of Stability (Test-Retest). The most often used technique for determining reliability is the test-retest method. A group of individuals is administered an instrument, and the same individuals receive a second administration of the same instrument. The second administration can occur immediately or after a time delay. Scores from both administrations are compared to determine the consistency of response. One of the drawbacks of this approach is the potential for practice effects or remembering items across administrations of the test. For example, Schneider and Daniels (1992) were interested in identifying the levels of peer acceptance of the social behaviors of gifted students. They identified the Sociometric Rating Scales (Asher, Singleton, Tinsley, & Hymel, 1979). The authors cited the developers' test-retest reliability data, which ranged from .74 to .81 as supportive evidence for their selection of the scale.

Coefficient of Equivalence (Parallel Forms). If practice effects are a concern, the researcher might choose the parallel-forms approach. In this case, an *equivalent form* of the test is used in the second administration. In addition to eliminating the practice effect, this approach enables the researcher to determine the degree to which performance might be influenced by new items. Of course, the major concern with the parallel-forms reliability check is the degree to which the tests are equivalent. For example, Schunk and Rice (1992) studied the influence of comprehension strategies on reading achievement in remedial readers. Because they believed that passage familiarity might confound measurement of performance on the dependent variable in a posttest administration, they developed a parallel form. The authors reported the parallel form's reliability as .87.

Internal Consistency (Method of Rational Equivalence)

The method of rational equivalence can be used with only one administration of an instrument. It is appropriate for use when the instrument has been designed to measure a particular attribute that is expected to manifest a high degree of internal consistency. Several statistical procedures can be used; however, the most frequently used are Cronbach's coefficient alpha and various Kuder-Richardson formulas (e.g., KR-20 and KR-21). These formulas can be used to compare responses within one administration of an instrument to determine its internal consistency. Most statistical packages for computer applications will calculate a reliability coefficient such as those named here. The Epilepsy Surgery Inventory, mentioned previously, consists of 11 scales (Vickrey, 1993). The author reported that reliability was established using Cronbach's alpha and that the reliability coefficients exceeded .76 for all ESI scales except social function (which was .68). Therefore, she concluded that the instrument was reliable.

Reliability With Observers

Interrater Reliability. In studies that use quantitative data that is collected through observation, the researcher needs to be concerned with the reliability between two independent observers or raters (thus, interrater reliability). The degree of interrater reliability can be expressed either as a reliability coefficient calculated between two sets of observations collected by independent observers, or it can be expressed as a simple percentage of agreement between the two observational data sets.

Intrarater Reliability. Intrarater reliability is similar to interrater reliability, except that the comparisons are made between two data collection efforts by the *same observer* (thus, intrarater reliability). The calculations are the same: either a reliability coefficient or a percentage of agreement.

Interpretive/Constructivist: Dependability

As you will recall in Chapter 7, Guba and Lincoln (1989) identify dependability as the interpretive/constructivists' parallel standard for reliability. Within this paradigm, change is expected, and therefore, the postpositivist notion of stability is not appropriate. However, the researcher who works within this paradigm does have a responsibility to track the change and provide a publicly documentable record of the change process. The quality of the data collection can be determined by means of a dependability audit in which the change process can be inspected to attest to the quality and appropriateness of the inquiry process.

Moss (1995) raises questions about the traditional psychometric approach to establishing reliability in the context of exploring what the interpretive paradigm of research could offer to educators and psychologists interested in the quality of measurement. She describes the traditional method of determining reliability as "operationalized by examining consistency, quantitatively defined, among independent observations or sets of observations that are intended as interchangeable—consistency among independent evaluations or readings of a performance, consistency among performances in response to independent tasks, and so on" (p. 6). This reliance on quantification of consistency across independent observations requires a significant level of standardization. Privileging standardization is problematic:

> There are certain intellectual activities that standardized assessments can neither document nor promote; these include encouraging students to find their own purposes for reading and writing, encouraging teachers to make informed instructional decisions consistent with the needs of individual students, and encouraging students and teachers to collaborate in developing criteria and standards to evaluate their work. (p. 6)

Moss (1995) continues with this explanation of an alternative to reliability grounded in the interpretive paradigm:

> A hermeneutic approach to assessment would involve holistic, integrative interpretations of collected performances that seek to understand the whole in light of its parts, that privilege readers who are most knowledgeable about the context in which the assessment occurs, and that ground those interpretations not only in the textual and contextual evidence available, but also in a rational debate among the community of interpreters. Here, the interpretations might be warranted by criteria like a reader's extensive knowledge of the learning context; multiple and varied sources of evidence; an ethic of disciplined, collaborative inquiry that encourages challenges and revision to initial interpretations; and the transparency of the trail of evidence leading to the interpretations, which allows users to evaluate the conclusions for themselves. (p. 7)

Moss suggests that such a process is already being used in many assessment situations, such as awarding of graduate degrees, granting tenure, and making decisions about hiring personnel. The people who make such decisions are selected because of their areas of expertise. They are then asked to reach and support a recommendation about the qualifications of the candidates. Decisions are made on the basis of available evidence and serious discussion.

Postpositivist: Validity

The appropriateness of a data collection instrument is only partially determined by its reliability or dependability. A second category of quality is validity of the meaning of scores derived from the data collection instrument. The conventional definition of the validity of an instrument is the extent to which it measures what it was intended to measure. In practice, however, the validity of an instrument is assessed in relation to the extent to which evidence can be generated that supports the claim that the instrument measures attributes targeted in the proposed research. For example, Dumas, Wolf, Fisman, and Culligan (1991) identify three measurement tools that had been used in previous research to measure the level of stress manifested by parents of children with disabilities. The authors reported validity information for each instrument to provide evidence that the instruments were appropriate for use within their study.

Messick (1989) and Moss (1992) consider validity to be the most essential consideration in test evaluation.[1] Messick (1995) broadly defines validity as "nothing less than an evaluative summary of both the evidence for and the actual—as well as potential—consequences of score interpretation and use" (p. 742). He argues for a unified concept of validity that integrates consideration of validity of content, criteria, and consequences under the concept of construct validity. He defines construct validity as the evidence and rationales that support the trustworthiness of score meaning. He further explains construct validity as follows: "In principle as well as in practice, construct validity is based on an integration of any evidence that bears on the interpretation or meaning of test scores—including content- and criterion-related evidence—which are thus subsumed as part of construct validity" (p. 742).

An overarching concern related to validity is the extent to which the instrument measures the attributes it was intended to measure rather than bias due to gender, race and ethnicity, class, or disability. To be valid, testing must be nondiscriminatory; that is, tests and procedures used to evaluate a person's characteristics, knowledge, or attributes must be free of bias based on gender, race and ethnicity, class, disability, or other cultural factors both in the way they are administered and in the content of the items on the test. Messick (1995) identifies two major threats to construct validity:

1. Construct underrepresentation in which the assessment is too narrow and fails to include important dimensions or facets of the construct.

2. Construct-irrelevant variance in which the assessment is too broad and contains excess variance because of intrusion of other constructs.

Construct-irrelevant variance can artificially lower scores for individuals with limited reading skills or limited English skills when undue reading comprehension is required in a test of subject matter knowledge (such as on a knowledge test in science). Or scores can be artificially inflated on a test of reading comprehension for a group that has greater familiarity with the subject matter.

Messick (1989) explains that a test could not be considered valid if adverse social consequences were attributable to construct underrepresentation or construct-irrelevant variance. Messick includes appraisal of the social consequences of testing, including an awareness of the intended and unintended outcomes of test interpretation and use, as an aspect of construct validity. Because of the central importance of this issue and the advances that have been made in understanding this threat to validity in data collection, the standard of quality related to avoidance of bias is discussed as a separate topic in this chapter.

Sources of Evidence for Construct Validity

The principal method of establishing validity involves "the appraisal of theoretically expected patterns of relationships among item scores or between test scores and other measures" (Messick, 1995, p. 743). I describe a number of different approaches to studying validity. It is important to remember that validity is a unified concept and that multiple sources of evidence are needed to support the meaning of scores. According to Messick (1995), validity cannot rely on any one form of evidence; however, it is not necessary to have every form of evidence explained here.

> What is required is a compelling argument that the available evidence justifies the test interpretation and use, even though some pertinent evidence had to be foregone. Hence, validity becomes a unified concept, and the unifying force is the meaningfulness or trustworthy interpretability of the test scores and their action implications, namely construct validity. (p. 744)

Researchers interested in measuring a hypothetical construct such as intelligence, anxiety, creativity, or the like need to explicate the theoretical model that underlies the constructs. Controversy frequently surrounds the establishment of construct validity in measurement because of cultural differences that can result in different performances. For example, with tests of intelligence, researchers need to be sensitive to the extent to which they are measuring intelligence, not language or cultural differences, or opportunities to learn specific information or practice certain skills.

According to Moss (1992), the purpose of construct validity is

> to justify a particular interpretation of a test score by explaining the behavior that the test score summarizes. The proposed interpretation is the construct of interest. A strong program of construct validation requires an explicit conceptual framework, testable hypotheses deduced from it, and multiple lines of relevant evidence to test the hypotheses. (pp. 233-234)

There are a number of different ways to establish construct validity. One way involves identifying a group of people who theoretically should perform differently from other groups on the task on the basis of a pre-identified trait. For example, if I had created a test of anxiety level, I could establish two or three groups that I would predict (on the basis of theory) would perform differently on that task. The three groups might be (a) college students on vacation on a Caribbean island, (b) people who had been hospitalized because of an anxiety-related condition, and (c) students in a research methodology course.

I would predict that the students on vacation would score very low on the anxiety measure and that the hospitalized patients would score very high. I just would not know what to do with the research students, so I would probably drop them from the sample. If those who were on vacation did score low on the instrument and those in the hospital scored high, I would say the instrument has construct validity.

Construct validity can also be established by correlation with other tests that have been validated as measuring the attribute of interest or by means of factor analysis to support the structure of the attribute as it has been designed by the researcher. For example, MacMillan, Widaman, Barlow, Hemsley, and Little (1992) reported factor analyses of the Survey of School Attitudes to support their claim that the instrument measured four hypothesized factors.

Campbell (1960) points out that tests should not only correlate highly with other related measures, they should also correlate weakly with measures that are irrelevant. He calls this *convergent* and *discriminant* validation. In other words, the convergent validation means that the test score correlates highly with a predicted value (such as another test of anxiety); but it does not correlate highly with an irrelevant variable such as creativity. (Although the argument might be made that anxiety and creativity are related, we will not pursue that here.) Examples of two strategies used to establish construct validity in the Quality of Life Study (Vickrey, 1993) are presented in Sample Study 11.1.

Content Validity

If the purpose of the research is to evaluate achievement of a specific body of knowledge, the researcher needs to be concerned with content validity. The researcher needs to be certain that the test covers the appropriate content. For example, if you were studying research methodology and you entered the classroom on "test" day and found a test on underwater photography, you would probably complain that that was not covered in the course. You would be right to say that the test was not content-valid for that purpose.

To establish content validity, you need to review the items or tasks in the measurement instrument to determine the degree to which they represent the sample of the behavior domain of interest in the research study. Sometimes, it is helpful to build a specifications matrix that lists the items and the content area domains covered by each item. The higher the degree of overlap, the better the representation of the behavioral domain, the higher the content validity.

Content validity is often established using content experts to make judgments. For example, Hughes and Shumaker (1991) investigated the influence of exposure to test-taking strategies on the performance of students with learning disabilities. One of the measures that they developed for use in their study centered on test-taking skills. To assess the content validity of the instrument, the authors asked a panel of experts in special education and measurement to review the new test. According to the authors, the panelists agreed that the test items would measure the skills that they were developed to measure.

Content validity is especially important in studies that purport to compare two (or more) different curricula, teaching strategies, or school placements. If all the students are taking the same test but all the students were not exposed to the same information, the test is not equally content valid for all the groups.

Predictive Validity[2]

Sometimes, a researcher wants to use a test score to predict some future behavior. In other words, I want to obtain a measure of some attribute today and then be able to estimate the likelihood that a person will perform some specific behavior later. For example, academic institutions want to know who will succeed in specific programs prior to admission.

SAMPLE STUDY 11.1 *Construct Validity: An Example From the Quality of Life Study*

Convergent-discriminant validation. The researcher hypothesized that scores on the mood profile measure should correlate significantly with the emotional well-being scale scores of the Epilepsy Surgery Instrument (ESI) because of the similarity of content of items on these two scales. The scale correlations ranged from .57 to .68. Thus, convergent validity was established. It was also hypothesized that correlations on the mood profile measure scales would be significantly greater with the emotional well-being scale of the ESI than with the physical function scale because the latter is not a mental health measure. The correlations between the mood profile measures and the physical health subscale ranged from .14 to .25, thus confirming discriminant validation.

Hypothesized group differences. The researcher then divided the sample into three groups based on postoperative seizure outcomes:

Group 1: Seizure-free

Group 2: Simple partial seizure

Group 3: Complex partial, grand, or both

As hypothesized, seizure-free patients scored better than did patients having seizures with loss of consciousness on all 11 scales of the ESI. In addition, scores of patients having simple partial seizures fell in between the scores of the other two groups on all 11 scales. "Patients with simple partial seizures scored significantly worse than did completely seizure-free patients on scales of health perception, energy/fatigue, role limitations due to emotional problems, cognitive function, and role limitations due to memory problems" (p. S26). Thus, the instrument was judged to be construct valid for epilepsy patients following surgery.

SOURCE: Vickrey (1993).

Therefore, tests such as the Graduate Record Examination (GRE) or the Medical Schools Admissions Test (MCAT) are used by universities to predict who will be successful in their programs. Predictive validity is also important for tests that purport to measure intelligence in infants or preschoolers, school readiness tests for slightly older children, and aptitude tests for any age group.

Although time-consuming, the typical approach to establishing the predictive validity of a measurement instrument is to administer the test, wait until the predicted behavior occurs, and correlate measures of this behavior with the student's performance on the original test. As the time between the administration of the test and the opportunity to observe the predicted behavior increases, the more likely the researcher would be better off using an established instrument.

As a researcher, you should be aware of a number of variables that can constrict the value of a predictive validity coefficient. In most complex human behaviors, a variety of variables influence performance. To establish the predictive validity of a test such as the GRE, university officials would have to (theoretically speaking) allow all applicants to enter regardless of their score on the GRE. Then they would have to wait to obtain the final grade point average (GPA) for all the entrants. They could then calculate a correlation between the GRE score and the final GPA to determine the predictive validity of the GRE. Of course, this approach is fraught with problems. Here are just a few:

■ Universities try to be selective as to whom they admit, so they are not likely to admit everyone regardless of GRE scores.

■ Typically, universities use more than one criterion for selecting students, so GRE scores are not the only basis for selection.

■ The students who are accepted probably represent a restricted range on the predictive variable (i.e., the students with the higher GRE scores would be accepted).

■ Students who actually complete the program will also represent a restricted range of values on the criterion variable (i.e., the GPA) because, generally, graduate students can make only As or Bs. If they get Cs or worse, they would be on probation or suspended.

■ Many personal factors influence a student's performance in graduate school, such as motivation, economic conditions, and family responsibilities.

Thus, as a researcher, you should be sensitive to the range of values possible for the predictive and criterion variables, as well as to the other variables that might influence performance on the criterion variables.

Concurrent Validity

Concurrent validity is conceptually similar to predictive validity, except your interest is in using a test or other measurement instrument to gauge a person's current behavior, interests, personality characteristics, or knowledge. In other words, the interest is in the relationship between a test score and *current* behavior or attributes. This type of validity can also be established in a method similar to predictive validity, except that the researcher does not have to wait any specific period of time to obtain the measure on the criterion variable. This type of validity is appropriate for such characteristics as personality traits or work attitudes.

For example, if I want to determine respondents' ability to handle interpersonal conflicts, I could give them a test and then either simulate or observe their performance in a natural setting that involved interpersonal conflict. I could then calculate a correlation coefficient between the two measures to obtain the concurrent validity value. Sometimes, researchers will identify an instrument that has already established concurrent validity for measuring a particular trait. They will then administer the new instrument along with the older instrument and calculate a correlation between the two scores. If the correlation is high, the new instrument is said to have concurrent validity.

One group of researchers used concurrent validity to justify using a shorter version of a measurement instrument that was designed to identify the prevalence of dysfunctional cognitions (negative thoughts) associated with depression in students with disabilities (Maag, Behrens, & DiGangi, 1992). To determine the concurrent validity of the shorter version, they correlated students' performance on the long and short versions. Correlations between the long and short forms were found to range from .87 to .96, indicating that the two tests measured the same attributes.

Consequential Validity

Consequential validity refers to the social consequences of test interpretation and use. Messick (1995) cautions that this type of validity should not be viewed in isolation as a separate type of validity because it is integrally connected with construct validity. The researcher needs to identify evidence of negative and positive, intended and unintended, outcomes of test interpretation and use.

> A major concern in practice is to distinguish adverse consequences that stem from valid descriptions of individual and group differences from adverse consequences that derive from sources of test invalidity such as construct underrepresentation and construct-irrelevant variance. The latter adverse consequences of test invalidity present measurement problems that need to be investigated in the validation process, whereas the former consequences of valid assessment represent problems of social policy. (p. 744)

The researcher must ensure that low scores do not occur because

> the assessment is missing something relevant to the focal construct that, if present, would have permitted the affected persons to display their competence. Moreover, low scores should not occur because the measurement contains something irrelevant that interferes with the affected persons' demonstration of competence. (p. 746)

Interpretive/Constructivist: Credibility

Guba and Lincoln (1989) identify credibility as the interpretive/constructivists' parallel to validity. The rationale that supports this criterion is the question, Is there a correspondence between the way the respondents actually perceive social constructs and the way the researcher portrays their viewpoints. The following research strategies can enhance credibility (see Chapter 7 for more details):

- Prolonged and substantial engagement
- Persistent observation
- Peer debriefing
- Negative case analysis
- Progressive subjectivity
- Member checks
- Triangulation

By these means, the researcher can increase the credibility of the results of a qualitative study.

Moss (1996) suggests that a more integrated approach to assessment would serve all researchers well who use educational and psychological tests. She points out that

> interpretive methods can illuminate some of the more subtle ways in which assessment choices interact with the local context, affecting the validity of the intended interpretation and the consequences of assessment use—how the local transforms and is transformed by the assessment practice. By drawing on the strengths of research traditions beyond our own, I believe we become better able to theorize and evaluate complex ways that assessment practices work within an educational system. (p. 23)

Specifically, Moss suggests that the psychometric tradition can be enhanced by adding alternative methodologies (less standardized) for assessments and by conducting case studies of the contexts in which assessments take place.

Postpositivist: Objectivity

In quantitative studies, objectivity refers to how much the measurement instrument is open to influence by the beliefs and biases of the individuals who administer, score, or interpret it. Objectivity is determined by the amount of judgment that is called for in these three processes. More objective measures consist of short-answer, multiple-choice, and true-false format options. Less objective measures include essay tests, although these can be made more objective by establishing criteria for scoring the responses. Standardized tests are often described as very objective because the instructions are read verbatim from the test manual; the manual tells the amount of time allowed and acceptable answers to students' questions; and answers are scored objectively with an answer key.

In some research situations, objectivity is deliberately sacrificed to allow the respondents a wider range of possible responses. Objectivity in projective tests can be exchanged for the value of having expert judgment involved in the administration, scoring, and interpretation of the test results. In cases such as this, it is important to know that the persons who are responsible for the test processes have received the necessary training in the administration, scoring, and interpretation of the tests. You should ask, What are the researchers' qualifications? What steps were taken to reduce bias? Was it possible to use "blind" testers (i.e., people who are unaware of the experimental condition of the respondent administrate the test)?

When the measurement instrument is a person who serves as an interviewer, observer, or reviewer of documents, the concern arises as to the objectivity of the person as instrument. Then you might ask, Are these data independent of the person doing the observations? Would another person come to the same conclusions? Would the observer have seen things the same way at a later date? These are issues that are addressed in the interpretive/constructivist paradigm.

Interpretive/Constructivist: Confirmability

Just as postpositivists seek to minimize the influence of the observer's judgment, the interpretive/constructivist researcher seeks to confirm that the data and their interpretation are not figments of the researcher's imagination (Guba & Lincoln, 1989). A confirmability audit can be used to trace the data to its original sources and to confirm the process of synthesizing data to reach conclusions using a chain of evidence.

Emancipatory Paradigm: Avoidance of Bias

All researchers, in all paradigms, must be sensitive to avoiding bias in data collection that results from differences in gender, race or ethnicity, sexual orientation, religion, disability, or socioeconomic status. As you read previously, psychometricians include assessment of the social consequences of test interpretation and use as a part of construct validity. Messick (1995) addresses the issue as follows:

> Some measurement specialists argue that adding value implications and social consequences to the validity framework unduly burdens the concept. However, it is simply not the case that values are being *added* to validity in this unified view. Rather, values are intrinsic to the meaning and outcomes of the testing and have always been. As opposed to adding values to validity as an adjunct or supplement, the unified view instead exposes the inherent value aspects of score meaning and outcome to open examination and debate as an integral part of the validation process (Messick, 1989b). This makes explicit what has been latent all along, namely, that validity judgments *are* value judgments. (p. 748)

Moss (1995) also reminds us that "If interpretations are warranted through critical dialogue, then the question of who participates in the dialogue becomes an issue of power" (p. 9). She criticizes the traditional psychometric approach because it "silences the voices of those who are most knowledgeable about the context and most directly affected by the results" (p. 10).

Because this is the central concern of the emancipatory paradigm, I describe specific examples of ways that data collection has been insensitive on these criteria and ways that it can be made to be more sensitive. My examples derive from writings about data collection from the perspectives of feminists, racial and ethnic minorities (African American, Native American Indian, and Latino American), and people with disabilities.

Feminists Issues in Data Collection

Eichler (1991) identifies a number of issues related to data collection that provide evidence of sexist bias in the collection of research data. Problems that researchers should avoid include the following:

1. Research instruments validated for one sex that are used for both sexes
2. Questions that use sexist language
3. Studies that do not take into account the fact that male and female researchers may elicit different responses from respondents
4. Questions premised on the notion of sex-inappropriate behavior, traits, or attributes
5. Research instruments that stress sex differences with the effect of minimizing the existence and importance of sex similarities
6. Gender insensitivity demonstrated by people being asked about the behaviors, traits, or attributes of members of the other sex and such information treated as fact rather than opinion

Lewin and Wild (1991) examined the impact of the feminist critique on tests, assessment, and methodology through an analysis of changes in psychological, vocational, and educational tests. They note,

> Tests that classify respondents on the basis of their similarity to people who are located in highly sex-stereotyped settings, such as the occupational world, risk reproducing patterns of past discrimination. It is easier for the feminist critique to call attention to a few blatantly sexist individual items on a scale than to get fundamental changes of familiar measures. (p. 585)

They compared the impact on testing in two different contexts: the Strong-Campbell Interest Inventory (successful) and the Minnesota Multiphasic Personality Inventory (MMPI) (not successful). The story of these two tests provides some insight into the issues that feminists raise about testing and measurement.

When the Strong Vocational Interest Blank was first published, women with interests in "typical male occupations" were compared with men in that occupational area. As a result of feminist critique, the test was revised so that women could be compared not only with men but also with other women who were in that occupation. The 1987 revised form, called the Strong-Campbell Interest Inventory, included sex-merged forms and an updated reference group. In that edition, only 5 of the 207 occupations lacked adequate samples of both genders (i.e., female agribusiness managers and male dental assistants, dental hygienists, home economics teachers, and secretaries).

Continuing problems with the MMPI illustrate that changes are still needed in psychological testing to avoid bias based on gender. One of the MMPI scales is called "Masculinity-Femininity" (Mf). The femininity score was originally validated in 1956 on a criterion group of 13 gay men. Yes, the scale that was supposed to assess the femininity of heterosexual women was based on a small number of gay men. When the test was revised in 1990, a new normative, nationally representative sample of the U.S. population was drawn; however, the Mf scores were not validated against any criterion whatsoever. The test manual describes various characteristics associated with high and low scorers on the Mf scale; however, it does not provide any validity data (concurrent or construct) to support the claims. Butcher (1989) states that although the manual uses characterizations such as males who score highly on the feminine scale are

> likely to be "sensitive, aesthetic, passive," and possibly have "low heterosexual drive," while low-scoring males are viewed as "aggressive, crude, adventurous, reckless, practical, and having narrow interests," no evidence is offered. Females who score highly "masculine" are seen as "rough, aggressive, self-confident, unemotional, and insensitive," whereas low-scoring (i.e., "feminine") women are seen as "passive, yielding, complaining, fault-finding, idealistic, and sensitive." (cited in Lewin & Wild, 1991, p. 586)

Lewin and Wild (1991) conclude that the MMPI Mf scale is ambiguous and open to bias and potential discrimination based on inappropriate use of it in contexts such as personnel hiring. They suggest that the scale should be dropped until such time as the developers can provide clear evidence of what they are measuring. They do recommend other sources in which a researcher can find more appropriate gender and sex role measures, such as Beere's (1990a) *Sex and Gender Issues: A Handbook of Tests and Measures.*

Lewin and Wild noted a number of other advances that have occurred in terms of avoidance of gender bias in testing and measurement:

1. The *Standards for Educational and Psychological Testing* (American Educational Research Association, American Psychological Association, and National Council on Measurement in Education, 1985b) includes reference to gender differences, item bias, predictive bias, and differential prediction that were not included in earlier editions. "The new standards that are most relevant to gender concerns suggest that when one is selecting content and type of items, consideration should be given to gender groups" (Standard 3.5, p. 598). The standards also suggest that criterion-related validity studies should be conducted for groups "for which previous research has established a substantial prior probability of differential prediction for the particular kind of test in question" (Standard 1.20, p. 17).

2. The *Code of Fair Testing Practices in Education* (American Psychological Association, Joint Committee on Testing Practices, 1988) recommends the revision of test questions that contain potentially insensitive content or language and that investigations be conducted into the performance of test takers of different races, gender, and ethnic backgrounds.

3. The Educational Testing Service (ETS) instituted some changes related to gender issues, specifically the introduction of the ETS Sensitivity Review Process, investigation of differential performance by gender and racial groups, and inclusion of women on committees responsible for test development.

People With Disabilities: Issues in Data Collection

The influence of the theoretical framework on the types of questions asked of people with disabilities is described in Chapter 5. You will recall that questions can be framed to suggest that the problem is "in" the individual with the disability or to suggest that the problem is "in" the societal response to the individual's needs.

Mertens and McLaughlin (1995) provide a summary of the types of accommodations that have been investigated for data collection with people with disabilities. On the basis of work by Thurlow, Ysseldyke, and Silverstein (1993) and Bennett and Ragosta (1988), the following types of accommodations have been identified: the use of Braille for tests, audio-cassette tapes, and large-print tests; oral reading of the text; large-type answer sheets; changing the test environment; flexible time arrangements (e.g., unlimited time or taking the test over several sessions to alleviate fatigue); signing instructions; and various assistive devices, such as Braillers, slate and stylus, magnifying glass, or tape recorder.

Bennett and Ragosta's (1988) work was based on research on the use of the GRE with people with disabilities. They reported that for students with learning disabilities, poor reading skills might prevent accurate performance, because of a lack of understanding of the test instructions and problems presented in context (e.g., word problems in math). Therefore, they recommend the use of modifications to testing conditions, such as using cassette tapes. For deaf students, they recommend use of sign language for instructions, videotapes, and performance-based rather than language-based measurement of cognitive and spatial abilities. For partially sighted people, they recommend large type, holding the page close, and magnification devices. People who are totally blind can augment their tactual or auditory senses by use of readers, Braille books, audiotapes, raised-line drawings, three-dimensional models, talking calculators, and Braille computers. For people who are physically disabled, the use of an *amanuensis* (person who records responses) and allowing extra time because of fatigue may be necessary.

In 1988, the Special Populations Group was established in the Division of Education Policy Research at ETS (Clewell, Brown, Mounty, & Villegas, 1993). This team of researchers focuses on research related to testing for racial and ethnic minorities, women, people of limited English proficiency, and people with disabilities. With specific reference to testing people with disabilities, they reported that the nonstandard versions of the SAT and GRE were comparable in most important psychometric respects (Ragosta, 1992, cited in Mounty & Anderson, 1993). For some learning disabled students, the test scores obtained under nonstandard conditions overpredicted first-year college performance. For deaf and hard of hearing students, the test scores underpredicted their first-year college performance. One possible explanation for these results is that the standardized tests do not capture the true capabilities of the deaf and hard of hearing students.

Ragosta and Wendler (1992) investigated the time requirements for people with different types of disabilities taking the SAT. They reported that time-and-a-half to double time was appropriate for deaf and hard of hearing examinees, candidates with physical or learning disabilities, and candidates with visual impairments less than total blindness. For persons using a reader or scribe or taking Braille or cassette versions of the test, double to triple time was found to be necessary. These time estimates need to be understood within the context that they were produced—that is, for testing in a multiple-choice, paper-and-pencil format. They should not be generalized to other formats, such as items that require a constructed response or essay. In addition, the time estimates might vary greatly for tests of a different purpose, such as professional certification tests.

The ETS is providing a model for other researchers by conducting research on the effects of test accommodations, considering specific issues pertaining to specific disabilities in the development of new tests, and including individuals with disabilities in pilot testing and field trials in all their major testing programs (Mounty & Anderson, 1993). The following is a description of one of the research projects that the ETS has been conducting in accommodation of testing for deaf individuals:

> Several projects have focused on prospective deaf teachers as nonnative speakers of English with unique testing needs. . . . [In one exploratory study,] . . . deaf students in teacher preparation programs provided both signed and written responses to essay prompts. The essays were holistically scored using essentially the same scoring rubric for signed and written responses. Mounty (1990, 1991) found that even without specific instruction in the process, some individuals produced high-quality signed responses, whereas after years of instruction in English composition, they produced mediocre to poor written essays. In that same study, one of two essay prompts elicited high-quality written essays as well as high-quality signed responses, while the responses to the other prompt tended to receive lower ratings, suggesting that the content of some essay items may be more congruent with the experiences of deaf individuals than others" (Mounty & Anderson, 1993, p. 32).

The ETS is also experimenting with computer-based testing accessible to examinees with disabilities in terms of videodisc systems that display written text simultaneously with an insert of a person translating the text into sign language, voice synthesizers that simulate speech for individuals who are blind, and movement controls that allow a person with difficulty speaking and limited hand movement to both enter text and respond to text presented on the monitor (ETS, 1992). In one study (Mounty & Anderson, 1993), four individuals participated in a computer-based pilot test of the GRE. One individual was deaf, one had a severe visual impairment, and two had learning disabilities. Despite the use of the computer-based technology, the researchers reported that many of the issues tied to test content and item construction that were problematic for paper-and-pencil tests remain unresolved in the experimental setting.

Many frontiers are opening through the use of technology; however, research is needed to determine the best way to make use of this technology for obtaining high-quality data. The National Center for Fair and Open Testing (FairTest, 1993) raised questions about the use of computers in testing with persons with disabilities: Is there adequate evidence that scores of computerized and paper-and-pencil tests are equivalent? Will computerized tests constrain users because they cannot underline, scratch out eliminated choices, or scan materials in the same way they can with paper-and-pencil tests? Additional research is needed in this area to answer these questions.

Another issue related to testing for people with disabilities relates to their inclusion in large-scale testing programs such as the National Assessment of Educational Progress

(NAEP). Researchers who are interested in using data from such existing databases to study the experiences of individuals with disabilities should be aware of the limitations imposed because of variations in inclusion of such individuals in the testing programs. Variations in the criteria for inclusion, and in the implementation of modifications to testing procedures, represent challenges for the researcher. The basis for inclusion of students with disabilities, and the types of acceptable modifications across states in minimum competency programs, is quite variable (McGrew, Thurlow, & Spiegel, 1993; Thurlow et al., 1993). In addition, McGrew et al. (1993) reported exclusion rates on the NAEP for students with disabilities that ranged from 33% to 87% across states. The variability in inclusion criteria and accommodations yield test results that are not easily interpretable across groups.

Racial and Ethnic Minorities: Issues in Data Collection

The use of standardized tests in particular have raised cause for concern about bias against members of racial and ethnic minority groups. The National Commission on Testing and Public Policy (1990) reported that performance on both educational and employment tests in the United States has been significantly lower for American Indians, some Asian Americans, Latinos, African Americans, Native Pacific Islanders, and other minority groups compared with their White counterparts. Lower test scores are particularly problematic in that test scores are used to allocate opportunities for higher education and improved employment.

McDowell (1992) recognizes the power factor in the determination of the nature of the tests that are constructed. The tests are generally constructed by the type of people who do well on that type of test. He calls for a reconceptualization of the methods of measurement and a reexamination of the methods for interpreting responses to make testing culturally appropriate.

Specific problems related to the use of standardized tests with racial and ethnic minorities have been identified by a number of authors. The following list is a synthesis of issues mentioned by Patton (1993) and Suzuki and Kugler (1995):

1. *Test content.* Inclusion of items that reflect White middle-class values and noninclusion of items and procedures that reflect various racial and ethnic minority groups.

2. *Examinee readiness, motivation, and response set.* Most middle-class children have been socialized to accept the cultural values that achievement is an individual accomplishment and that such accomplishment should be publicly displayed (Davis, 1992). However, many non-middle-class children and children from other cultures do not share those values. Thus, many children have no clear idea of what testing is when they encounter it for the first time in school, nor have they grown up in environments in which children are asked to give information to adults. Davis (1992) uses as an example many American Indian cultures that socialize children through nonverbal communication, emphasizing visual and spatial memory, visual and motor skills, and sequential visual memory over verbal skills. Many of these cultures also emphasize sharing and working together. The tests that these children

encounter in school focus on verbal skills and force children to work alone. Because of the patterns of teaching in Navajo society, many Navajo children encountering a test for the first time see it literally as a game, not as an evaluation tool (McShane, 1989).[3]

3. *Standardization level.* Racial and ethnic groups are often underrepresented in standardization samples. National norms more commonly reflect predominantly White, middle-class samples, for which results may be inappropriately applied to minorities.

4. *Examiner bias and language differences.* Noninclusion of individuals knowledgeable of and sensitive to language and cultural differences can result in bias in the results. The test administrator can misjudge, stereotype, or intimidate the respondent because of difficulties in verbal and nonverbal communication.

5. *Reliability and validity issues.* Because tests are developed with specific populations, the reliability and validity for racial and ethnic minority groups may be questionable. Tests may actually measure different attributes when used with individuals from different cultures (construct validity), and the predictive validity may be inaccurate in comparison to White, middle-class individuals.

6. *Societal inequities.* Because of histories of oppression and discrimination, members of racial and ethnic minority groups are already at a disadvantage in educational and vocational achievement. Thus, discrepancies between groups may reflect systemic problems rather than deficits inherent in the individuals providing the data.

Suzuki and Kugler (1995) suggest the following issues in the use of intellectual and personality instruments with different racial and ethnic groups:

---

1. *Conceptual equivalence.* The researcher needs to check that the concepts being measured have the same meaning across and within different cultural groups (called *concept equivalence*).

2. *Demographic and environmental variables.* Demographic and environmental variables, such as language, socioeconomic status, educational level, acculturation status, and region of the country, must be taken into consideration. Be aware of the multiplicity of factors that can influence performance, such as poverty, educational failure, malnutrition, and other health-related concerns.

3. *Racial identity and level of acculturation.* Knowing how the people in your research study perceive their own racial identities can be important because it may influence the impact of cultural influences such as the nature and configuration of symptoms, the way in which problems are reported, strategies of problem solving, attributions regarding the origin of the presenting concerns, and appropriate interventions. Some individuals of different racial and ethnic groups may adhere strongly to the beliefs and values of the dominant White culture to the exclusion of their own racial identity. Others may value their own culture to the exclusion of the dominant culture. Information regarding identity development and acculturation may be obtained through interviews or standardized measures.

4. *Use of translated measures.* Translated materials can be helpful; however, they should be used cautiously. The problem of concept equivalence must be addressed, because psychological constructs may not have such a direct translation in another culture. The researcher should also check to see if the format is acceptable to people in that culture and that validity and reliability are established for the different cultural group. You should also investigate the method of translation that was used to be sure that a back translation yields similar concepts. Here is an example of the challenges in translating a Spanish Version of the Expectations About Counseling Questionnaire.

> Campbell, Brislin, Stewart, and Werner (as cited in Brislin, 1970) described four techniques for translation for cross-cultural research: back-translation, bilingual technique, committee approach, and pretest procedure. All four translation techniques were used in this study. Combining the back-translation and committee procedures, the EAC-B was first translated from English to Spanish by a committee of bilingual individuals and then back-translated into English. Translators and back-translators were four graduate students in counseling who had been schooled in both English and Spanish. Three were foreign-born, nonnative English speakers from Cuba, the Dominican Republic, or El Salvador. Average length of time in the United States was 12.67 years (range 8-18). The fourth translator was Cuban American and born in the United States. The English versions were then compared, and discrepant items were retranslated and back-translated, again using the committee procedure. After a comparable Spanish version was obtained via this procedure, both versions were examined by another bilingual individual who completed the fine-tuning of the Spanish version. This person was a Cuban-born, nonnative English speaking university professor who had received formal schooling in both English and Spanish and had been in the United States for 31 years. (Burhke & Jorge, 1992, p. 366)

5. *Language Dominance.* The researcher should determine the individual's dominant language and make arrangements to collect the information using the person's dominant language. Suzuki and Kugler (1995) suggest that assessment be made in both English and the person's primary language.

Quantitative Measurement Topics

A researcher needs to decide whether to (a) use a measurement instrument that is commercially available or that has been developed by other researchers, (b) adapt an existing instrument, or (c) create a new one to meet the needs of the proposed research. In quantitative research, your decision will be clearer if you understand some of the common terms used in describing different types of measurement instruments.

Standardized and Nonstandardized Tests

Standardized tests, such as the SAT and the GRE, have been mentioned in the previous sections of this chapter. Other commonly used standardized tests include many intelligence and personality instruments. The distinguishing characteristic of standardized tests is that they have uniformity in directions for administering and scoring the instrument, as well as having been through rigorous developmental cycles. The nonstandardized test is usually not developed through a rigorous process and has a limited purpose and application, such as a teacher-made test or that developed by a researcher for a specific study.

With norm-referenced standardized tests, a reference group of people participated in the standardization of the test, to which researchers can compare the performance of their respondents. This reference group is referred to as the *norm group*. The norm group's raw scores on the test are compiled into norm tables, often in the form of percentile ranks, which furnish the percentage of students in the norm group who received the same score or lower. Researchers using the test can compare the performance of their respondents to the norm tables.

As mentioned in the previous section concerning bias based on race or ethnicity, gender, and disability, researchers who choose to use standardized measures are faced with the challenge of locating an instrument that was developed with a norm group that matches the group in the proposed research study. If the research sample is composed of students with learning disabilities, the researcher would have to check the test manual to identify the characteristics of the norm group to determine if students with learning disabilities were in the norm group and if there was a norm table specifically for this group.

Unfortunately, standardized tests are usually globally referenced to the general population. Thus, most of them do not contain information about the performance of persons with specific disabilities, and persons with more severe disabilities are most frequently omitted. This does not mean that the test could not be used in the research study. However, the researcher should not use the norms for interpretations or generalizations. Parallel problems face the researcher who wishes to use standardized instruments with racial and ethnic minority groups.

The researcher should be sensitive to the composition of the norm group, the heterogeneity of the population, the possibility of regression toward the mean for extreme groups, adaptations that might violate standardized administration procedures, development of local norms, language differences, and cultural bias.

Individual and Group Tests: Speed and Power Tests

Some tests are administered on an individual basis, and others are administered to groups. This is an important distinction, especially with groups that might not be part of the dominant language or culture. For example, in special education, some attributes, such as intelligence, might be more appropriately measured individually than in a group. Another category of measurement is known as *speed* or *power* tests. Speed tests are made up of relatively simple items, and the administration requires a specified, and usually fairly short, response time. On the other hand, power tests are composed of difficult items that are responded to in a more liberal time frame. This distinction is important for members of nondominant cultural or language groups, as well as for people with disabilities. Such respondents might require additional time and thus would be penalized on speed tests.

Norm-Referenced and Criterion-Referenced Testing

Most standardized tests are norm referenced; that is, the research samples' performance can be compared with the performance of individuals in a well-defined, previously tested group (the norm group). In criterion-referenced testing, the test is designed to address the content or domain of the attribute being tested. The concept of criterion is applied when the researcher identifies a particular level of performance that test takers should reach as a result of being exposed to a particular intervention.

Performance and Portfolio Assessment

Performance assessment (sometimes called authentic assessment) is an emerging form of measurement that involves determining how well individuals can do something, as opposed to what they know about doing it (ETS, 1995). Performance assessments are not new in the sense that teachers have used them for years to determine students' abilities to swim, dance, play music, drive a car, or repair a car engine. However, in other academic disciplines, performance tests have been less common. Performance assessment in disciplines such as mathematics, science, or language arts can be designed to evoke complex cognitive behaviors, such as high-level thinking, communication, and analytical skills.

In education, portfolios are used as one method of implementing performance assessments. Portfolios take different forms but might consist of an accordion folder with a variety of products that each student produces such as audiotapes, videotapes, pictures, and copies of students' written work (Wesson & King, 1996). Rather than multiple-choice tests, the portfolio work would consist of authentic tasks, such as students' written reactions to a novel, a position statement on issues, and lists of books read. Wesson and King provide two examples of portfolios in special education that document the social progress of a boy with serious emotional disturbance and transitional vocational experiences for a 16-year-old student with severe disabilities.

Performance and portfolio assessment strategies are not without challenges psychometrically. Moss (1992) discusses the particular challenges related to the validity of performance measures in which she notes that the consequences of performance assessment are likely to be more beneficial to teaching and learning than are the consequences of multiple-choice assessments when used alone. The performance tasks themselves are not easy to develop, and considerable training is necessary for their proper administration (ETS, 1995). The issue of interjudge and intrajudge reliability is an issue in scoring solutions to performance tasks. Judges must have a common understanding of what constitutes high-quality work. Performance tasks can elicit any number of solutions; therefore, judges need sophisticated scoring criteria that can differentiate between diverse levels of student performance. The Center for Research on Evaluation, Standards, and Student Testing has studied the applicability of performance testing in schools and research. Additional information can be found in their newsletters: the *CRESST Line* (1992-1995) and *Evaluation Comment* (1993).

Curriculum-Based Assessment

Curriculum-based assessment was developed within the context of special education to determine the student's achievement of "enroute" and terminal objectives (Fuchs & Deno,

1991). It is designed to collect information on the instructional needs of students through the continuous, direct observation of student performance. The information collected reflects both the student's approach to the learning task and the products developed. Generally, such information is used to make decisions about the individual; however, Fuchs, Fuchs, and Fernstrom (1992) used curriculum-based assessment as one of their dependent measures in a study of the reintegration of special education students into mainstream classrooms.

Secondary Data Sources

Secondary sources of data can be found, for example, in sources such as administrative records and previous research studies. Analysis of existing documents is discussed in a subsequent section of this chapter on qualitative data collection methods. However, there are considerable quantitative databases that researchers should know about. Several examples were mentioned in Chapter 5 of this text on survey research. Other examples include the National Assessment of Educational Progress, the High School and Beyond Longitudinal Studies, and the National Longitudinal Transition Study of Special Education Students.

Such databases can provide a wealth of information; however, they should be used with appropriate caution. Some national databases do not allow for disaggregation by variables such as race, gender, or type of disability. In others, certain categories of persons have actually been excluded. For example, NAEP excludes educable mentally retarded students and those with functional disabilities (unless they can respond to the tasks) (National Association of State Directors of Special Education [NASDSE], 1988). The exclusion decision is the responsibility of the local school division. McGrew et al. (1993) report that the basis for inclusion of students with disabilities and the types of acceptable modifications across states were quite variable. Exclusion rates on the NAEP for students with disabilities ranged from 33% to 87% across states.

Selection and Development of Quantitative Instruments

Now that you have a basic understanding of the "language" of psychometrics, measurement, and data collection, you are in a position to decide on the best method for collecting your data. Qualitative data collection methods are discussed in the final section of this chapter. In this section, I address the sources and criteria for choosing to use an existing instrument for quantitative research.

Identifying an Instrument: Sources of Information

In your literature review, you may have come across a measurement instrument that was used in previous research that seems "just right" for your purposes. If so, that is great! It will give you a place to start to determine if that is, indeed, the appropriate instrument for you. I will first explain sources of information about tests and other data collection instruments, and then I will discuss criteria for the selection of existing instruments. Your first source of information about possible data collection instruments for your own research is the literature review. If you have not zeroed in on a particular instrument through your initial searching, now is the time to go back to the databases described in Chapter 2 and conduct a more focused search to determine what instruments have been used to measure your constructs of interest.

In addition, other sources, listed here, have been created specifically to make your search for a data collection instrument easier and more thorough.

> Kramer, J. J., & Conoley, J. C. (1992). *The eleventh mental measurement yearbook.* Lincoln: University of Nebraska Press.

The *Mental Measurement Yearbooks* (MMY) have been published periodically since 1938. New yearbooks are published about every second year, with a supplement published during alternate years. (The *Supplement to the Tenth Mental Measurements Yearbook* was published in December 1990, with Jack J. Kramer, Jane Close Conoley, and Linda L. Murphy as editors.) The 11th yearbook contains descriptive information on 477 tests in 18 major categories. Each new yearbook contains information about tests that have been published or revised since the last edition or that have generated 20 or more references since the last *MMY.* The information about each test in the *MMY* is quite extensive, including the title, group for which the test is intended, its acronym, available subscale scores, criticism of the test, whether it is for individuals or groups, how many forms are available, its cost, the author and publisher, and references on construction, validity, use, and limitations. In addition, test reviews are printed that are written specifically for the *MMY.*

Tests in the *MMY* are printed in alphabetical order by title. However, each test also has an entry number that you can use to locate the test from the indexes in the *MMY.* A variety of indexes are provided, including by title, acronym, classified subject (the 18 major categories), publisher, and author.

> Murphy, Linda L., Conoley, Jane Close, & Impara, James C. (1994). *Tests in print IV: An index to tests, test reviews, and the literature on specific tests.* Lincoln: University of Nebraska—Lincoln, Buros Institute of Mental Measurements.

Tests in Print (TIP) serves as a supplemental source of information to the *MMY* in that it contains a comprehensive bibliography of all tests that appeared in preceding *MMYs.* However, *TIP* is not limited to tests that have been published, revised, or generated 20 or more references since the last *MMY.* Rather, it contains information about any test that is *in print and available for purchase or use.* Like the *MMY,* the *TIP* is organized alphabetically by test name and contains a number of indexes that use entry numbers to refer to specific tests. The information about each test is not as extensive in the *TIP* as in the *MMY.* However, the *TIP* does provide references to the appropriate *MMY* for readers who require more detailed information.

The Educational Testing Service

The Educational Testing Service (ETS) provides a wide range of means to access information about tests. It maintains a test collection that contains over 17,000 tests and other measurement devices from the United States and a few other countries (Canada, England, and Australia). The test collection is accessible to any qualified person, based on publishers' restrictions. The ETS publishes over 200 annotated test bibliographies in specific subject areas, available for a modest fee. The bibliographies include the following information about each test: title, author, publication date, target population, publisher or source, and an annotation indicating the purpose of the instrument.

The test collection file is now available as a publicly searchable database on the Internet on the World Wide Web. The test collection provides current information on available published and unpublished tests and related activities. The online database (label ETSF) uses ERIC descriptors and can be searched using the same search strategies used to access ERIC. For more information, contact ETS at (609) 734-5667 in Princeton, New Jersey.

Some tests are not available commercially. Therefore, ETS makes many of these test available on microfiche through their program called Tests in Microfiche. Sets of tests are prepared annually, and they may be purchased individually or as a complete set.

> Beere, Carole A. (1990). *Gender roles: A handbook of tests and measures.* Westport, CT: Greenwood.

In this volume, Beere lists 190 scales that concern gender roles or attitudes related to gender or gender issues. The information includes title, author(s), date of publication (and revision, if appropriate), variable(s) measured, type of instrument, description, sample items, previous subjects, appropriate subjects, administration, scoring, development, reliability, validity, where the scale is available, publications that used the scale, and additional bibliography.

> Beere, Carole A. (1990). *Sex and gender issues: A handbook of tests and measures.* Westport, CT: Greenwood.

This volume also presents information for each scale reviewed in a format consistent with that found in *Gender Roles*. The second volume contains descriptions of scales (also 190 in number) on the topics of heterosexual relations, sexuality, contraception and abortion, pregnancy and childbirth, somatic issues (primarily menstrual cycle), homosexuality, rape and sexual coercion, family violence, body image and appearance, and eating disorders.

The Test Publisher. If you feel fairly certain that you want to use a particular measurement instrument, you can request a copy directly from the publisher. Most instruments come with a manual that explains administration procedures and other background information about the test. You should be cautious about using the test manual as your sole source of information about a test, because it may not present information that is critical of the test. Always be sure to check multiple sources for information about any instrument that you decide to use.

Criteria for Selecting an Instrument

The following list can be used to help you in selecting your data collection instrument:

1. Identify the intended purpose of the instrument as it was conceptualized by the author.
2. Identify your own purpose in collecting data; who do you intend to use it with and for what reason.
3. Identify the variables that the instrument measures; are subscales and multiple constructs involved?
4. Examine the validity information available for the instrument. What type of validity is reported; how was it established?
5. Examine the reliability information that is available. What type and level of reliability is reported? How was it established?
6. What is the age range and type of person for whom the instrument is appropriate? If it is a norm-referenced instrument, what is the composition of the norm group?
7. What are the conditions for administration? Is it group or individual?
8. What type of training is needed for administration, scoring, and interpretation?
9. Are alternate or short forms available?
10. How much time is required for administration and scoring the instrument?
11. What is the cost of the instrument? Can it be scored by hand? Is it possible to score it with a computer? Can you do it yourself, or do you have to send in the responses to the publisher or distributor?
12. Does the instrument satisfy concerns about language and culture in terms of avoiding bias on the basis of gender, race and ethnicity, and disability?
13. What is the format of the instrument? How much time is needed for administration? To what extent do these features promote or restrict accuracy of assessment for the people in the proposed research?

If modifications are made in an available instrument, Thurlow et al. (1993) suggest that the researcher ask the following questions:

1. If accommodation is made on the basis of a specific characteristic (e.g., a disability), how should eligibility for accommodation be determined?
2. What type of modifications should be allowed?
3. Do scores achieved under nonstandard conditions have the same meaning?
4. If there is a difference in performance levels between standard and nonstandard administrations, are these due to actual differences in the construct being measured, or are they artifacts of modifications of the testing process?

Researchers can use pilot tests to determine the impact of modifications of existing instruments.

Developing a Data Collection Instrument

Development of a data collection instrument is a complex and time-consuming task. After an exhaustive search of the literature, you may determine that no existing instrument will measure exactly the construct in which you are interested. Thus, you will find it necessary to develop your own data collection instrument. The steps outlined here give you a rough guide to this complex process. If you really intend to get involved in instrument development, you should check on other sources that provide more detail, such as DeVellis (1991), Gable (1986), and Morris, Fitz-Gibbon, and Lindheim (1987). The American Educational Research Association's (1985b) *Standards for Educational and Psychological Tests* is another good resource.

The following steps are adapted from Devellis (1991) and Borg and Gall (1989). Similar steps can be found in most test and measurement texts. These steps relate to the measurement of a construct such as optimism or anxiety. If you are interested in collecting information from a general survey instrument, review the steps for constructing a questionnaire in Chapter 5. In this section, I use the development of the Epilepsy Surgery Inventory (Vickrey, 1993) as an example of the instrument development process.

Step 1: Define the Objective of Your Instrument. What is the specific purpose of the proposed measurement instrument? What information do you want on what attribute? Vickrey (1993) defines the purpose of the ESI this way: "The goal of our group of researchers was to supplement traditional seizure outcome assessment with a HRQOL [Health-Related Quality of Life] measure that was psychometrically sound and practical to administer" (p. S22). The purpose is to determine the extent to which an individual's functioning is improved following surgery.

Step 2: Identify the Intended Respondents. The relevance of the criterion centers on the persons for whom the measurement is intended. Factors related to the administration of the instrument should be considered, such as amount of time required to complete it, reading level, format for items, response option formats, and test setting.

Format options include true-false, matching, multiple-choice, sentence completion, ranking items, Likert-type scales, and open-ended, essay-type questions. Examples of several of these formats can be found in Chapter 5. You are probably familiar with most of these formats simply by virtue of having been a student and taking tests yourself. However, being able to recognize an item type and being able to write good, high-quality items are two entirely different matters. You should review one of the measurement texts cited earlier for rules for item construction of the different types.

The Likert-type scale is a type that you may well have responded to on instruments rating the quality of your instruction in your university courses, but you may not recognize the name itself. Quite simply, this is the type of item that makes a statement, such as the following:

"My emotional problems interfere with my usual daily activities."

Then you would indicate the strength of your agreement or disagreement with that statement on a 4- or 5-point scale that might look like this: 1 (*strongly agree*), 2 (*moderately agree*), 3 (*neutral*), 4 (*moderately disagree*), 5 (*strongly disagree*). The intended respondents for the ESI were adult patients who had undergone surgery for epilepsy. The researchers wanted to have a comprehensive but brief questionnaire for research purposes. They also wanted it to be self-administering.

Step 3. Review Existing Measures. You already did this to decide that you needed to create your own. However, methods for formatting and administering the measure as well as for determining its reliability and validity can be identified from the developmental work conducted by other researchers. In Vickrey's (1993) study of the ESI, the literature review supported the inclusion of the physical, mental, social, and general health dimensions for determining quality of life. In addition, the researchers identified an existing instrument, the 36-item RAND Health Survey, that could serve as the generic core for the new instrument (RAND, 1992). The RAND instrument had accumulated a body of evidence supporting its reliability and validity.

Step 4. Develop an Item Pool. There are many avenues open to the researcher in preparing draft items for the new measurement device. Some may be adopted or adapted from current measures. Others might be developed using experts or program staff responsible for the program being studied.

The item pool for the ESI was developed by an interdisciplinary group of experts, including health services researchers, epilepsy specialists, an epidemiologist, and a social scientist. They used the RAND instrument and added 19 items to tap domains specific to epilepsy, such as cognitive functions and role limitations due to memory problems.

Covert (1977) suggests that you should take some time to think of an appropriate title for your data collection instrument. This is the first thing that the respondent will read, so you want it to be motivating and conceptually consistent with the content of the instrument. Following the title, you might want to include a short, introductory paragraph explaining the purpose of the instrument and its intended use. (This information is sometimes more extensively described in a cover letter). The introductory statement can be used to explain how you got the person's name or why he or she was selected, as well as to provide assurances of confidentiality or anonymity. Obviously, the introductory paragraph (and all statements on the instrument) should be written in language that is understandable to the intended respondents.

Directions for how to complete the instrument should be included next. These could be as simple as, "Circle the appropriate response." If a separate answer sheet is to used, more complex instructions may be necessary. It is also possible to start with general directions and then supply more specific directions for individual parts as appropriate. As mentioned in

Chapter 5, it is important to tell the respondent who to give or send the instrument to after completion.

Step 5. Prepare and Pilot Test the Prototype. After the item pool has been developed, the researcher will assemble the first draft of the instrument. To develop a good instrument, you need to go through a number of pilot tests. At first, it is recommended that the developer ask other professionals knowledgeable about the attribute and its measurement in the targeted sample to review the prototype. These experts will be looking for content validity in addition to relevance for the target population.

After revisions have been made as a result of the first review, the prototype can be tried out on a small sample of the intended respondents. Typically, this is done by the researcher under expected administration procedures to get a general idea of the quality of the information as well as any problems in administration and scoring. The researcher should provide a means for the members of the pilot group to give feedback on the instrument in terms of items that might need additional clarification. This can be done after they complete the instrument through written comments, some type of modified focus group format, or both.

The final pilot test should be conducted with a large enough sample to enable the researcher to gather reliability and validity information. If the instrument depends on the use of interviewers, observers, or document reviewers, the researcher must collect interrater and intrarater reliability indices at this time.

Vickrey (1993) used a series of pilot tests in the development of the ESI: First, seven health care professionals specializing in epilepsy and two health services researchers reviewed the draft instrument for content validity and clarity of wording. The reviewers were asked to judge whether the items appeared to tap into health-related quality of life domains as hypothesized.

Second, the test battery was then pilot tested by administering it to eight people with epilepsy. Minor modifications in wording were made based on this evaluation.

Finally, 224 postoperative epilepsy patients were mailed a questionnaire that included the ESI, a mood profile measure, questions on medication regimen and seizure occurrence over the preceding 12 months, a $15 cash incentive, and a cover letter. Of these patients, 89% responded to the questionnaire either on the first mailing or after one or two mailed follow-up reminders.

Step 6. Conduct an Item Analysis and Revise the Measure. The answers to each item should be reviewed to determine if a pattern suggests ambiguity or bias in the item. The final revisions of the instrument can then be made. The researcher should be careful to document all the pilot test procedures and revisions in the instrument so that these can be presented in the research report as evidence of the quality of the measurement.

For additional examples of reliability and validity studies, and discussion of relevant issues the reader is referred to the following sources:

Gribbons, B. C., Tobey, P. E., & Michael, W. B. (1995). Internal-consistency reliability and construct and criterion-related validity of an academic self-concept scale. *Educational and Psychological Measurement, 55*(5), 858-867.

Millar, R., & Gallagher, M. (1996). The "Things I Worry About" Scale: Further developments in surveying the worries of postprimary school pupils. *Educational and Psychological Measurement, 56*(6), 972-994.

Sun, A. (1995). Development and factor analysis of Student Resistance to Schooling Inventory. *Educational and Psychological Measurement, 55*(5), 841-849.

Thompson, B., & Daniel, L. G. (1996). Seminal readings on reliability and validity: A "hit parade" bibliography. *Educational and Psychological Measurement, 56*(5), 741-745.

Thompson, B., & Daniel, L. G. (1996). Factor analytic evidence for the construct validity of scores: A historical overview and some guidelines. *Educational and Psychological Measurement, 56*(2), 197-208.

Thompson, B., Wasserman, J. D., & Matula, K. (1996). The factor structure of the behavior rating scale of the Bayley Scales of Infant Development-II. *Educational and Psychological Measurement, 56*(3), 460-474.

Sensitivity to Multicultural Concerns

Several sources have provided information about how to be sensitive to concerns about inclusion of a multicultural perspective in the construction of data collection instruments. Covert (1995) makes the following suggestions:

1. Understand your own prejudices and biases. As researchers, we should be aware that even though we strive to be "objective," we all have our prejudices. These might be related to a person's ethnicity, gender, sexual orientation, religion, disability, or socioeconomic status.

2. Be sensitive to the language used in the research process to describe the different groups involved:
   a. Are explicitly derogatory terms used in describing people from "other" groups?
   b. Are subtly derogatory terms used, such as "those people" when describing clients in a program?

3. Is the language used in the data collection instruments understandable to the respondents?

4. How sensitive to cultural issues are the members of the research team? Have they been trained to deal with people who are culturally different from themselves?

5. Are the various different cultural groups involved in planning, implementing, and reviewing results from the research?

6. Are multicultural issues addressed openly at all stages of the research process?

7. Is the sample representative of the cultural diversity of the population being served?

8. What evidence exists about the multicultural validity of the instruments being selected or developed for the research (do men score significantly differently than women, do minority people score differently than nonminority people)?

9. Will the results of the research be viewed differently by different cultural groups? What provision has been made to ensure that their perspectives are included?

Additional concerns about multicultural issues in the construction of data collection instruments have been addressed in the *Handbook of Multicultural Counseling* (Ponterotto, Casas, Suzuki, & Alexander, 1995). Two sets of guidelines/principles are included in that text:

1. American Psychological Association. (1993). Guidelines for providers of psychological services to ethnic, linguistic, and culturally diverse populations. *American Psychologist, 48,* 45-48.

2. Tapp, J. J., Kelman, H., Triandia, H., Wrightsman, L., & Coelho, G. (1973). Advisory principles for ethical considerations in the conduct of cross-cultural research: Fall 1973 Revision. *International Journal of Psychology, 9*(3), 240-249.

Qualitative Data Collection Methods

As discussed in Chapter 7, the researcher is the instrument in qualitative research studies. In other words, instead of using a test or questionnaire to collect data, the researcher is the instrument that collects data by observing, interviewing, examining records and documents in the research setting, or using some combination of these methods. Many issues related to the role of the researcher as instrument are discussed in Chapter 7. In this chapter, I focus on the three main qualitative data collection methods: observation, interview, and document and records review.

Observation

Qualitative observation occurs in naturalistic settings without using predetermined categories of measurement or response (Adler & Adler, 1994). The researcher is interested in observing people's behaviors as they naturally occur in terms that appear to be meaningful to the people involved. Adler and Adler distinguish between observation and participant observation, suggesting that qualitative researchers tend to use more of the latter, probably because of the theoretical roots associated with symbolic interactionism. In that type of qualitative research, the researcher usually wants to interact with the participants while collecting data from them. This contrasts with the less interactive, more "pure" observation appropriate for qualitative researchers who are conducting ethnomethodological research.

Spradley (1980) identifies five types of participation:

1. *Nonparticipation:* The lowest level of involvement is usually accomplished by watching a videotape of the situation. For example, a researcher could ask a teacher to turn on a video camera at selected times when a student with disabilities is in her class. The researcher would then review the tape at a later time.

2. *Passive participation:* The researcher is present but does not interact with the participants. Keller (1993) used this approach in observing a girl with Down's syndrome who was integrated in a regular education classroom.

3. *Moderate participation:* The researcher attempts to balance the insider and outsider roles by observing and by participating in some but not all of the activities. Keller (1993) used this approach when he taught three lessons in the sixth-grade classroom in which the girl with Down's syndrome was integrated.

4. *Active participation:* The researcher does what the others do, generally, but does not try to blend in completely. Mertens (1991b) used this approach in a study of gifted deaf adolescents in a summer enrichment program. She was with the students all day in the classroom, on field trips, and at meals. However, she did not sleep in the students' dorms at night, and thus, she maintained some distance from the participants (and some semblance of sanity).

5. *Complete participation:* The researcher becomes a natural participant, which has the disadvantage of trying to collect data and maintain a questioning and reflective stance. This approach was used by Ferguson who was a special education teacher for students with learning disabilities (Davis & Ferguson, 1992). She continued with her role as the special education teacher while collecting qualitative data by observation and interviews.

Adler and Adler (1994) reconceptualize the most common qualitative researcher observational roles as these:

Peripheral-member-researcher: Observing and interacting closely enough with members to establish an insider's perspective, without participating in the activities of the core group (e.g., drug dealing)

Active-member-researcher: Becoming more involved in the group's central activities but not fully committing to the group's values and goals

Complete-member-researcher: Studying scenes in which you are already a member or becoming a complete member during the study

They state that the qualitative research field has shifted to value more the "insider" perspective, and thus, researchers have tended to take on more of a membership role, either overtly or covertly.

So then, what do observers observe? Patton (1990) suggests the following list as ideas for an observer to attend to:

1. *Program setting.* The physical environment within which the program takes place should be described in sufficient detail to permit the reader to visualize the setting. Avoid interpretive adjectives unless they represent quotations from the participants (e.g., *comfortable, beautiful,* and *stimulating* are interpretive); colors, measurements, and purpose are less interpretive (e.g., "a blue room with a green chalkboard at one end measuring 40' by 25'" or "a library with the walls lined with books"). Describe the way the walls look in the room, the amount of space available, how the space is used, the nature of the lighting, how people are organized in the space, and the interpretive reactions of program participants to the physical setting. If I am entering a new setting for observation, I often take the first few minutes to sketch out a picture of the room, furniture, salient objects, and persons. I will sometimes label people as S1, S2, S3, or T (teacher). Once I have finished my "drawing," usually the people in the room have started to forget that I am there. Then I continue my observations.

2. *Human and social environment.* Look for ways in which people organize themselves into groups and subgroups. Patterns of interaction, frequency of interaction, direction of communication patterns (from staff to participants and participants to staff), and changes in these patterns. Characteristics of people in the different groups (male and female group interactions, different background characteristics, racial and ethnicity differences, and different ages). Decision-making patterns: Who makes decisions about the activities that take place? To what extent are decisions made openly so that participants are aware of the decision-making process? How are decisions by staff presented to the full group? How are decisions communicated?

3. *Program activities and participant behaviors.*

> What do people do in the program?
>
> How do they experience the program?
>
> What is it like to be a participant in the program?
>
> What would one see if one were watching the program in progress?

Find a unit of activity—for example, a class session, mealtime, or meeting. A comprehensive description of an activity includes the following:

At the *beginning:*

> How is the activity introduced or begun?
>
> Who is present at the beginning?
>
> What exactly was said at the beginning?
>
> How did participants respond or react to what was said?

In the *middle:*

> Who is involved?
>
> What is being said by staff?
>
> What are participants doing?
>
> What is being said by participants?
>
> What are the variations in how participants are engaging in the activity being observed?
>
> How does it feel to be engaged in this activity (observer records own feelings).

In the *end:*

What are the signals that the activity unit is ending?

Who is present at the time?

What is said?

How do participants react to the ending of the activity?

How is completion of this unit of activity related to the other program activities and future plans?

4. *Informal interactions and unplanned activities.* Simply continue to gather descriptive information about what people do and, in particular, what people are saying to each other. Data include things such as the following:

None of the participants talk about a session when it is over.

Everyone splits in a different direction when a session is over.

People talk about personal interests and share gossip that has nothing to do with the program.

Learning occurs in unstructured moments through personal interactions.

Observe body language and nonverbal cues.

5. *The native language of the program participants should be attended to.* Part of the observer's task is to learn the native language of the program—that is, the literal meanings, connotations, and symbolism. The field notes of the observer should include the exact language used by the participants to describe their experiences so that patterns of word usage can emerge.

6. *Nonverbal communication.* In many settings, nonverbal communication includes patterns established for the participants to get the attention of or otherwise approach another person. Fidgeting, moving about, or trying to get comfortable can communicate things about attention to and concentration on group processes. Dress, expression of affection, physical spacing, and arrangements are nonverbal cues.

7. *Unobtrusive measures.* These include physical clues about program activities—for example, "wear" spots on the floor, dusty equipment, areas used a lot or a little.

8. *Observing what does not happen.* If the program goals, implementation design, or proposal suggest that certain things ought to happen or are expected to happen, it is appropriate for the observer to note that those things did not happen. When your basic experience with a program suggests that the absence of some particular activity or factor is noteworthy, be sure to note what did not happen.

Quality in Observational Research

Adler and Adler (1994) suggest the following ideas for enhancing the validity and reliability of observational data:

1. Use multiple observers or teams, diverse in age and gender, if possible.

2. Cross-check observational findings with other researchers and eliminate inaccurate interpretations.

3. Search for negative cases to test emergent propositions.

4. Describe the research setting and findings in such a way that the reader can "see" and "feel" what it was like.

5. Address reliability by making observations in various settings, at various times of the day, days of the week, and months of the year.

Interviewing: Individual and Focus Group

Although observation allows collection of data through the researcher's direct contact in the setting, it is not always possible to have intimate, repeated, and prolonged involvement in the life and community of the respondents (McCracken, 1988). Interviews can be structured or unstructured, group or individual. Typically, interviews in a qualitative study are done with an unstructured or minimally structured format. Interviewing can be conducted as a part of participant observation or even as a casual conversation. The questions emerge as the researcher is sensitized to the meanings that the participants bring to the situation. As the study evolves, interviewing can become more structured and formal.

Interviews can be conducted individually or in a group. The *focus group* approach was described in Chapter 7. Although focus groups have been used extensively in market research, they can also be used in needs sensing for training and service programs, for instrument review, and for many other research purposes (Mertens, 1989a). Because the focus group is a "guided" discussion, the facilitator usually has a list of five to seven questions to ask during a 1.5- to 2-hour session. The questions are used in a semistructured way to ensure coverage of important issues yet allow for flexibility in responding to group-initiated concerns. One of the benefits of focus group research is the additional insight gained from the interaction of ideas among the group participants.

The characteristics of questions for focus group interviews have been delineated by Krueger (1988) as follows:

1. Usually, focus group interviews include less than 10 questions and often around 5 or 6 total.

2. Focus group interviews use open-ended questions. So instead of asking, "Does your child play at the playground?" ask, "Where does your child usually play?"

3. Avoid using "why" questions. These questions can set off a defensive reaction by the respondent. Modify the question, such as "What prompted you to want to participate in the program?"

4. Carefully develop the questions. Brainstorming sessions with colleagues or audience members is one way to generate questions. Many questions can be generated this way and then priorities can be established to determine critical questions.

5. Establish the context for questions so participants are ready to respond. Provide enough information in each question so that the participants understand what you are asking for.

6. Questions should be arranged in a logical order, sometimes from general to specific.

The box labeled "Sample Focus Group Questions" provides examples of focus group questions from counseling and community education focus group studies. The role of the focus group facilitator is a challenging one. He or she needs to be able to control the interview process so that all participants can express themselves, one or a few people do not dominate the discussion, more introverted people are encouraged to speak, and all important topics are covered.

Generally speaking, qualitative researchers tend to favor semistructured or unstructured individual interview formats. (See the box labeled "Using a Questionnaire in Interviewing" for McCracken's, 1988, views on the necessity of having a questionnaire for long interviews.)

■ **SAMPLE FOCUS GROUP QUESTIONS**

Sessions and Yanos (1987) conducted focus group interviews to determine desirable characteristics of a counseling agency. They asked such questions as these:

1. What qualities would one look for in a counselor?

2. What types of office setting would be preferable for the provision of counseling services?

3. If a person was seeking counseling, what days or hours would be most desirable?

4. What sort of services would be most desired—individual counseling, group counseling, or family counseling?

5. What other factors should be considered in providing a counseling service to persons living, say, in the eastern suburbs of a particular city?

Krueger (1988) also presents many excellent examples of focus group questions. The following illustrates a focus group question that could be used to develop a strategic plan for community education:

"I'd like each of you to take a few moments and fill out this list. [pass out page]. I've listed several categories of problems or issues that may affect you and others in your community. The categories include the following: work and business, family, leisure, community, and environment. Take a moment and jot down what you think to be the most important issues in each of these categories. . . . Which of the issues that you mentioned on your list could be solved or lessened by education or information" (p. 70)? ■

■ USING A QUESTIONNAIRE IN INTERVIEWING

"The use of a questionnaire is sometimes regarded as a discretionary matter in qualitative research interview. But, for the purposes of the long qualitative interview, it is indispensable. . . .

"The questionnaire has several functions. Its first responsibility is to ensure that the investigator covers all the terrain in the same order for each respondent (preserving in a rough way the conversational context of each interview). The second function is the care and scheduling of the prompts necessary to manufacture distance. . . . The third function of the questionnaire is that it establishes channels for the direction and scope of discourse. The really open-ended interview is an ever-expanding realm of possibility in which the generative power of language is unleashed to potentially chaotic effect. The fourth function of the questionnaire is that it allows the investigator to give all his or her attention to the informant's testimony. . . .

"It is important to emphasize that the use of the questionnaire does not preempt the 'open-ended' nature of the qualitative interview. Within each of the questions, the opportunity for exploratory, unstructured responses remains. . . . The interviewer must be able to take full advantage of the contingency of the interview and pursue any opportunity that may present itself. In sum, the questionnaire that is used to order data and free the interviewer must not be allowed to destroy the elements of freedom and variability within the interview." ■

SOURCE: McCracken (1988, pp. 24-25).

Adler and Adler (1994) describe unstructured interviews in the ethnographic sense as including formal and informal interviewing in which the interviewer freely answers questions asked by respondents and expresses his or her own feelings during the interview. The goal is to have a human-to-human relationship with respondents and to understand their perspective. This requires building rapport with the respondents.

Feminists have endorsed the idea that interviews should "allow the development of a closer relation between interviewer and respondent, attempting to minimize status differences and doing away with the traditional hierarchical situation in interviewing" (Adler & Adler, 1994, p. 370). Some of these issues were discussed in Chapter 5 on survey research interviewing.

Interviewing *people with disabilities* can present challenges because of the capabilities or communication needs of the respondents. For example, Ferguson (1992) did a case study of autistic students in which he conducted interviews with adults who had various connections to autistic individuals at the school, including regular and special education teachers, administrators, and support staff. He commented, "Because of the limited verbal skills of the students in Mel's class, I did not conduct formal interviews with any of them. I did have short, informal conversations with the students when I was there doing observations" (p. 166).

Mertens (1991b) interviewed gifted deaf adolescents and found that it was necessary to train herself to take notes while watching the respondent in order to not miss any of their signs. She found that she could accommodate to this situation by using a clipboard that was tilted enough for her to see with her peripheral vision that the writing was going onto the right part of the page. She also paused between questions to finish writing each response and then spent time immediately after each interview filling in any holes that had been created by this interview process. As mentioned in Chapter 5, several researchers have suggested that the researcher explicitly turn control of the interview over to the person with the disability in view of his or her position of least power (Abberley, 1987; Foster, 1993a, 1993b). Saying "turn over control," means allowing the person to end the interview at any time, choose not to answer specific questions, raise issues that the researcher did not bring up, and have the opportunity to review his or her comments before they are made part of the official record for the research data.

Document and Records Review

All organizations leave trails composed of documents and records that trace their history and current status. Documents and records include not only the typical paper products, such as memos, reports, and plans, but also computer files, tapes (audio and video), and other artifacts. The qualitative researcher must turn to these documents and records to get the necessary background of the situation and insights into the dynamics of everyday functioning. The researcher cannot be in all places at all times; therefore, documents and records give the researcher access to information that would otherwise be unavailable. In special education research, documents that might be important include report cards, special education files, discipline records, individualized education plans (IEPs), IEP meeting minutes, curriculum materials, and test scores. Access to records and documents needs to be negotiated up front. You should be sensitive to the types of records and documents that might be associated with a particular setting.

Lincoln and Guba (1985) distinguish between documents and records as follows:

Type	Purpose	Examples
Records	Prepared for official reasons	Marriage certificates Driving licenses Bank statements File records
Documents	Prepared for personal reasons	Diaries Memos Letters Field notes

Researchers may find it easier to access documents but be restricted by law regarding privacy for access to records (Hodder, 1994).

This distinction between records and documents is also important in that use of extant materials must always be tempered with an understanding of the time, context, and intended use for which the materials were created (Hodder, 1994). As noted in Chapter 8, particularly with historical research, it may not be possible to interact with the people who produced the materials. The researcher then faces the challenge of how to interpret the meaning of such materials. Hodder suggests that the qualitative researcher use the same rules of thumb that guide other types of qualitative data and ask questions such as, "How does what is said fit into more general understanding?" (p. 398). Then examine patterns and inconsistencies in the evidence. When the authors or users are still alive, the researcher can conduct "member checks" to determine various perspectives for the interpretation of the data.

▶ *Questions for Critically Analyzing Data Collection*

1. What evidence is provided of the quality of the data collection instruments in terms of the following:

   a. Reliability or dependability

   b. Validity or credibility

   c. Objectivity or confirmability

   d. Freedom from bias based on gender, race and ethnicity, or disability?

2. Are the procedures used by the test developers to establish reliability, validity, objectivity, and fairness appropriate for the intended use of the proposed data collection techniques? Was the research instrument developed and validated with representatives of both sexes and of diverse ethnic and disability groups?

3. Is the proposed data collection tool appropriate for the people and conditions of the proposed research?

4. Given the research questions of the proposed research, when and from whom is it best to collect information?

5. Does the instrument contain language that is biased, based on gender, race and ethnicity, class, or disability?

6. If observers are used, what are the observers' qualifications? What steps were taken to reduce bias? Was it possible or reasonable to use "blind" observers? Are the data independent of the person doing the observations? Should they be? What is the influence of the nature of the person doing the observations? Is this discussed? Would another person come to the same conclusions? What unique insights and sensitivities can or does the observer claim? Would the observer have seen things the same way at a later date?

7. Were instruments explored for gender bias; for example, were instruments used for both sexes that had only been validated for one sex? Did questions use sexist language? Was consideration given to the sex of the test administrator? Were questions premised on the notion of sex-inappropriate behavior, traits, or attributes? Did the research instruments stress sex differences with the effect of minimizing the existence and importance of sex similarities? Was information about one sex obtained by asking people of the other sex about their behaviors, traits, or attributes and then treating such information as fact rather than opinion?

8. In terms of race and ethnicity biases, were the data collection instruments screened so that the test content reflected various racial and ethnic minority

groups? Was consideration given to cultural differences in terms of examinee readiness, motivation, and response set? Were racial and ethnic groups appropriately represented in the standardization group? Were examiner bias and language differences considered? Was reliability and validity established for racial and ethnic minority groups? Were systemic problems that might lead to differences in performance considered? Did the researcher check on the conceptual equivalence of the items for the different cultural groups? Was the researcher aware of the level of acculturation for members of minority racial and ethnic groups? Were translated measures used appropriately? Did the researcher investigate the dominant language for the respondents?

9. If the instrument is to be or was used with people with disabilities, was the accommodation made on the basis of a specific disability? How was eligibility determined for the accommodation? What type of modification was or should be allowed? Do the scores achieved under the nonstandard conditions have the same meaning? If there is a difference in performance levels between standard and nonstandard administrations, are these due to actual differences in the construct being measured, or are they artifacts of modifications of the testing process?

10. Did the researcher consider his or her own prejudices and biases that might effect data collection? If a research team was used, how sensitive were team members to cultural issues? Was training provided to people in dealing with people who are culturally different from themselves?

11. Were the various different cultural groups involved in planning, implementing, and reviewing the data collection instruments? In the results?

12. Were multicultural issues addressed openly at all stages of the research process?

13. In observational research, was it possible or reasonable to use multiple observers or teams, diverse in age, gender, or ethnicity? Were observational findings crosschecked with other researchers? Were negative cases sought out to test emergent propositions? Were the research setting and findings described in such a way that the reader can "see" and "feel" what it was like there? Was reliability addressed by making observations in various settings, at various times of the day, days of the week, and months of the year?

■ *Activities and Questions for Discussion and Application*

1. Select a specific research question, either one from your own research proposal or one from published literature. Brainstorm ideas for data collection strategies for both quantitative and qualitative techniques. Which would be most appropriate for your question? On what basis did you make that decision?

2. Locate a commercially developed measure and review the manual to determine how the developers have treated the concepts of reliability, validity, objectivity, and bias based on gender, ethnicity, class, and disability. Compare the informa-

tion available in the test manual with that from an independent source, such as the MMY or TIP.

3. Review the same test and determine to what extent you think it is appropriate for both males and females, people of different racial and ethnic backgrounds, languages other than English, and people with different types of disabilities. What kinds of accommodations would be needed to administer the instrument to people with different types of disabilities? What would be the impact of those accommodations? What could you do to determine the answer to these questions?

4. Identify several of the main journals in education and psychology. Examine their instructions to potential authors to see what the journal editors require in the way of evidence of measurement reliability, validity, objectivity, and lack of bias based on gender, ethnicity, and disability. Compare these instructions with those found in journals that specialize in publishing research about multicultural, gender, or disability issues mentioned in Chapter 2 of this text. Do you see any differences in the instructions related to this issue?

5. Identify attributes of people that might be the focus of research (such as gender, race and ethnicity, or disability) and describe how the impact of each attribute on data collection strategies might be investigated.

6. Identify an attribute that you might want to investigate in a research study. Following the steps for instrument development in this chapter, develop a draft instrument to measure the intended attribute. Try it out on a small group of appropriate respondents.

7. Identify several research articles that provide descriptions of their data collection strategies (of course, they all should have such sections). Using the questions for critical analysis provided in this chapter, analyze the strengths and weaknesses of the data collection sections of the research articles. Be sure to look at examples of both qualitative and quantitative research studies.

8. Using the research proposal that you have been developing as you move through this text (assuming that you are developing one), write out the data collection plan for your study. Be sure to include information about how you will ensure the quality of the data that you propose to collect.

Notes

1. The *term test score* is used in a generic sense as explained by Messick (1995): "The term *score* is used generically in its broadest sense to mean any coding or summarization of observed consistencies, or performance regularities on a test, questionnaire, observation procedure, or other assessment devices such as work samples, portfolios, and realistic problem simulations" (p. 741).

2. Predictive validity and concurrent validity are sometimes combined into one category called *criterion validity*.

3. Note: For additional information about testing and assessment with Native American Indian populations, see Chavers and Locke (1989) and McShane (1988).

In This Chapter

■ *Common types of statistics used for quantitative data analysis are defined, along with a method for choosing among them.*

■ *Interpretation issues relevant to quantitative data analysis are discussed, including randomization, sample size, statistical versus practical significance, cultural bias, generalizability, and options for reporting quantitative results, such as effect sizes and variance accounted for, replication, use of nonparametric statistics, exploration of competing explanations, and recognition of a study's limitations.*

■ *Statistical synthesis (i.e., meta-analysis) as a literature review method is explained.*

■ *Options for qualitative analysis are described, along with selected computer programs that are available.*

■ *Interpretation issues related to qualitative data analysis are discussed, including use of triangulated data, audits, cultural bias, and generalization of results.*

■ *Development of a management plan for conducting a research study is described as a tool to be included in the research proposal.*

■ *Writing research reports is described in terms of dissertation and thesis requirements, alternative reporting formats, and publication issues.*

■ *Strategies are discussed for ensuring utilization of your research results.*

Data Analysis, Interpretation, and Reporting

By reading and studying this book, you have moved through the steps of preparing a research proposal or critiquing a research study to the point of data analysis. If you are preparing a research proposal, your next step is to describe the data analysis strategies that you plan to use. In most research proposals, this section is followed by a management plan that specifies what tasks you will complete within a specified time frame and what resources will be required to complete the research project. Then you would be in a position to complete the research study itself, and to write up the results. Thus, the organizing framework for this chapter is designed to take you through the data analysis decisions, the design of a management plan, and ideas concerning writing research. If your goal is to critique research (rather than conduct it yourself), you will find guidelines that will help you identify the strengths and weaknesses of this portion of a research study.

A final section addresses the idea of utilization of research results. Although this section appears at the end of this text, ideas to enhance utilization have been integrated throughout the descriptions of the research planning process in this text. If you wait until after the research is finished to consider utilization, chances are your research could become a "dust catcher" on someone's shelf. That would not be a happy ending after all your work, so it is important to build in strategies for utilization during your planning process.

Quantitative Analysis Strategies

How effective are monetary incentives for improving response rates to surveys? What is the relationship between holding Africentric values and avoidance of harmful drugs? These are the types of questions that researchers have used quantitative research methods to investigate. Brief descriptions of two studies that explored answers to these questions are provided in Sample Study 12.1. The analytic and interpretive strategies used in these studies are used as examples of the various concepts described in this section of the chapter.

Commonly Used Quantitative Data Analysis Techniques

It is not possible to explain all the different types of statistics, the derivation of their formulas, and their appropriate uses in this chapter. The reader is referred to general statistics books for more specific information on this topic (see Hays, 1988; Heiman, 1992; Moore & McCabe, 1993; Popham & Sirotnik, 1992). First, I define and give examples of some of the more commonly used quantitative data analysis techniques. Then, I provide you with a model to aid you in making decisions about the most appropriate data analysis techniques. Finally, I discuss issues related to the interpretation of quantitative data analysis results.

Statistics can be thought of as being descriptive (i.e., they describe characteristics of your sample), correlational (i.e., they describe the strength and direction of relationships), and inferential (i.e., they allow you to make group comparisons). The box labeled "Definitions of Commonly Used Statistics" provides definitions of the most commonly used descriptive, correlational, and inferential statistics.

Descriptive Statistics

Belgrave et al. (1994) reported the following statistical values for the children's performance on the African Value Scale: a mean of 2.3, with a standard deviation of .51, and a range from 1.00 to 3.00. With this kind of information, you would still be unable to determine the meaning of the statistics presented. However, they also reported that each participant's scores were summed and then averaged to obtain a composite score that could range from 1 (*high Africentric values*) to 3 (*low Africentric values*). The statistical values reported for the Drug Attitude Scale were a mean of 1.3, a standard deviation of .25, and a range between 1.00 and 2.00. The children's responses to this scale were also derived by averaging across the items on the scale so that they could range from 1 (*very harmful*) to 3 (*not harmful*). Thus, on both measures, a lower number reflects a more favorable attitude.

Correlational Statistics

Belgrave et al. (1994) wanted to test the strength of the relationship between their predictor variables and the children's attitudes toward drugs. They reported simple correlation coefficients between the variables (e.g., attitudes toward drugs correlated .29 with African values). They also chose to use a multiple regression technique that allowed them to test the relationship of all three predictor variables in the same statistical analysis. They

---

SAMPLE STUDY 12.1 *Brief Descriptions of Two Sample Quantitative Studies*

Study 1: Effects of Respondents' Socioeconomic Status and Timing and Amount of Incentive Payment on Mailed Questionnaire Response Rates (Parthasarathy, Sailor, & Worthen, 1995):

> The researchers investigated how response rate to a mailed questionnaire was influenced by the socioeconomic status (SES) of respondents (high, middle, or low); amount of payment of a monetary incentive (none, $1, or $2); and time of payment (prepaid or promised after return of completed questionnaire). One hundred and twenty-five people in each SES group (low, middle, and high) were randomly assigned to one of five incentive conditions: prepaid $1, prepaid $2, promised $1, promised $2, or an unpaid control group. The actual contents of the survey related to the economic well-being of one county's residents.

Study 2: The Influence of Africentric Values, Self-Esteem, and Black Identity on Drug Attitudes Among African American Fifth Graders: A Preliminary Study (Belgrave et al., 1994):

> This team of researchers conducted a study to determine the influence of three predictor variables on fifth-grade African American students' attitudes toward drugs:
>
> 1. Africentric values, defined as the extent to which the children value collective responsibility—that is, beliefs that Blacks are responsible for and should collectively look out for one another
>
> 2. Black identity, defined as the child's identification with the Black race
>
> 3. Self-esteem, defined as a global measure of how the child feels about himself or herself
>
> Fifty-four fifth-grade students completed the three measurement instruments and a short attitude questionnaire designed to assess the extent to which they felt that seven commonly used drugs were dangerous.

---

reported that Africentric values was the only variable that significantly contributed to explaining drug attitudes (beta $= .29$, $R^2 = .08$, $F[1,47] = 4.3$, $p = .04$). In English, this paranthetical expression would be read: Beta equals .29, R^2 equals .08, F equals 4.3 with 1 and 47 degrees of freedom, and a significance level of p equal to .04.

Beta is a standardized regression coefficient obtained by multiplying the regression coefficient by the ratio of the standard deviation of the explanatory variable to the standard deviation of the response variable. Thus, a standardized regression coefficient is one that

■ **DEFINITIONS OF COMMONLY USED STATISTICS**

Descriptive statistics: Statistics whose function it is to describe or indicate several characteristics common to the entire sample. Descriptive statistics summarize data on a single variable (e.g., mean, median, mode, standard deviation)

1. Measures of central tendency

   Mean: The mean is a summary of a set of numbers in terms of centrality; it is what we commonly think of as the arithmetic average. In graphic terms, it is the point in a distribution around which the sum of deviations (from the mean point) are zero. It is calculated by adding up all the scores and dividing by the number of scores. It is usually designated by an X with a bar over it (X) or the capital letter M.

   Median: The median is the midpoint in a distribution of scores. This is a measure of central tendency that is equidistant from low to high; the median is the point at which the same number of scores lay on one side of that point as the other.

   Mode: The mode is a measure of central tendency that is the most frequently occurring score in the distribution.

2. Measures of variability

   Range: The range is a measure of variability that indicates the total extension of the data; for example, the numbers range from 1 to 10. It gives the idea of the outer limits of the distribution and is unstable with extreme scores.

   Standard deviation: The standard deviation is the measure of variability that is the sum of the deviations from the mean squared. It is a useful statistic for interpreting the meaning of a score and for use in more sophisticated statistical analyses. The standard deviation and mean are often reported together in research tables because the standard deviation is an indication of how adequate the mean is as a summary statistic for a set of data.

   Variance: The variance is the standard deviation squared and is a statistic used in more sophisticated analyses.

Correlational statistics: Statistics whose function it is to describe the strength and direction of a relationship between two or more variables.

   Simple correlation coefficient: The simple correlation coefficient describes the strength and direction of a relationship between two variables. It is designated by the small letter r.

   Coefficient of determination: This statistic is the correlation coefficient squared. It depicts the amount of variance that is accounted for by the explanatory variable in the response variable.

would result if the explanatory and response variables had been converted to standard z scores prior to the regression analysis. This standardization is done to make the size of beta weights from regression analysis easier to compare for the various explanatory variables.

R^2 is the proportion of variation in the response variable (in this case drug attitudes) explained by the explanatory variable (in this case Africentric values) in this multiple regression.

Multiple regression: If the researcher has several independent (predictor) variables, multiple regression can be used to indicate the amount of variance that all of the predictor variables explain.

Inferential statistics: Statistics used to determine whether sample scores differ significantly from each other or from population values. Inferential statistics are used to compare differences between groups.

1. *Parametric statistics:* Statistical techniques used for group comparison when the characteristic of interest (e.g., achievement) is normally distributed in the population, randomization was used in sample selection (see Chapter 10) and/or assignment (see Chapter 3), and the interval or ratio level of measurement is used (e.g., many test scores).

   t test: Inferential statistical tests are used when you have two groups to compare. If the groups are independent (i.e., different people are in each group), the *t* test for independent samples is used. If two sets of scores are available for the same people (or matched groups), the *t* test for correlated samples is used.

   ANOVA: The analysis of variance is used when you have more than two groups to compare or when you have more than one independent variable.

   ANCOVA: The analysis of covariance is similar to the ANOVA except that it allows you to control for the influence of an independent variables (often some background characteristic) that may vary between your groups before the treatment is introduced.

   MANOVA: The multivariate analysis of variance is used in the same circumstances as ANOVA except that you have more than one dependent variable.

2. *Nonparametric statistics:* Statistical techniques used when the assumption of normality cannot be met, with small samples sizes, and with ordinal (rank) or nominal (categorical) data.

   Chi-square: Used with nominal level data to test the statistical independence of two variables.

   Wilcoxon matched pairs signed-ranks test: Used with two related samples and ordinal level data.

   The Mann-Whitney U test: Used with two independent samples and ordinal level data.

   The Friedman two-way analysis of variance: Used with more than two related samples and ordinal level data.

   The Kruskal-Wallis one-way analysis of variance: Used with more than two independent samples and ordinal-level data. ■

F is the statistic used to determine the statistical significance of this result. That is, is the contribution of the explanatory variable to the prediction of the response variable statistically significant?

And p is the level of statistical significance associated with F. (Statistical significance is explained in the next section.)

Degrees of freedom indicate the appropriate degrees of freedom for determining the significance of the reported F statistic. F distributions are a family of distributions with two parameters—the degrees of freedom in the numerator of the F statistic (based on the number of predictor variables or groups) and those associated with the denominator (based on the sample size). If you know the number of explanatory variables and the sample size, the computer program will calculate the appropriate degrees of freedom and will use the appropriate sampling distribution to determine the level of statistical significance.

Based on these results, Belgrave et al. (1994) reported that self-esteem and Black identity were not significant contributors. They also concluded that even though Africentric values was found to be a statistically significant predictor, its contribution to understanding drug attitudes was small (based on the $R^2 = .08$).

Statistical Significance

Shaver (1992) defines a test of statistical significance as a method that "provides a statement of probability of occurrence in the long run, with repeated random sampling (or assignment) under the null hypothesis" (p. 12). The null hypothesis is the statement that the groups in the experiment do not differ from one another or that there is no statistically significant relationship between two or more variables. In the Belgrave et al. (1994) study, their null hypothesis would read as follows: There will be no statistically significant relationship between fifth-grade students' attitudes toward drugs and their Africentric values, self-esteem, and Black identity.

A test of statistical significance will tell researchers if they can accept or reject the null hypothesis and the level of confidence they could have in their decision. When you read in a research report that the results were significant at the .05 level (usually depicted as $p < .05$), the researcher is telling you that there is a 5% chance that he or she rejected a null hypothesis that was true. In other words, there is a 5% chance that the researcher made a mistake and said there is a statistically significant difference (or relationship) when there really is not. This is called a Type I error. (The converse of this is called a Type II error; that is, the researcher fails to reject a false hypothesis.) In the Belgrave et al. (1994) study, the multiple regression analysis resulted in a statistical significance level of .04. Thus, the researchers rejected the null hypothesis that no statistically significant relationship existed between attitudes toward drugs and Africentric values.

Inferential Statistics

In the Parthasarathy, Sailor, and Worthen (1995) study, the researchers needed to use a different statistical technique because they were interested in determining the statistical significance of group differences. They chose to conduct a 3 × 2 × 2 analysis of variance (ANOVA). The 3 × 2 × 2 in the previous sentence is a code that statisticians use to indicate how many independent variables there are (three) and how many levels for each variable. For example,

Variable A: 3 socioeconomic levels
Variable B: 2 amounts of payment
Variable C: 2 times of payment

The control group (those who would not receive any payment) was not included in this analysis, because people who were to receive no payment could not be divided into two groups according to time of payment—think about it.

The ANOVA allows you to test for main effects (i.e., is there a significant effect for each of the independent variables). Their results indicated that response rates were significantly different for socioeconomic (SES) ($F[2,288 = 7.78, p = .001$), amount of payment ($F[1,288] = 4.40, p = .037$), and time of payment ($F[1,288] = 3.63, p = .000$). The results for SES will be used to give another example of how paranthetical statistical results would be read in English. You would say, F equals 7.78 with 2 and 288 degrees of freedom, with a statistical significance at the p equals .001 level. On the basis of this result, you could conclude that people in different SES groups perform differently in terms of their response rates at a level higher than could be expected by chance.

However, before drawing conclusions, it was important to also test if there were any interaction effects of the variables (i.e., did any of the independent variables vary systematically with each other). In this study, the researchers also reported a significant interaction between SES and time ($F[2,288] = 3.70, p = .026$). None of the other interactions were significant. To reach a conclusion about the meaning of the interaction effect, the researchers had to examine the return rates for the individual groups, disaggregated by SES and timing. When they did that, they reported that timing had little effect on the return rate for the high-SES people. However, timing was found to have a substantial effect on the return rates for middle- and low-SES people, with prepaid people returning a far higher percentage of questionnaires than those promised payment. Interpretation of interaction effects is made far easier by graphing the disaggregated results, as can be seen in Figure 12.1.

The graphical display makes it clear that the people in the high-SES group uniformly responded at a high rate, whether or not they were prepaid or were promised payment. However, for the middle- and low-SES groups, prepayment resulted in statistically significant higher response rates than were found in the "promised" payment condition. On the bases of the results of their analysis, the authors concluded that in surveys of people of lower SES, prepaying the incentive can boost response rates to levels comparable to those of high- and middle-SES populations, whereas promising later payment is no better, and perhaps worse, than no payment at all.

Choice of Statistic

Before explaining in detail the decision strategy for choosing a statistical procedure, I wish to digress for a moment to describe one concept on which the basis for choosing a statistical procedure rests—the *scale of measurement*. As a researcher you need to ask, What is the scale of measurement for the data? for both the independent and dependent variables.

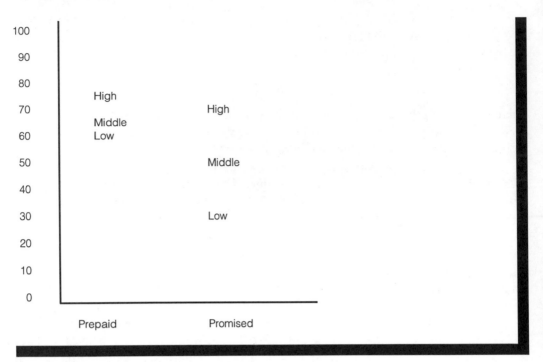

Figure 12.1. Graphical Depiction of an Interaction Effect
SOURCE: Parthasarathy, Sailor, and Worthen (1995).

Scale of Measurement

The four scales of measurement are defined and examples of each are provided in Table 12.1. The scale of measurement is important because it determines which type of statistical procedure is appropriate. As you will see later, this has an influence on deciding between parametric or nonparametric statistics as well as on the appropriate choice of correlation coefficient.

The choice of a statistical procedure is outlined in Table 12.2. Your choice will depend on the following factors:

1. Your research question, which can be descriptive, concerns the extent of relationships between variables, determine significance of group differences, make predictions of group membership, or examine the structure of variables

2. The type of groups that you have (i.e., independent, dependent, repeated measures, matched groups, randomized blocks, or mixed groups)

3. The number of independent and dependent variables you have

4. The scale of measurement

5. Your ability to satisfy the assumptions underlying the use of parametric statistics

Each type of research question leads you to a different statistical choice; thus, this is the most important starting point for your decisions.

TABLE 12.1 Scales of Measurement		
Scale of Measurement	Definition	Example
Nominal	Categorical data	Color: red, green, blue Label: male, female
Ordinal	Ranked data organized according to increasing or decreasing presence of a characteristic	Tallest to shortest Sweetest to sourest Heaviest to lightest
Interval	Equal intervals, but zero is arbitrary	Temperature
Ratio	Equal intervals and zero is defined as meaning the absence of the characteristic	Weight, age, IQ, many personality and educational tests

Before jumping into complex statistical analysis, it is important to really understand what your data "looks like." Statisticians recommend that you always graph your data before you start conducting analyses. This will help you in several respects. First, you will be closer to your data and know it better in terms of what it is capable of telling you. Second, it will help you determine if you have met the appropriate assumptions required for different types of analyses. Third, you will be able to see if you have any "outliers"—that is, values for variables that are very different from the general group response on your measure.

Table 12.2 can be used as a flowchart to logically think through your statistical choices. For example, in the Belgrave et al. (1994) study, the researchers first wanted to know to what extent the students in their study held Africentric values (i.e., believed that Blacks are responsible for and should collectively look out for each other). This portion of their study is descriptive; therefore, they could go to the first section in Table 12.2 to identify their statistical options. Their scale of measurement is assumed to be interval (ranging from 1.00 to 3.00), so they determined that the mean was the appropriate measure of central tendency.

Belgrave et al. (1994) had an additional research question: What was the influence of the students' Africentric values, their Black identity, and their self-esteem on their attitudes toward drugs? In other words, they wanted to test the relationship between three predictor variables and drug attitudes. Therefore, they could go to the second section in Table 12.2 because their research question was one of relationships. They have more than two predictor variables, with interval data, so they chose to conduct multiple regression analysis.

Assumptions for Parametric Statistics

As mentioned in the box labeled "Definitions of Commonly Used Statistics," it is important for you to be aware of the assumptions that underlie the use of parametric statistics. These include (a) normal distribution of the characteristic of interest in the population, (b) randomization for sample selection or group assignment (experimental vs.

TABLE 12.2 Choice of a Statistical Procedure	
Research question: Descriptive	
For *interval or ratio data:*	Mean, median or mode, and variance
For *ordinal* data:	Median
For *nominal* data:	Mode
Research question: Relationship	
For *two variables:*	
For *interval or ratio data:*	Pearson product-moment coefficient of correlation
For *ordinal data:*	Spearman rank order coefficient of correlation or Kendall rank correlation
For *interval and nominal or ordinal data:*	Point biserial
For *interval and artificial dichotomy on an ordinal scale (dichotomy is artificial because there is an underlying continuous distribution):*	Biserial
For *nominal data:*	Contingency coefficient
For *more than two variables:*	
For *interval or ratio data:*	Multiple regression analysis
For *ordinal data:*[a]	Kendall partial rank correlation
For *nominal data:*	Discriminant analysis
Research question: Group differences	
For *Two Variables:*	
For *related samples:*	
For *interval or ratio data:*	*t* test for correlated samples[b]
For *ordinal data:*	Wilcoxon matched-pairs signed-ranks test
For *nominal data:*	McNemar test for the significance of changes
For *independent samples:*	
For *interval or ratio data:*	*t* test for independent samples
For *ordinal data:*	Mann-Whitney U test or Kolmogorov-Smirnov two-sample test
For *nominal data:*	Chi-square test
For *more than two variables:*	
For *related samples:*	
For *interval or ratio data:*	Repeated measures analysis of variance (ANOVA)
For *ordinal data:*	Friedman two-way analysis of variance
For *nominal data:*	Cochran Q test
For *independent samples:*	
For *interval or ratio data:*	Analysis of variance
For *ordinal data:*	Kruskal-Wallis one-way analysis of variance
For *nominal data:*	Chi-square test for *k* independent samples
Research question: Prediction of group membership	
For *all data:*	Discriminant function[c]
Research question: Structure of variables	
For *interval or ratio data:*	Factor analysis

a. Ordinal and nominal data can be used in multiple regression equations through a process called "dummying-up" a variable. Refer to one of the statistical texts cited at the beginning of this chapter for more details on this procedure.

b. All *t* tests and variations on ANOVA require that the data satisfy the assumptions for parametric statistical procedures.

c. Discriminant functions can be one-way, hierarchical, or factorial depending on the number of independent and dependent variables.

control), and (c) an interval or ratio level of measurement. The assumption that the population is normal rules out outliers in your data, so the presence of outliers shows that this assumption is not valid. Also, if the distribution of the characteristic in the population is skewed (i.e., bunched up at one end of the continuum or the other), the assumption of normality is not met. In the case of skewness, it may be possible to transform the data to approximate a normal distribution using a logarithmic transformation (Moore & McCabe, 1993). If the assumptions cannot be met, you need to consider alternative data analysis strategies. That is where the choice of nonparametric statistics becomes attractive (sometimes called distribution-free inference procedures)[1.]

Variations on ANOVA

Several variations on ANOVA are listed in the box labeled "Definitions of Commonly Used Statistics." These include statistical procedures to use when you have different combinations of independent and dependent variables. The choice of ANOVA in Table 12.2 is a bit oversimplified. Actually, if you have more than one independent variable, you will need to use a factorial ANOVA. An example of a factorial ANOVA is the A × B × C ANOVA described in the analysis in the Parthasarathy et al. (1995) study. It is also possible to have another type of "independent" variable—one that is not of central interest for the researcher but that needs to be measured and accounted for in the analysis. This type of variable is called a *covariate*. It might be entry-level test scores for two different groups, or socio-economic indicators. In this case, the researcher would used an analysis of covariance or ANCOVA. If you have included more than one dependent measure in your design, you may need to use a MANOVA or a multivariate analysis of variance. If you are getting into this level of complexity in your analysis, you definitely need to refer to a statistics book.

Post Hoc Analysis

Once you have completed an analysis such as a two-way factorial ANOVA, you need to determine where the significant effects are. This can be done using multiple-comparison *t* tests or other post hoc procedures, such as Tukey's or Scheffe's post hoc tests. Such post hoc tests allow you to focus on which of several variables exhibit the main effect demonstrated by your initial analysis.

Interpretation Issues in Quantitative Analysis

A number of challenges are presented for quantitative researchers for the interpretation of the results of their data analysis:

1. The influence of randomization (or lack of same) on statistical choices and interpretation of results
2. The analytic implications of using intact groups
3. The influence of sample size on achieving statistical significance
4. Statistical versus practical significance
5. Issues related to cultural bias
6. Variables related to generalizability

Options for responding to some of these challenges are considered, such as reporting effect sizes and amount of variance accounted for, replication, use of nonparametric statistics and exploration of competing explanations, and recognition of a study's limitations.

Randomization

Randomization is a necessary condition for the use of typical tests of parametric statistics (Shaver, 1992). Randomness can be achieved by either random sampling or random assignment to conditions. Random sampling has to do with how the participants were chosen from the population (see Chapter 10). Random assignment has to do with how participants were assigned to levels of the independent variable so that variability between groups is statistically evened out (see Chapter 3). Random sampling is a very difficult condition to meet in most educational and psychological research, and random assignment is not always possible.

For example, the researchers in the Parthasarathy et al. (1995) study were able to randomly select people from the larger population in the county from the telephone directory (although the researchers acknowledge that this omits people with unlisted numbers, about 6% of the county population). In addition, the original random sampling was used to determine people's SES, and thus, the final sample was selected only if the respondents to the original survey answered the SES-related questions. The authors acknowledge that "although most respondents did answer these questions, the fact some chose not to makes this technically a volunteer sample" (p. 9). They were also able to randomly assign the people to conditions in terms of time and amount of payment; however, they were unable (obviously) to assign individuals to SES categories.

In many situations, it is not possible for ethical or practical reasons to assign people randomly, and it may not be possible to randomly select individuals from a larger population. Much research in education and psychology is done with available populations, and therefore, the use of parametric statistics is questionable.

If intact classes are used, the class becomes the unit of analysis thus necessitating having a large number of classes involved in the research to conduct meaningful statistical analysis. Maruyama and Deno (1992) suggest an alternative statistical analysis scheme that uses classes and subjects within classes as variables in the experimental design. This requires use of an ANOVA model in which class becomes a variable nested within treatments, unless all treatments occur in each class, with students nested within class. The treatment effects can then be compared with their interaction with subjects within classes.

In studies with intact classes or groups, researchers can choose to use a regression analysis rather than ANOVA. In regression analysis, there is no need to create small groups based on collapsing scores on variables. Thus, this approach can provide a more desirable option because it would not require expanding the sample size.

Sample Size

Sample size is a basic influence on statistical significance (Thompson, 1992). Virtually any study can have statistically significant results if a large enough sample size is used. For example, with a standard deviation of 10 and a sample size of 20, a difference of 9.4 between two independent means is necessary for statistical significance at the .05 level in a nondirectional test. However, if the sample size is 100, a difference of only 4.0 is required, and with a sample size of 1,000, a difference of only 1.2 is required (Shaver, 1992). An overly large sample size can result in obtaining statistical significance, even though the results may have little practical significance (see the next paragraph for further elaboration of this idea). When researchers are working with low-incidence populations, as commonly happens in special education research, the small sample size itself might prevent the researcher from obtaining statistical significance. Small sample sizes also have implications for the researcher's ability to disaggregate results by characteristics such as gender, ethnicity, or type of disability. In such cases, the researcher needs to plan a sample of sufficient size to make the disaggregation meaningful.

Statistical Versus Practical Significance

The influence of the size of the sample on the ease or difficulty of finding statistical significance brings up the issue of statistical versus practical significance. Simply because it is easier to obtain statistical significance with larger samples, researchers need to be sensitive to the practical significance of their results. For example, statistical significance may be obtained in a study that compares two drug treatment interventions. In examining the size of the difference, the data may indicate that there is only 2 days longer abstinence for the experimental group. Thus, the researcher needs to be aware of the practical significance of the results, particularly if there are big differences in the costs of the two programs. Is it worth changing to a much more expensive program to keep someone off drugs for 2 additional days?

Cultural Bias

Davis (1992) explored the meaning of using a label to indicate race when investigating the effects of various social programs. He writes that researchers avoid the complexity of participants' experiences and social locations by categorizing people uncritically according to their race and thereby assuming homogeneity in their conditions. This is a point also supported in the writings of Stanfield (1993a, b, c) who warns against the use of racial categorization in an overly simplistic way in research.

Davis (1992) criticizes researchers who lack a basic understanding of the way programs and target populations function, particularly with poor minority populations:

> For instance, in the absence of such knowledge, randomization serves as a safety net and as a way of dealing with threats to internal validity. This dependence on design and method often results in program evaluations that employ poor program conceptualization, insensitive measures, and inappropriate generalization of findings. (p. 56)

He cites as an example of this lack of cultural sensitivity research on social programs such as those designed to prevent teenage pregnancy and sexually transmitted diseases in African American communities, in which assumptions are made that are in conflict with the pervasive religious values. Or in employment training programs for Black men, assumptions are made that are in conflict with the perceptions of self-worth and values as they are related to motivation and behavior with respect to employment. "Most job training programs were developed with inadequate understanding of the target population, and the result has been program evaluations that have reinforced negative stereotypes of African American men" (p. 57).

Davis (1992) notes that different populations are often classified on the basis of phenotypic and genotypic criteria. Then researchers who lack knowledge in biology and genetics often interpret correlates with race on the basis of biogenetic meanings, either implicitly or explicitly. "Such practices rule out cultural or economic explanations of race differences such as income, trust in program personnel, and program delivery" (p. 58). If the researcher erroneously privileges the biogenetic meanings over other meanings, recommendations might follow the path of sterilization or abandonment of current social interventions. However, researchers who critically examine race as a distinct cultural pattern realize that interpretations must be tied to the socioeconomic and environmental context. Thus, policy and program decisions based on this perspective can be more responsive to the social and cultural settings of programs.

Davis (1992) thus brings us full circle from the perspectives discussed in Chapter 1. If the researcher starts from a "deficit" view of the minority population, the interpretation of the data will focus on the dysfunctions found within that community. If the researcher starts with an emancipatory perspective, the researcher will attempt to identify the broader cultural context within which the population functions. For example, African Americans are at greater risk than other populations for living in poverty. These circumstances are important because of the causal relationship between poverty and oppressive social consequences. Rather than focusing on the "deficit" of being raised in a single-parent household, researchers need to understand the notion of extended family and its particular importance for African American children. They also need to understand the contextual information about the experiences and characteristics of racial communities concerning the environments in which children live that make them less likely to perceive the benefits of high educational achievement.

Marín and Marín (1991) note that in less acculturated Hispanic populations, research has suggested that there is a tendency to use the extreme response categories on a Likert-type scale. That is, Hispanic respondents are less likely to use the middle response categories when presented with response scales and more likely to choose the extremes such *definitely true* or *agree a lot*. The authors speculate that the reason for this response pattern is the cultural value placed on sincerity in expression of feelings and that choosing a middle response might be viewed as a way of hiding a person's real feelings. They suggest that researchers be aware of this tendency and examine the pattern of responses obtained to determine if it is evident in their data set. If it is, researchers might want to consider aggregating the responses to both the *strongly agree* and *agree* items to moderate the effect of having a preponderance of extreme responses.

Marín and Marín (1991) also note that there has been some research suggesting that Hispanic populations may be more likely to provide socially desirable responses and to underreport socially undesirable behaviors. Although the research supporting such reporting biases is not abundant, the authors do suggest that researchers examine their data carefully to detect if any reporting biases appear to be present, be sensitive to the need to match ethnic characteristics of the participants and research staff, and disaggregate by educational levels (because lower educational levels tend to be associated with more response biases of these types).

Generalizability

As mentioned in previous chapters, external validity is defined in terms of the generalizability of the results of one particular research study to a broader population. Randomized sampling strategies are supposed to ensure that the results can be generalized back to the population from which the sample was drawn. Randomized sampling is not always possible, and therefore, researchers need to be careful in the generalizations they make based on their results.

When working with racial and ethnic minority groups or people with disabilities, generalizations about group differences are often put forward without much attention to within-group variation and the influence of particular contexts. Davis (1992) describes this problem within the African American community in that many social prevention programs have been conceived from dominant middle-class perspectives, and many of these programs have been implemented in African American communities. Although researchers sometimes acknowledge that culturally specific approaches are needed, there have been few serious efforts to design and evaluate programs based on culturally diverse perspectives. When researchers use inappropriate measurement strategies with minority groups, they can erroneously reach conclusions that the programs are not effective. The people who are hurt by such inappropriate conclusions are those who have the least power. The following comments by Davis summarize the problems with reliance on statistical outcomes without proper sensitivity to contextual variables:

> Data-analytical techniques should not completely replace informed program analysis based on knowledge obtained in the context of program participants' lives and experience. An enormous amount of information about the location and contexts of programs is missing from the discussion of programs' causal claims. Often, knowledge of a program's clientele and the program's appropriateness for its environment is needed to advance thinking about the program's causal assertions. Unfortunately for African Americans and other U.S. racial minorities, this information is, at best, partially known but discarded or, at worst, not known or even cared about. This is not to say that experimental and quasi-experimental studies are not useful for program evaluation; to the contrary. These methods are very powerful in revealing program effects, but results must be examined more carefully, and with sensitivity to diverse populations.
>
> A comparative analytical approach works from the assumption that because African Americans are homogeneous in their condition and experience, programs are homogeneous in their effects. There is relatively little information about the many sources of variation within the Black population. African Americans are the largest racial minority in this country, but much within-group

variation and in-depth understanding will be completely lost with traditional race-comparative analysis in program evaluation. (p. 63)

Options for Reporting Statistical Results

Researchers have offered a number of options for reporting statistical results of quantitative research that include effect sizes, percentage of variance accounted for, and examining within- and between-group differences. For studies that use means to compare an experimental and control group, the *effect size* is defined as the distance between the two group means in terms of their common standard deviation (Cooper, 1989). Thus, an effect size of .5 means that the two means are separated by one half of a standard deviation. This is a way of describing how well the average student or client who received the treatment performed relative to the average student or client who did not receive the treatment. For example, if an experimental group of persons with behavioral problems received a drug treatment and the control group received a placebo, an effect size of .8 would indicate that the experimental group's mean was .8 standard deviation above the control group. Shaver (1992) and Carver (1992) recommend that researchers report their effect sizes rather than statistical significance when that is inappropriate. Later in this chapter, I describe how to use effect sizes for meta-analysis—that is, a statistical synthesis of previously conducted research.

Snyder and Lawson (1992) warn against a blind interpretation of effect size based on magnitude and suggest that the judgment of significance rests with the researcher's, user's and reviewer's personal value systems; the research questions posed; societal concerns; and the design of a particular study. For more detailed information on effect size, the reader is referred to Lipsey (1990).

Lewin and Wild (1991) contrast two ways that researchers could report information about the *amount of variance accounted for* in a correlational study:

> If we read that a sample of men score "significantly higher at the .01 level" than do women on some scale or test, the implication is quite different from that of a report that reads, "Sex differences, although significant at the .01 level, account for only 3% of the variance on this scale. A combined index of the level of training on three skills: X, Y, and Z, plus months of experience in two settings: P and Q, jointly accounts for 73% of the variance in scale scores." (p. 584)

They note that both of these statements could well be accurate descriptions of exactly the same research study. However, the conclusions that would be drawn from each statement might differ markedly. The first statement suggests that women do not do as well as men. The second description indicates that training and experience are very important, whereas the impact of gender is trivial.

Davis (1992) suggests that reporting differences between identified racial groups is overemphasized and suggested that more attention be given to important variations within racial groups. For example, differences between urban and rural African American families could account for much of what appears to be cross-race difference. He also recommended having members of racial and ethnic groups review the research results before they are disseminated to help detect bias and inaccuracies.

Replication

When the data do not meet the assumptions necessary for reaching conclusions about statistical significance, Carver (1992) recommends that researchers replicate the study's results as the best replacement for information about statistical significance. Building replication into research helps eliminate chance or sampling error as a threat to the internal validity of the results. This also emphasizes the importance of the literature review, discussed in Chapter 2, as a means of providing support for the generalizability of the results.

Use of Nonparametric Statistics

Nonparametric statistics provide an alternative for researchers when their data do not meet the basic assumptions of normality and randomization, they have small samples, or they use data of an ordinal or nominal nature.

Competing Explanations

No matter what design, paradigm, or type of data collected, researchers always need to consider competing explanations. (In the postpositivist paradigm, these are called threats to internal and external validity.) Such competing explanations become critical when it is time to interpret the results. In the study of African American children's attitudes toward drugs (Belgrave et al., 1994, summarized in Sample Study 12.1), the authors acknowledge that they had expected to find a relationship between Africentric values and self-esteem. They hypothesized that the unexpected lack of relationship between the two variables may be because they used a global measure of self-esteem that did not tap the dimensions of self-esteem that may be more relevant to African American children and youths. They suggest that a more relevant dimension of self-esteem for this population might include aspects of the family and community as well as more social and recreational areas, such as sports, physical activities, and peer relationships.

Recognizing Limitations

As should be clear by now, it is not possible to design and conduct the "perfect" research study in education or psychology. Therefore, it is incumbent on the researcher to recognize and discuss the limitations of a study. For example, Belgrave et al. (1994) recognized that they had used a small convenience sample; only children who had agreed to participate in an intervention program were available for research purposes. It is possible that these individuals were already different in some ways on measures of beliefs and drug attitudes. Also, although the researchers attempted to revise the instruments so that they were culturally relevant, they acknowledge that the measures were not as robust and strong psychometrically as they would have liked. Future research is recommended that uses a larger, random sample with more psychometrically sound instruments.

Special Application: Statistical Synthesis as Literature Review

Statistical syntheses are appropriate for experimental, quasi-experimental, causal comparative, and correlational research. However, even within these types, constraints apply. Cooper (1989) identifies the following three situations in which the use of statistical syntheses are not appropriate:

1. If the researcher's goal is to trace the historical development of a concept or practice, statistical synthesis is not appropriate.

2. If comparable treatment and control groups are not included in the reviewed studies, it may be inappropriate to lump the studies together. Aggregation of dissimilar groups can obscure effects.

3. Studies should be aggregated only if they share sufficient similarity in the conceptual definition of the variables.

Statistical Synthesis

Meta-analysis is one statistical approach to research synthesis that uses additional analyses to aggregate the findings of studies and reach conclusions. Meta-analysis is a quantitative synthesis of the existing research. Using primary source information from the literature, the meta-analyst establishes empirical evidence to increase understandings about a particular theory.

In meta-analysis, the researcher addresses studies that have attempted to establish a causal relationship between some intervention and an outcome based on a review of available literature. For example, Hyde and Linn (1988) were able to identify 165 studies of gender differences in verbal ability. Typically, an effect size is established for each study in the sample of studies drawn for the meta-analysis. The effect size is then compared across studies the analyst has identified in the literature.

For studies that use means to compare an experimental and control group, the effect size is defined as the distance between the two group means in terms of their common standard deviation (Cooper, 1989). It is calculated as follows:

$$d = \frac{M_1 - M_2}{s}$$

where

M_1 is the mean or average for one group (e.g., experimental group),
M_2 is the mean or average for the other group (e.g., control group), and
s is the within-group standard deviation (measure of variability within groups).

Thus, an effect size of .5 means that the two means are separated by half a standard deviation. This is a way of describing how well the average student who received the treatment performed relative to the average student who did not receive the treatment. For example, if an experimental group of students with behavioral problems received a drug treatment and the control group received a placebo, an effect size of .8 would indicate that the experimental group's mean was .8 standard deviation above the control group. (Statistical terms are defined in the box labeled "Definitions of Commonly Used Statistics.")

Once the effect size for each study has been computed, an average effect size is calculated by combining the d for each study. For example, based on a meta-analysis of gender difference in cognitive abilities, Hyde (1981) reported that $d = .45$ for spatial ability, $-.24$ in verbal ability, and .43 for mathematical ability.

Interpretation of effect sizes is not clear-cut. Cohen (1988) proposes the following (somewhat arbitrary) guideline:

.20 is small

.50 is medium

.80 is large

Hyde (1990) suggests comparing the obtained d with effect sizes reported for either related studies in the same field or for quite different studies. For example, one might compare effect sizes for verbal and spatial abilities. Or the effect size of spatial abilities for gender differences could be compared with effect sizes for the magnitude of the effects of psychotherapy (which Smith & Glass, 1977, cited in Hyde, 1990, reported to be $d = .68$). Hyde believes it will be beneficial for feminist researchers to compare gender difference effects with the magnitude of other effects on the same phenomenon (e.g., social class or differences in attitude toward mathematics).

Gender Differences in Meta-Analysis

The calculation of d using within-group standard deviation has certain advantages for studying gender differences because it takes into account not only gender differences but also male and female variability (Hyde, 1990). This procedure recognizes that each sex is not homogeneous and calculates exactly how large or small the differences are within groups.

Gender differences in abilities have sometimes been used as an explanation for lopsided gender ratios in some occupations. Hyde's (1981, 1990) work in meta-analysis makes it possible to determine whether such explanations are adequate. For example, she observed that fewer than 5% of engineers in the United States are women and that possessing a high level of spatial ability is generally considered important for success at engineering. Assuming that spatial ability at least at the 95th percentile is required to become an engineer and that $d = .40$ for gender differences in spatial ability, about 7.35% of men and 3.22% of women would possess sufficiently high spatial ability to be engineers. That would support a 2:1 ratio of males:females in the profession, or 67% men and 33% women. Therefore, she concluded that, if women constitute fewer than 5% of engineers, they are seriously underrepresented in comparison with their spatial ability test performance, and other factors must be considered to account for the lopsided gender ratio.

Hyde (1990) describes further steps in the meta-analytic process that can provide additional insights into gender differences based on various features of the study (see also Hedges & Becker, 1986). *The homogeneity analysis* analyzes the extent to which the values of *d* in the set are uniform or homogeneous. When the values of *d* vary widely across studies, the meta-analysis must account for these differences. One strategy for handling this problem is to group the studies with similar values for *d* into subsets and explore the data for underlying similarities in method or characteristics of subjects.

Race, Ethnicity, and Disability in Meta-Analysis

Fuchs and Fuchs (1989) conducted a meta-analysis on the effects of familiarity of the test administrator to the test taker for special education placement in early childhood programs to study racial and ethnic factors in assessment. On the basis of the use of 14 studies in their sample, they concluded that Hispanic and Black students scored significantly higher with familiar examiners; Caucasian students showed no such interaction effects. Fuchs and Fuchs note that the racial and ethnic variable was confounded with socioeconomic status, and therefore, their conclusions were tentative.

Beaudry (1992) identifies a number of challenges in conducting meta-analysis on ethnically diverse populations. Specifically, complex variables are reduced for statistical purposes to dichotomies. For example, ethnicity and race must be dichotomized to fit statistical models. Thus, the operational definition of variables requires an aggregation of ethnic groups into Black versus non-Black or Hispanic versus non-Hispanic. This may result in sample sizes that are too small to warrant analysis disaggregated by ethnicity.

There are many pros and cons for deciding to use meta-analysis. It does offer a systematic and objective method of aggregating the results of a large number of studies on a specific topic. On the other hand, this approach suffers from the same threats faced in other research efforts—the exhaustive nature of the retrieval process and the diversity of research quality in the studies selected.

Qualitative Analytic Strategies

As mentioned before, but repeated here for emphasis, data analysis in qualitative studies is an ongoing process. It does not occur only at the end of the study as is typical in most quantitative studies. The fact that the topic is explored in depth here is simply an artifact of the way the human brain works. It is not possible to learn about everything all at once. So realize that analysis in qualitative studies designed within the ethnographic or phenomenological traditions is *recursive;* findings are generated and systematically built as successive pieces of data are gathered (Stainback & Stainback, 1988).

Qualitative data analysis has sometimes been portrayed as a somewhat mysterious process in which the findings gradually "emerge" from the data through some type of mystical relationship between the researcher and the sources of data. Anyone who has conducted in-depth qualitative analysis will testify that a considerable amount of work occurs during the data collection and analysis phases of a qualitative study. Several authors have attempted to describe that process of transforming qualitative data in recent texts:

> Feldman, M. S. (1995). *Strategies for interpreting qualitative data.* Thousand Oaks, CA: Sage.

Feldman describes four qualitative strategies: ethnomethodology, semiotics, dramaturgical analysis, and deconstruction.

> Miles, M. B., & Huberman, A. M. (1994). *Qualitative data analysis* (2nd ed.). Thousand Oaks, CA: Sage.

This sourcebook can be used to guide the novice researcher through the entire process of managing, analyzing (within and across cases), conclusion drawing and verification tactics, matrix building and use, ethics, and report writing.

> Silverman, D. (1993). *Interpreting qualitative data: Methods for analyzing talk, text, and interaction.* Thousand Oaks, CA: Sage.

Silverman's text is written as an introductory text for sociology students and therefore covers more than just data analysis and interpretation. However, the author structured the book to integrate opportunities to analyze samples of qualitative data throughout the text, thereby emphasizing this aspect of doing qualitative research.

> Tesch, R. (1990). *Qualitative research: Analysis types and software tools.* New York: Falmer.

Tesch provides a diagram of different types of qualitative research within the disciplines of education, psychology, and sociology. She then describes various analytic strategies and computer packages that can be used for qualitative analysis.

> Weitzman, E. A., & Miles, M. B. (1995). *A software sourcebook: Computer programs for qualitative data analysis.* Thousand Oaks, CA: Sage.

The authors review the major computer programs that can be used to aid in qualitative data analysis, with a matrix that guides readers through a selection process to suit their own needs.

> Wolcott, H. F. (1994). *Transforming qualitative data: Description, analysis, and interpretation.* Thousand Oaks, CA: Sage.

Wolcott focuses on what the researcher does with data that have already been collected (i.e., not on the data collection process itself) and provides examples of nine of his own qualitative studies to further elucidate the process of transforming qualitative data.

Based on a qualitative analysis of texts that describe qualitative principles and procedures, Tesch (1990) identifies principles and practices that hold true for most types of qualitative research analysis and interpretation. Researchers should be aware of the following principles and practices in qualitative data analysis:

1. Analysis occurs throughout the data collection process. Stainback and Stainback (1988) identify different levels of data analysis that occur during the course of a study. Initially, while the researcher is in the field, he or she reflects on impressions, relationships, patterns, commonalities, and so on. For example, during a study of special education training in Egypt, Mertens (1995) shared the results of her initial impressions with participants who were deaf, blind, or nondisabled on a daily basis. This allowed the participants to be informed of any hypotheses that the researcher was formulating and to add their own interpretations to the data. The second level of analysis occurs when the researcher sits down to organize and develop the variety of data collected in the field to make detailed notes. The researcher analyzes the logic and the correspondence of data to initial impressions in the field. Periodically throughout the study, the researcher carefully and thoroughly studies all the data, seeking similarities, differences, correspondence, categories, themes, concepts and ideas, and analyzes the logic of previous analytic outcomes, categories, and weakness or gaps in the data. To gain a fresh perspective on the nature of the data and the problems, some methodologists recommend that the researcher wait up to a month before conducting the final analysis of the data (Bogdan & Biklen, 1992; Stainback & Stainback, 1988).

2. "The analysis process is systematic and comprehensive, but not rigid" (Tesch, 1990, p. 95). Unlike quantitative statistical analysis, there is no test of statistical significance to tell the researcher that the data analysis is at an end. Lincoln and Guba (1985) recommend that the data analysis be stopped with the emergence of regularities: That is, no new information emerges with additional data analysis.

3. Data analysis includes reflective activities that result in a set of notes that record the analytic process, thus providing accountability. Procedures (also discussed in Chapter 7) include the inquiry audit in which an "auditor" examines the fairness of the research process and accuracy of the product in terms of internal coherence and support by data (Lincoln & Guba, 1985). Keller (1993) used peer debriefing in his case study of a girl with Down's syndrome by exposing his research findings to an uninvolved peer. Outside referees can be asked to review the data analysis procedures and results.

4. The analysis process begins with reading all the data at once and then dividing the data into smaller, more meaningful units. For example, in Mertens's (1992) study of contextual factors that influence the success of total-inclusion program planning, she identified categories such as the state's least restrictive environment policy, the quality of existing services, the strength of advocacy groups, the process of communicating information to parents and staff, and the number and characteristics of the students involved.

5. The data segments are organized into a system that is predominately derived from the data; that is, the data analysis process is inductive. Some guiding research questions can be formulated at the beginning of the process; however, additional categories or themes are allowed to emerge from the data. In the total-inclusion study, Mertens (1992) used a semi-structured interview guide based on previous research on factors that influence the success of total-inclusion programs. However, the participants were first asked an open-ended question about advice they would give to others who might want to implement a total-inclusion program.

6. The main analytic process is comparison; that is, the researcher uses comparison to build and refine categories, define conceptual similarities, find negative evidence, and discover patterns. Mertens (1992) discovered that a top-down approach to implementing a total-inclusion program created more negative feelings than a shared governance approach. Other problems were common to all the schools studied, such as the need for additional training and support staff; however, the feelings expressed by students, parents, and staff were more negative in the top-down schools.

7. The categories are flexible and are modified as further data analysis occurs. For example, a researcher might start with a category called "finances" and find later that it is more functional to divide that category into "current finances" and "future financial needs."

8. Qualitative data analysis is not mechanistic. The basis for judging the quality of analysis in a qualitative study rests on corroboration to be sure that the research findings reflect people's perceptions (Stainback & Stainback, 1988). Several of the criteria presented in Chapter 7 for judging the quality of qualitative studies in general have relevance for the quality of the data analysis in particular. Specifically, triangulation requires the convergence of multiple data sources from a variety of participants under a variety of conditions. It should be noted that all people and sources may not agree, and this difference in opinion should be made explicit in the report.

9. The result of an analysis is some type of higher-order synthesis in the form of a descriptive picture, patterns or themes, or emerging or substantive theory. The results of the study of total-inclusion planning processes consisted of a framework for decisions related to implementing a program to bring students with disabilities into their neighborhood schools (Mertens, 1992). Factors that were identified fit into the following broad categories: planning and contextual factors, parental involvement, training, logistics, curriculum issues, and spillover effects.

Steps in Qualitative Data Analysis

Miles and Huberman (1994) sequence the steps for qualitative data analysis as follows:

1. Give codes to your first set of field notes drawn from observations, interviews, or document reviews.

2. Note personal reflections or other comments in the margin.

3. Sort and sift through the materials to identify similar phrases, relationships between variables, patterns, themes, distinct differences between subgroups, and common sequences.

4. Identify these patterns and processes, commonalities, and differences and take them out to the field in the next wave of data collection.

5. Begin elaborating a small set of generalizations that cover the consistencies discerned in the database.

6. Examine those generalizations in light of a formalized body of knowledge in the form of constructs or theories.

The researcher would then continue the process of data collection and analysis until the regularities that were mentioned previously emerged.

Grounded Theory Analysis Strategies

As mentioned in Chapter 7, grounded theory is a type of qualitative research developed by Strauss and Corbin (1990). I outline the steps for analysis as Strauss and Corbin explain them within this approach to qualitative inquiry as one example of how to approach qualitative analysis. Strauss and Corbin caution the researcher-analyst to be sensitive to the nonlinear nature of qualitative analysis; that is, even though the analytic process is described in terms of three steps, the researcher is actually moving back and forth with the data, analyzing and then collecting more data, and then analyzing some more. The steps rarely occur in a linear fashion but recur as often as is necessary to reach the appropriate conclusions.

Grounded theory is an interactional method of theory building. It involves making comparisons and asking questions of the data. It is sometimes called the constant comparative method of analysis. Strauss and Corbin (1990) identify three steps in the grounded theory analytic process:

Step 1: *Open coding* is the part of analysis that pertains specifically to naming and categorizing phenomena through close examination of data. During this phase, the data are broken down into discrete parts, closely examined, compared for similarities and differences, and questions are asked about the phenomena as reflected in the data. Thus, the researcher must take apart an observation, a sentence, or a paragraph and give each discrete incident, idea, or event, a name or label that stands for or represents a phenomenon. They suggest that the researcher ask basic questions of the data, such as Who? When? Where? What? How? How much? and Why?

Step 2: *Axial coding* is the part of the analytic process in which the researcher puts the parts of the data identified and separated in open coding back together to make connections between categories. This is an important step in the coding process because this is how you bring the complexity of the context back into the picture. During this phase, you build a model of the phenomena that includes the conditions under which it occurs (or does not occur), the context in which it occurs, the action and interactional strategies that describe the phenomena, and the consequences of these actions. You continue to ask questions of the data; however, now the questions focus on relationships between the categories. You begin to formulate possible relationships and continue to search the data for verification or negation of the hypothesized relationships. Strauss and Corbin (1990) describe it as a "constant interplay between proposing and checking" (p. 111). If your interest is in theme analysis or concept development, your analysis is complete at the end of this step. However, if you are interested in building theory, you need to continue to Step 3.

Step 3: *Selective coding* involves the process of selecting one, main core category (the story line) and relating the other categories to it. You validate the hypothesized relationships with the data available to you and fill in categories that need further refinement and development.

This step is similar to axial coding in that it is integrative and relational; however, Strauss and Corbin (1990) state that it is "done at a higher more abstract level of analysis" (p. 117). During this phase of analysis, the first step is to identify the core category, or story line, and then relate the subsidiary categories to the core through a model. (Strauss and Corbin use the term *paradigm* instead of model; however, I use the term *model* because paradigm has a different meaning in this book.[2]) The model includes an explication of the conditions, context, strategies, and consequences identified in the axial coding phase. You then validate your theory by grounding it in the data; if necessary, you seek additional data to test the theory.

Using Computers in Qualitative Analysis

Because qualitative studies tend to result in mountains of data (literally), many researchers have turned to computerized systems for storing, analyzing, and retrieving information. Presently, a large number of computer programs are available (e.g., The Ethnograph and NUD•IST), and this is an area in which rapid changes are occurring. Weitzman and Miles (1995) divide the possible computer programs for qualitative data analysis into the following categories:

1. *Text retrievers:* These are dedicated, sophisticated text search programs that can find all instances of words, phrases, and combinations that you are interested in locating. Examples include Metamorph, Orbis, Sonar Professional, The Text Collector, WordCruncher, or ZyINDEX.

2. *Textbase managers:* These programs provide more help in organizing, sorting, and making subsets of text systematically and then conducting search and retrieval activities. Examples include askSam, Folio VIEWS, Tabletop, and MAX.

3. *Code-and-retrieve programs:* These specialize in helping you divide text into segments or chunks, attaching codes to the chunks, and finding and displaying all the chunks with a given code (or combination of codes). Examples include HyperQual2, Kwalitan, QUALPRO, Martin, and The Ethnograph.

4. *Code-based theory builders:* These contain features similar to the code-and-retrieve programs; however, they provide greater support for theory building by helping you make connections between codes to develop higher-order classifications and categories, formulate propositions or assertions that imply a conceptual structure that fits the data, or test such propositions to see if they apply. Examples include AQUAD, ATLAS/ti, HyperRESEARCH, NUD•IST, and QCA.

5. *Conceptual network builders:* These programs take theory building one step further by providing the researcher with the capability of graphically representing relationships in the data. Data are depicted as nodes (typically in the form of rectangles or ellipses), linked to other nodes by lines or arrows that represent specific relationships. Examples include ATLAS/ti, MECA, and SemNet.

Before making a decision about which software program to use, you should review the texts cited in this chapter (as well as any more recent developments in this rapidly changing field). You need to pick a system that is compatible with your hardware as well as with your research purposes. One caution: No matter how attractive the software, nothing should separate you from active involvement with your data. Qualitative data analysis is really about *you* thinking about your data and hypothesizing possible relationships and meanings. A computer can be an important aid in this process, but you should not let it become a means of separating you from the process of knowing what your data has to say.

Interpretation Issues in Qualitative Data Analysis

Triangulating Data

Triangulation, as it was discussed in Chapter 7, involves the use of multiple methods and multiple data sources to support the strength of interpretations and conclusions in qualitative research. As Guba and Lincoln (1989) note, triangulation should not be used to gloss over legitimate differences in interpretations of data. Such diversity should be preserved in the report so that the "voices" of the least empowered are not lost.

Audits

Two types of audits were described in Chapter 7: the dependability audit and the confirmability audit. Through the use of these two strategies, the researcher can document the changes that occurred during the research and the supporting data for interpretations and conclusions. Questions to guide an audit for reviewing qualitative studies were suggested by Schwandt and Halpern (1988) whose work was cited in Miles and Huberman (1994). The questions are as follows:

1. Are findings grounded in the data? (Is sampling appropriate? Are data weighted correctly?)
2. Are inferences logical (Are analytic strategies applied correctly? Are alternative explanations accounted for?)
3. Is the category structure appropriate?
4. Can inquiry decisions and methodological shifts be justified? (Were sampling decisions linked to working hypotheses?)
5. What is the degree of researcher bias (premature closure, unexplored data in field notes, lack of search for negative cases, feelings of empathy)?
6. What strategies were used for increasing credibility (second readers, feedback to informants, peer review, adequate time in the field)? (p. 439)

Cultural Bias

The comments included in the section on cultural bias for quantitative research are equally appropriate when analyzing and interpreting qualitative research. The opportunity to see things from your own cultural bias is recognized as a potential problem in qualitative research. Many of the safeguards discussed in Chapter 7 are useful for minimizing this source of bias or for recognizing the influence of the researcher's own framework. You should begin by describing your own values and cultural framework for the reader. Then you should keep a journal or log of how your perspectives change through the study. Discussing your progress with a peer debriefer can enhance your ability to detect when your cultural lens is becoming problematic. Conducting member checks with participants who are members of the culture under study can help you see where divergence in viewpoints may be based on culturally different interpretations.

Generalization

Firestone (1993) recognized that the postpositivist conceptualization of generalization based on sample to population extrapolation was not appropriate for qualitative research. He describes two other perspectives for generalization that appear to be more compatible with the qualitative approach. The first of these is the case-to-case translation, which Lincoln and Guba (1985) explain as transferability. With this approach, the burden of proof for "generalizability" lies with the reader, and the researcher is responsible for providing the "thick description" that allows the reader to make a judgment about the applicability of the research to another setting.

The second type of generalizability described by Firestone (1993) is analytic generalization, based on the researcher's generalizing from a particular set of results to a broader theory. To enhance the researcher's ability to make this type of generalization, Firestone recommends a number of strategies, such as using multisite case studies with the cases being selected on a theoretical basis. He argues that the use of critical and deviant cases can facilitate the exploration and extension of existing theories by allowing for the examination of threats to generalizability within cases: "The multicase studies can use the logic of replication and comparison to strengthen conclusions drawn in single sites and provide evidence for both their broader utility and the conditions under which they hold" (p. 22).

Even still, the notion of generalizability through multisite studies is not an uncontested strategy. As Miles and Huberman (1994) commented,

> Thus there is a danger that multiple cases will be analyzed at high levels of inference, aggregating out the local webs of causality and ending with a smoothed set of generalizations that may not apply to any single case. This happens more often than we care to remember. (p. 435)

So aggregating across cases must be done cautiously and without loss of the uniqueness in the context of each case.

A Research Plan: The Management Plan and Budget

A research plan is needed to outline the steps that must be taken to complete the research study within a specific time frame and to identify the resources needed to accomplish this complex task. The research plan consists of two parts: the management plan and budget. Together, these can be used to guide you as you conduct your research and to monitor your progress.

The Management Plan

To develop a management plan, you need to analyze the major steps in the research process—for example, the literature review, design of the study, implementation of the study, and analysis and report of the study. Then, for each major step, you should list the substeps that you need to accomplish to conduct your research. A sample management plan is presented in Table 12.3. You can use the management plan to monitor your progress and to make any midcourse corrections that might be necessary. In addition, it can serve as a trail that documents your actions, which would allow researchers to audit your work, including any divergences from the original plan and the reasons for those changes. Particularly in qualitative research, the divergences are important because they are expected to occur. Thus, you are able to establish a trail of evidence for decisions that influenced the direction of the project and to support any conclusions you reached based on the research outcomes.

If you are involved in a large-scale research project, it might be helpful to divide the work that will be done by people (defined in terms of positions—e.g., project director, research assistant) and identify the amount of time that each person will devote to the various activities. Such a "person loading" chart can help with budgeting and justification for funding requests.

The Research Budget

Many dissertations and theses are written with very little or even no external funding. However, it is common for institutions to offer small grants to support such research or even for advanced students to seek outside funding. A sample budget sheet is presented in Table 12.4. General budget categories include personnel and nonpersonnel items. Under personnel, you should list all the people who will be involved in the research process, the amount of time each will be expected to work, and the rate at which each will be paid. Typical nonpersonnel items include travel, materials, supplies, equipment, communication expenses (telephone, postage), and copying. If you plan to pay people who participate in your research that should be included as well. If you are seeking funds from an external source, you will need to include "indirect costs." This is typically a percentage of the overall amount requested that your institution will expect to receive to cover costs such as maintaining the building in which you have an office, the heat, the water, and other "indirect costs" of supporting you as you conduct your research.

TABLE 12.3 Sample Management Plan for Research Proposal

Research Function	Subtasks	Person Responsible	Start Date	End Date
1. Literature review	1.1 Identify key terms 1.2 Identify data-bases 1.3 Conduct electronic search 1.4 Conduct hand search of journals 1.5 Contact experts in the field etc.	Research director	September 1996	November 1996
2. Instrument development	etc.[a]	Research director	November 1996	September 1996
3. Data collection	etc.	Research director	January 1997	March 1997
4. Data analysis	etc.	Research director	March 1997	April 1997
5. Reporting	etc.	Research director	April 1997	May 1997

a. You will be clearer about the other subtasks needed after you complete your literature review.

The budget can be arranged by research activities, to indicate which categories or activities require varying proportions of the funds. Arranging the budget this way makes it possible to show the impact of budget cuts on the research activities themselves. For example, if funds are budgeted for a follow-up of nonrespondents and this amount is cut from the budget, it would have deleterious effects on the quality of the research.

Writing Research Reports

The benchmark style manual for writing educational and psychological research reports is the *Publication Manual of the American Psychological Association* (4th ed.) (American Psychological Association [APA], 1994). This style manual has been "translated" specifically for students who are writing dissertations and theses; the translation is titled *Dissertations and Theses From Start to Finish* (Cone & Foster, 1993). In some disciplines (e.g., history), other style manuals may be recommended such as *The Chicago Manual of Style* (University

TABLE 12.4 Sample Budget (in dollars)	
Personnel	
Research director (9 months @ 2,000/month)	18,000[a]
Nonpersonnel	
Travel (2 trips at 1,000/trip)	2,000[b]
Communication costs	
Postage	
100 surveys @ .32	32
Second mailing 80 surveys @ .32	25
Third follow-up 50 surveys @ .32	16
Telephone (30 calls to nonrespondents @ 10)	300
Copying (5 pages × 230 surveys @ .10/page)	115
Total	20,488

a. Most institutional small grant programs disallow you paying yourself to complete your dissertation or thesis research. However, you might be able to obtain funds to support a research assistant to help with the copying, mailing, coding, or entry of data.

b. Typically, a budget would require specific justification for travel expenditure in terms of the cost of an airline ticket, hotel room, meals (sometimes calculated as a per diem), and so on.

of Chicago Press, 1993) or Turabian's (1987) *A Manual for Writers of Term Papers, Theses and Dissertations* (5th ed.). The APA also publishes a number of references on nondiscriminatory use of language, available from their publications office located in Washington, D.C.:

□ *Guidelines for Nonsexist Language in APA Journals* (1977)
□ *Guidelines for Avoiding Racial/Ethnic Bias in Language* (1989)
□ *Guidelines for Nonhandicapping Language in APA Journals* (1992)
□ *Avoiding Heterosexual Bias in Language* (1991)

Other professional organizations publish similar sets of guidelines, such as the American Educational Research Association, also located in Washington, D.C.

Students should check with their university regarding local style requirements. Individuals who wish to publish their research should check with prospective publishers for their requirements. Journals generally tend to include publication requirements in the front or back of each issue.

Dissertations and Theses

Most dissertations and theses consist of the same first three chapters:

Chapter 1: Introduction
Chapter 2: Literature Review
Chapter 3: Methodology

Quantitative dissertations and theses typically have two additional chapters:

Chapter 4: Results
Chapter 5: Discussion and Conclusions

Meloy (1994) found that qualitative dissertations tended to have different formats for the final chapters, such as chapters on emergent analyses, individual case study reports, and conclusions and implications. An outline for writing dissertation and thesis proposals for different paradigms is provided in the Appendix.

Before you start writing, you should determine if your institution has a formal style manual. In addition, ask questions to determine the general practices at your school:

---

1. What is the acceptable number of chapters in a dissertation or thesis? What flexibility exists for alternative formats?

2. How much control do students, faculty members, and the graduate school have in determining the appearance and style of the dissertation or thesis? Which decisions, if any, are negotiable?

3. Do you write in first person or third person? Do you use past, present, or future tense?

4. What are the local guidelines and requirements for selecting a committee? How many committee members must you have? What is the recommended or acceptable role for the committee members?

5. How supportive is the environment at your university or college for postpositivist, interpretive/constructivist, or emancipatory research?

Alternative Formats

Although you may have been working in the mind-set of producing a dissertation or thesis, you will want to be cognizant of alternative reporting formats for your academic research, as well as for your future research studies. Researchers have a wide range of options available to them for reporting their research: for example, presentations at professional meetings, journal articles, and technical reports. Typically, a research report includes an introduction (with a literature review) and sections for method, results, and discussion. The exact structure differs dependent on the type of research (quantitative or qualitative), the audience, and purpose of the report. Research reports can have multiple uses for different audiences; thus, alternative reporting formats should be considered for dissemination.

In both quantitative and qualitative studies, the researcher should tie the results back to the purpose for the study and to the literature in the discussion section of the report. Furthermore, findings should be based on data, and caution should be exercised in recommendations for practice. Limitations of the work should be recognized.

Quantitative Reports. In this format, results are typically reported by the use of tables and graphs. Researchers also tend to write in a detached style, avoiding the use of the first person and employing the passive voice. Although qualitative reports can use tables and graphs (Miles & Huberman, 1994), they typically present results in a more narrative style and include more personal revelations about the author (Van Maanen, 1988).

Moore (1991) identifies problems in writing the results of quantitative data analyses. She explains three problems commonly related to the use of the term *significant* in such reports. First, writers frequently use the term significant without the appropriate accompanying modifier term—for example, *statistically*—in the description of the results. The reader cannot infer that the term significant implies statistical significance. However, without that modifying term, the intended meaning of significance is not clear in this context. Second, writers sometimes assume that the use of the term *statistically significant* means that the results are important or meaningful. As mentioned in the section on the difference between statistical and practical significance, you know that having statistical significance does not necessarily equate with being important. Third, writers sometimes talk about *approaching significance.* This is not appropriate language in a research report. Results are either statistically significant or not; they do not approach (or avoid) significance.

In Thompson's (1988) analysis of common errors found in quantitative dissertations, he also notes this problem with language that describes statistical significance: Writers will sometimes interpret significance tests as if they were effect sizes (e.g., results were highly significant or results approached statistical significance). In addition, he notes the following common errors:

1. When the sample size is small and the effect size is large, the results are often underinterpreted. (As you will recall, it is harder to get statistical significance with a small sample, so if a large effect size is found under these conditions, it should be noted.) And if the sample size is large and effect sizes are modest, the results can be overinterpreted.

2. Researchers sometimes use many univariate tests of statistical significance when a multivariate test would be more appropriate. The probability of making a Type I error is increased when multiple univariate tests are applied to one data set.

3. Researchers sometimes convert continuous (ratio or interval) data to categorical (nominal) data to conduct a chi-square or some type of ANOVA. Thompson (1988) points out that much variance is lost by this conversion and suggests that researchers ask themselves whether a regression analysis might be more appropriate as a way of preserving the variance in the data.

4. Analysis of Covariance (ANCOVA) is sometimes employed to provide statistical control when random assignment was not performed with the expectation that the statistical adjustments will magically make groups equivalent. However, when the data cannot satisfy the underlying assumption of homogeneity of regression, it is not appropriate to use ANCOVA. The assumption states that the relationship between the covariate and the dependent variable is equivalent in all experimental groups; for example, children in a treatment group learn at the same rate as children in the control group. If the relationship between the dependent variable

and the covariate is different under different treatments, the ANCOVA should not be used. The effect of not satisfying the homogeneity of regression assumption can be to suppress evidence of program effects.

5. Researchers who use regression analysis should apply the regression equation to a fresh sample of data to see how well it does predict values on the criterion variable (replication and validation).

6. Researchers should always report the psychometric integrity of the measures they use.

Qualitative Reports. For this format, Stainback and Stainback (1988) recommend that the reader look for a deep and valid description and for well-grounded hypotheses and theories that emerge from a wide variety of data gathered over an extended period of time. The researcher should also seek contextual meaning—that is, attempt to understand the social and cultural context of the situation in which the statements are made and the behaviors exhibited. This includes a description of relevant contextual variables, such as home, community, history, educational background, physical arrangements, emotional climate, and rules.

Writing up qualitative research has emerged as an area of controversy. Wolcott (1994) describes the situation:

> One of the . . . strategies . . . [used] during the reporting phase of a study is for researchers to remove themselves from the picture, leaving the setting to communicate directly with the reader, as early ethnographic accounts often did. Another is to have informants present their accounts "entirely" in their own words or faithfully (alas, sometimes too faithfully) to preserve and report *every word* spoken by both interviewer and interviewee in formally taped sessions. This strategy, passing on "raw" rather than "cooked" data, presupposes a reader capable of overcoming all the problems that the researcher tried to avoid. Done in good faith—although built on a misunderstanding of how to keep an account "scientific" or "objective"—it falls of its own weight unless the neophyte realizes in time that there is no such thing as "pure" description. (p. 13)

This struggle of how to present qualitative data has sometimes been framed as a question of whose *voice* is represented in the written report.

McGee-Brown (1994) struggled with the implications for representing different voices in research in a way that would be meaningful for those who would be affected by the results. She notes that participants' constructions of meaning in social context often vary radically from the researcher's constructions because of different histories or experiences. She says that such variations do not discourage her from conducting and reporting research of a qualitative nature. Indeed, she views the variations as an impetus to seek the most accurate understanding possible of what is happening in contexts from as many perspectives as possible. She suggests that structural change is necessary to create formats for data dissemination that include all voices meaningfully in the discourse. Researchers need to establish mechanisms for speaking with the people for whom the research is conducted. For example, in education, researchers need to communicate about the research with students, teachers, and administrators. Currently, there is little value attached to such discourse, because a researcher is rewarded for publication in scholarly journals and presentations at professional meetings that the students, teachers, and administrators typically do not attend.

Organizing Qualitative Writing. Qualitative researchers often end up with a mountain of data that needs to be reduced to some manageable form so that others will be able and willing to read it. Wolcott (1994) suggests the following possibilities for organizing the presentation of the results:

---

1. Events can be presented in *chronological order* as they occurred in the data collection setting.

2. Events can be presented in the order in which the *narrators* revealed them to the researcher.

3. The researcher can write using *progressive focusing*—that is, describing a broad context and then progressively focusing on the details of the particular case.

4. You can report events as a *day-in-the-life* description of what life is like for people in that setting.

5. You can focus on one or two *critical or key events.*

6. You can introduce the *main characters* and then tell the story, revealing the *plot* as in a stage play.

7. The main *groups* in the setting can be described along with the way they *interact* with each other.

8. You can use an *analytic framework* (described earlier in the chapter in the section on grounded theory analysis) to organize the writing.

9. You can tell the *story several different ways,* from the viewpoint of different actors in the setting. Wolf (1992) used such a strategy in her book *A Thrice Told Tale* in which she reports the same field study as a work of fiction, in the form of field notes, and as a self-reflexive account.

10. You can present the research problem as a *mystery* to be solved, and then bring the pieces of data into the story as a way of solving the mystery.

Clarity in Writing

Clarity of writing seems, at first glance, to be an essential characteristic of a research report, especially one that purports to be directed at political change—a goal toward which emancipatory researchers strive. As obvious as this criteria might seem, it is not uncontested in the scholarly world. Lather (1995) was criticized because her published writings are not considered to be easily accessible to many audiences because of complex language and complicated writing style. In her own defense, and as a point to be made more broadly about language, she warns that simple, clear writing might disguise the complexity of an issue. She says, "Sometimes we need a density that fits the thoughts being expressed" (p. 4). She raises some provocative questions:

> What would it mean to position language as revealing or productive of new spaces, practices, and values? What might be the value of encouraging a plurality of theoretical discourses and forms of writing in a way that refuses the binary between so-called "plain speaking" and complex writing? What are the power issues involved in assumptions of clear language as a mobilizing strategy? What are the responsibilities of a reader in the face of correspondence theories of truth and transparent theories of language? What is the violence of clarity, its non-innocence? (p. 4)

She contends that writing that the reader is able to understand is accomplished at the cost of filtering the information to minimize demands on the reader. To make use of a text, a reader needs to see it as an opportunity to wrestle with ideas, become reflective, read it again, and come up with a personal understanding.

Utilization of the Research Results

Utilization of research results is more likely to occur when the researcher integrates strategies to enhance utilization into the research proposal. As mentioned in Chapter 9, scholars who work primarily in the area of program evaluation listed utilization as the first, and most important, criteria for judging the quality of an investigative effort. Although their focus was on investigations for evaluation purposes, the importance of utilization of research in education and psychology should not be overlooked. The following strategies have been identified to enhance utilization of research:

1. Identification and involvement of appropriate audiences for the proposed research, including representation of those who would be most likely to benefit from, or be hurt by, the research.

2. Frequent and appropriate methods of communication with the intended users of the research, including targeting reports to appropriate audiences.

3. Provision of reports that clearly describe the theoretical framework for the study, the procedures, and the rules for interpretation of the data.

4. Reaching intended users of the research through a variety of dissemination modes, with presentation of the research results in a timely manner, such that the information can be used for decision making.

Researchers should be cognizant of evaluating their own research (meta-evaluation) during the planning, implementation, and reporting phases of their studies.

Writing for Publication

Journals vary in what they are looking for and will find acceptable for publication. Inside the front or back covers of most journals, you will find a publication policy statement. Typically, the journal editors prepare a statement that describes the type of articles that they want to publish. Some journals specialize in theoretical work, others focus on empirical research studies, and some publish a combination of both. You generally find a description of the content that the editors view as being appropriate for that journal as well. You can sort of guess what that description will say by the title of the journal; however, it is good to review the statement, as well as a sampling of the articles that have been recently published in that source.

When you submit a manuscript for consideration to a journal, if it is a refereed journal, the editors will send the manuscript to several reviewers. The reviewers are given a checklist that allows them to make suggestions about your manuscript:

- That it be published as is (if you receive such a letter, save it, frame it, and hang it on the wall)
- That it be published with minor changes
- That it be revised and resubmitted for another review
- That it be rejected as inappropriate for that journal

Reviewers are typically given some type of checklist on which they can record their ratings of various aspects of the manuscript. Usually, they will be asked to rate things such as the following:

- The clarity of the problem
- The logical progression of ideas
- The significance of the issues raised (for the readers of that journal, specifically)
- The appropriateness of the research design for that problem
- The appropriateness of the conclusions based on the data analysis
- The readability of the text
- Appropriateness of tone (not overly emotional)
- Need for additional editing
- Appropriateness of references (in terms of quantity, quality, inclusion of important studies, and timeliness).

If you are thinking about publishing your research as a book, you should do some research on publishers to see who is publishing books on similar topics. This is important not just to determine potential interest on the part of the publisher but also to assess the publisher's ability to market the book to appropriate audiences for you. When you have identified one or a few potential publishers, it is appropriate to contact them and ask for their prospectus guidelines. Although publishers vary somewhat, they typically have an outline that delineates the type of information they need about your intended book to make a decision about their desire to publish it for you. Some publishers will request a sample chapter, whereas others will be satisfied with a detailed outline. Your prospectus is usually sent out to reviewers by the publisher who then uses their comments as a basis for deciding to accept or reject your book proposal.

▶ Questions for Critically Analyzing Data Analysis and Interpretation

▶ Quantitative Research

The reader is referred to the general statistical texts referenced at the beginning of this chapter for further explanations of the statistical terms and concepts used in these questions.

1. What types of statistical analysis were used? Were they appropriate to the level of measurement, hypotheses, and the design of the study? What alpha level was used to determine statistical significance?

2. Is there statistical significance? What was the effect size?

Note: Criteria 3 through 6 were adapted from Thompson (1988).

3. Does the researcher interpret significance tests correctly (i.e., avoid saying the results were highly significant or approached significance)?

4. When the sample size is small and the effect size large, are the results underinterpreted? Or if the sample size is large and effect sizes modest, are the results overinterpreted?

5. Are many univariate tests of significance used when a multivariate test would be more appropriate?

6. Are basic assumptions for parametric, inferential statistics met (i.e., normal distribution, level of measurement, and randomization)?

▶ Qualitative Research

1. Did regularities emerge from the data such that addition of new information would not change the results?

2. Was there corroboration between the reported results and people's perceptions? Was triangulation used? Were differences of opinions made explicit?

3. Was an audit used to determine the fairness of the research process and the accuracy of the product in terms of internal coherence and support by data?

4. Was peer debriefing used? Outside referees? Negative case analysis? Member checks?

5. Is the report long and rambling, thus making the findings unclear to the reader?

6. Was the correct conclusion missed by premature closure, resulting in superficial or wrong interpretations?

7. Did the researcher provide sufficient description?

Interpretation Issues

1. How do you account for the results? What are the competing explanations; how did the authors deal with them? What competing explanations can you think of other than those the author discussed?

2. How would the results be influenced if applied to different types of people (e.g., rural or urban)?

3. What were the processes that caused the outcomes?

4. What conclusions and interpretations are made? Are they appropriate to the sample, type of study, duration of the study, and findings? Does the author over- or undergeneralize the results?

5. Is enough information given so that an independent researcher could replicate the study?

6. Does the researcher relate the results to the hypotheses, objectives, and other literature?

7. Does the researcher overconclude? Are the conclusions supported by the results?

8. What extraneous variables might have affected the outcomes of this study? Does the author mention them? What were the controls? Were they sufficient?

9. Did the author acknowledge the limitations of the study?

■ Questions and Activities for Discussion and Application

1. How can sample size influence statistical significance? Why is this particularly important in special education research?

2. Why is randomization an important consideration in the choice of a statistical test? Why is this particularly important for research that uses small, heterogeneous, or culturally diverse samples?

3. What can a researcher do when the basic assumptions for parametric inferential statistics are not met?

4. Answer the questions for critically analyzing data analysis and interpretation in quantitative research for a study that you identified in your literature search.

5. What is the basis for judging the quality of data analysis and interpretation in qualitative research?

6. Answer the questions for critically analyzing data analysis and interpretation in qualitative research for a study that you identified in your literature search.

7. Elijah Anderson (1990) conducted research in a run-down neighborhood of poor and working-class Blacks. In an article in *The Chronicle of Higher Education,* Anderson was described as feeling frustration at the way various groups interpret and use his work (Coughlin, 1994). The following passage appeared in the article:

> Lingering racism and lack of jobs, he insists repeatedly, almost like a mantra, are at the root of the ghetto's chaos and despair.
>
> So it is a particular frustration to Mr. Anderson that conservative pundits and others have seized on his work, reading it as evidence for the necessity of cracking down on crime and reforming the welfare system. . . .
>
> "Conservatives, liberals, whoever, pick pieces of it to make their points," he (Anderson) says. "My job is to describe and represent and analyze in such a way that people who have no experience in that setting can learn something." (p. A9)

Critically analyze Anderson's description of the role of the researcher in terms of representation, interpretation, and utilization of research.

8. Reread the passage in this chapter in which Lather (1995) contests the "innocence" of clear, simplistic writing. She further explains her own way of writing as follows:

> Across the sweep of post-humanist theory, I find confirmations of and challenges and directions to my efforts. I am on to something, inchoate as it often is, turning to the theory that helps me articulate the investments and effectivities of what I have wrought, reading both the affirmations of my efforts and the critiques of it in a way that lets me keep on keeping on, stubbornly holding on to the rhythms of the unfoldings of a book that is as much writing me as the other way around. This exploration of possibilities in the face of limit questions marks my desire to "trouble" the dualism between calls for accessibility and the assumption that academic "High Theory" is a sort of masturbatory activity aimed at a privileged few that can have no "real" effect in the material world. (p. 12)

What is your view of the dichotomy set up (and rejected) by Lather (1995) in this passage: accessibility versus High Theory? What do you think Lather means when she says that simple, clear writing is not "innocent"? Can you think of examples of things you have struggled to read and then found that you gained new, deeper, and different understandings with rereading?

9. Causality is a much contested issue in the research world. As you will recall from Chapter 3, postpositivists contend that demonstration of causality can be

achieved only through experimental designs. Miles and Huberman (1994) address the issue of causality in qualitative research as follows:

> Can qualitative studies establish causal relationships at all? That possibility is often attacked from both the right ("Only controlled quantitative experiments can do that") and the left ("Causality is an unworkable concept in human behavior—people are not billiard balls"). In line with our epistemological stance, mentioned at the outset, the position we take here is that qualitative studies (see Van Maanen, 1979, 1983) are especially well suited to finding causal relationships; they look directly and longitudinally at the local processes underlying a temporal series of events and states, showing how these led to specific outcomes, and ruling out rival hypotheses. In effect, we get inside the black box; we can understand not just that a particular thing happened, but how and why it happened. (p. 434)

Contrast the viewpoint expressed by Miles and Huberman (1994) in the preceding passage with the viewpoints expressed in the following passage from a study of appropriate research methodologies to be used to determine the effectiveness of programs to prevent teenage pregnancy:

> To identify strategies that will have substantial impacts on levels of adolescent sexual activity, contraceptive use, and pregnancy, it will be necessary to conduct a coherent set of evaluation studies, based on theory and existing research, using rigorous experimental methods. (Moore, Sugland, Blumenthal, Glei, & Snyder, 1995, p. x)

> Qualitative studies can suggest hypotheses and fine-tune questions and methodologies. However, only rigorously-executed experimental studies can aspire to address questions of causal impact. (Moore et al., 1995, p. xii)

> Information obtained from anthropological investigations, focus groups, and qualitative interviews cannot be viewed as evaluation studies. (Moore et al., 1995, p. 107)

10. Reread the section of this chapter that describes Firestone's (1993) and Miles and Huberman's (1994) views on multisite case studies as a potential solution to the generalization issue for qualitative research. Contrast the two viewpoints in terms of the pros and cons of multisite case studies for this purpose. What is your position with regard to this issue?

11. McGee-Brown (1994) addresses the need to bring researchers and practitioners closer together in the following comments:

> Once educators are directly involved in the research process, then natural interactive discourse among educational researchers in higher education and public school will take place. We will not have to try to discover formats through which voices of all participants emerge, nor will we have to structure presentation formats which encourage interaction. Educational researchers who participate in AERA are hungry for discourse. Teachers

are no less hungry for that dialogue in research which will make the culture of schooling not only more effective for student learning, but more tolerable as a culture for them and their students. The stress of multiple competing responsibilities among teachers is at a peak. Can we ask them to take on yet another one, research, without providing them the resources and knowledge they need to accomplish it? Can we afford to continue to exclude them from the discourse by suggesting that they share their own research among themselves in journals and meetings where they talk to each other as we talk to each other through our professional channels? It is time for the two discourses to meet. (p. 5)

What kind of changes are necessary to bring about a true discourse between researchers and practitioners? McGee-Brown's comments were made within the context of educational research. What are the parallel issues for researchers in psychology? What can be done to make research more "usable" for practitioners? What responsibility do researchers have for interacting with the people who will be affected by the research results?

Notes

1. It should be noted that the choice of an analytic strategy is not without controversy. Carver (1992) and Shaver (1992) contend that researchers who cannot satisfy the assumptions for parametric statistics must use alternative analytic strategies. In practice, many researchers assume that the parametric statistics are robust—that is, the assumptions can be violated without serious consequences.

2. I reserve the use of the term *paradigm* for one's overarching view of the world, including one's philosophical assumptions about the nature and truth of knowledge.

APPENDIX

Writing the Research Proposal

Getting the Research Idea

Many students reading this document will already have some idea of what they want to study for their research. However, several sources of research ideas (for students who are still searching for the right topic) include your personal experience, reading in the professional literature, discussions with professors or students, and current issues in your field.

Research Abstract

Before proceeding with a full proposal, you should start with a research concept paper that is used for discussion purposes with the professor. This provides a basis for further development of the proposal itself. The purpose is to describe the research idea, present a brief commentary on the literature, and propose an appropriate methodology to conduct the inquiry.

Formal Research Proposal

The formal research proposal is begun after the professor approves the research concept or topic. Typically, the formal research proposal is written in the future tense and includes the specific information that will form the basis of the first three chapters of your proposal.

Educational researchers are engaged in a paradigm struggle in defining approaches to research. A paradigm is a worldview that includes certain philosophical assumptions about the nature of knowledge (i.e., epistemology). The dominant orientation in educational research historically has been derived from the philosophical orientation of positivism. Epistemologically, positivism is represented by the rationalistic paradigm, which typically employs a preordinate, quantitative design. In the positivist paradigm, a preordinate, quantitative design means that the researcher establishes the research questions prior to data collection (research questions are "preordained"). The positivist approach to research evolved into the postpositivist viewpoint with the introduction of quasi-experimental methods in the 1960s.

A second paradigm, that of interpretive/constructivism, is typically associated with qualitative research designs that are described as contextual, inclusive, involved, and emergent. In the constructivist paradigm, an emergent, qualitative design means that the research questions are allowed to emerge from the data as the study progresses.

The emancipatory paradigm represents a third worldview that explicitly addresses the issues of oppression, power, and politics in research. Feminists, ethnic minorities, and persons with disabilities are among those who have written about the philosophical assumptions and methodological implications of this paradigm.

It is beyond the scope of these guidelines to explore the underlying axioms of each paradigm; however, researchers should be familiar with the paradigm debate, read and reflect on this topic, and establish their own worldview as it affects their research activities.

The researcher's worldview influences the nature of the research questions and proposed methodology. These three elements (i.e., worldview, research questions, and proposed methodology) places you in one of the major research paradigms discussed in the professional literature concerning the researcher's philosophical orientation. Currently, the postpositivist paradigm is most closely associated with quantitative methods and the constructivist paradigm is associated with qualitative methods. In the emancipatory paradigm, scholars generally tend to use qualitative methods; however, they can use quantitative methods also. You should not confuse paradigm with method. You may choose to use a design that mixes both quantitative and qualitative data collection; however, the study will reflect one philosophical orientation by the philosophical assumptions that guide the research.

You should place yourself within one of the major paradigms for your research based on the correspondence with your worldview and the assumptions associated with each paradigm. The suggestions that follow describe the three chapters that make up the proposal (i.e., problem statement, literature review, and methodology).

Proposal Considerations

Chapter 1: Problem Statement

A. *Area of Study.* This provides a general introduction to the area of study. It briefly outlines the problem to be investigated, the purpose of the study, and significance of the problem and the justification for investigating it. If you are proposing to use *qualitative methods,* you should recognize the evolving nature of the problem statement and acknowledge that this is just a beginning point for the study.

B. *Definition of Terms.* Important terms and concepts should be defined. If you are proposing a *qualitative study,* initial definitions for important terms and concepts should be included, while recognizing that these will change as the study proceeds.

C. *Paradigm and Assumptions.* You should discuss your choice of the paradigm for the proposed study and explain the philosophical assumptions that make that paradigm choice appropriate.

Chapter 2: Literature Review

A. *History.* Chapter 2 provides a review of the historical background and the theory relevant to the major questions of the research.

B. *Current Literature.* A review of current relevant literature should be included. To exhibit adequate mastery of the literature, both supporting and opposing views should be presented. Emphasis should be placed on critically analyzing the strengths and weaknesses of previous research.

C. *Research Problem.* The literature review should build to the description of the research problem described in Chapter 2 and the research questions described in Chapter 3. If you are proposing *qualitative research,* acknowledge that the study may uncover other areas of literature that will need to be explored as the study progresses.

Chapter 3: Methodology

A. *Research Questions and Hypothesis.* For *quantitative research,* you should present major and minor research questions that emanate from the literature review. These questions should be translated into researchable hypotheses when the design requires the use of such. For *qualitative research,* you should present the initial questions and objectives that will focus the study. A qualitative study must focus on a specific phenomenon (e.g., rules for classroom interaction) that emanates from the inadequacies of current theory and research. The precise nature of the questions to be researched evolves in the process of collecting and analyzing data. The initial questions may be vague, but stating the questions is important because they frame the procedures for collecting and analyzing data. The questions should follow from the theoretical and research background and should guide the design of the study.

B. *Research Design.* The research design should be described. Many available references discuss research design; therefore, that information will not be repeated here. For *quantitative research,* you may conduct research using a variety of approaches, such as experimental, survey, and comparative data analysis. Basic assumptions of the selected designs must be addressed. If you are using an experimental or quasi-experimental design, inclusion of a schematic drawing of the design is appropriate. For *qualitative research,* many different design options are available to a student who works in the emergent, qualitative tradition. You should describe the design that will be used, such as ethnography or phenomenology. This will communicate to the reader whether the emphasis will be on cultural issues or individual, subjective experiences. You should present a rationale for the design of choice in terms of the research problems identified.

C. *Sample.* For *quantitative research,* you should describe the general characteristics of the population from which data will be collected. In addition, the sampling technique must be fully described, as well as the rationale for the method used for selecting the sample. Choice of sample size should be defended. For *qualitative research,* you should discuss the criteria for the selection of the participants and the setting of the study. Qualitative studies typically occur in naturally occurring settings and all individuals in the settings are considered as participants. You should describe the method that will be used to identify those participants who will serve as a subsample to provide in-depth information.

For *all research,* research involving human beings, no matter where those people are located (on or off campus), must be reviewed by the university's institutional review board (IRB). This is necessary prior to conducting any research. (Even research that will ultimately be ruled "exempt" from IRB approval, must be reviewed by an IRB.) The current members of the board and procedures for submitting a research proposal are generally available from the graduate school. Approval for the study should occur after the proposal is accepted by the committee and before beginning to collect any data.

D. *Measures.* For *quantitative research,* you should describe the variables that will be measured and delineate how they will be operationalized. You must address the issues of reliability and validity in measurement. In many studies, pilot testing of the instrument and procedures is necessary. For *qualitative research,* the researcher is the data collection instrument in the collection of much of the data. Therefore, the researchers must describe themselves in terms of closeness to the topic, values, and the like.

E. *Data Collection Procedures.* For *quantitative research,* you should describe the procedures by which the data will be collected (e.g., survey, test, observation, etc.; administered by mail, researcher, collaborating teacher, etc.). For *qualitative research,* you should describe the design for the data collection, including a clear description of the procedures that will be used. The researcher's role should be described in terms of the degree of participation in which the researcher will engage. Supplemental methods of data collection such as videotapes, audiotapes, diary notes, or journal entries should be described. The time period for data collection should be identified. You should acknowledge that data collection and analysis overlap in qualitative studies and should reflect on possible changes in the type of data or the focus, time, or strategies used in the study. You should address the qualitative parallels to reliability and validity in measurement as they are explicated in the literature, including credibility, transferability, dependability, and confirmability and describe the methodological strategies that will be used to ensure that high-quality data are collected.

F. *Pilot Testing.* In many studies, pilot testing of the instrument and procedures is necessary. This is especially important in qualitative studies, because pilot studies are often necessary in qualitative studies to help provide a framework and research questions. You should describe the pilot study procedures and results as well as insights from the pilot study that will affect the research itself.

G. *Data Analysis Procedures.* For *quantitative research,* the data analysis section should describe how you plan to handle the data in terms of processing of data, data coding and entry, and accuracy checks. In addition, you should provide information on which statistical procedures will be used for each research question. For *qualitative research,* data analysis strategies should be described. If triangulation is planned, you should explain the multiple sources of data and the conditions under which corroboration of evidence will be sought.

H. *Limitations of the Study.* Anticipated limitations of the study should be explained. For example, limitations may arise because of the nature of the available sample or instruments. You should explore the limitations and any strategies that will be used to minimize their impact. Implications for conducting and generalizing the study should be discussed.

I. *Time-Lines.* You should include a proposed time-line that clearly depicts the approximate time each research activity will be completed (e.g., instrument selected or developed, pilot test conducted, etc.).

Recommended Proposal Document Format Sequencing Layout of Proposal

Title page
Abstract
Table of contents
List of tables (if any)

List of illustrations (if any)
Chapter 1: Statement of the problem
Chapter 2: Review of the literature
Chapter 3: Methodology
Appendixes
References

References

Abberley, P. (1987). The concept of oppression and the development of a social theory of disability. *Disability, Handicap, and Society, 2*(1) 5-19.

Adler, P. A., & Adler, P. (1994). Observational techniques. In N. K. Denzin & Y. S. Lincoln (Eds.), *Handbook of qualitative research* (pp. 377-392). Thousand Oaks, CA: Sage.

Alcoff, L., & Potter, E. (1993). Introduction: When feminisms intersect epistemology. In L. Alcoff & E. Potter (Eds.), *Feminist epistemologies* (pp. 1-14). New York: Routledge.

Anderson, E. (1990). *Streetwise: Race, class, and change in an urban community.* Chicago: University of Chicago Press.

American Association of University Women Educational Foundation. (1993). *The AAUW survey on sexual harassment in America's schools: Hostile hallways.* Washington, DC: Author.

American Council of Learned Societies. (Ed.). (1927-1994). *Dictionary of American biography* (20 vols., 7 suppl., & index guide). New York: Scribner.

American Educational Research Association. (1985a). Guidelines for eliminating race and sex bias in educational research and evaluation. *Educational Researcher, 14*(6), 16-17.

American Educational Research Association, American Psychological Association, & National Council on Measurement in Education. (1985b). *Standards for educational and psychological testing.* Washington, DC: American Psychological Association.

American Historical Association. (1992). *Statement on standards of professional conduct.* Washington, DC: Author.

American Psychological Association. (1977). *Guidelines for nonsexist language in APA journals.* Washington, DC: Author.

American Psychological Association. (1982). *Ethical principles in the conduct of research with human participants.* Washington, DC: Author.

American Psychological Association. (1989). *Guidelines for avoiding racial/ethnic bias in language.* Washington, DC: Author.

American Psychological Association. (1991). *Avoiding heterosexual bias in language.* Washington, DC: Author.

American Psychological Association. (1992). *Guidelines for nonhandicapping language in APA journals*. Washington, DC: Author.

American Psychological Association. (1993). Guidelines for providers of psychological services to ethnic, linguistic, and culturally diverse populations. *American Psychologist, 48,* 45-48.

American Psychological Association. (1994). *Publication manual of the American Psychological Association* (4th ed.). Washington, DC: Author.

Anastasi, A. (1988). *Psychological testing* (6th ed.). New York: Macmillan.

Anderson, B. T. (1993). Minority females in the science pipeline: Activities to enhance readiness, recruitment, and retention. *Initiatives, 55*(3), 31-38.

Anderson, M. L. (1993). Studying across differences: Race, class, and gender in qualitative research. In J. H. Stanfield & R. M. Dennis (Eds.), *Race and ethnicity in research methods* (pp. 39-52). Newbury Park, CA: Sage.

Andrews, J. F., & Mason, J. M. (1986). How do deaf children learn about prereading? *American Annals of the Deaf, 131*(3), 210-216.

Appleby, J. O., Hunt, L. A., & Jacob, M. C. (1994). *Telling the truth about history*. New York: Norton.

Aquilino, W. S. (1994). Interview mode effects in surveys of drug and alcohol use: A field experiment. *Public Opinion Quarterly, 58,* 210-240.

Arias, B., & Casanova, U. (Eds.). (1993). *Bilingual education: Politics, practice, and research: Vol. 92. Yearbook of National Society for the Study of Education*. Chicago: University of Chicago Press.

Asher, S. R., Singleton, L. C., Tinsley, B. R., & Hymel, S. (1979). A reliable socio-metric measure for preschool children. *Developmental Psychology, 15,* 443-444.

Atkinson, D. R., Abreu, J., Ortiz-Bush, Y., & Brewer, S. (1994). Mexican American and European American ratings of four alcoholism treatment programs. *Hispanic Journal of Behavior Sciences, 16*(3), 265-280.

Atkinson, P., & Hammersley, M. (1994). Ethnography and participant observation. In N. K. Denzin & Y. S. Lincoln (Eds.), *Handbook of qualitative research* (pp. 248-261). Thousand Oaks, CA: Sage.

Auchter, J. C., & Skaggs, G. (1994, April). *The performance of 1993 graduating high school seniors: How do U.S. high schools measure up?* Paper presented at the annual meeting of the National Council on Measurement in Education, New Orleans, LA.

Babbie, E. (1990). *Survey research methods* (2nd ed.). Belmont, CA: Wadsworth.

Baker, E., & Linn, R. (1992, Spring). Performance based assessments. *CRESST,* pp. 1-8. (Newsletter of the National Center for Research on Evaluation, Standards, and Student Testing at UCLA)

Balay, R., & Sheehy, E. P. (1992). *Guide to reference books. Supplement to the tenth edition*. Chicago: American Library Association.

Banks, J. A. (1993). The canon debate, knowledge construction, and multicultural education. *Educational Researcher, 22*(5), 4-14.

Banks, J. A. (1995). Multicultural education: Historical development, dimensions, and practice. In J. A. Banks & C. A. McGee-Banks (Eds.), *Handbook of research on multicultural education* (pp. 3-24). New York: Macmillan.

Barlow, D. H., & Hersen, M. (1984). *Single-case experimental designs: Strategies for studying behavior change*. New York: Pergamon.

Barrios, B. A., & Hartmann, D. P. (1988). Recent developments in single subject methodology: Methods for analyzing generalization, maintenance, and muti-component treatments. In M. Hersen, R. M. Eisler, & P. M. Miller (Eds.), *Progress in behavior modification* (Vol. 22, pp. 11-47). New York: Academic Press.

Barzun, J., & Graff, H. F. (1992). *The modern researcher* (5th ed.). Boston: Houghton Mifflin.

Beaudry, J. S. (1992). Synthesizing research in multicultural teacher education. In A. Madison (Ed.), *Minority issues in program evaluation* (New Directions for Program Evaluation, Vol. 53, pp. 69-86). San Francisco: Jossey-Bass.

Beere, C. A. (1990a). *Gender roles: A handbook of tests and measures.* Westport, CT: Greenwood.

Beere, C. A. (1990b). *Sex and gender issues: A handbook of tests and measures.* Westport, CT: Greenwood.

Begg, C. B. (1994). Publication bias. In H. Cooper & L. V. Hedges (Eds.), *The handbook of research synthesis* (pp. 399-410). New York: Russell Sage.

Beins, B. (1993, Fall). Examples of spuriousness. *Teaching Methods, 2,* 3.

Belgrave, F. Z., Cherry, V. R., Cunningham, D., Walwyn, S., Letlaka-Rennert, K., & Phillips, F. (1994). The influence of Africentric values, self-esteem, and black identity on drug attitudes among African American fifth graders: A preliminary study. *Journal of Black Psychology, 20*(2), 128-142.

Benhabib, S. (1995). *Feminist contentions: A philosophical exchange.* New York: Routledge.

Bennett, R. E., & Ragosta, M. (1988). Handicapped people. In W. W. Willingham, M. Ragosta, R. W. Bennett, H. Braun, D. A. Rock, & D. A. Powers (Eds.), *Testing handicapped people.* Boston, MA: Allyn & Bacon.

Berdie, D. R. (1990, April). *High interview response rates: Much ado about nothing?* Paper presented at the annual meeting of the American Educational Research Association, Boston.

Bibliographic Index. *A cumulative bibliography of bibliographies.* (1938-1994). New York: H. W. Wilson.

Biklen, D., Ferguson, D. L., & Ford, A. (Eds.). (1989). *Schooling and disabilities: Vol. 88. Yearbook of National Society for the Study of Education.* Chicago: University of Chicago Press.

Biklen, S. K., & Pollard, D. (Eds.). (1993). *Gender and education: Vol. 92. Yearbook of National Society for the Study of Education.* Chicago: University of Chicago Press.

Bloch, M. (1963). *The historian's craft.* New York: Knopf.

Bogdan, R. C., & Biklen, S. K. (1992). *Qualitative research for education.* Boston, MA: Allyn & Bacon.

Borg, W. R., & Gall, M. D. (1989). *Educational research.* White Plains, NY: Longman.

Born, T. (1993). Shared leadership: A study of change at middle college high school. In F. Pignatelli & S. W. Pflaum (Eds.), *Celebrating diverse voices* (pp. 64-86). Thousand Oaks, CA: Corwin.

Bowe, F. G. (1991). Access to tele-communications: The views of blind and visually impaired adults. *Journal of Visual Impairment and Blindness, 85*(8), 328-331.

Bowker, A. (1993). *Sisters in the blood.* Newton, MA: WEEA.

Bracht, H. G., & Glass, V. G. (1968). The external validity of experiments. *Journal of the American Educational Research Association, 5*(4), 437-474.

Braverman, M. T. (1996). Sources of survey error: Implications for evaluation studies. In M. T. Braverman & J. K. Slater (Eds.), *Advances in survey research* (New Directions for Program Evaluation, Vol. 70, pp. 17-27). San Francisco: Jossey-Bass.

Breisach, E. (1994). *Historiography: Ancient, medieval, and modern.* Chicago: University of Chicago Press.

Brinkerhoff, R. O., Brethower, D. M., Hluchyji, T., & Nowakowski, J. R. (1983). *Program evaluation.* Hingham, MA: Kluwer Boston.

Brunner, I., & Guzman, A. (1989). Participatory evaluation: A tool to assess projects and empower people. In R. F. Conner & M. Hendricks (Eds.), *International innovations in evaluation methodology* (New Directions for Program Evaluation, Vol. 42, pp. 9-17). San Francisco: Jossey-Bass.

Buhrke, R. A., & Jorge, M. (1992). A Spanish version of the Expectations About Counseling Questionnaire: Translation and validation. *Hispanic Journal of Behavioral Science, 14*(3), 363-372.

Bullis, M., & Anderson, G. (1986). Single subject research methodology: An underutilized tool in the field of deafness. *America Annals of the Deaf, 132(5),* 344-348.

Burd, S. (1995, March 31). Two courts put limits on research involving the mentally ill. *Chronicle of Higher Education,* p. A27.

Burke, P. (1992). *New perspectives on historical writing.* University Park: Pennsylvania State University Press.

Burns, G. (1984). *Dr. Burns' prescription for happiness.* New York: G. P. Putnam.

Busk, P. L., & Marscuilo, L. A. (1992). Statistical analysis in single-case research: Issues, procedures, and recommendations, with applications to multiple behaviors. In T. R. Kratochill & J. R. Levin (Eds.), *Single-case research design and analysis* (pp. 159-182). Hillsdale, NJ: Lawrence Erlbaum.

Buss, F. (1985). *Dignity: Lower income women tell of their lives and struggles.* Ann Arbor: University of Michigan Press.

Campbell, D. T., & Stanley, J. C. (1963). Experimental and quasi-experimental designs for research on teaching. In N. L. Gage (Ed.), *Handbook of research on teaching* (pp. 171-246). Chicago: Rand McNally.

Campbell, D. T., & Stanley, J. C. (1966). *Experimental and quasi-experimental designs for research.* Skokie, IL: Rand McNally.

Campbell, D. T. (1960). Recommendations for the APA test standards regarding construct, trait, and discriminant validity. *American Psychologist, 15,* 546-553.

Campbell, P. B. (1988). *Rethinking research: Challenges for new and not so new researchers.* Groton, CT: P. Campbell.

Campbell, P. B. (1989). *The hidden discriminator: Sex and race bias in educational research.* Newton, MA: WEEA Publishing Center.

Canning, K. (1994, Winter). Feminist history after the linguistic turn: Historicizing discourse and experience. *Signs: Journal of Women in Culture and Society,* pp. 368-404.

Carlson, R. (1972). Understanding women: Implications for personality theory and research. *Journal of Social Issues, 28*(2), 112.

Carr, E. H. (1986). *What is history?* (2nd ed.). London: Macmillan.

Carver, R. P. (1992, April). *The case against statistical significance testing, revisited.* Paper presented at the annual meeting of the American Educational Research Association, San Francisco.

Chartier, R. (1988). *Cultural history.* Ithaca, NY: Cornell University Press.

Chavers, D., & Locke, P. (1989). *The effects of testing on Native Americans.* Albuquerque, NM: Native American Scholarship Fund.

Chen, H. T. (1990a). Issues in constructing program theory. In L. Bickman (Ed.), *Advances in program theory* (New Directions in Program Evaluation, Vol. 47, pp. 7-18). San Francisco: Jossey-Bass.

Chen, H. T. (1990b). *Theory-driven evaluations.* Newbury Park, CA: Sage.

Chen, H. T. (1994). Current trends and future directions in program evaluation. *Evaluation Practice, 15*(3), 229-238.

Chen, H. T., & Rossi, P. H. (1992). *Using theory to improve program and policy evaluation.* Westport, CT: Greenwood.

Clewell, A., Brown, J., Mounty, J., & Villegas, A. M. (1993, April). *Research of the special populations group.* Paper presented at the annual meeting of the American Educational Research Association, Atlanta, GA.

Cohen, J. (1988). *Statistical power analysis for the behavioral sciences.* Hillsdale, NJ: Lawrence Erlbaum.

Cohen, J. (1992). A power primer. *Psychological Bulletin, 112*(1), 155-159.

Collins, P. H. (1990). *Black feminist thought*. New York: Routledge.

Cone, J. D., & Foster, S. L. (1993). *Dissertations and theses from start to finish*. Washington, DC: American Psychological Association.

Conference of Executives of American Schools for the Deaf. (1979). Suggested guidelines for research in educational programs. *American Annals of the Deaf, 124*, 770-784.

Conley, H., & Fink, L. (1992). *Using statistical sampling*. Washington, DC: U.S. General Accounting Office.

Cook, T. D., & Campbell, D. T. (1979). *Quasi-experimentation: Design and analysis issues for field settings*. Chicago: Rand McNally.

Cooper, H., & Hedges, L. V. (1994a). Potentials and limitations of research synthesis. In H. Cooper & L. V. Hedges (Eds.), *The handbook of research synthesis* (pp. 521-530). New York: Russell Sage.

Cooper, H., & Hedges, L. V. (Eds.). (1994b). *The handbook of research synthesis*. New York: Russell Sage.

Cooper, H. M. (1989). *Integrating research*. Newbury Park: Sage.

Cotterill, P. (1992). Interviewing women-issues of friendship, vulnerability, and power. *Women's Studies International Forum, 15*(5/6), 593-606.

Coughlin, E. K. (1994, September 21). Mean streets are a scholar's lab. *Chronicle of Higher Education*, pp. 8, 9, 14.

Council for Exceptional Children. (1983). Code of ethics and standards for professional practice. *Exceptional Children, 50*, 205-209.

Cousins, J. B., & Earl, L. (Eds.). (1995). *Participatory evaluation in education*. London: Falmer.

Covert, R. W. (1977). *Guidelines and criteria for constructing questionnaires*. Unpublished manuscript, University of Virginia, Charlottesville.

Covert, W. (1995, November). *Designing questionnaires*. Paper presented at the International Conference on Evaluation, Vancouver, B.C.

Crabtree, C., & Nash, G. B. (1994). *National standards for history for grades K-4: Expanding children's world in time and space*. Los Angeles: University of California at Los Angeles, National Center for History. (ERIC Document Reproduction Service No. ED 375 075)

Cronbach, L. J., & Associates. (1980). *Toward reform of program evaluation*. San Francisco: Jossey-Bass.

Davis, C., & Ferguson, D. L. (1992). Trying something completely different: Report of a collaborative research venture. In P. M. Ferguson, D. L. Ferguson, & S. J. Taylor (Eds.), *Interpreting disability: A qualitative reader*. New York: Teachers College Press.

Davis, J. E. (1992). Reconsidering the use of race as an explanatory variable in program evaluation. In A. Madison (Ed.), *Minority issues in program evaluation* (New Directions for Program Evaluation, Vol. 53, pp. 55-68). San Francisco: Jossey-Bass.

DeKoning, K., & Martin, M. (Eds.). (1996). *Participatory research in health*. London: Zed Books.

Denzin, N. K. (1994). The art and politics of interpretation. In N. K. Denzin & Y. S. Lincoln (Eds.), *Handbook of qualitative research* (pp. 500-515). Thousand Oaks, CA: Sage.

Denzin, N. K., & Lincoln, Y. S. (1994). Strategies of inquiry. In N. K. Denzin & Y. S. Lincoln (Eds.), *Handbook of qualitative research* (pp. 199-208). Thousand Oaks, CA: Sage.

DeStefano, L., & Wagner, M. (1991). *Outcome assessment in special education: Lessons learned*. Menlo Park, CA: SRI International.

DeVellis, R. F. (1991). *Scale development: Theory and applications*. Newbury Park, CA: Sage.

Dewey, J., Cashin, J., Stockdale, M., & Shearer, V. (1994, November). *Women in the university: Assessing the chilly campus climate.* Paper presented at the annual meeting of the American Evaluation Association, Boston, MA.

Dietel, R. (1993, Spring). What works in performance assessment? *Evaluation Comment,* pp. 1-15. (Newsletter published by CRESST at UCLA)

Doe, T. (1996, June). *Doing participatory action research.* Paper presented at the annual meeting of the Society for Disability Studies, Washington, DC.

Doren, B., Bullis, M., & Benz, M. R. (1996). Predictors of victimization experiences of adolescents with disabilities in transition. *Exceptional Children, 63*(1), 7-18.

Dumas, J. E., Wolf, L. C., Fisman, S. N., & Culligan, A. (1991). Parenting stress, child behavior problems, and dysphoria in parents of children with autism, Down syndrome, behavior disorders, and normal development. *Exceptionality: A Research Journal, 2*(2), 97-110.

Eagly, A. H., & Carli, L. L. (1981). Sex of researchers and sex-typed communications as determinants of sex differences in influenceability: A meta-analysis of social influence studies. *Psychological Bulletin, 90,* 1-20.

Eagly, A. H., & Wood, W. (1994). Using research synthesis to plan future research. In H. Cooper & L. V. Hedges (Eds.), *The handbook of research synthesis* (pp. 485-500). New York: Russell Sage.

Echevarria, J. (1995). Interactive reading instruction: A comparison of provincial and distal effects of instructional conversations. *Exceptional Children, 61*(6), 535-552.

Edgington, E. S. (1992). Nonparametric tests for single-case experiments. In T. R. Kratochwill & J. R. Levin (Eds.), *Single-case research design and analysis* (pp. 133-157). Hillsdale, NJ: Lawrence Erlbaum.

Educational Testing Service. (1992). *ETS conference examines the technology of computer-based testing for people with disabilities.* Princeton, NJ: Author.

Educational Testing Service. (1995). *Performance assessment: Different needs difficult answers* [Brochure]. Princeton, NJ: ETS Trustees' Colloquy.

Eichelberger, R. T. (1989). *Disciplined inquiry: Understanding and doing educational research.* New York: Longman.

Eichler, M. (1991). *Nonsexist research methods.* New York: Routledge.

Ellis, D., Reid, G., & Barnsley, J. (1990). *Keeping on track: An evaluation guide for community groups.* Vancouver, BC: Women's Research Centre.

Fabre, G., & O'Meally, R. G. (1994). *History and memory in African American culture.* New York: Oxford University Press.

FairTest. (1993). *Computerized testing: More questions than answers.* Cambridge, MA: National Center for Fair and Open Testing.

Fals-Borda, O., & Ralman, M. A. (Eds.). (1991). *Action and knowledge: Breaking the monopoly with participatory action research.* New York: Intermediate Technology/Apex.

Feldman, M. S. (1995). *Strategies for interpreting qualitative data.* Thousand Oaks, CA: Sage.

Fendrich, M., & Vaughn, C. M. (1994). Diminished lifetime substance use over time: An inquiry into differential reporting. *Public Opinion Quarterly, 58,* 96-123.

Ferguson, M. (1993). *The history of Mary Prince: A West Indian slave, related by herself.* Ann Arbor: University of Michigan Press.

Ferguson, P. M. (1992). The puzzle of inclusion: A case study of autistic students in the life of one high school. In P. M. Ferguson, D. L. Ferguson, & S. J. Taylor (Eds.), *Interpreting disability: A qualitative reader.* New York: Teachers College Press.

Fetterman, D. M. (1989). *Ethnography: Step by step.* Newbury Park, CA: Sage.

Fetterman, D. M. (1994). Empowerment evaluation. *Evaluation Practice, 15*(1), 1-15.

Fetterman, D. M. (1995). In response to Dr. Daniel Stufflebeam's empowerment evaluation, objectivist evaluation, and evaluation standards: Where the future of evaluation should not go and where it needs to go. *Evaluation Practice, 16*(2), 179-199.

Fidell, L. S. (1970). Empirical verification of sex discrimination in hiring practices in psychology. *American Psychologist, 25*(12), 1094-1097.

Fine, G., & Sandstrom, K. L. (1988). *Knowing children: Participant observation with minors.* Newbury Park, CA: Sage.

Fine, M. (1992). Passions, politics, and power: Feminist research possibilities. In M. Fine (Ed.), *Disruptive voices* (pp. 205-232). Ann Arbor: University of Michigan Press.

Fine, M. (1994a). Dis-stance and other stances: Negotiations of power inside feminist research. In A. Gitlin (Ed.), *Power and method* (pp. 13-35). New York: Routledge.

Fine, M. (1994b). Working the hyphens: Reinventing self and other in qualitative research. In N. K. Denzin & Y. S. Lincoln (Eds.), *Handbook of qualitative research* (pp. 70-82). Thousand Oaks, CA: Sage.

Fine, M., & Gordon, S. M. (1992). Feminist transformation of/despite psychology. In M. Fine (Ed.), *Disruptive voices* (pp. 1-25). Ann Arbor: University of Michigan Press.

Firestone, W. A. (1993). Alternative arguments for generalizing from data as applied to qualitative research. *Educational Researcher, 22*(4), 16-23.

Foster, S. (1993a, August). *Ethnographic interviews in disability studies: The case of research with people who are deaf.* Paper presented at the annual meeting of the American Sociological Association, Miami, FL.

Foster, S. (1993b, April). *Outsider in the deaf world: Reflections of an ethnographic researcher.* Paper presented at the annual meeting of the American Educational Research Association, Atlanta, GA.

Fowler, F. J., Jr. (1993). *Survey research methods* (2nd ed.). Newbury Park, CA: Sage.

Fox, L., & Westling, D. (1991). A preliminary evaluation of training parents to use facilitative strategies with their children with profound disabilities. *Journal of the Association for Persons With Severe Handicaps, 16*(3), 168-176.

Freeman, R. D., Goetz, E., Richards, D. P., & Groenveld, M. (1991). Defiers of negative prediction: A 14-year follow-up study of legally blind children. *Journal of Visual Impairment and Blindness, 85*(9), 365-370.

Freire, P. (1971). *Pedagogy of the oppressed.* New York: Hender & Hender.

Fuchs, D., & Fuchs, L. S. (1989). Effects of examiner familiarity on Black, Caucasian, and Hispanic children: A meta-analysis. *Exceptional Children, 55,* 303-308.

Fuchs, D., Fuchs, L. S., & Fernstrom, P. (1992, April). *A conservative approach to special education reform: Mainstreaming through transenvironmental programming and curriculum based measurement.* Paper presented at the annual meeting of the American Educational Research Association, San Francisco.

Fuchs, L. S., & Deno, S. L. (1991). Paradigmatic distinctions between instructionally relevant measurement models. *Exceptional Children, 57*(6), 488-500.

Furumoto, L. (1980). Mary Whiton Calkins (1863-1930). *Psychology of Women Quarterly, 5*(1), 55-68.

Gable, R. K. (1986). *Instrument development in the affective domain.* Boston: Kluwer-Nijhoff.

Gay, L. R. (1992). *Educational research* (4th ed.). New York: Merrill.

Gaylord-Ross, R. (Ed.). (1990). *Issues and research in special education* (Vol. 1). New York: Teachers College Press.

Geilheiser, L. M., & Meyers, J. (1992, April). *Pull-in and pull-out programs: A comparative case study.* Paper presented at the Annual Meeting of the American Educational Research Association, San Francisco, CA.

Gaylord-Ross, R. (Ed.). (1992). *Issues and research in special education* (Vol. 2). New York: Teachers College Press.

Gilligan, C. (1982). *In a different voice.* Cambridge, MA: Harvard University Press.

Gitlin, A. (Ed.). (1994). *Power and method.* New York: Routledge.

Goh, H-L., & Iwata, B. A. (1994). Behavioral persistence and variability during extinction of self-injury maintained by escape. *Journal of Applied Behavior Analysis, 27*(1), 173-174.

Goode, D. (1994). *A world without words.* Philadelphia: Temple University Press.

Gordon, B. M. (1995). Knowledge construction, competing critical theories, and education. In J. Banks & C. A. McGee-Banks (Eds.), *Handbook of research on multicultural education* (pp. 184-202). New York: Macmillan.

Grace, N. C., Sung, W. K., & Fisher, W. W. (1994). Balancing social acceptability with treatment effectiveness of an intrusive procedure: A case report. *Journal of Applied Behavior Analysis, 27*(1), 171-172.

Grant, G. (Ed.). (1991). *Review of research in education* (Vol. 17). Washington, DC: American Educational Research Association.

Grant, G. (Ed.). (1993a). *Review of research in education* (Vol. 18). Washington, DC: American Educational Research Association.

Grant, G. (Ed.). (1993b). *Review of research in education* (Vol. 19). Washington, DC: American Educational Research Association.

Greene, J. C. (1994). Qualitative program evaluation: Practice and promise. In N. K. Denzin & Y. S. Lincoln (Eds.), *The handbook of qualitative research* (pp. 530-544). Thousand Oaks, CA: Sage.

Gribbons, B. C., Tobey, P. E., & Michael, W. B. (1995). Internal-consistency reliability and construct and criterion-related validity of an academic self-concept scale. *Educational and Psychological Measurement, 55*(5), 858-867.

Guba, E. G., & Lincoln, Y. S. (1989). *Fourth generation evaluation.* Newbury Park, CA: Sage.

Guba, E. G., & Lincoln, Y. S. (1994). Competing paradigms in qualitative research. In N. K. Denzin & Y. S. Lincoln (Eds.), *The handbook of qualitative research* (pp. 105-117). Thousand Oaks, CA: Sage.

Haaken, J. (1988). Field dependence research: A historical analysis of a psychological construct. *Signs: Journal of Women in Culture and Society, 13*(2), 311-329.

Hadley, R. G., & Mitchell, L. K. (1995). *Counseling research and program evaluation.* Pacific Grove, CA: Brooks/Cole.

Haraway, D. (1988). Situated knowledge: The science question in feminism and the privilege of partial perspective. *Feminist Studies, 14*(3), 575-599.

Harding, S. (1993). Rethinking standpoint epistemology: What is "strong objectivity"? In L. Alcoff & E. Potter (Eds.), *Feminist epistemologies* (pp. 49-82). New York: Routledge.

Hartsock, N. (1983). The feminist standpoint: Developing the ground for specifically feminist historical materialism. In S. Harding & M. B. Hintikka (Eds.), *Discovering reality* (pp. 283-310). Amsterdam: D. Reidel.

Hartsock, N. (1985). *Money, sex and power: Towards a feminist historical materialism.* Boston, MA: Northeastern University Press.

Hays, W. L. (1988). *Statistics (for psychologists).* New York: Holt, Rinehart & Winston.

Hedges, L. H., & Becker, B. J. (1986). Statistical methods in the meta-analysis of research on gender differences. In J. S. Hyde & M. C. Linn (Eds.), *The psychology of gender: Advances through meta-analysis*. Baltimore, MD: Johns Hopkins University Press.

Hedrick, T. E., Bickman, L., & Rog, D. (1993). *Applied research design: A practical guide*. Newbury Park, CA: Sage.

Heiman, G. W. (1992). *Basic statistics for the behavioral sciences*. Boston, MA: Houghton Mifflin.

Henry, G. T. (1990). *Practical sampling*. Newbury Park, CA: Sage.

Henry, G. T. (1996). Does the public have a role in evaluation? In M. T. Braverman & J. K. Slater (Eds.), *Advances in survey research* (New Directions for Program Evaluation, Vol. 70, pp. 3-16). San Francisco: Jossey-Bass.

Herrnstein, J., & Murray, C. (1994). *The bell curve*. New York: Free Press.

Hess, I. (1985). *Sampling for social research surveys 1947-1980*. Ann Arbor: University of Michigan.

Hine, D. C. (Ed.). (1990). *Black women's history: Theory and practice* (Black women in United States history, Vols. 9-10). Brooklyn, NY: Carlson.

Hodder, I. (1994). The interpretation of documents and material culture. In N. K. Denzin & Y. S. Lincoln (Eds.), *The handbook of qualitative research* (pp. 393-402). Thousand Oaks, CA: Sage.

Holstein, J. A., & Gubrium, J. F. (1994). Phenomenology, ethnomethodology, and interpretive practice. In N. K. Denzin & Y. S. Lincoln (Eds.), *The handbook of qualitative research* (pp. 262-272). Thousand Oaks, CA: Sage.

hooks, b. (1990). *Yearning: Race, gender, and cultural politics*. Boston: South End.

House, E. (1993). *Professional evaluation: Social impact and political consequences*. Newbury Park, CA: Sage.

Howard, A. (Ed.). (1995). *The changing nature of work*. San Francisco: Jossey-Bass.

Howe, K. R., & Miramontes, O. B. (1991). A framework for ethical deliberation in special education. *Journal of Special Education, 25*(1), 7-25.

Hughes, C. A., & Shumaker, J. B. (1991). Test-taking strategy instruction for adolescents with learning disabilities. *Exceptionality: A Research Journal, 2*(4), 205-221.

Humphries, B., & Truman, C. (Eds.). (1994). *Re-thinking social research*. Aldershot, UK: Avebury.

Hyde, J. S. (1981). How large are cognitive gender differences? *American Psychologist, 36*(8), 892-901.

Hyde, J. S. (1990). Meta-analysis and the psychology of gender differences. *Signs: Journal of Women in Culture and Society, 16*(1), 55-73.

Hyde, J. S., & Linn, M. C. (1988). Gender differences in verbal ability: A meta-analysis. *Psychological Bulletin, 104*(1), 53-69.

Jackson, P. W., & Haroutunian-Gordon, S. (1989). *From Socrates to software: The teacher as text and the text as teacher: Vol. 88. Yearbook of National Society for the Study of Education*. Chicago: University of Chicago Press.

James, S., & Busia, A. (1993). *Theorizing black feminisms*. New York: Routledge.

Janney, R., Snell, M., Beers, M, & Raynes, M. (1995). Integrating students with moderate and severe disabilities into general education classes. *Exceptional Children, 61*(5), 425-438.

Jensen, A. (1969). How much can we boost IQ and achievement. *Harvard Educational Review, 39*, 1-39.

Joint Committee on Standards for Educational Evaluation. (1988). *The personnel evaluation standards*. Newbury Park, CA: Sage.

Joint Committee on Standards for Educational Evaluation. (1994). *The program evaluation standards: How to assess evaluations of educational programs*. Thousand Oaks, CA: Sage.

Jones, J. A. (1995, April). *An illustration of the danger of nonresponse for survey research.* Paper presented at the annual meeting of the American Educational Research Association, San Francisco.

Jones, J. H. (1992). *Bad blood: The Tuskegee syphilis experiment* (Rev. ed.). New York: Free Press.

Josselson, R. (1993). A narrative introduction. In R. Josselson & R. Lieblich (Eds.), *The narrative study of lives* (Vol. 1). Newbury Park, CA: Sage.

Judy, R. A. T. (1993). *(Dis)forming the American canon: African Arabic slave narratives and the vernacular.* Minneapolis: University of Minnesota Press.

Kaestle, C. F. (1993). The awful reputation of educational research. *Educational Researcher, 22*(1), 22-31.

Kagan, S. L. (1991). *The care and education of America's young children: Vol. 90. Yearbook of National Society for the Study of Education.* Chicago: University of Chicago Press.

Katz, E., Green, K. E., & Kluever, R. C. (1995, April). *First impressions: The cover letter.* Paper presented at the annual meeting of the American Educational Research Association, San Francisco.

Keller, C. (1993, April). *Paula: A girl with Down syndrome integrated in a sixth-grade classroom.* Paper presented at the annual meeting of the American Educational Research Association, Atlanta, GA.

Keller, C., Karp, J., & Carlson, H. L. (1993, April). *The community and school contexts for the integration of students with disabilities in general education.* Paper presented at the annual meeting of the American Educational Research Association, Atlanta, GA.

Kelly, L., Burton, S., & Regan, L. (1994). Researching women's lives or studying women's oppression? Reflections on what constitutes feminist research. In M. Maynard & J. Purvis (Eds.), *Researching women's lives from a feminist perspective* (pp. 27-48). Bristol, PA: Taylor & Francis.

Kerlinger, F. N. (1973). *Foundations of behavioral research.* New York: Holt, Rinehart & Winston.

Kirkhart, K. E. (1995). Seeking multicultural validity: A postcard from the road. *Evaluation Practice, 16*(1), 1-12.

Koppenhaver, D. A., & Yoder, D. A. (1992). Literacy issues in persons with impairments. In R. Gaylord-Ross (Ed.), *Issues and research in special education* (Vol. 2). New York: Teachers College Press.

Kozicki, H. (1993). *Developments in modern historiography.* New York: St. Martin's.

Kramer, J. J., & Conoley, J. C. (1992). *The eleventh mental measurement yearbook.* Lincoln: University of Nebraska Press.

Krathwohl, D. R. (1993). *Methods of educational and social science research.* White Plains, NY: Longman.

Kratochwill, T. R. (1992). Single-case research design and analysis: An overview. In T. R. Kratochwill & J. R. Levin (Eds.), *Single-case research design and analysis* (pp. 1-12). Hillsdale, NJ: Lawrence Erlbaum.

Kratochwill, T. R., & Levin, J. R. (Eds.). (1992). *Single-case research design and analysis.* Hillsdale, NJ: Lawrence Erlbaum.

Krosnick, J. A., Narayan, S., & Smith, W. R. (1996). Satisficing in surveys: Initial evidence. In M. T. Braverman & J. K. Slater (Eds.), *Advances in survey research* (New Directions for Program Evaluation, Vol. 70). San Francisco: Jossey-Bass.

Krueger, R. A. (1988). *Focus groups: A practical guide for applied research.* Newbury Park, CA: Sage.

Langenbach, M., Vaughn, C., & Aagaard, L. (1994). *An introduction to educational research.* Needham Heights, MA: Allyn & Bacon.

Lanham, B. A., & Mehaffy, G. L. (1988). *Oral history in the secondary school classroom.* Los Angeles: Oral History Association.

Lather, P. (1992). Critical frames in educational research: Feminist and post-structural perspectives. *Theory and Practice, 31*(2), 1-13.

Lather, P. (1995, April). *Troubling clarity: The politics of accessible language.* Paper presented at the annual meeting of the American Educational Research Association, San Francisco.

Levin, J. R. (1992). Single-case research design and analysis: Comments and concerns. In T. R. Kratochwill & J. R. Levin (Eds.), *Single-case research design and analysis* (pp. 213-222). Hillsdale, NJ: Lawrence Erlbaum.

Lewin, M., & Wild, C. L. (1991). The impact of the feminist critique on tests, assessment, and methodology. *Psychology of Women Quarterly, 15,* 581-596.

Lieberman, A. (Ed.). (1992). *The changing contexts of teaching: Vol. 92. Yearbook of National Society for the Study of Education.* Chicago: University of Chicago Press.

Lincoln, Y. S. (1995, April). *Standards for qualitative research.* Paper presented at the annual meeting of the American Educational Research Association, San Francisco.

Lincoln, Y. S., & Guba, E. G. (1985). *Naturalistic inquiry.* Newbury Park, CA: Sage.

Lincoln, Y. S., & Guba, E. G. (1994). R. S. V. P.: We are pleased to accept your invitation. *Evaluation Practice, 15*(2), 179-192.

Linn, R. L. (Ed.). (1989). *Educational measurement* (3rd ed.). New York: American Council on Education, Macmillan.

Lips, H. M. (1993). Bifurcation of a common path: Gender splitting on the road to engineering and physical science careers. *Initiatives, 55*(3), 13-22.

Lipsey, M. K. (1990). *Design sensitivity.* Newbury Park, CA: Sage.

Locke, L. F., Spirduso, W. W., & Silverman, S. J. (1993). *Proposals that work.* Newbury Park, CA: Sage.

Lopez, S., & Mertens, D. M. (1993, April). *Integrating the feminist perspective in educational research classes.* Paper presented at the annual meeting of the American Educational Research Association, Atlanta, GA.

Maag, J. W., Behrens, J. T., & DiGangi, S. A. (1992). Dysfunctional cognitions associated with adolescent depression: Findings across special populations. *Exceptionality: A Research Journal, 3*(1), 31-47.

Mac an Ghaill, M. (1993). Beyond the white norm: The use of qualitative methods in the study of black youths' schooling in England. In P. Woods & M. Hammersley (Eds.), *Gender and ethnicity in schools* (pp. 145-165). London: Routledge.

MacDonald, V. M. (1995, April). *Portraits in black and white: A micro and macro view of Southern teachers before and after the Civil War.* Paper presented at the annual meeting of the American Educational Research Association, San Francisco.

Macias, R. F. (1993). Language and ethnic classification of language minorities: Chicano and Latino students in the 1990's. *Hispanic Journal of Behavioral Sciences, 75*(2), 230-257.

MacLeod-Gallinger, J. (1992). The career status of deaf women: A comparative look. *American Annals of the Deaf, 137*(4), 315-325.

MacMillan, D. L., Widaman, K. F., Barlow, I. H., Hemsley, R. E., & Little, T. D. (1992). Difference in adolescent school attitudes as a function of academic level, ethnicity, and gender. *Learning Disabilities Quarterly, 15*(1), 39-50.

Madaus, G. F., Stufflebeam, D. L., & Scriven, M. S. (1983). Program evaluation: A historical overview. In G. F. Madaus, M. Scriven, & D. L. Stufflebeam (Eds.), *Evaluation models* (pp. 3-22). Boston: Kluwer-Nijhoff.

Madison, A. M. (Ed.). (1992). *Minority issues in program evaluation* (New Directions for Program Evaluation, Vol. 53). San Francisco, CA: Jossey-Bass.

Malone, W., & Mastropieri, M. A. (1992, December/January). Reading comprehension instruction: Summarization and self-monitoring training for students with learning disabilities. *Exceptional Children,* pp. 270-279.

Marcus, L. S. (1993). The here and now comes of age: Margaret Wise Brown, Lucy Sprague Mitchell, and the early days of writing for children at Bank Street. In F. Pignatelli & S. W. Pflaum (Eds.), *Celebrating diverse voices* (pp. 177-196). Thousand Oaks, CA: Corwin.

Marder, C., & Cox, R. (1990). More than a label: Characteristics of youth with disabilities. In M. Wagner, L. Newman, & D. L. Shaver (Eds.), *Young people with disabilities: How are they doing? A comprehensive report from wave 1 of the National Longitudinal Transition Study of Special Education.* Menlo Park, CA: SRI International.

Marín, G., & Marín, B. V. (1991). *Research with Hispanic populations.* Newbury Park, CA: Sage.

Marshall, C., & Rossman, G. B. (1989). *Designing qualitative research.* Newbury Park, CA: Sage.

Martusewicz, R. A., & Reynolds, W. M. (1994). Introduction: Turning the study of education inside/out. In R. A. Martusewicz & W. M. Reynolds (Eds.), *Inside out: Contemporary critical perspectives in education.* New York: St. Martin's.

Maruyama, G., & Deno, S. (1992). *Research in educational settings.* Newbury Park, CA: Sage.

Massey, D. S., Zambrana, R. E., & Bell, S. A. (1995). Contemporary issues in Latino families: Future directions for research, policy, and practice. In R. E. Zambrana (Ed.), *Understanding Latino families* (pp. 190-192). Thousand Oaks, CA: Sage.

Matt, G. E., & Cook, T. D. (1994). Threats to the validity of research synthesis. In H. Cooper & L. V. Hedges (Eds.), *The handbook of research synthesis* (pp. 503-520). New York: Russell Sage.

McCracken, G. (1988). *The long interview* (Qualitative research methods series, Vol. 13). Newbury Park, CA: Sage.

McCrank, L. J., et al. (1989). *Bibliographic services of the American Historical Association: Recently published articles and writings on American History.* Washington, DC: American Historical Association. (ERIC Document Reproduction Service No. ED 312 200)

McDowell, C. L. (1992). Standardized tests and program evaluation: Inappropriate measures in critical times. In A. Madison (Ed.), *Minority issues in program evaluation* (pp. 45-54). San Francisco: Jossey-Bass.

McGee-Brown, M. J. (1994, April). *Accuracy in data collection, representation, and presentation: Towards an ethics of educational research.* Paper presented at the annual meeting of the American Educational Research Association, New Orleans, LA.

McGrew, K. S., Thurlow, M. L., & Spiegel, A. N. (1993). An investigation of the exclusion of students with disabilities in national data collection programs. *Educational Evaluation and Policy Analysis, 15*(3), 339-352.

McKay, R. B., Breslow, M. J., Sangster, R. L., Gabbard, S. M., Reynolds, R. W., Nakamoto, J. M., & Tarnai, J. (1996). Translating survey questionnaires: Lessons learned. In M. T. Braverman & J. K. Slater (Eds.), *Advances in survey research* (New Directions for Program Evaluation, Vol. 70, pp. 93-104). San Francisco: Jossey-Bass.

McKee, N. (1992). Lexical and semantic pitfalls in the use of survey interviews: An example from the Texas-Mexico border. *Hispanic Journal of Behavioral Sciences, 14*(3), 353-362.

Mclaughlin, M. W., & Phillips, D. C. (1991). *Evaluation in education: At quarter century: Vol. 90. Yearbook of National Society for the Study of Education.* Chicago: University of Chicago Press.

McShane, D. (1988). Mental abilities testing research with American Indians: A reprise. *Canadian Journal of Native Education, 15*(3), 92-100.

McShane, D. (1989, April). *Testing American Natives and Alaskan Natives*. Paper presented at Native American Hearing of the National Commission on Testing and Public Policy, Albuquerque, NM.

Melosh, B. (1993). *Gender and American history since 1890*. London: Routledge.

Meloy, J. M. (1994). *Writing the qualitative dissertation*. Hillsdale, NJ: Lawrence Erlbaum.

Merten, D. E. (1996). Visibility and vulnerability: Responses to rejection by nonaggressive junior high school boys. *Journal of Early Adolescence, 16*(1), 5-26.

Mertens, D. M. (1989a). Developing focus group questions for needs assessment. In D. M. Mertens (Ed.), *Creative ideas for teaching evaluation* (pp. 213-219). Boston, MA: Kluwer Academic.

Mertens, D. M. (1989b). Social experiences of hearing-impaired high school youth. *American Annals of the Deaf, 134*(1), 15-19.

Mertens, D. M. (1990). Practical evidence of the feasibility of the utilization-focused approach to evaluation. *Studies in Educational Evaluation, 16*, 181-194.

Mertens, D. M. (1991a). Implications from the cognitive paradigm for teacher effectiveness research in deaf education. In D. S. Martin (Ed.), *Advances in cognition, education, and deafness* (pp. 342-347). Washington, DC: Gallaudet University Press.

Mertens, D. M. (1991b). Instructional factors related to hearing impaired adolescents' interest in science. *Science Education, 75*(4), 429-441.

Mertens, D. M. (1992, November). *Increasing utilization through a collaborative model of evaluation in an international setting: Holding hands across the culture gap*. Paper presented at the 1992 annual meeting of the American Evaluation Association, Seattle, WA.

Mertens, D. M. (1994). Training evaluators: Unique skills and knowledge. In J. Altschuld & M. Engle (Eds.), *The preparation of professional evaluators: Issues, perspectives, and current status* (pp. 17-28). San Francisco: Jossey-Bass.

Mertens, D. M. (1995). Identify and respect differences among participants in evaluation studies. In W. Shadish, D. Newman, M. A. Scheirer, & C. Wye (Eds.), *The American Evaluation Association's guiding principles* (pp. 91-98). San Francisco: Jossey-Bass.

Mertens, D. M. (1996). Breaking the silence about sexual abuse of deaf youth. *American Annals of the Deaf, 141*(5), 352-358.

Mertens, D. M., Berkeley, T. R., & Lopez, S. (1995). Using participatory evaluation in an international context. In J. B. Cousins & L. M. Earl (Eds.), *Participatory evaluation in education* (pp. 140-156). Washington, DC: Falmer.

Mertens, D. M., Farley, J., Madison, A., & Singleton, P. (1994). Diverse voices in evaluation practice: Feminists, minorities, and persons with disabilities. *Evaluation Practice, 15*(2), 123-129.

Mertens, D. M., & McLaughlin, J. (1995). *Research methods in special education*. Thousand Oaks, CA: Sage.

Messick, S. (1989). Meaning and values in test validation. *Education Researcher, 18*(2), 5-11.

Messick, S. (1995). Validity of psychological assessment. *American Psychologist, 50*(9), 741-749.

Miles, M. B., & Huberman, A. M. (1994). *Qualitative data analysis* (2nd ed.). Newbury Park, CA: Sage.

Millar, R., & Gallagher, M. (1996). The "Things I Worry About" Scale: Further developments in surveying the worries of postprimary school pupils. *Educational and Psychological Measurement, 56*(6), 972-994.

Miller, N., & Pollock, V. E. (1994). Meta-analytic synthesis for theory development. In H. Cooper & L. V. Hedges (Eds.), *The handbook of research synthesis* (pp. 457-484). New York: Russell Sage.

Miller, W. L., & Crabtree, B. F. (1994). Clinical research. In N. K. Denzin & Y. S. Lincoln (Eds.), *The handbook of qualitative research* (pp. 340-352). Thousand Oaks, CA: Sage.

Millman, J., & Darling-Hammond, L. (Eds.). (1990). *The new handbook of teacher evaluation.* Newbury Park, CA: Sage.

Mio, J. S., & Iwamasa, G. (1993). To do or not to do: That is the question for white cross-cultural researchers. *The Counseling Psychologist, 21*(2), 197-212.

Moore, D., & McCabe, D. (1993). *Introduction to the practice of statistics.* New York: Freeman.

Moore, K. A., Sugland, B. W., Blumenthal, C., Glei, D., & Snyder, N. (1995). *Adolescent pregnancy prevention programs: Intervention and evaluations.* Washington, DC: Child Trends.

Moore, M. A. (1991, April). *The place of significance testing in contemporary social sciences.* Paper presented at the annual meeting of the American Educational Research Association, Chicago. (ERIC Document Reproduction Service No. Ed 333 036)

Morgan, D. L. (1988). *Focus groups as qualitative research.* Newbury Park, CA: Sage.

Morra, L. G. (1994). *School-age children: Poverty and diversity challenge schools nationwide* (GAO/T-HEHS-94-125). Washington, DC: U.S. General Accounting Office.

Morris, L. L., Fitz-Gibbon, C. T., & Lindheim, E. (1987). *How to measure performance and use tests.* Newbury Park, CA: Sage.

Morse, J. M. (1994). Designing funded qualitative research. In N. K. Denzin & Y. S. Lincoln (Eds.), *The handbook of qualitative research* (pp. 220-235). Thousand Oaks, CA: Sage.

Moss, P. A. (1992). Shifting conceptions of validity in educational measurement: Implications for performance assessment. *Review of Educational Research, 62*(3), 229-258.

Moss, P. A. (1995). Can there be validity without reliability? *Educational Researcher, 23*(2), 5-12.

Moss, P. A. (1996). Enlarging the dialogue in educational measurement: Voices from interpretive research traditions. *Educational Researcher, 25*(1), 20-28.

Mounty, J. L., & Anderson, B. T. (1993, April). Assessment. In A. Clewell, J. Brown, J. Mounty, & A. M. Villegas (Eds.), *Research of the special population group* (pp. 28-37). Paper presented at the annual meeting of the American Educational Research Association, Atlanta, GA.

Murphy, L. L., Conoley, J. C., Close, J., & Impara, J. C. (1994). *Tests in print IV: An index to tests, test reviews, and the literature on specific tests.* Lincoln: University of Nebraska—Lincoln, Buros Institute of Mental Measurements.

Nash, G. B. (1995, April 21). The history children should study. *Chronicle of Higher Education,* p. A60.

National Association of State Directors of Special Education. (1988). *NAEP testing for state comparisons: Issues related to inclusion of handicapped students.* Washington, DC: Author.

National Commission for Protection of Human Subjects of Biomedical and Behavioral Research. (1978). *The Belmont Report: Ethical principles and guidelines for the protection of human subjects of research* (DHEW Publication No. OS 78-0012). Washington, DC: Government Printing Office.

National Commission on Testing and Public Policy. (1990). *From gatekeeper to gateway: Transforming testing in America.* Boston, MA: Author.

National Historical Publications and Records Commission. (1988). *Directory of archives and manuscript repositories in the United States.* Washington, DC: Author.

National inventory of documentary resources in the United States. (1988). Teaneck, NJ: Chadwyck-Healey.

Neuenschwander, J. A. (1993). *Oral history and the law* (Rev ed., Pamphlet series No. 1). Albuquerque, NM: Oral History Association.

Neustadt, R. E., & May, E. R. (1986). *Thinking in time: The uses of history for decision makers.* New York: Free Press.

Norton, M. B., & Gerardi, P. (Eds.). (1995). *The American Historical Association's guide to historical literature* (3rd ed.). New York: Oxford University Press.

Oakes, J., & Guiton, G. (1995). Matchmaking: The dynamics of high school tracking decisions. *American Educational Research Journal, 32*(1), 3-33.

Oakley, A. (1981). Interviewing women: A contradiction in terms. In H. Roberts (Ed.), *Doing feminist research* (pp. 30-61). London: Routledge.

Odom, S. (1988). Research in early childhood special education: Methodologies and paradigms. In S. L. Odom & M. B. Karnes (Eds.), *Early intervention for infants and children with handicaps* (pp. 1-22). Baltimore, MD: Paul H. Brookes.

Ogawa, R. T., & Malen, B. (1991). Towards rigor in reviews of multivocal literatures: Applying the exploratory case study method. *Review of Educational Research, 61*(3), 265-286.

Olesen, V. (1994). Feminisms and models of qualitative research. In N. K. Denzin & Y. S. Lincoln (Eds.), *The handbook of qualitative research* (pp. 158-174). Thousand Oaks, CA: Sage.

Oliver, M. (1992). Changing the social relations of research production? *Disability, Handicap, & Society, 7*(2), 101-114.

Oral History Association. (1992). *Oral history evaluation guidelines* (Pamphlet No. 3). Los Angeles, CA: Author.

Ottenbacher, K. J., & Cusick, A. (1991). An empirical investigation of interrater agreement for single-subject data using graphs with and without trend lines. *JASH, 16*(1), 48-55.

Owano, A., & Jones, C. (1995, March). *Participatory evaluation handbook: A resource for resident evaluators.* Paper presented at the Washington Evaluator's Conference, Washington, DC.

Oxford Dictionary of Quotations (3rd ed.). (1979). Oxford, UK: Oxford University Press.

Padilla, A. M., & Lindholm, K. S. (1995). Quantitative educational research with ethnic minorities. In J. A. Banks & C. A. McGee-Banks (Eds.), *Handbook of research on multicultural education* (pp. 97-113). New York: Macmillan.

Parsonson, B. S., & Baer, D. M. (1992). The visual analysis of data and current research into the stimuli controlling it. In T. R. Kratochwill & J. R. Levin (Eds.), *Single-case research design and analysis* (pp. 15-38). Hillsdale, NJ: Lawrence Erlbaum.

Parthasarathy, A., Sailor, P., & Worthen, B. (1995, April). *Effects of respondents' socioeconomic status and timing and amount of incentive payment on mailed questionnaire response rates.* Paper presented at the annual meeting of the American Educational Research Association, Atlanta, GA.

Patai, D. (1994). (Response) When method becomes power. In A. Gitlin (Ed.), *Power and method* (pp. 61-76). New York: Routledge.

Patton, J. M. (1993). Psychoeducational assessment of gifted and talented African Americans. In J. H. Stanfield, II & R. M. Dennis (Eds.), *Race and ethnicity in research methods* (pp. 198-216). Newbury Park, CA: Sage.

Patton, M. Q. (1986). *Utilization-focused evaluation* (2nd ed.). Beverly Hills, CA: Sage.

Patton, M. Q. (1987). Evaluation's political inherency: Practical implications for design and use. In D. J. Palumbo (Ed.), *The politics of program theory* (pp. 100-145). Newbury Park, CA: Sage.

Patton, M. Q. (1988). Paradigms and pragmatism. In D. M. Fetterman (Ed.), *Qualitative approaches to evaluation in education: The silent/scientific revolution* (pp. 116-137). New York: Praeger.

Patton, M. Q. (1990). *Qualitative evaluation and research methods.* Newbury Park, CA: Sage.

Patton, M. Q. (1991). Towards utility in reviews in multivocal literatures. *Review of Educational Research, 61*(3), 287-292.

Patton, M. Q. (1994). Developmental evaluation. *Evaluation Practice, 15*(3), 311-320.

Peck, C. A., & Furman, G. C. (1992). Qualitative research in special education: An evaluative review. In R. Gaylord-Ross (Ed.), *Issues and research in special education* (pp. 1-42). New York: Teachers College Press.

Perlmann, J., & Margo, R. (1989). Who were America's teachers? Toward a social history and a data archive. *Historical Methods, 22*(2), 68-73.

Phoenix, A. (1994). Practicing feminist research: The intersection of gender and race in the research process. In M. Maynard & J. Purvis (Eds.), *Researching women's lives from a feminist perspective* (pp. 49-71). Bristol, PA: Taylor & Francis.

Pok, A. (1992). *A selected bibliography of modern historiography.* New York: Greenwood.

Pollard, D. S. (1992, February). Toward a pluralistic perspective on equity. *Women's Education Equity Act Publishing Center Digest,* pp. 1-2, 7.

Ponterotto, J. G., & Casas, J. M. (1991). *Handbook of racial/ethnic minority counseling research.* Springfield, IL: Charles C Thomas.

Ponterotto, J. G., Casas, J. M., Suzuki, L. A., & Alexander, C. M. (Eds.). (1995). *Handbook of multicultural counseling.* Thousand Oaks, CA: Sage.

Popham, W. J. (1988). *Educational evaluation.* Englewood Cliffs, NJ: Prentice Hall.

Popham, W. J., & Sirotnik, K. A. (1992). *Understanding statistics in education.* Itasca, IL: F. E. Peacock.

Posavac, E. J., & Carey, R. G. (1992). *Program evaluation: Methods and case studies.* Englewood Cliffs, NJ: Prentice Hall.

Purvis, J. (1994). Doing feminist women's history: Researching the lives of women in the Suffragette Movement in Edwardian England. In M. Maynard & J. Purvis (Eds.), *Researching women's lives from a feminist perspective* (pp. 166-189). London: Taylor & Francis.

Ragin, C. C., & Hein, J. (1993). The comparative study of ethnicity: Methodological and conceptual issues. In J. H. Stanfield, II & R. M. Dennis (Eds.), *Race and ethnicity in research methods.* Newbury Park, CA: Sage.

Ragosta, M., & Wendler, C. (1992). *Eligibility issues and comparable time limits for disabled SAT examinees* (Research report No. 92-35). Princeton, NJ: Educational Testing Service.

RAND. (1992). *36-item health survey 1. 0.* Santa Monica, CA: Author.

Reason, P. (Ed.). (1994a). *Participation in human inquiry.* London: Sage.

Reason, P. (1994b). Three approaches to participative inquiry. In N. K. Denzin & Y. S. Lincoln (Eds.), *The handbook of qualitative research* (pp. 324-339). Thousand Oaks, CA: Sage.

Reichardt, C. S., & Rallis, S. F. (1994). Qualitative and quantitative inquiries are not incompatible: A call for a new partnership. In C. S. Reichardt & S. F. Rallis (Eds.), *The qualitative/quantitative debate* (New Directions for Program Evaluation, Vol. 61, pp. 85-91). San Francisco, CA: Jossey-Bass.

Reimer, B., & Smith, R. A. (Eds.). (1992). *The arts, education, and aesthetic knowing: Vol. 91. Yearbook of National Society for the Study of Education.* Chicago: University of Chicago Press.

Reinharz, S. (1992). *Feminist methods in social research.* New York: Oxford University Press.

Reinharz, S. (1994). Feminist biography: The pains, the joys, the dilemmas. In A. Lieblich & R. Josselson (Eds.), *Exploring identity and gender: Vol 2. The narrative study of lives* (pp. 37-82). Thousand Oaks, CA: Sage.

Richardson, L. (1994). Writing: A method of inquiry. In N. K. Denzin & Y. S. Lincoln (Eds.), *The handbook of qualitative research* (pp. 516-529). Thousand Oaks, CA: Sage.

Ritchie, D. A. (1995). *Doing oral history.* New York: Twayne.

Roethlisberger, F. J., & Dickson, W. J. (1939). *Management and the worker.* Cambridge, MA: Harvard University Press.

Rogers, A. G., Brown, L. M., & Tappan, M. B. (1994). Interpreting loss in ego development in girls: Regression or resistance? In A. Lieblich & R. Josselson (Eds.), *Exploring identity and gender: Vol. 2. The narrative study of lives* (pp. 1-36). Thousand Oaks, CA: Sage.

Rortverdt, A. K., & Miltenberger, R. G. (1994). Analysis of a high probability instructional sequence and timeout in the treatment of child noncompliance. *Journal of Applied Behavior Analysis, 27*(2), 327-330.

Ross, L. (1992). *Mothers behind bars: A comparative study of the experiences of imprisoned American Indian and white women.* Unpublished doctoral dissertation, University of Oregon.

Ross, L. (1995, June). *Imprisoned Native American women and denial of culture.* Paper presented at the annual meeting of the Sociologists for Women in Society, Washington, DC.

Rossi, P. H., & Freeman, H. E. (1993). *Evaluation: A systematic approach.* Newbury Park, CA: Sage.

Sadker, M., & Sadker, D. (1991). Sexism in the classroom: From grade school to graduate school. In M. H. Dembo (Ed.), *Applying educational psychology* (pp. 450-452). Los Angeles: Longman.

Sanders, J. R. (1994, November). *What the program evaluation standards say about social justice.* Paper presented at the annual meeting of the American Evaluation Association, Boston.

Sands, R. G., & Nuccio, K. (1992). Postmodern feminist theory and social work. *Social Work, 37*(6), 489-494.

Scarr, S., & Eisenberg, M. (1993). Child care research: Issues, perspectives, and results. *Annual Review of Psychology, 44,* 613-644.

Schneider, B., & Daniels, T. (1992). Peer acceptance and social play of gifted kindergarten children. *Exceptionality: A Research Journal, 3*(1), 17-29.

Schofield, J. W. (1991). School desegregation and intergroup relations: A review of literature. In G. Grant (Ed.), *Review of research in education* (Vol. 17). Washington, DC: American Educational Research Association.

Schunk, D. H., & Rice, J. M. (1992). Influence of reading-comprehension strategy information on children's achievement outcomes. *Learning Disability Quarterly, 15*(1), 51-64.

Schwandt, T. A. (1994). Constructivist, interpretivist approaches to human inquiry. In N. K. Denzin & Y. S. Lincoln (Eds.), *Handbook of qualitative research* (pp. 118-137). Thousand Oaks, CA: Sage.

Scott, J. W. (1986). Gender: A useful category of historical analysis. *American Historical Review, 91*(5), 1053-1075.

Scott-Jones, D. (1993, April). *Ethical issues in reporting and referring in research with minority and low-income populations.* Paper presented at the biennial meeting of the Society for Research in Child Development, New Orleans, LA.

Scriven, M. (1967). The methodology of evaluation. *AERA Monograph Series in Curriculum Evaluation, 1,* 39-83.

Scriven, M. (1991). *Evaluation thesaurus* (4th ed.). Newbury Park, CA: Sage.

Sessions, J. T., & Yanos, J. H. (1987, November). *Desirable characteristics of a counseling agency.* Paper presented at the 1987 annual meeting of the American Evaluation Association, Boston.

Shadish, W. R. (1994). Need-based evaluation: Good evaluation and what you need to know about it. *Evaluation Practice, 15*(3), 347-358.

Shadish, W. R., Jr., Cook, T. D., & Leviton, L. C. (1991). *Foundations of program evaluation.* Newbury Park, CA: Sage.

Shadish, W. R., Newman, D., Scheirer, M. A., & Wye, C. (Eds.). (1995). *The American Evaluation Association's guiding principles.* San Francisco: Jossey-Bass.

Shakeshaft, C., Campbell, P., & Karp, K. (1992). Sexism and racism in educational research. In M. C. Alkin (Ed.), *Encyclopedia of educational research* (6th ed., Vol. 4, pp. 1210-1216). New York: Macmillan.

Shapiro, A. L. (1994). *Feminist revision history.* New Brunswick, NJ: Rutgers University Press.

Shapiro, E., & Lentz, F. E. (1991). Vocational-technical programs: Follow-up of students with learning disabilities. *Exceptional Children, 58*(1), 47-59.

Shaver, J. P. (1992, April). *What statistical significance testing is, and what it is not.* Paper presented at the annual meeting of the American Educational Research Association, San Francisco.

Sheehy, E. P. (1986). *Guide to reference books* (10th ed.). Chicago: American Library Association.

Sherman, P. R. (1993). What do you want to be when you grow up? The ideology of vocational choice. In F. Pignatelli & S. W. Pflaum (Eds.), *Celebrating diverse voices* (pp. 197-220). Newbury Park, CA: Corwin.

Shipman, S., MacColl, G. S., Vaurio, E., & Chennareddy, V. (1995). *Program evaluation: Improving the flow of information to the Congress* (Report to the ranking minority members, Committee on Labor and Human Resources, U. S. Senate). Washington, DC: U.S. General Accounting Office.

Sicherman, B., & Green, C. H. (1980). *Notable American women: The modern period.* Cambridge, MA: Harvard University Press.

Sieber, J. (1992). *Planning ethically responsible research.* Newbury Park, CA: Sage.

Silverman, D. (1993). *Interpreting qualitative data analysis.* Newbury Park, CA: Sage.

Singh, A., & Lidsky, D. (1996, December 3). All-out search. *PC Magazine,* pp. 213-249.

Sirotnik, K. A. (Ed.). (1990). *Evaluation and social justice: Issues in public education* (New Directions for Program Evaluation, Vol. 45). San Francisco: Jossey-Bass.

Sirotnik, K. A., & Oakes, J. (1990). Evaluation as critical inquiry: School improvement as a case in point. In K. A. Sirotnik (Ed.), *Evaluation and social justice* (New Directions in Program Evaluation, Vol. 45, pp. 37-60). San Francisco: Jossey-Bass.

Skrtic, T. M. (1991). *Behind special education.* Denver, CO: Love Publishing.

Sleeter, C. (1994). Resisting racial awareness. In R. A. Martusewicz & W. R. Reynolds (Eds.), *Inside out: Contemporary critical perspectives in education* (pp. 237-263). New York: St. Martin's.

Smith, D. E. (1987). *The everyday world as problematic.* Boston, MA: Northeastern University Press.

Smith, M. (1994). Enhancing the quality of survey data on violence against women: A feminist approach. *Gender & Society, 8*(1), 109-127.

Smith, M. F. (1994). Evaluation: Review of the past, preview of the future. *Evaluation Practice, 15*(3), 215-227.

Smith, W. (1993). Survey research on African Americans. In J. Stanfield & R. Dennis (Eds.), *Race and ethnicity in research methods* (pp. 217-229). Newbury Park, CA: Sage.

Snyder, P., & Lawson, S. (1992, April). *Evaluating statistical significance using corrected and uncorrected magnitude of effect size estimates.* Paper presented at the annual meeting of the American Educational Research Association, San Francisco.

Solberg, V. S., Valdez, J., & Villarreal, P. (1994). Social support, stress, and Hispanic college adjustment: Test of a diathesis-stress model. *Hispanic Journal of Behavioral Sciences, 16*(3), 230-239.

Spalter-Roth, R., & Hartmann, H. (1989). *Unnecessary losses: Costs to America of the lack of family and medical leave.* Washington, DC: Institute for Women's Policy Research.

Spradley, J. P. (1980). *Participant observation.* New York: Holt, Rinehart & Winston.

Stainback, S., & Stainback, W. (1988). *Understanding and conducting qualitative research.* Dubuque, IA: Kendall/Hunt.

Stake, R. E. (1983). The case study method in social inquiry. In G. F. Madaus, M. Scriven, & D. L. Stufflebeam (Eds.), *Evaluation models* (pp. 279-286). Boston: Kluwer-Nijhoff.

Stake, R. E. (1994). Case studies. In N. K. Denzin & Y. S. Lincoln (Eds.), *Handbook of qualitative research* (pp. 236-247). Thousand Oaks, CA: Sage.

Stake, R. E. (1995). *The art of case study research.* Thousand Oaks, CA: Sage.

Stanfield, J. H., II. (1993a). Epistomological considerations. In J. H. Stanfield & R. M. Dennis (Eds.), *Race and ethnicity in research methods* (pp. 16-36). Newbury Park, CA: Sage.

Stanfield, J. H., II. (1993b). In the archives. In J. H. Stanfield & R. M. Dennis (Eds.), *Race and ethnicity in research methods* (pp. 273-283). Newbury Park, CA: Sage.

Stanfield, J. H., II. (1993c). Methodological reflections: An introduction. In J. H. Stanfield & R. M. Dennis (Eds.), *Race and ethnicity in research methods* (pp. 3-15). Newbury Park, CA: Sage.

Stanfield, J. H., II. (1994). Ethnic modeling in qualitative research. In N. K. Denzin & Y. S. Lincoln (Eds.), *Handbook of qualitative research* (pp. 175-188). Thousand Oaks, CA: Sage.

Stanfield, J. H., II, & Dennis, R. M. (Eds.). (1993). *Race and ethnicity in research methods.* Newbury Park, CA: Sage.

Steady, F. C. (1993). Women and collective action. In S. M. James & A. P. A. Busia (Eds.), *Theorizing black feminisms* (pp. 90-101). London: Routledge.

Stevens, R. J., & Slavin, R. E. (1995). The cooperative elementary school: Effects on students' achievement, attitudes, and social relations. *American Educational Research Journal, 32*(2), 321-351.

Stinson, D. M., Gast, D. L., Wolery, M., & Collins, B. C. (1991). Acquisition of nontargeted information during small group instruction. *Exceptionality, 2*(2), 65-80.

Stock, W. A. (1994). Systematic coding for research synthesis. In H. Cooper & L. V. Hedges (Eds.), *The handbook of research synthesis* (pp. 125-138). New York: Russell Sage.

Stockdill, S. H., Duhon-Sells, R. M., Olsen, R. A., & Patton, M. Q. (1992). Voices in the design and evaluation of a multicultural education program: A developmental approach. In A. M. Madison (Ed.), *Minority issues in program evaluation* (New Directions for Program Evaluation, Vol. 53, pp. 17-34). San Francisco: Jossey-Bass.

Stone, G. (Ed.). (1993). White American researchers and multicultural counseling [Special edition]. *The Counseling Psychologist, 21*(2).

Storey, K., & Horner, R. H. (1991). An evaluative review of social validation research involving persons with handicaps. *Journal of Special Education, 25*(3), 352-401.

Strauss, A., & Corbin, J. (1990). *Basics of qualitative research.* Newbury Park, CA: Sage.

Strauss, A., & Corbin, J. (1994). Grounded theory methodology: An overview. In N. K. Denzin & Y. S. Lincoln (Eds.), *Handbook of qualitative research* (pp. 273-285). Thousand Oaks, CA: Sage.

Stufflebeam, D. L. (1983). The CIPP model for program evaluation. In G. F. Madaus, M. Scriven, & D. L. Stufflebeam (Eds.), *Evaluation models* (pp. 117-142). Boston: Kluwer-Nijhoff.

Stufflebeam, D. L. (1994). Empowerment evaluation, objectivist evaluation, and evaluation standards: Where the future of evaluation should not go and where it needs to go. *Evaluation Practice, 15*(3), 321-338.

Sudman, S., & Bradburn, N. M. (1982). *Asking questions.* San Francisco: Jossey-Bass.

Sullivan, P. M. (1992). The effects of psychotherapy on behavior problems of sexually abused deaf children. *Child Abuse and Neglect: The International Journal, 16*(2), 297-307.

Sullivan, P. M., Vernon, M., & Scanlan, J. M. (1987). Sexual abuse of deaf youth. *American Annals of the Deaf, 132*(4), 256-262.

Sun, A. (1995). Development and factor analysis of the student resistance to schooling inventory. *Educational and Psychological Measurement, 55*(5), 841-849.

Suzuki, L. A., & Kugler, J. F. (1995). Intelligence and personality assessment: Multicultural perspectives. In J. G. Ponterotto, J. M. Casas, L. A. Suzuki, & C. M. Alexander (Eds.), *Handbook of multicultural counseling* (pp. 493-515). Thousand Oaks, CA: Sage.

Tapp, J. J., Kelman, H., Triandia, H., Wrightsman, L., & Coelho, G. (1973). Advisory principles for ethical considerations in the conduct of cross-cultural research: Fall 1973 revision. *International Journal of Psychology, 9*(3), 240-249.

Tawney, J. W., & Gast, D. (1984). *Single subject research in special education.* Columbus, OH: Merrill.

Tesch, R. (1990). *Qualitative research analysis types and software tools.* New York: Falmer.

Thompson, B. (1988, January). *Common methodology mistakes in dissertations: Improving dissertation quality.* Paper presented at the annual meeting of the Mid-South Education Research Association, Louisville, KY.

Thompson, B. (1992, April). *The use of statistical significance tests in research: Some criticisms and alternatives.* Paper presented at the annual meeting of the American Educational Research Association, San Francisco.

Thompson, B., & Daniel, L. G. (1996a). Factor analytic evidence for the construct validity of scores: A historical overview and some guidelines. *Educational and Psychological Measurement, 56*(2), 197-208.

Thompson, B., & Daniel, L. G. (1996b). Seminal readings on reliability and validity: A "hit parade" bibliography. *Educational and Psychological Measurement, 56*(2), 741-745.

Thompson, B., Wasserman, J. D., & Matula, K. (1996). The factor structure of the Behavior Rating Scale of the Bayley Scales of Infant Development-II. *Educational and Psychological Measurement, 56*(3), 460-474.

Thurlow, M. L., Ysseldyke, J. E., & Silverstein, B. (1993). *Testing accommodations for students with disabilities.* Minneapolis: University of Minnesota, National Center on Educational Outcomes.

Tirapella, L., & Cipani, E. (1992). Developing functional requesting: Acquisition, durability, and generalization of effects. *Exceptional Children, 58,* 260-269.

Tong, R. (1989). *Feminist thought: A comprehensive introduction.* San Francisco: Westview.

Tosh, J. (1991). *The pursuit of history* (2nd ed.). New York: Longman.

Truman, C. (1995, November). *Feminist perspectives in research and evaluation: The challenge of "difference."* Paper presented at the International Evaluation Conference, Vancouver, Canada.

Tuchman, B. W. (1978). *A distant mirror: The calamitous 14th century.* New York: Knopf.

Tuchman, G. (1994). Historical social science: Methodologies, methods, and meanings. In N. K. Denzin & Y. S. Lincoln (Eds.), *Handbook of qualitative research* (pp. 306-323). Thousand Oaks, CA: Sage.

Turabian, K. L. (1987). *A manual for writers of term papers, theses and dissertations* (5th ed.). Chicago: University of Chicago Press.

U.S. Department of Education. (1989). *"To assume the fair appropriate public education of all handicapped children": Eleventh annual report to Congress on the implementation of the Education of the Handicapped Act.* Washington, DC: Author.

U.S. Department of Education. (1993). *OSEP data dictionary.* Washington, DC: U.S. Department of Education, Office of Special Education Programs.

U.S. Department of Health, Education, and Welfare. (1977). Nondiscrimination on the basis of handicap. *Federal Register, 42,* 22676-22702.

U.S. General Accounting Office. (1990). *Case study evaluations* (Transfer paper 10.1.9: Case study evaluations). Washington, DC: Author.

U.S. General Accounting Office. (1993). *Initial accessibility good but important barriers remain: Americans With Disabilities Act.* Washington, DC: Author.

University of Chicago Press. (1993). *The Chicago manual of style* (14th Ed.). Chicago: Author.

Van Maanen, J. (1988). *Tales of the field.* Chicago: University of Chicago Press.

Vickrey, B. G. (1993). A procedure for developing a quality-of-life measure for epilepsy surgery patients. *Epilepsia, 34*(4), S22-S27.

Villegas, A. M. (1991). *Culturally responsive pedagogy for the 1990s and beyond* (Monograph). Princeton, NJ: Educational Testing Service.

Walford, A. J., Mullay, M., & Schlicke, P. (1993). *Walford's guide to reference material.* London: Library Association Publishing.

Walkowitz, J. (1992). *City of dreadful delight: Narratives of sexual danger in Late-Victorian London.* London: Virago.

Wallerstein, N., & Martinez, L. (1994). Empowerment evaluation: A case study of an adolescent substance abuse prevention program in New Mexico. *Evaluation Practice, 15*(2), 131-138.

Wang, M. C., Reynolds, M. C., & Walberg, H. J. (1987-1989). *Handbook of special education: Research and practice* (Vol. 1-3). Oxford, UK: Pergamon.

Wang, M. C., Reynolds, M. C., & Walberg, H. J. (1990). *Special education research and practice.* Oxford, UK: Pergamon.

Warren, C. A. B. (1988). *Gender issues in field research.* Newbury Park, CA: Sage.

Weiss, C. H. (1987). Where politics and evaluation research meet. In D. J. Palumbo (Ed.), *The politics of program evaluation* (pp. 47-70). Newbury Park, CA: Sage.

Weitzman, E. A., & Miles, M. B. (1995). *A software sourcebook: Computer programs for qualitative data analysis.* Thousand Oaks, CA: Sage.

Wesson, C. L., & King, R. P. (1996). Portfolio assessment and special education students. *Teaching Exceptional Children, 28*, 44-48.

Wheeler, D. L. (1995, February 17). A growing number of scientists reject race. *Chronicle of Higher Education,* pp. A8, A9, A15.

White, D. G. (1987). Mining the forgotten: Manuscript resources for Black women's history. *Journal of American History, 74*, 237-242.

Whitmore, E. (1991). Evaluation and empowerment: It's the process that counts. *Networking bulletin: Empowerment and Family Support, 2*, 1-7. Ithaca, NY: Cornell University, Cornell Empowerment Project.

Whitmore, E. (1996). *Ideology in evaluation.* Unpublished manuscript.

Wilson, C. L., & Sindelar, P. T. (1991). Direct instruction in math word problems: Students with disabilities. *Exceptional Children, 57*(6), 512-519.

Witkin, B. R., & Altschuld, J. W. (1995). *Planning and conducting needs assessment.* Thousand Oaks, CA: Sage.

Wittrock, M. C. (1986). Students' thought processes. In M. C. Wittrock (Ed.), *Handbook of research on teaching* (pp. 297-314). New York: Macmillan.

Wolcott, H. F. (1994). *Transforming qualitative data.* Thousand Oaks, CA: Sage.

Wolf, M. (1992). *A thrice-told tale: Feminism, postmodernism, and ethnographic responsibility.* Stanford, CA: Stanford University Press.

Woodworth, G. (1994). Managing meta-analytic databases. In H. Cooper & L. V. Hedges (Eds.), *The handbook of research synthesis.* New York: Russell Sage.

Worthen, B. R., Sanders, J. R., & Fitzpatrick, J. (1997). *Program evaluation.* New York: Addison Wesley, Longman.

Yammarino, R. S., Skinner, S. S., & Childers, T. L. (1991). Understanding mail survey response behavior: A meta-analysis. *Public Opinion Quarterly, 55*, 613-639.

Yin, R. K. (1991). Advancing rigorous methodologies. *Review of Educational Research, 61*(3), 299-306.

Yin, R. K. (1993). *Applications of case study research.* Newbury Park, CA: Sage.

Yin, R. K. (1994). *Case study research design methods* (2nd ed.). Thousand Oaks, CA: Sage.

Yow, V. R. (1994). *Recording oral history: A practical guide for social scientists*. Thousand Oaks, CA: Sage.

Ysseldyke, J., Algozzine, B., & Epps, S. (1983). A logical and empirical analysis of current practice in classifying students as handicapped. *Exceptional Children, 50*(2), 160-166.

Zambrana, R. E. (Ed.). (1995). *Understanding Latino families*. Thousand Oaks, CA: Sage.

Author Index

Subject Index

About the Author

Donna M. Mertens is Professor in the Department of Educational Foundations and Research at Gallaudet University. She teaches research methods, program evaluation, statistics, and educational psychology to deaf and hearing students at the BA, MA, and PhD levels. She has conducted research and evaluation studies on topics such as improvement of special education services in international settings, planning for the inclusion of students with disabilities in neighborhood schools, enhancing the educational experiences of students with disabilities, preventing sexual abuse in residential schools for deaf students, and improving access to the court systems for deaf and hard of hearing people. Her research focuses on improving methods of inquiry by integrating the perspectives of those who have experienced oppression in our society. She draws on the writings of feminists, minorities, and people with disabilities who have addressed the issues of power and oppression and their implications for research methodology. She has made numerous presentations at the meetings of the American Educational Research Association, the American Evaluation Association, the Convention of American Instructors of the Deaf, and various international organizations that explore these themes. She was elected President-Elect of the American Evaluation Association for 1997 and will serve as president of that organization in 1998. Her publications include an edited volume, titled *Creative Ideas for Teaching Evaluation,* and a text co-authored with John McLaughlin titled *Research Methods in Special Education.* She has also published many articles in journals such as *New Directions for Program Evaluation, Evaluation Practice, American Annals of the Deaf, Studies in Educational Evaluation,* and *Educational Evaluation and Policy Analysis.*